THE GOSPEL
ACCORDING TO PAUL

THE GOSPEL
ACCORDING TO PAUL

A Reappraisal

Graham H. Twelftree

CASCADE *Books* • Eugene, Oregon

THE GOSPEL ACCORDING TO PAUL
A Reappraisal

Copyright © 2019 Graham H. Twelftree. All rights reserved. Except for brief quotations in critical publications or reviews, no part of this book may be reproduced in any manner without prior written permission from the publisher. Write: Permissions, Wipf and Stock Publishers, 199 W. 8th Ave., Suite 3, Eugene, OR 97401.

Cascade Books
An Imprint of Wipf and Stock Publishers
199 W. 8th Ave., Suite 3
Eugene, OR 97401

www.wipfandstock.com

PAPERBACK ISBN: 978-1-5326-8703-7
HARDCOVER ISBN: 978-1-5326-8704-4
EBOOK ISBN: 978-1-5326-8705-1

Cataloguing-in-Publication data:

Names: Twelftree, Graham H.
Title: The gospel according to Paul : a reappraisal / Graham H. Twelftree.
Description: Eugene, OR: Cascade Books, 2019. | Includes bibliographical references and index.
Identifiers: ISBN 978-1-5326-8703-7 (paperback) | ISBN 978-1-5326-8704-4 (hardcover) | ISBN 978-1-5326-8705-1 (ebook)
Subjects: LCSH: Paul, the Apostle, Saint. | Bible. Epistles of Paul—Criticism, interpretation, etc.
Classification: BS2506.3 T84 2019 (paperback) | BS2506.3 (ebook)

Manufactured in the U.S.A.   11/19/19

To
Randall and Estella Kay Pannell

"When Christianity (precisely because it is not a doctrine) is not reduplicated in the life of the person presenting it, it is not Christianity he presents."

SØREN KIEKEGAARD (1813–1855)

Contents

Preface | ix
Abbreviations | xiii

1 Paul's Gospel? | 1
2 The Gospel Paul Inherited | 25
3 The Gospel Paul Promoted:
    Thessalonians, Galatians, and Philippians | 78
4 The Gospel Paul Promoted:
    Corinthians, Philemon, and Romans | 132
5 The Gospel According to Paul | 178

Appendix: The Vocabulary of "Gospel" | 207

Bibliography | 211
Biblical and Ancient Literature Index | 239
Name Index | 279
Subject Index | 289

Preface

PAUL'S GOSPEL IS MISUNDERSTOOD. At least that is the argument of this book. Paul's gospel is not simply his message or even his empowered message. The misunderstanding of Paul's gospel has become obvious with new interpretive lenses available as a result of the change in the theological center of gravity of the global church, and of many local churches in the West.

The Reformation continues to dominate most of the theological landscape against which Pauline studies are conducted. Paul is seen primarily as an intellectual and a theologian. Debates over his intellectual and theological achievements continue to center around his understanding of what became the Reformation's *shibboleths* of "law," "grace," and "justification by faith alone." The unspoken assumption is that if these and related terms are understood, Paul—and Christianity—is understood. Large sectors of the church and academy would agree with Günther Bornkamm that, as "the gospel of justification by faith alone was the article by which the church stood or fell . . . an effort is required to reintroduce Paul's doctrine and rekindle the fire with which it once burned."[1]

However, the modern Pentecostal and charismatic movements have brought an increasing theological and ecclesial sensitivity to, and interest in, the affective and ecstatic aspects of Paul's thought and work. Though I am not a Pentecostal, nor am I the son or even father of one, this study seeks to take into account the new landscape in which Paul is more broadly read than through the myopic lens of Reformation concerns.

In particular, in this study we will see that the generally agreed notion of Paul's "gospel," inherited from the Reformers, if not simply wrong because of its narrow denotation, is profoundly different and poorer from the one he had. For example, we will see that even to describe Paul's gospel as his God-empowered message is a gross oversimplification and misunderstanding of what he had in mind.

1. Bornkamm, *Paul*, 136.

It was near the end of working on *Paul and the Miraculous: A Historical Reconstruction* (Grand Rapids: Baker Academic, 2013) that I became aware that Paul's description and understanding of his gospel appeared to be very different from what it is generally supposed to have been. In this book I want to take up, explore, develop, and test ideas that were emerging towards the end of that project.

However, research has led to different conclusions from what I expected. The earlier project carried my conclusion that, "For Paul, *no more could the gospel be proclaimed without words than it could come or be experienced without miracles. Without the miraculous Paul may have had a message, but he would not have had a gospel. Without the miraculous there was no gospel, only preaching.*"[2] While this remains true, it turns out to be only partly true. Only now, completing this book, has the richness and all-encompassing depth and breadth of the gospel according to Paul become apparent to me. I hope the reader is able grasp not only how different Paul's idea of the gospel is from how it is generally seen, but how rich and polyvalent that different gospel is.

Given the significance of "gospel" in Paul's writings, his understanding of it can be expected to have implications across his thinking. His theology and writing are so tightly woven that to pull at any one thread is to tug at and unravel the whole cloth. To keep this study within manageable limits (or a readable length!) and to maintain focus on what will be argued to be the principle ongoing misunderstanding of "gospel" in Paul, attention here will be directed to elucidating the core of his views and attending to the most immediate associations he makes with the motif, rather than exploring their broader implications. Therefore, for example, in the pages that follow no particular attention is given to the sociological or political implications of Paul's gospel. Rather the attention of this project is on the core meaning and Paul's immediate use of the term "gospel." Wider implications of "gospel" (verb and noun) and the connections with other motifs will have to be left to others, and other projects, to explore and develop.

When I was invited to be the first incumbent of the Charles L. Holman Professorship of New Testament and Early Christianity at Regent University, I had the opportunity to try out aspects of my ideas in the inaugural lecture. This book is a development of the ideas set out in that lecture. I met Charles Holman (1935–2006) in 1978 when we were both reading for our doctorates at Nottingham University under James Dunn. At Regent University, where years later we became colleagues, Charles was a greatly

---

2. Twelftree, *Paul and the Miraculous*, 317 (emphasis original). On Paul's understanding of the miraculous see the brief discussion below (§3.2 [a] 3) and in more detail see Twelftree, *Paul and the Miraculous*, 20–26, 313–14.

loved professor. He was also the quintessential absentminded professor. For example, one evening my wife and I went with Charles and Rose, his wife, to the Pavilion in Virginia Beach. On emerging after hearing Beethoven's ninth symphony, Charles wandered off to get the car, I assume in some state of musically induced ecstasy. He brought the car around in front of us and I opened the doors for the ladies to get in. As I closed the doors for them, Charles promptly drove off. Thankfully, the shouts of our wives caused him to return for me. Others who knew Charles treasure equally interesting memories of this dear man. Charles did most of his scholarly work looking over the shoulders of Paul the apostle. It is a privilege to follow Charles in looking over those same shoulders.

Looking back on the life of this project I am grateful for the help of those who have made its completion possible. At the top of the list are the librarians, Patty Hughson, Keith Lang, and Bob Sivigny. With great patience, grace, and perseverance, they have made hard-to-find resources available. Particular thanks is due to John Nelson for a summer of research assistance and lively interaction, and to Douglas Campbell, Michael Gorman, Kenneth D. Litwak, Petr Pokorný, Steve Rumens, Andy Steere, Jerry Sumney, Barbara Twelftree, Brenton Wait, and Catherine Wait, who read and interacted with parts or the whole of the project. Two anonymous reviewers were also most helpful in raising questions and pointing to problems in what they read. In that I have not always heeded their advice none of these people should be held responsible for what follows. I am most grateful to Michael Thomson, Acquisitions Editor at Wipf and Stock, who has been an enthusiastic, informed, and helpful supporter of the project. I am thankful to Thomas Casemore, Jonathan Dendy, Amaris Rivera Mercado, and Sarah Parsons, for their essential help in the final stages of the project. Rachel Bennett, a remarkable and long-suffering PA, has made this and so many other projects possible.

Once again, Barbara, my wife, has gone beyond any reasonable expectations of companionship to constructing bibliographies and spending countless hours proofreading. Thank you!

Unless noted as my own, translations of biblical texts are from the NRSV. Much of this project revolves around a discussion of the use of particular Greek words Paul used—or did not use. Notwithstanding, throughout this book care has been taken to keep in mind readers who are not familiar with Greek.

The body of secondary literature relating to the study of Paul of Tarsus is astonishingly large and continues to grow unabated. Not surprisingly, not even the footnotes can contain everything; only a small fraction of the mountain can be mentioned. Also, the bibliography contains only those items referred to in the project.

In January 2002, when we went to live in the United States for what turned out to be fourteen special years, Randall and Kay Pannell were warmly welcoming and went to great lengths to help us settle and feel at home. Randall, an Old Testament specialist, was my supportive colleague, then caring, tireless leader as Associate Dean of the School of Divinity, and then with compassion and singular integrity, Acting Vice President for Academic Affairs at Regent University. Kay became and remains my wife's most special and longtime loyal friend. This book is dedicated to them as a token of the gratitude Barbara and I owe to them.

Graham H. Twelftree
London School of Theology

Abbreviations

AB	Anchor Bible
Abbott-Smith	G. Abbott-Smith, *A Manual Greek Lexicon of the New Testament*. Edinburgh: T. & T. Clark, 1973
ABS	T. & T. Clark Approaches to Biblical Studies
ABG	Arbeiten zur Bibel und Ihrer Geschichte
ACCS	Ancient Christian Commentary on Scripture
ACW	Ancient Christian Writers
AnBib	Analecta Biblica
ANTC	Abingdon New Testament Commentaries
ACCS	Ancient Christian Commentary on Scripture
APAMS	American Philological Monograph Series
ASV	American Standard Version
ATR	*Anglican Theological Review*
BAGD	Walter Bauer, et al., eds., *A Greek-English Lexicon of the New Testament and other Early Christian Literature*. Chicago: University of Chicago Press, 1979
BBE	The Bible in Basic English
BBR	*Bulletin for Biblical Research*
BDAG	Frederick William Danker, et al., eds., *A Greek-English Lexicon of the New Testament and other Early Christian Literature*. Chicago: University of Chicago Press, 2000
BDF	Friedrich Blass, et al., *A Greek Grammar of the New Testament and Other Early Christian Literature*. Chicago: University of Chicago Press, 1961

BECNT	Baker Exegetical Commentary on the New Testament
BETL	Bibliotheca Ephemeridum Theologicarum Lovaniensium
BGBE	Beiträge zur Geschichte der biblischen Exegese
BHT	Beiträge zur Historischen Theologie
Bib	*Biblica*
BiBh	*Bible Bhashyam*
BN	*Biblische Notizen*
BNTC	Black's New Testament Commentary
BSac	*Bibliotheca Sacra*
BST	The Bible Speaks Today
BT	*Biblical Translator*
BTB	*Biblical Theology Bulletin*
BZ	*Biblische Zeitschrift*
BZNW	Beihefte zur Zeitschrift für die neutestamentliche Wissenschaft
CBC	The Cambridge Bible Commentary
CBET	Contributions to Biblical Exegesis and Theology
CBQ	*Catholic Biblical Quarterly*
CBR	*Currents in Biblical Research*
CGTC	Cambridge Greek Testament Commentary
CGTSC	Cambridge Greek Testament for Schools and Colleges
ChrCent	*Christian Century*
Colloq	*Colloquium*
Conc	*Concilium*
CSB	Holman Christian Standard Bible
CTQ	*Concordia Theological Quarterly*
CTR	*Criswell Theological Review*
CurBR	*Currents in Biblical Research*
DBY	The Darby Bible
DJD	Discoveries in the Judaean Desert

DJG²	*Dictionary of Jesus and the Gospels.* Edited by Joel B. Green, et al. 2nd ed. Downers Grove, IL: InterVarsity, 2013.
DRA	Duay-Rheims Amercian Edition (1899)
DSD	*Dead Sea Discoveries*
EC	Epworth Commentaries
EDNT	Horst Balz and Gerhard Schneider, eds., *Exegetical Dictionary of the New Testament*. 3 vols. Grand Rapids: Eerdmans, 1990, 1991, 1993
EGGNT	Exegetical Guide to the Greek New Testament
EGT	The Expositor's Greek Testament
EKKNT	Evangelisch-katholischer Kommentar zum Neuen Testament
ERV	English Revised Version
ESV	English Standard Version
ETL	*Ephemerides Theologicae Lovanienses*
EvQ	*Evangelical Quarterly*
EvT	*Evangelische Theologie*
ExAud	*Ex Auditu*
ExpTim	*Expository Times*
FRLANT	Forschung zur Religion und Literatur des Alten und Neuen Testaments
GNV	Geneva Bible
GNT⁴	Barbara Aland, et al., eds. *The Greek New Testament.* Stuttgart: Deutsche Bibelgesellschaft and United Bible Societies, 1993.
GR	*Greece & Rome*
GWN	God's Word to the Nations Version
HBT	*Horizons in Biblical Theology*
HNT	Handbuch zum Neuen Testament
HThKNT	Herder Theologischer Kommentar zum Neuen Testament
HTR	*Harvard Theological Review*

IBS		*Irish Biblical Studies*
ICC		International Critical Commentary
IG		*Inscriptiones Graecae. Editio Minor.* Berlin: de Gruyter, 1924–
IGRR		*Inscriptiones Graecae ad res romanas pertinentes avctoritate et impensis*, edited by Rene Cagnat, et al. Paris: Librairie Ernest Leroux, 1901
Int		*Interpretation*
ITC		International Theological Commentary
ITQ		*Irish Theological Quarterly*
JAJSup		Journal of Ancient Judaism Supplements
JBL		*Journal of Biblical Literature*
JCTCRS		Jewish and Christian Texts in Contexts and Related Studies
JETS		*Journal of the Evangelical Theological Society*
JHC		*Journal of Higher Criticism*
JSHJ		*Journal for the Study of the Historical Jesus*
JSJSup		Journal for the Study of Judaism Supplement
JSNT		*Journal for the Study of The New Testament*
JSNTSupp		Supplement to the Journal for the Study of the New Testament
JSP		*Journal for the Study of The Pseudepigrapha*
JTC		*Journal for Theology and the Church*
JTS		*Journal of Theological Studies*
KEK		*Kritisch-exegetischer Kommentar über das Neue Testament*
KJV		King James Version
KKS		Konfessionskundliche und Kontroverstheologische Studien
LCL		Loeb Classical Library
LNTS		Library of New Testament Studies
LQ		*Lutheran Quarterly*

LSJ	Liddell, H. G., R. Scott, and H. S. Jones, eds. *A Greek-English Lexicon*. 9th ed., with revised supplement. Oxford: Clarendon, 1996
LXX	Septuagint
MGS	Franco Montanari, et al., *The Brill Dictionary of Ancient Greek*. Leiden: Brill, 2015
MIT	MacDonald Idiomatic Translation
MM	James H. Moulton and George Milligan, *The Vocabulary of the Greek Testament*. London: Hodder and Stoughton, 1930
MNTC	Moffatt New Testament Commentary
NA^{25}	Barbara Aland, et al., eds., *Novum Testamenum Graece*. Stuttgart: Deutsche Bibelgesellschaft, 1975
NA^{26}	Barbara Aland, et al., eds., *Novum Testamenum Graece*. Stuttgart: Deutsche Bibelgesellschaft, 1979
NA^{27}	Barbara Aland, et al., eds., *Novum Testamenum Graece*. Stuttgart: Deutsche Bibelgesellschaft, 1993
NA^{28}	Barbara Aland, et al., eds., *Novum Testamenum Graece*. Stuttgart: Deutsche Bibelgesellschaft, 2012
NAB	The New American Bible
NAS	New American Standard Bible (1977)
NAU	New American Standard Bible (1995)
NCB	New Century Bible
NClB	New Clarendon Bible
NCBC	New Cambridge Bible Commentary
NEB	New English Bible
NET	New English Translation
NETS	Albert Pietersma and Benjamin G. Wright. *A New English Translation of the Septuagint: And the Other Greek Translations Traditionally Included Under That Title*. New York: Oxford University Press, 2007
NewDocs	G. H. R. Horsley, *New Documents Illustrating Early Christianity*, vol. 3. North Ryde, NSW: Macquarie University Press, 1983

NIB	New International Version (UK)
NIBC	New International Bible Commentary
NICNT	New International Commentary on the New Testament
NIDB	*The New Interpreter's Dictionary of the Bible*, edited by Katharine Doob Sakenfeld, et al. 5 vols. Nashville: Abingdon, 2006–2010
NIDNTTE	Moisés Silva, revision editor, *New International Dictionary of New Testament Theology and Exegesis*. 5 vols. Grand Rapids: Zondervan, 2014
NIGTC	New International Greek Testament Commentary
NIRV	New International Reader's Version
NIV	New International Version
NJB	New Jerusalem Bible
NKJ	New King James
NLT	New Living Translation
NovT	*Novum Testamentum*
NovTSup	Novum Testamentum Supplement
NRSV	New Revised Standard Version
NT	New Testament
NTAbh	Neutestamentliche Abhandlungen
NTCC	New Testament in Context Commentaries
NTD	Das Neue Testament Deutsch
NTL	New Testament Library
NTOA	Novum Testamentum et Orbis Antiquus
NTM	New Testament Message
NTS	*New Testament Studies*
NTTS	New Testament Tools and Studies
OGIS	*Orientis Graeci Inscriptiones Selectae*
OTL	Old Testament Library
OTP	*Old Testament Pseudepigrapha*. Edited by James H. Charlesworth. 2 vols. New York: Doubleday, 1983, 1985
PBM	Paternoster Biblical Monographs

PCNT	Paideia Commentaries on the New Testament
PG	Patrologia Graeca [= Patrologiae Cursus Completus: Series Graeca]. Edited by Jacques-Paul Migne. 162 vols. Paris, 1857–1886
PMS	Patristic Monograph Series
PNT	Bishop's New Testament (1595)
PNTC	Pelican New Testament Commentaries
PNTCS	Pillar New Testament Commentary Series
PPS	Past and Present Series
PSB	*Princeton Seminary Bulletin*
PthS	Paderborner theologische Studien
RB	*Revue Biblique*
RCT	*Revista catalana de teología*
ResQ	*Restoration Quarterly*
RevExp	*Review and Expositor*
RBS	Resources for Biblical Study
RNT	Regensburger Neues Testament
RSV	Revised Standard Version
RWB	Revised Webster Update
SBLDS	Society of Biblical Literature Dissertation Series
SBLSP	Society of Biblical Literature Seminar Papers
SBT	Studies in Biblical Theology
SC	Sources Chrétiennes
ScEccl	*Sciences ecclésiastiques*
SCJR	*Studies in Christian-Jewish Relations*
SCO	Studi classici e orientali
SComS	Septuagint Commentary Series
SD	Studies and Documents
SEG	Supplementum epigraphicum graecum
SJT	*Scottish Journal of Theology*
SNT	Studien zum Neuen Testament

SNTSMS	Society for New Testament Studies Monograph Series
SNTSU	Studien zum Neuen Testament und seiner Umwelt
SNTW	Studies of the New Testament and its World
SP	Sacra Pagina
SPIB	Scripta Pontificii Instituti Biblici
SSEJC	Studies in Scripture in Early Judaism and Christianity
ST	*Studia Theologica*
Str-B	Hermann L. Strack and Paul Billerbeck. *Kommentar zum Neuen Testament aus Talmud und Midrasch.* 6 vols. Munich, 1922–1961
STRev	*Sewanee Theological Review*
StTh	*Studia Theologica*
SUNT	Studien zur Umwelt des Neuen Testaments
SVTP	*Studia in Veteris Testamenti Pseudepigraphica*
TDNT	*Theological Dictionary of the New Testament.* Edited by Gerhard Kittel and Gerhard Friedrich. Translated by Geoffrey Bromiley. 10 vols. Grand Rapids: Eerdmans, 1964–1976
THKNT	Theologischer Handkommentar zum Neuen Testament
THNTC	Two Horizons New Testament Commentary
ThTo	*Theology Today*
TLG	THESAURUS LINGUAE GRAECAE®, A Digital Library of Greek Literature, University of California, Irvine
TNIV	Today's New International Version
TNT	Tyndale's New Testament (1534)
TNTC	Tyndale New Testament Commentaries
TPINTC	Trinity Press International New Testament Commentaries
TynBul	*Tyndale Bulletin*
TZ	*Theologische Zeitschrift*
UBW	Understanding the Bible and its World
UCBS	Understanding the Bible Commentary Series
WBC	Word Bible Commentary

WC	Westminster Commentaries
WEB	Webster Bible (1833)
WesTJ	*Wesleyan Theological Journal*
WUNT	Wissenschaftliche Untersuchungen zum Neuen Testament
WW	Word and World
YLT	Young's Literal Translation (1862/1898)
ZNW	*Zeitschrift für die neutestamentliche Wissenschaft und die Kunde der älteren Kirche*
ZTK	*Zeitschrift für Theologie und Kirche*
ZWB	Zürcher Werkkommentare zur Bibel

1

Paul's Gospel?

FEW FIGURES IN HUMAN history have been or remain as influential as Paul.[1] In Christian history Paul's impact has been profound. His early influence is seen both in the enduring impact of his own letters, and the influence of his thought found in the other texts collected in the New Testament, including those written by others under his name. Perhaps only the Fourth Gospel shows no evidence of Pauline influence. Subsequently, many of the leading figures of Church history—Augustine (354–430), Martin Luther (1483–1546), John Wesley (1703–1791), and Karl Barth (1886–1968), for example—claim to have been decisively influenced by Paul.[2] In our time, Paul is seen as the inventor[3] or founder of Christianity[4] or its theology.[5] Few would dissent from the view that, if theological significance is measured in terms of originality, skilled articulation, and later influence, even if he is not deemed the founder of Christianity, Paul has no equal.[6] Given such impact through history, including such early interpretive significance and such ongoing influence and scholarly veneration, it is important we continue to

---

1. E.g., Hart, *100*, ranks Paul after Muhammad, Isaac Newton, Jesus Christ, Buddha, and Confucius, and ahead of, for example, Johannes Gutenberg, Albert Einstein, Galileo Galilei, and Aristotle.

2. E.g., Bruce, *Romans*, 58–60.

3. See Maccoby, *Mythmaker*; Tabor, *Paul and Jesus*; Wilson, *How Jesus Became Christian*; and the discussion by Sumney, *Steward of God's Mysteries*, 1–9.

4. E.g., Lüdemann, *Paul.* Cf. Wrede, *Paul*, 179–80.

5. E.g., Schnelle, *Apostle Paul.* Cf. the discussion by Dunn, *Theology of Paul the Apostle*, 2.

6. Cf. Dunn, *Theology of Paul the Apostle*, 2–3.

interact with Paul's writings so they can be read with as much understanding as possible in our time.[7]

§1.1 WHAT IS THE GOSPEL?

Where do we begin in understanding Paul's highly original, articulate and influential ideas? "Justification by faith"[8] or "reconciliation"[9] are often championed as the center of his theology, but so is being "in Christ."[10] Going a step further, Douglas Campbell says that, "Christ *himself* (in some sense), rather than Paul's conceptual and linguistic construction *of* Christ, is at the center of Paul."[11] Or perhaps it is from his understanding of the cross that his theology radiates.[12] Ever since the groundbreaking book, *Paul and Palestinian Judaism: A Comparison of Patterns of Religion* (1977), by E. P. Sanders (1939–), some have used his phrase "participationist" to sum up the essence of Paul's theology.[13] Also recently, Udo Schnelle has suggested that Paul was so overwhelmed by the experience and insight of ultimate experience in Jesus Christ that in him Paul saw the eschatological presence of God's salvation as the basis and center of his thought.[14] Alternatively, perhaps the center of Pauline thinking is a cluster of key ideas, such as "the whole and undivided richness and mystery of Christ and of the Father's saving purpose through his Son," as Joseph Plevnik put it.[15] Some interpreters looking for a central organizing principle for his ideas[16] even see discovering this center as the fundamental problem in Pauline studies.[17]

I do not intend to claim the gospel is the central, organizing principle of Paul's theology. However, I do want to demonstrate broadly that the term

---

7. Cf. Furnish, "On Putting Paul in His Place," 17.

8. Notably, Käsemann, "'Righteousness of God' in Paul," 168–69, and the discussion by Campbell, *Deliverance of God*, 11–218.

9. Martin, *Reconciliation*.

10. Cf. Schweitzer, *Mysticism of Paul the Apostle*. For a discussion of the Spirit and the center of Paul, see Pretorius, "Theological Centre of Pauline Theology," 253–62.

11. Campbell, *Quest for Paul's Gospel*, 32 (emphasis original).

12. E.g., Wilckens, *Brief an die Römer*; Gorman, *Cruciformity*.

13. Cf. Gorman, *Becoming the Gospel*, 26–36.

14. Schnelle, *Apostle Paul*, 389.

15. Plevnik, "Center of Paul's Theology," 477–78. Also, see the discussion by Lincoln, "Ephesians 2:8–10," 617–30.

16. Cf. Campbell, *Quest for Paul's Gospel*, 17–28. For brief, earlier discussions, e.g., see Boers, "Foundations of Paul's Thought," 55–68; Bishop, "Gospel(s) According to Paul," and Dunn, *Theology of Paul the Apostle*, 19–21.

17. Boers, cited by Beker, "Paul the Theologian," 354.

"gospel," and what it signifies, is of such importance to Paul as one of the central and centralizing concepts in his thought and theology[18] that we would advance the cause of understanding him if we grasped the understanding he had of the term.[19] In turn, given that large tracts of the academy articulate notions of the Christian gospel that are explicitly or implicitly dependent primarily on Paul's writings,[20] and that large swaths of the church take their theological bearings not simply from Paul's theology or writings but, in particular, from his understanding of the gospel,[21] a reexamination of his views is of enormous potential contemporary importance.

We begin to see the significance of the word "gospel" (noun and verb) for Paul when we notice that over half of its occurrences in the New Testament are found in his writings.[22] The importance of the term also becomes obvious when we note that in more than half of his use, "gospel" is in the absolute, needing no adjective or other term to describe it.[23] More significant than statistics, Paul understood himself in relation to the gospel. He talks of "my gospel" (Rom 2:16; cf. 16:25) or "our gospel" (2 Cor 4:3) and of being "set aside for the gospel."[24] Whatever the nature of this gospel, it is clearly very important to him and his self-understanding. Further, much of what he writes appears to be an explanation of the gospel,[25] or a defense of it.[26] Paul can even use the verb, and describe his work as, "gospelling,"[27] as it

---

18. Cf. Becker, "Gospel, Evangelize, Evangelist," 111: "In Paul *euangelion* has become a central concept in his theology."

19. Cf. §5.3 and 5.5 below.

20. E.g., see McFarland, "Gospel," 200–201.

21. E.g., biblical support for The Southern Baptist Convention's statement on "The Centrality of the Gospel" is selected primarily from Paul's letters: http://www.sbc.net/resolutions/1199/on-the-centrality-of-the-gospel.

22. The noun εὐαγγέλιον ("gospel") occurs seventy-six times in the NT, and forty-eight times in Paul's letters: at least once in each of the seven generally-agreed-authentic letters of Paul: Romans 9x; 1 Corinthians 8x; 2 Corinthians 8x; Galatians 7x; Philippians 9x; 1 Thessalonians 6x; and Philemon 1x. The verb εὐαγγελίζειν ("to gospel") occurs fifty-four times in the NT, and nineteen times in Paul's letters: Romans 3x; 1 Corinthians 6x; 2 Corinthians 2x; Galatians 7x; and 1 Thessalonians 1x. In more detail see the Appendix below.

23. Rom 1:16; 10:16; 11:28; 1 Cor 4:15; 9:14 (x2), 18 (x2), 23; 2 Cor 8:18; Gal 2:5, 14; Phil 1:5, 7, 12, 16, 27; 2:22; 4:3, 15; 1 Thess 2:4; Phlm 13. Cf. Friedrich, "εὐαγγελίζομαι, κτλ," 729n65.

24. Rom 1:1; cf. 1:9, 16; 15:16; Gal 2:7.

25. E.g., see Rom 1:16; 2:16; 15:14–29; 1 Cor 4:1–21; Gal 1:6–9.

26. E.g., at Gal 1:6; cf. 2 Cor 11:1–6. At 1 Cor 9:3 and Phil 1:7, 16, Paul uses ἀπολογία ("defense") in relation to his work.

27. See εὐαγγελίζω in Rom 1:15; 15:20; 1 Cor 1:17; 9:16, 18; 15:1; 2 Cor 10:16; 11:7; Gal 1:8, 9, 11, 16, 23; 4:13; 1 Thess 3:6.

can be translated. For example, he says he was sent (1 Cor 1:17), or is eager, to "gospel" (Rom 1:15; 15:20). It is reasonable, then, to suppose that without a comprehensive understanding of Paul's "gospel" we will not understand him or his work as well as we might.[28]

The purpose of this book is, therefore, to answer this question: What is the gospel according to Paul?[29] In order to answer this fundamental question, along the way a number of other and subsidiary questions will be answered: What did the word—noun and verb—mean in Paul's world? Where did Paul get the term—noun and verb? Did he introduce the term to Christianity, or did he receive it from earlier followers of Jesus? What role did Paul's Scriptures play in his understanding of the gospel? Is the gospel, for Paul, his preached message? Is the gospel his empowered message, a message embodying God's transforming power? Or, is the gospel something else?

In answering these questions, the project exposes the disconnect between the gospel according to Paul and his gospel as it is now generally understood. In part, this book develops ideas in my *Paul and the Miraculous: A Historical Reconstruction*, particularly the statement near the end that "Paul's message was not his gospel."[30] Positively, through close attention to what he says, this project is able to set out what Paul most likely meant when he used the term "gospel." As a result, we will see his multifaceted understanding of the gospel.

This first chapter, "Paul's Gospel?," takes a look across the recent history of Pauline studies, as well as at current studies, through discussing the representative work of James Dunn, Tom Wright, Udo Schnelle, Michael Gorman, Michael Wolter, and Douglas Campbell, and along the way taking into account other significant voices. We will see that, over against what appears to be Paul's richer and more nuanced perspective, his gospel has been, and continues to be, taken as his message about Jesus. Sometimes, particularly more recently, that gospel message is taken to embody God's transforming power. By the time we reach the end of our study it will become patently clear that this view of Paul's gospel stands in stark contrast to what he most probably had in mind.

Chapter 2, "The Gospel Paul Inherited," sets out the idea of "gospel" in Paul's Jewish and Greco-Roman traditions, and among his predecessors in the Jesus movement. Through this exercise it becomes clear that,

---

28. Cf. Furnish, "On Putting Paul in His Place," 17.

29. As his title suggests, the study by Calhoun, *Paul's Definitions of the Gospel*, is confined to a small part of Paul's writings and analyzes only a part of what Paul understood by the gospel.

30. Twelftree, *Paul and the Miraculous*, 316.

particularly among earlier followers of Jesus, the term "gospel" was far more than the content of preaching. In turn, this helps explain the origin of Paul's approach, as well as highlights the novelty of his views and practices.

A careful reading of his letters in chapter 3, "The Gospel Paul Promoted: Thessalonians, Galatians, and Philippians," and chapter 4, "The Gospel Paul Promoted: Corinthians, Philemon, and Romans," the core of this project, shows that although the term "gospel" was polyvalent for Paul, it generally referred to something that could be experienced or seen as well as described or preached. Notwithstanding, in his first letter (that to the Thessalonians), Paul has left clear traces of the missional message that he preached to those who became believers. Reconstructing what he initially preached to the Thessalonians helps us understand the relationship Paul saw between the gospel and what he said, particularly in relation to the coming of the gospel. Also, in Romans, at the other end of his brief letter-writing career, Paul gives an extensive treatment of his understanding of the gospel that we will be able to set out in outline.[31] The final chapter, "The Gospel According to Paul," chapter 5, will draw together the results of the study, including an attempt to reconstruct what Paul meant by "gospel." The brief Contemporary Coda that ends the final chapter notes some of the implications of our conclusions that, given the credibility of the results of this study, need urgent attention by theologians, pastors, preachers, and teachers.

To contextualize this project and to demonstrate its need, we begin by doing two things. First, in the next few sections of this chapter (§§1.2–4), through sampling some key studies on Paul, we will see how his gospel has been, and continues to be, understood. It will become obvious that the prevailing view has been, and remains, that Paul's message was his gospel or that his gospel was his message. Then, to provide the raw material to test the credibility of this prevailing view, in the next section (§1.5) Paul's uses of "gospel" (noun and verb) will be set out.[32] The conclusion (§1.6) draws attention to what appear to be the main contours of the differences between what Paul says and what the prevailing views assert. In this difference is the reason for this project.

§1.2 EARLIER VOICES

If this was a history of the understanding of Paul's gospel we would be taking into account much earlier voices such as Origen (c.185–c.254), Jerome

---

31. See §3.2 (a) 1 below.

32. In the Appendix below, Paul's use is set out statistically in the context of the wider use of the "gospel" word group.

(c.342–420), John Chrysostom (c.347–407), Theodore of Mopsuestia (c.350–428), and Augustine of Hippo (354–430).[33] However, our primary concern is with how Paul's gospel is understood in contemporary discussions.

The first systematic study of Pauline theology was published in 1824 by the Zürich theologian Leonhard Usteri (1799–1833).[34] In *Entwicklung des Paulinischen Lehrbegriffs* (*The Development of Pauline Doctrine*), Usteri describes the treasure and wisdom of the gospel as a preached message of salvation about the love of God in Christ.[35] Around two decades later, in 1845, Pauline studies took a new direction in the work of Ferdinand Christian Baur (1792–1860), the founder of the Tübingen School.[36] In *Paulus der Apostel Jesu Christi* (*Paul the Apostle of Jesus Christ*), he advanced the novel and still-debated view that Paul developed his theology over against others in early Christianity.[37] Nevertheless, in line with other students of Paul, Baur saw the gospel by its nature as having intellectual principles or content, and being proclaimed and heard.[38] Notably, he supposed that, in character, the gospel was inconsistent with the miraculous, which hides historical truth.[39] For example, concerning the story Luke has of the conversion of Cornelius (Acts 10:1–48) Baur said that it was "wanting in historical connexion." He went on to say that, "No satisfactory aim seems to be furthered by such a miracle." He then enquired, assuming a negative answer: "How does so studied and complicated a series of miraculous occurrences agree with the character of the Gospel history?"[40] Similarly, toward the end of the nineteenth century, J. B. Lightfoot (1828–1889), who interacted with Baur,[41] describes the gospel as a doctrine preached, taught, and learnt.[42]

---

33. On Romans, e.g., see Greenman and Larsen, *Reading Romans through the Centuries*; Bray and Oden, *Romans*.

34. Kümmel, *New Testament*, 95.

35. Usteri, *Entwicklung des Paulinischen Lehrbegriffs*, 160, 265–66, 279–80, 291, 342. The first edition of 1824 was revised in 1829, 1830, and 1832 by Usteri. After his death two more editions appeared, in 1834 and 1851. Schweitzer, *Paul and His Interpreters*, 9n1.

36. See Harris, *Tubingen School*.

37. Cf. Goulder, *St Paul Vs St Peter*, a reworking of Bauer's proposal, and the discussion in the review by Elliott, "Tale of Two Missions," 295–98.

38. Baur, *Paul the Apostle*, 1:37, 39, 60, 107–8, 112, 115–18, 130–131n, 164, 176, 177, 226, 240, 260, 261, 280, 288, 324, 334, 336, 338, 340, 345, 348, 374–76, 378, 2:13n, 56, 58, 86, 87, 149, 217, 319.

39. Baur, *Paul the Apostle*, 1:83, 153.

40. Baur, *Paul the Apostle*, 1:82, 83.

41. E.g., see Lightfoot, *Saint Paul's Epistle to the Philippians*, 15n1, 23n2, 74, 170, 177n2, and 296n2, and the discussion by Kaye, "Lightfoot and Baur," 193–224.

42. Lightfoot, *Saint Paul's Epistle to the Galatians*, 76, 107, 173; Lightfoot, *Colossians*

In the early part of the twentieth century, the historian and theologian Adolf von Harnack (1851–1930) of Berlin, perhaps the most important patristics scholar of his time, appended a study of "gospel" to his *The Constitution and Law of the Church in the First Two Centuries*.⁴³ In the section on the gospel in Paul, Harnack rightly notes that, like εὐαγγελίζεσθαι ("to gospel"), εὐαγγέλιον ("gospel") most frequently stands by itself since Paul assumed his readers knew its meaning. However, in light of evidence from Paul we will have to call into question Harnack translating εὐαγγελίζεσθαι "to preach."⁴⁴ Given that Harnack takes εὐαγγελίζεσθαι to refer to preaching, he takes the content of the εὐαγγέλιον to be Paul's message: "God's plan of salvation, contained in the Old Testament as a promise, and realized through Jesus Christ."⁴⁵ He also notes that the term εὐαγγελίζεσθαι is not exclusively a technical term for the apostle in that he can use it of Timothy bringing news of the Thessalonians (1 Thess 3:6). Harnack's brief study is one of the few studies dedicated to "gospel," and will occasionally be taken into account in this study.

Around the same time, Adolf Schlatter (1852–1938) produced a two-volume New Testament theology in which he gave considerable attention to Paul.⁴⁶ For Schlatter, Paul's gospel is a message of "the good news of God." Notably, he also says the message "has power, because it not merely promises God's gift but also grants it." This gift centers around Jesus Christ and forgiveness.⁴⁷ A year later, in 1910, Julius Schniewind (1883–1948) published his inaugural dissertation at Friedrichs University Halle-Wittenberg on the terms "word" and "gospel," concluding they mean one and the same thing, looked at from two different angles.⁴⁸

In his survey of the discussion of how the life and work of Jesus became the basis of the theology of Paul, Albert Schweitzer (1875–1965) also refers

and to Philemon, 132; Lightfoot, *Notes on Epistles of St Paul*, 12, 13, 120, 244; Lightfoot, *Saint Paul's Epistle to the Philippians*, 85.

43. Harnack, *Constitution and Law*, 275–331, esp. 292–303.

44. Harnack, *Constitution and Law*, 293. Cf. Asting, *Die Verkündigung des Wortes*, 388–408, esp. 408: "The gospel and the proclamation stand in an inseparable relationship (*Das Evangelium und die Verkündigung stehen also in einem unlösbaren Verhältnis*)."

45. Harnack, *Constitution and Law*, 294.

46. Schlatter, *Theology of the Apostles*, 187–321. Cf. Schlatter, *History of the Christ*, 375–89.

47. Schlatter, *Theology of the Apostles*, 191; cf. 264, 279, 311.

48. Schniewind, *Die Begriffe Wort und Evangelium*, 114.

to the gospel as a message[49] and implies no more than that it is a set of ideas.[50] In *The Mysticism of Paul the Apostle,* Schweitzer works with the same set of assumptions and ideas.[51] Not surprisingly, then, Paul's gospel, a recasting of Jesus' doctrine of his redemptive death and his expectation of the kingdom of God, is preached.[52]

Arguably the most significant British New Testament scholar of the early-to-mid twentieth century, C. H. Dodd (1884-1973) described Paul's gospel as transforming the apostle and was, in turn, something that he preached.[53] Dodd says that the content of this preached gospel is the revelation of God's righteousness by faith and for faith (Rom 1:17).[54] In turn, the key words of the Pauline gospel are "redemption," "atonement,"[55] "righteousness," and "faith."[56] A hint from him that Paul's gospel is more than his message is in Dodd's understanding of faith. He says that faith does not "mean belief in a proposition, though doubtless intellectual beliefs are involved when we come to think it out." Rather, Dodd says, faith "is an act which is the negation of all activity, a moment of passivity out of which the strength for action comes, because in it God acts."[57] We can note, however, that Dodd is at one with those who have seen, and continue to see, Paul's gospel as a message.

Adolf Deissmann (1866-1937), a pastor and then professor of New Testament at Heidelberg and Berlin, resorting to hyperbole to make his point, took the Greek "gospel" (εὐαγγέλιον) to be "a word that is one of the greatest creations of mankind."[58] For Deissmann, Paul's gospel incorporated a religious faith in Christ with the gospel of Jesus concerning God and the nearness of his kingdom.[59] In turn, the gospel was something Paul

---

49. Schweitzer, *Paul and His Interpreters,* 62.
50. Schweitzer, *Paul and His Interpreters,* 64, 82.
51. Schweitzer, *Mysticism of Paul the Apostle,* 389-90.
52. Schweitzer, *Mysticism of Paul the Apostle,* 390, 393-94.
53. Dodd, *Meaning of Paul for Today,* 7, 36, 42; Dodd, *Epistle of Paul to the Romans,* 9.
54. Dodd, *Epistle of Paul to the Romans,* 9.
55. Dodd, *Meaning of Paul for Today,* 54.
56. Dodd, *Epistle of Paul to the Romans,* 9.
57. Dodd, *Epistle of Paul to the Romans,* 16.
58. Deissmann, *Religion of Jesus,* 102. His discussion of the English history of "gospel" remains instructive (102-4).
59. Deissmann, *Paul,* 257.

preached⁶⁰ and which could be characterized as propaganda.⁶¹ His gospel was not something different from that of Jesus' but the experience one had of God secured for many.⁶²

With Martin Dibelius (1883-1947), also of Heidelberg, we reach the end of the first half of the twentieth century and still find Paul's gospel described as his proclamation. In a small book, *Paul*, which his student Werner Kümmel completed, Paul's gospel is taken to be his message that is preached and heard.⁶³ Accordingly, what Paul handed on in his preaching were the accounts he had received of the news of salvation that had appeared in Christ (e.g., 1 Cor 15:3, 5), along with an interpretation of the why and the how of that salvation.⁶⁴

§1.3 RECENT VIEWS

Even though most of his work was undertaken in the first half of the twentieth century, Rudolf Bultmann (1884-1976) remains part of the conversation about Paul.⁶⁵ In the first volume of his classic, *Theology of the New Testament*, published in English in 1952, he says that "the proclamation of salvation can . . . be called 'gospel.'"⁶⁶ Paul's gospel is "truth," knowledge, or a message, and something proclaimed by a prophet and teacher which is heard, understood, obeyed, and crystalized into creeds and literature.⁶⁷ In the same period, others such as Johannes Munck (1904-1965) of the University of Aarhus, and the Jewish scholar, Hans J. Schoeps (1909-1980) of the University of Erlangen, for example, continued to hold the view that the gospel was what Paul preached.⁶⁸ Schoeps notes Paul mentioning

---

60. Deissmann, *Paul*, viii.
61. Deissmann, *Paul*, 128.
62. Deissmann, *Paul*, 258-59.
63. Dibelius, *Paul*, 56, 68, 69, 95, 97, 119, 149, 155, 157, 159.
64. Dibelius, *Paul*, 88-89.
65. E.g., Zahl, "New Source for Understanding German Theology," 413-22. However, Wright, "Paul in Current Anglophone Scholarship," 367, suggests that Bultmann is no longer a key discussion partner.
66. Bultmann, *Theology of the New Testament*, 1:34.
67. Bultmann, *Theology of the New Testament*, 1:67, 86, 89, 120, 269, 271, 274, 275, 280, 283, 286, 288, 314-15, 318.
68. Munck, *Paul and the Salvation of Mankind*, 16, 41, 42, 49, 51, 191, 264, 298, 300; Schoeps, *Paul*, 58, 72, 78, 79, 80, 85, 102, 107, 230. Cf. Whiteley, *Theology of St. Paul*, 73.

Spirit-inspired signs and wonders (2 Cor 12:12), but connects them not so much with the gospel as with the justification of Paul's ministry.[69]

In what Victor Furnish called "a magnificent achievement,"[70] Günther Bornkamm (1905–1990) set out in his book, *Paul*, to give both an account of Paul's life as well as an exposition of his gospel and theology. Bornkamm wrote of "the intellectual range" of Paul's gospel,[71] which was a development of the primitive Christian *kerygma*.[72] As one would then expect, Paul's gospel is preached and proclaimed.[73] As Paul Bormann put it, writing at the same time, Paul's "Gospel is the oral, actual spoken word."[74] Yet, for Bornkamm, Paul's theological statements resist being systematized, not because of the changing situation of his letters, but because his mode of thought is "so much dominated by the *encounter between God, man, and the world*" that there is no place for "stock phrases."[75] Importantly, even though Bornkamm distances Paul's gospel from "signs," (1 Cor 2:18–25)[76] he notes that "his gospel and theology in general, exhibit oddly 'enthusiastic' features."[77] Unfortunately, however, Bornkamm does not develop these comments. Ernst Käsemann (1906–98) also distanced Paul's gospel from miracles: "Not individual miracle and ecstatic experiences, but the continuity of . . . service by the congregation is the actual apostolic sign . . . . Thus, the ministry of the Gospel is separated from any kind of enthusiasm (*Schwärmerei*) and a conspicuous boundary is established against enthusiasm as well as traditionalism."[78]

Werner Kümmel (1905–1995) of the University of Marburg said that Paul's gospel, which he preached, revealed God acting righteously to acquit

---

69. Schoeps, *Paul*, 81.

70. Furnish, Review of *Paul*, 501.

71. Bornkamm, *Paul*, xxvi.

72. Bornkamm, *Paul*, 114.

73. Bornkamm, *Paul*, 18, 19, 21, 29, 33, 36, 49, 51, 53, 62, 65, 67, 92, 104, 112, 139.

74. Bormann, *Die Heilswirksamkeit der Verkündigung*, 201: "*Evangelium is das mündliche, das aktuell gesprochene Wort*," which is expressed in the subtitle of the book: *Ein Beitrag zur Theologie der Verkündigung* (A Contribution to a Theology of Proclamation.) Cf. Thrall, *II Corinthians*, 2:668, who says that εὐαγγέλιον ("gospel") "is Paul's frequent term for his own apostolic message (1 Cor 4:15; 9:12, 14, 18, 23; 15:1; 2 Cor 2:12; 4:3–4; 8:18; 9:13)."

75. Bornkamm, *Paul*, 118 (emphasis original).

76. Bornkamm, *Paul*, 159.

77. Bornkamm, *Paul*, 20, 64.

78. Käsemann, "Die Legitimität des Apostels," 70–71. Translation in Klaiber, "Ernst Käsemann as Theological Exegete," 29.

the godless and cause them to become righteous.[79] Using Paul's letter to the Romans as his principle source, F. F. Bruce (1910–1990) of Manchester arrived at similar results.[80]

Leonhard Goppelt (1911–1973) of Munich's Ludwig Maximilian University concluded that in essence Paul's gospel—the preaching of which was the focus of his life—was "both historical tradition and pneumatic kerygma." That is, it grew out of both information handed on about Jesus' life, ministry, and person, as well as Paul's Damascus Road experience. This became gospel when "encountered as kerygmatic address."[81] In other words, the uttered gospel was God's active involvement in Jesus at work in the present.[82]

Ed Sanders, most recently of Duke University, also characterizes Paul's gospel as his preaching of "the saving action of God in Jesus Christ and how his hearers could participate in that action."[83] Notably Sanders goes on to say that Paul explicitly called the gospel "the power of God" (Rom 1:16) suggesting that the gift of salvation is the "presence of the giver who demands obedience," which he calls a "transformation of existence."[84] Also, Sanders notes that Paul reminded his readers that "he brought his gospel not only with the word but also with manifestations of the Spirit," proof of the Christians' present possession of the Spirit.[85] Unfortunately, Sanders offers no comment beyond citing references that become important in this project. Nevertheless, and notably, with Sanders there is a breaking of ranks in him seeing the gospel as more than words.

The comprehensive treatment of Paul's theology by J. Christiaan Beker (1924–1999), professor of biblical theology at Princeton Theological Seminary, included a discussion of Paul's gospel.[86] Beker says that Paul's gospel was not a written text but both the content of an oral proclamation

---

79. Kümmel, *Theology of the New Testament*, 196, 199, 201.

80. Bruce, *Paul*, 325–38. Here could be added Hunter, *Interpreting Paul's Gospel*, 13.

81. Goppelt, *Theology of the New Testament*, 2:41, cf. 2:40.

82. Goppelt, *Theology of the New Testament*, 2:117.

83. Sanders, *Paul and Palestinian Judaism*, 447. Cf. 443–47, 492, 496.

84. Sanders, *Paul and Palestinian Judaism*, 528.

85. Sanders, *Paul and Palestinian Judaism*, 450, citing 1 Cor 2:4; 2 Cor 12:12, and 1 Thess 1:5.

86. Beker, *Paul the Apostle*, 121–23. Cf. Becker, "Gospel, Evangelize, Evangelist," 107–15, who notes that, as used by Paul, εὐαγγέλιον "does not mean only the content of what is preached, but also the act, process and execution of the proclamation." Becker goes on to say that "Content and process of preaching are one" so that "in the very act of proclamation its content becomes reality and brings about the salvation which it contains" (111).

and the act of preaching.[87] The power of the gospel (Rom 1:16), which depends for its truth on its specific identity as of "Jesus Christ and him crucified" (1 Cor 2:2), is verified in its empirical effectiveness.[88] In essence, however, Paul's gospel remains a message that is proclaimed.

In a brief and finely nuanced treatment, Joseph A. Fitzmyer defined Paul's gospel as "the good news of Jesus Christ."[89] In general, according to Fitzmyer, the gospel designated Paul's presentation of the Christ-event; it was "what he preached, proclaimed, announced, spoke about."[90] Fitzmyer noted that Paul's gospel originated in the pre-Pauline kerygmatic tradition, that it was revelatory, normative for the Christian life, promissory in nature in that it continues God's promises made of old, and was universal in character.[91] Also, although Paul did not create a narrative form of the gospel, it was not an abstraction but a salvific force that came "not in words alone, but with power and the holy Spirit" (1 Thess 1:5).[92] Unfortunately, Fitzmyer does not elaborate on "not in words alone." Nevertheless, in this sketch we see Fitzmyer joining Sanders in moving beyond taking Paul's gospel as more than just his message; "it is a 'power' unleashed in the word of . . . human beings, challenging them to accept it," as he put it in his commentary on Romans.[93]

Up to this point it is clear that the broad view is that, in Fitzmyer's words, Paul's gospel is "what he preached, proclaimed, announced, spoke about."[94] Yet, on the eve of the current discussion we can see that there are hints of the idea that Paul's gospel may not be understood in terms of Paul's message alone. Bornkamm noted the oddly enthusiastic features of Paul's gospel and theology; Sanders said that Paul reminded his readers that his gospel came not only in word but also with manifestations of the Spirit; and we have seen even Fitzmyer describe Paul's gospel in terms of a salvific force that came not only in words. Remarkably, in the recent studies of Paul to which we will now turn, these hints are not picked up. Rather, there are slight and subtle developments of the understanding of the gospel in other ways.

---

87. Beker, *Paul the Apostle*, 121–22; cf. Dickson, "Gospel as News," 212–30.
88. Beker, *Paul the Apostle*, 34, 122.
89. Fitzmyer, *Paul and His Theology*, 38.
90. Fitzmyer, *Paul and His Theology*, 38; cf. Fitzmyer, *Romans*, 256.
91. Fitzmyer, *Paul and His Theology*, 39–41.
92. Fitzmyer, *Paul and His Theology*, 40.
93. Fitzmyer, *Romans*, 254.
94. Fitzmyer, *Paul and His Theology*, 38.

§1.4 THE CURRENT DISCUSSION

From the work of some leading, high-profile Pauline scholars of our day the question of the nature of Paul's gospel appears settled, with some slight nuancing of ideas emerging most recently. We will discuss the contributions in order of their publication.

James D. G. Dunn. Lightfoot Professor Emeritus of Divinity at Durham University, Dunn has had a profound and defining influence on Pauline studies. In his magisterial treatment, *The Theology of Paul the Apostle*, Dunn says much the same as will N. T. Wright. He says Paul used the term "gospel" "in talking about the good news proclaimed by and about Jesus."[95] It was for Paul, Dunn says, a "technical term for his own proclamation."[96] In other words, the "gospel" is Paul's message.[97] This news in its "full roundedness"[98] encompassed or touched on justification by faith, participation in Christ, becoming like Christ, the gift of the Spirit, and the Spirit and the outworking of the gospel in ethical corollaries.[99] However, Dunn notes that in his letter to the Romans Paul says the gospel is "the power of God" (Rom 1:16). Taking this into account, Dunn says Paul "clearly has in mind a force that operates with marked effect on people, transforming them—as evident particularly in conversion and resurrection—and providing a source of energy to sustain that qualitatively different life."[100] In other words, for Dunn, the power of God is embodied and mediated through the message or gospel.[101]

N. T. Wright. Presently a professor at the University of St. Andrews, Scotland, Tom Wright is probably the highest-profile, and certainly the most popular and prolific, student of Paul in our time. In a relatively recent article he says Paul's "gospel . . . is a message about Jesus."[102] In his massive, two-volume, 1,660-page *Paul and the Faithfulness of God*, Wright says of Paul's

---

95. Dunn, *Theology of Paul the Apostle*, 168.

96. Dunn, *Theology of Paul the Apostle*, 168. Cf. Dunn, "Gospel According to St. Paul," 140.

97. Dunn, *Theology of Paul the Apostle*, 168. Scot McKnight, a doctoral student of Dunn's, maintains the same view in McKnight, *King Jesus Gospel*, 49–50, and McKnight, *Sermon on the Mount*, 239.

98. Dunn, "Gospel According to St. Paul," 152.

99. Dunn, "Gospel According to St. Paul," 139–53.

100. Dunn, *Romans 1–8*, 39. Hultgren, *Paul's Letter to the Romans*, 72, uses the term, "a message of dynamic 'power'"; cf. Gräbe, *Power of God in Paul's Letters*, 177.

101. Dunn, *Theology of Paul the Apostle*, 168. Cf., e.g., Dunn, "From Jesus' Proclamation to Paul's Gospel," 417–37n.

102. Wright, "Paul as Preacher," 138, cf. 137. Cf., e.g., Wright, *What Saint Paul Really Said*, 151; Wright, "Romans," 423–24; Wright, *Paul in Fresh Perspectives*, 100; Wright, *Paul and the Faithfulness of God*, 410, 914–18.

gospel: "It defined Paul. It defined his work. It defined his communities. It was the shorthand summary of the theology . . . . . It carried God's power."[103] Through what Paul says, according to Wright, "God's power is unleashed, the power of Christ's spirit (1 Cor 2:5)."[104] Thus, when Paul tells the great final—or ultimate or eschatological—story about what has taken place in Jesus, Wright says, "God's spirit goes to work. . . . Human hearts and minds, to their own surprise, are opened, warmed, challenged, broken and healed and remade, all through the word and the Spirit."[105] Clearly, for Wright, the gospel is, as he plainly says in more than one place, Paul's message about Jesus through which the Spirit works.[106] On this view, shared by a considerable number of students of Paul, the gospel is characterized in terms of a narrative or story that is centered around Jesus, in Wright's case at least, through which the Spirit works.[107]

Udo Schnelle. Writing extensively on Paul, Udo Schnelle from Martin-Luther-Universität Halle-Wittenberg has gained wide attention.[108] Again, we have views with which we are now familiar from Dunn and Wright. Schnelle says that "the gospel is the message of salvation."[109] He is quick to point out though that the gospel is more than words. He says "the gospel is mediated through the human word of the apostle, but it cannot be reduced to that; it is the word of God that encounters his hearers in his own preaching."[110] Schnelle says that the gospel is "much more than 'good news'; it is an effective means by which salvation is communicated, a faith-generating event and a faith-effecting power."[111]

---

103. Wright, *Paul and the Faithfulness of God*, 411, cf. 518, where 1 Cor 15:3–8 is taken to sum up the good news. Also, see Wright, "New Perspectives on Paul," 278: "My proposal is this. When Paul refers to 'the gospel,' he is not referring to a system of salvation . . . . But rather to the proclamation that the crucified Jesus of Nazareth has been raised from the dead and thereby demonstrated to both Israel's Messiah and the world's true Lord."

104. Wright, "Paul as Preacher," 137.

105. Wright, "Paul as Preacher," 137. Cf. Conzelmann, *1 Corinthians*, 249, cited p. 146n109 below.

106. Wright, "Paul as Preacher," 138, cf. 137. Cf., e.g., Wright, *What Saint Paul Really Said*, 151; Wright, "Romans," 423–24; Wright, *Paul in Fresh Perspectives*, 100; Wright, *Paul and the Faithfulness of God*, 410, 914–18.

107. See the summary discussion by Longenecker, "Narrative Interest," 3–16.

108. Cf. Cousar, "Apostle Paul," 478–79; Carson, "Locating Udo Schnelle's *Theology*," 133–41.

109. Schnelle, *Apostle Paul*, 405.

110. Schnelle, *Apostle Paul*, 404, citing 1 Thess 2:13; 2 Cor 4:4–6; 5:20. Also, see Bourke, "Holy Spirit as the Controlling Dynamic," 149–50.

111. Schnelle, *Apostle Paul*, 403–4.

Michael J. Gorman. Reading Paul through the lens of missional hermeneutics, Gorman of St. Mary's Seminary and University, Baltimore, argues that for Paul, "gospel" is "a story of salvation"[112] that is both narrated and embodied.[113] Gorman notes Paul saying that he did "not venture to speak of anything except what Christ has accomplished through me to win obedience from the Gentiles, by word and deed, by the power of signs and wonders, by the power of the Spirit of God" (Rom 15:18–19). However, Gorman says: "It would be a mistake to limit the deeds to the signs and wonders . . . . Rather, Paul claims, Christ has lived and worked in him, giving him his mind and empowered him to speak and to live the gospel fully. *This is what the indwelling and empowering Spirit does to people.*"[114] Gorman concludes that Paul is saying that in coming to the gentiles he embodied the gospel—and expected his readers or hearers also to "*become* the gospel."[115]

More recently, in a rich and evocative chapter on "Paul's Gospel,"[116] Gorman continues to emphasize that Paul's gospel is his message, even if a performative one. He says, "For Paul the gospel is not, however, just words; it is *power*—'the power of God for salvation' (Rom 1:16; cf. 1 Thess 2:13)." He goes on to say, "It is God's efficacious or performative utterance."[117] In discussing the "nature of this power and the substance of this good news" Gorman considers "the content of Paul's gospel according to summary statements in his letters"[118] under a number of headings: "Christ Crucified and Raised," "The Gospel in Creed and Verse," "Paul's Master Story," "The Story of God's Faithfulness and Salvation," "A Theopolitical Gospel," and "The Benefits of the Gospel"[119]—all this is "in continuity with the story of Israel and in distinction to the imperial gospel of Rome."[120] Toward the end of the chapter on Paul's gospel, staying with the notion that the gospel is performative utterance, he says that he has "stressed the narrative character of Paul's gospel as the announcement of the good news." This good news, he

112. Gorman, *Reading Paul*, 54.
113. Gorman, *Becoming the Gospel*, e.g., 11, 15–16, 18.
114. Gorman, *Becoming the Gospel*, 45 (emphasis original).
115. Gorman, *Becoming the Gospel*, 45 (emphasis original).
116. Gorman, *Apostle of the Crucified Lord*, 120–39.
117. Gorman, *Apostle of the Crucified Lord*, 120 (emphasis original). Gorman acknowledges that the term "performative utterance" is Luke Timothy Johnson's "commenting on Romans 1:16–17 and referring to the gospel as the power of God to effect salvation." See Gorman, *Inhabiting the Cruciform God*, 101n171, citing Johnson, *Reading Romans*, 25.
118. Gorman, *Apostle of the Crucified Lord*, 120.
119. Gorman, *Apostle of the Crucified Lord*, 121–33.
120. Gorman, *Apostle of the Crucified Lord*, 183.

goes on to say, has "social and political dimensions as well as 'spiritual' or (narrowly construed) 'religious' ones."[121] A little later, as part of a very long sentence synthesizing Paul's big ideas, Gorman says, "Paul preached ... a narrative, apocalyptic, theopolitical gospel of God's shocking faithfulness and grace."[122]

Michael Wolter. A finely nuanced treatment of Paul's concept of gospel, with close attention to Paul's use of the term (verb and noun), enables Wolter to suggest that "Paul's theology of the gospel is that the gospel does not merely *speak* about the power of God ..., but that it itself *is* also God's power that rescues and brings about salvation."[123] Wolter, of the faculty of Protestant Theology at the University of Bonn, goes on to say that, "When Paul labels his gospel 'God's power,' he wishes to express thereby that it does not merely make known the justice of God that creates salvation or give information about it, but that it allows God's justice to become a reality among humans."[124] In turn, it is faith that "unleashes God's salvific work," that "makes Paul's gospel the 'power of God' that brings about salvation."[125] Nevertheless, the gospel remains Paul's words, even if they become God's salvific power.

Douglas A. Campbell. Currently at Duke Divinity School, Duke University, Campbell tantalizingly entitled one of his books, *The Quest for Paul's Gospel: A Suggested Strategy*. From the first lines it is clear that this project "is essentially a sketch of what we might dub the 'grand strategic' level in the debate concerning Paul's theology."[126] Campbell is seeking an outline of Paul's gospel, by which he means he is seeking a coherent explanatory model for Paul's thinking. In the process Campbell considers the justification by faith model, the so-called Lutheran view, in which an individual sinner's faith triggers a transference from a negative state of Jewish legalism to a new state of salvation. This is because the sinner's transgressions are imputed to Christ on the cross and Christ's perfect righteousness is credited to the sinner. This model is set aside because of its distortion of Judaism as contractual, conditional, and individualistic.[127] Campbell also sets aside the Salvation-History model. In this scheme, in

---

121. Gorman, *Apostle of the Crucified Lord*, 133. Cf. Gorman, *Reading Paul*.

122. Gorman, *Apostle of the Crucified Lord*, 183. Cf. Gorman, *Inhabiting the Cruciform God*, 139.

123. Wolter, *Paul*, 64, his emphases.

124. Wolter, *Paul*, 66.

125. Wolter, *Paul*, 67.

126. Campbell, *Quest for Paul's Gospel*, 1.

127. Campbell, *Quest for Paul's Gospel*, 146–78.

which Campbell places W. D. Davies, Oscar Cullmann, and N. T. Wright,[128] Paul is driven by a historical schema of salvation, drawn from a particular reading of the Jewish Scriptures, that links salvific promise in Judaism with its fulfillment in the Messiah Jesus so that those receiving this promise are the "new people of God."[129] This model of Paul's gospel is rejected because it emphasizes Paul's Jewish background rather than the central role of Christ as God with us. Also, it "tends to elevate historical Israel into something of a sacred nation."[130] In turn, this view can give rise to the idea that the church displaces Israel and, sickeningly, is ethnically cleansed.[131]

Campbell instead offers what he calls the "pneumatologically, participatory, martyrological eschatology," or as he (mercifully!) abbreviates it, the PPME strategy. He notes that this model is often referred to more briefly by a single term, "apocalyptic," "eschatological," or "participatory."[132] Campbell explains that in an interchange "The very being of the sinful believer is taken up into Christ's on the Cross, crucified, buried, then resurrected in a transformed state, and here free from sin, according to Paul." Campbell goes on immediately to say that "In a sense, then, a person is absorbed into the Easter events, and transformed through them and by them."[133] For Paul, according to Campbell, this process takes place in relation to the Spirit for "the presence of the Spirit in the lives of Christians is the main testimony of the reality of the event."[134] For Campbell this gospel is, to repeat, the coherent explanatory model for Paul's thinking which, as Campbell discusses it, is something that Paul preaches or proclaims and writes about.[135]

We could turn the pages of others involved in current discussions who have described what they think Paul means by "gospel." But we would come to the same general results: fundamentally, Paul's gospel is his message[136]

---

128. Campbell, *Quest for Paul's Gospel*, 36–38.
129. Campbell, *Quest for Paul's Gospel*, 37.
130. Campbell, *Quest for Paul's Gospel*, 37.
131. Campbell, *Quest for Paul's Gospel*, 37–38.
132. Campbell, *Quest for Paul's Gospel*, 4.
133. Campbell, *Quest for Paul's Gospel*, 39.

134. Campbell, *Quest for Paul's Gospel*, 40. For his summary of Paul's gospel, see Campbell, *Paul*, 139. For a helpful article that articulates a key aspect of his understanding of Paul see Campbell, "Covenant or Contract."

135. E.g., Campbell, *Quest for Paul's Gospel*, 21–26, 246, 252, 257.

136. E.g., see Harnack, *Constitution and Law*, 275–331; Hunter, *Interpreting Paul's Gospel*, 13; Bornkamm, *Paul*, 115; Gaston, *Paul and the Torah*, e.g., 13, 47, 57, 73, 78, 144; Fitzmyer, *Paul and His Theology*, §35; Hays, *Echoes of Scripture*, x; Elliott, *Rhetoric of Romans*, 85, 103, 111; Stuhlmacher, "Pauline Gospel," 149; Stowers, *Rereading of*

that embodies or through faith, as we have seen for Wolter, becomes God's transforming power.[137] In the case of Gorman, the gospel can and is to be embodied. In the case of Campbell, the gospel is the outline of Paul's thinking. It is to be noted that in no case did any of these individuals state or give the impression that in describing Paul's gospel as his message they were defining or dealing with only an aspect of his gospel.

In his contribution to *The Cambridge Companion to St Paul*, Graham Stanton (1940–2009) concludes with a very brief and tantalizing discussion of Paul's gospel coming in power, and in the Spirit. Stanton notes that, for Paul, the gospel was "not merely a set of statements to be affirmed in response to the rhetorical persuasion of a street-corner philosopher." He goes on to say that "the gospel did not make its impact on the basis of his own powers of rhetorical persuasion, but through the power of and conviction of God's Spirit."[138] However, from an examination of what Paul says, we will see that this still does not capture Paul's understanding of either the gospel or its coming.

We have seen that recent discussions of Paul's gospel are dominated by the idea that his gospel is his message or proclamation, even if that proclamation is Spirit-empowered. In turn, this has inevitably led to conclusions about the importance of Paul's theological articulation for the success of his mission. His theological achievement—through which the knowledge "inherent in faith itself" was raised by him "into the clarity of conscious knowing," as Rudolf Bultmann put it[139]—has been taken to be the explanation of Paul's missionary effectiveness, not least among the gentiles. For example, his vision of God's impartiality[140] as intrinsic to the gospel obliged and authorized Paul to act in mission.[141] In turn, if the gospel is

---

Romans, e.g., 217–18, 245, 306–7, 310; Wenham, *Paul*, 63; Nanos, *Mystery of Romans*, 212, 225, 257; Schreiner, *Paul*, 22, 64; Witherington, *Paul's Letter to the Romans*, 50; Schnelle, *Apostle Paul*, 403–5; Watson, *Paul, Judaism, and the Gentiles*, 78; Campbell, *Deliverance of God*, 379; Pokorný, *From the Gospel to the Gospels*, 58; Nanos, *Reading Paul within Judaism*, 7, 9, 78.

137. Wolter, *Paul*, 66–67.

138. Stanton, "Paul's Gospel," 182.

139. Bultmann, *Theology of the New Testament*, 1:190.

140. Those of the so-called "Paul within Judaism" perspective maintain that this impartiality needs to be reexpressed in terms of "the Jew first" approach in which Paul hoped, as Nanos put it, "to ensure the restoration of the dispersed of Israel in the synagogues of Rome *first*, there after bringing the good news to the gentiles *also*" (*Mystery of Romans* 26; emphasis original). Also, e.g., note Nanos and Zetterholm, *Paul within Judaism*, esp. Zetterholm, "Paul within Judaism," 31–51.

141. Furnish, "On Putting Paul in His Place," 16–17.

Paul's message, its propagation is through talking.[142] As Scot McKnight put it, *"to gospel is to tell the story that Jesus is Lord."*[143]

Yet, in the slight breaking of ranks by Sanders and Fitzmyer, and in the work of Gorman and Wolter, there has been a perceptible change in how Paul's gospel is characterized. The missional hermeneutics of Gorman supposes that Paul's gospel was not only what he may have said in his preaching, but also the example of his transformed life that, participating in the life and character of God as revealed in Jesus, embodied the message. Wolter's close attention to Paul's use of the term leads him to conclude that, through faith, the gospel of Paul's message becomes the gospel of the power of God. Nevertheless, from the work of these high-profile interpreters of Paul, his gospel remains understood as centered around his message, in some cases taken to embody and mediate God's power. The inadequacy of even these nuanced views of Paul's gospel as his message will become clear through this project and begins to come into view when we set out in brief what Paul said.

§1.5 THE GOSPEL IN PAUL'S LETTERS

For ease of reference, and to gain an overall impression of what Paul said directly about "gospel," his uses of the term and those closely related to it can be listed, in my translations, in canonical order. *Verbs* (εὐαγγελίζω, "gospel") are identified by italics, nouns (εὐαγγέλιον, "gospel") by underlining.[144]

> "Paul, a servant of Christ Jesus, called to be an apostle set apart to the gospel of God, which he promised beforehand through his prophets in the holy scriptures, the gospel concerning his Son." (Rom 1:1–3a)

> "For God is my witness, whom I serve in my spirit in the gospel of his Son, that without ceasing I remember you always in my prayers." (Rom 1:9–10)

> "hence my eagerness to *gospel* to you also in Rome." (Rom 1:15)

> "For I am not ashamed of the gospel; for it is the power of God to salvation for everyone who has faith." (Rom 1:16)

---

142. Cf. Bormann, *Die Heilswirksamkeit der Verkündigung*, 201.

143. McKnight, "Atonement and Gospel," 138 (emphasis original). Also, see McKnight, *King Jesus Gospel*, 49–50.

144. In order to convey different aspects of Paul's ideas, translations of his texts sometimes vary throughout this project. Also, space prevents setting out Paul's use of all related words, some of which can be seen in the chart in the Appendix below.

"in the day when God will judge the secret thoughts of people according to my gospel through Christ Jesus." (Rom 2:16)

"But how are they to preach unless they are sent? As it is written, 'How beautiful are the feet of those *gospelling* [the][145] good things.'" (Rom 10:15)

"not all have obeyed the gospel." (Rom 10:16)

"Regarding the gospel they are enemies of God for your sake." (Rom 11:28)

"because of the grace given me by God to be a servant of Christ Jesus to the Gentiles, serving the gospel of God, so that the offering of the Gentiles may be acceptable, sanctified by the Holy Spirit." (Rom 15:15b–16)

"For I will not venture to speak of anything except what Christ has accomplished through me to win obedience from the Gentiles, by word and deed, by the power of signs and wonders, by the power of the Spirit of God, so that from Jerusalem and as far around to Illyricum I have fulfilled the gospel of Christ." (Rom 15:18–19)

"Thus I am eager *to gospel* where Christ is not known." (Rom 15:20)

"Now to him who is able to strengthen you according to my gospel and the proclamation of Jesus Christ." (Rom 16:25)

"For Christ did not send me to baptize but *to gospel*, and not in eloquent wisdom, so that the cross of Christ might not be made void." (1 Cor 1:17)

"For in Christ Jesus I became a father to you through the gospel." (1 Cor 4:15)

"but we endure all things in order not to provide any obstacle to the gospel of Christ." (1 Cor 9:12)

"Those who proclaim the gospel should get their living from the gospel." (1 Cor 9:14)

"If I *gospel*, this is not me boasting, for an obligation is laid on me; for woe betide me if I do not *gospel*!" (1 Cor 9:16)

"What is my reward? To *gospel* without charging for the gospel, not to make full use of my authority in the gospel." (1 Cor 9:18)

"I do everything because of the gospel in order to share in it." (1 Cor 9:23)

---

145. On the status of the article τά ("the") see p. 61n247 below.

"Now I make known to you, brothers, the gospel that I *gospelled* to you, and which you received, in which also you stand, through which also you are being saved, if you hold firmly to the message that I *gospelled* to you, unless you have come to believe in vain." (1 Cor 15:1–2)

"Coming to Troas for the gospel of Christ an opportunity for me opened in the Lord." (2 Cor 2:12)

"But if, indeed, our gospel is veiled, to those who are perishing it is veiled. In their case the god of this age has blinded the minds of the unbelievers to keep them from seeing the light of the gospel of the glory of Christ, who is the image of God." (2 Cor 4:3–4)

"With him [Titus] we are sending the brother who is famous in the gospel among all the churches." (2 Cor 8:18)

"Through the approval of this ministry you are glorifying God by the obedience to the confession of the gospel of Christ and by the generosity of your sharing with them and with all others." (2 Cor 9:13)

"For we were not overstepping our limits when we reached you; we were the first to come to you with the gospel of Christ." (2 Cor 10:14)

"so that we may *gospel* beyond you." (2 Cor 10:16)

"For if someone comes and preaches another Jesus whom we did not preach—or if you receive a different spirit from the one you received, or a different gospel from the one you accepted—you tolerate it readily enough." (2 Cor 11:4)

"Did I commit a sin by humbling myself so that you might be exalted, because I freely *gospelled* God's gospel to you?" (2 Cor 11:7)

"I am amazed that you are so quickly deserting the one who called you in the grace of Christ and are turning to a different gospel—not that there is another, but there are some who are confusing you and want to pervert the gospel of Christ." (Gal 1:6–7)

"even if we or an angel from heaven should *gospel* to you different from what we *gospelled* to you, let that one be accursed! As we have said before, and now again I say, if someone *gospels* different from what you have received, let that one be accursed!" (Gal 1:8–9)

"For I want you to know, brothers, my gospel *gospelled* by me is not of human origin." (Gal 1:11)

"[God was] pleased to reveal his Son in me so that I might *gospel* him among the Gentiles." (Gal 1:15b–16)

"'The one persecuting us previously now *gospels* the faith which he previously destroyed.'" (Gal 1:23)

"I laid before them the gospel which I preached among the Gentiles." (Gal 2:2)

"in order that the truth of the gospel might remain with you." (Gal 2:5)

"I had been entrusted with the gospel." (Gal 2:7)

"They were not acting consistently with the truth of the gospel." (Gal 2:14)

"But you know that it was because of physical weakness that I first *gospelled* to you." (Gal 4:13)

"You share in the gospel from the first day until now." (Phil 1:5)

"In my chains and in the defense and confirming of the gospel you are all my partners in the grace" (of God)." (Phil 1:7)

"Rather, I wish you to know brothers that the things that have happened to me have helped advance the gospel." (Phil 1:12)

"These out of love, knowing that for the defense of the gospel I have been put here, . . . *gospel*." (Phil 1:17)

"Live only worthy of the gospel of Christ, so that whether I come and see you or I am absent I hear that you are standing firm in one spirit, one mind, striving together for the faith of the gospel." (Phil 1:27)

"As a son with a father he has served for the gospel." (Phil 2:22)

"in the gospel they have struggled with me and with Clement and my other fellow workers." (Phil 4:3)

"in the beginning of the gospel, when I left from Macedonia." (Phil 4:15)

"our gospel did not come to you in word only but also in power and in the Holy Spirit and in much fullness." (1 Thess 1:5)

"to speak to you the gospel of God." (1 Thess 2:2)

"we have been approved by God to be entrusted with the gospel, thus we speak not to please people but God." (1 Thess 2:4) "we are determined to share with you not only the <u>gospel</u>, but also ourselves." (1 Thess 2:8)

"night and day we work in order not to be a burden to any of you preaching to you the <u>gospel</u> of God." (1 Thess 2:9)

"Timothy our brother and fellow worker of God in the <u>gospel</u> of Christ." (1 Thess 3:2)

"But just now Timothy has come to us from you and *gospelled* to us your faith and love." (1 Thess 3:6)

"I wanted to keep him [Onesimus] with me so that for you he may be of service to me in the imprisonment for the <u>gospel</u>." (Phlm 13)

Listing Paul's use of "gospel" in its various forms and showing how often he used it gives the clear impression that it was very important to him. Even a cursory examination of this list also raises the question of adequacy of the current view that Paul's gospel was his message that embodies or becomes God's transforming power.

§1.6 CONCLUSION

Earlier studies in this survey appear agreed that Paul's gospel was his message—what he preached. With Bornkamm noting that Paul's gospel exhibited oddly "enthusiastic" features,[146] by the middle of the twentieth century there are hints of a change. While for some, Paul's gospel remained the message he preached, others expressed the view that his gospel was more than words. In recent discussions, represented here by Dunn, Wright, Schnelle, and Wolter, Paul's gospel remains his message. Yet, as Dunn put it, that message embodied and mediated the power of God.[147] Even more recently, Paul's gospel in Gorman's missional hermeneutics is an embodiment of the transformative participation in God's life and character revealed in Jesus.[148]

On one reading of Paul, as we will see, it is reasonable to conclude that the gospel is his message and that this message is the foundation of his mission and the reason for its success. However, as we can see from the list of Paul's use of the word, and as we will see more clearly in this

---

146. Bornkamm, *Paul*, 20, 64.

147. Dunn, *Theology of Paul the Apostle*, 168. Cf., e.g., Dunn, "From Jesus' Proclamation to Paul's Gospel," 417–37n.

148. More recently Gorman's missional theosis perspective is explored in Gorman, *Abide and Go*.

project, even when Paul occasionally uses the term "gospel" to refer to his message,[149] or the word implies a message,[150] not only does he have in mind more than empowered ideas,[151] there are a number of places in his letters where we catch a glimpse of his much richer conception of the gospel that underpins his understanding of "gospel." We will also see that, although Paul understood that he embodied the gospel, that embodiment expressed more than the mind or character of Christ.[152]

In the next chapter an exploration of the idea of gospel in the traditions that Paul inherited—Hebraic, Greco-Roman, and Christian—is important. These traditions bring to light what the term "gospel" (verb and noun) would have meant generally to Paul and his readers, and in particular what the term meant for believers who, it will be argued, were using it before Paul. This exercise contributes to understanding what Paul would have meant by "gospel" and will help us see the novelty in his use of the idea "gospel."[153]

---

149. Gal 2:2; 1 Thess 2:2, 4.

150. Rom 2:16; 10:16; 1 Cor 9:14; Phil 1:16.

151. Rom 1:1–6; (cf. 1:3–5); 1 Thess 2:2, 9; cf. 1:5. Notably, in 1 Cor 15:1–8, where Paul describes what has been handed on to him, he begins with propositions with historical content (15:3–4), which lead into and are inextricably related to the encounter with the risen Jesus (15:5–8).

152. See §5.2 (f), §5.5 and §5.6.

153. Cf. §5.5 below.

2

The Gospel Paul Inherited

PAUL WAS NOT THE first person to use the word "gospel." Before him "gospel" had a long history, even if not a very distinguished one. Yet, in his letters Paul uses the term relatively frequently and has given it an important function in his theology and ministry. Paul's self-understanding also revolved around "the gospel," both in terms of his identity in relation to the gospel (noun) and his activity as "gospelling" (verb).[1] Indeed, we have already seen that over half the occurrences of "gospel," or around two thirds (63 percent) of occurrences of the noun "gospel" and just over a third (35 percent) of the occurrences of the verb in the New Testament are found in his correspondence.[2]

As there are so few uses of the term before Paul, especially as a noun,[3] two questions are to be answered in this chapter: (1) where did Paul get this relatively obscure term from, and (2) what did it mean when he borrowed it to use as one of the key terms in his vocabulary? For knowing the source and meaning of the term as Paul took it up can be expected to help explain why he found the term so useful. Also, eventually seeing in relief what Paul received and how he developed and used the term will highlight the emphases and any novelty involved in his views.

There has been no shortage of suggestions as to where Paul got the term "gospel" from. For example, it could be that Paul took over the term, at least as a noun, from its use in the imperial cult,[4] or indirectly from such

   1. See the list of Paul's use of the verb and noun at §1.5 above.
   2. Cf. p.3n22 above and see the chart below in the Appendix.
   3. See the chart below in the Appendix.
   4. Schneemelcher, "Gospel," 72–73; Strecker, "Das Evangelium Jesu Christi,"

a source.⁵ Or, countering that the gospel as "a sacral term of the emperor-cult cannot be maintained," Rudolf Bultmann said that the "absolute use of the word seems to have developed in Hellenistic Christianity gradually, but relatively quickly."⁶ Yet, it could be, as Petr Pokorný says, that "the gospel" was already used among post-Easter followers of Jesus before Paul.⁷ Or, as Peter Stuhlmacher argued, perhaps the use of the term among early Christians derives from Jesus and his use of Isaiah.⁸ Alternatively, as James Dunn suggests: it could be "Paul himself who introduced into Christian vocabulary the noun form of the term ['gospel'] familiar to him both from Isaiah and from the Jesus tradition."⁹ Perhaps, however, echoing Bultmann, we will have to be content with Graham Stanton's conclusion: "I do not think that we can be certain about the *origin* of Christian use of the 'gospel' word group."¹⁰ Along the way, in enquiring where he got the term "gospel" from, we will be able to test the view that Paul or early followers of Jesus developed the noun from the verb.¹¹

In considering the source of "gospel" in Paul's letters we have to keep in mind that there were a number of influences on his intellectual life: the Greco-Roman world, his Jewish culture, including his Scriptures, and earlier tradents of the Jesus traditions. Paul himself may also provide clues as to where he got this word from and perhaps, therefore, its meaning and why it became so important to him. A brief but careful history of the term in the context of our study will help us determine what the term meant generally in Paul's time and what it meant for those who provided him with the term.

183–228; Strecker, "εὐαγγέλιον," 71 (4).

5. Friedrich, "εὐαγγελίζομαι, κτλ," 724–25.

6. Bultmann, *Theology of the New Testament*, 1:87. Cf. Krodel, "Gospel According to Paul," 99.

7. Pokorný, *From the Gospel to the Gospels*, 13. Cf. Harnack, *Constitution and Law*, 294; Tasmuth, "Paul's *Gospel* to the Romans," 312.

8. Isa 61:1. Cf. Matt 11:5/Luke 7:22; 4:18; Acts 10:36; Stuhlmacher, *Das paulinische Evangelium*; Stuhlmacher, "Theme," 1–25; Stuhlmacher, "Pauline Gospel," 149–72.

9. Dunn, "Gospel and the Gospels," 293.

10. Stanton, *Jesus and Gospel*, 35 (emphasis original). Cf. Bultmann, *Theology of the New Testament*, 1:87–88.

11. Cf., e.g., Bowman, "Term *Gospel* and its Cognates," 67: "the idea of a gospel must have followed the path designated by the steps: Hebrew verb −> Galilean Aramaic verb and noun −> NT Greek verb and noun"; Krodel, "Gospel According to Paul," 97; Kümmel, *Introduction to the New Testament*, 35–36.

§2.1 A BRIEF HISTORY OF "GOSPEL"

We cannot be sure when "gospel" entered the Greek language for only a fraction of ancient literature has come down to us.[12] In any case, it is in Homer's epic poetry of the eighth century BCE that we first find "gospel," by which he means primarily the reward good news brings rather than the news itself. He says: "Let me have the good news (εὐαγγέλιον) as soon as he comes to his house, and you can dress me in a cloak and tunic, good clothes."[13] The only other use of εὐαγγέλιον in Homer appears in the same context a few lines later: "Old man, neither shall I pay you this reward for bearing good news (εὐαγγέλιον), nor will Odysseus ever come home."[14] Incredibly, we have no further record of the use of the neuter singular noun "gospel" (εὐαγγέλιον)—the term so important to Paul—from Homer until the apostle's letters.

However, by the time of Aeschylus (?525/4–456/5 BCE), the Greek dramatist, the next extant occurrence of the word group refers not to the reward of good news but to the good news itself. In the introduction to his *Agamemnon* the Watchman says: "But now may there be a happy release from misery, by the appearance in the darkness of the fire that brings good news (εὐαγγέλου)."[15] A little later Aeschylus has the chorus use εὐαγγέλοισιν (plural dative adjective), for a messenger's good news[16] and Clytaemestra[17] uses εὐάγγελος for a messenger of good news. The word "gospel," however, remained of little interest in Greek literature.[18] When a word in the group was used it was across its three meanings:[19] for the reward of good news,[20]

---

12. Discussions and bibliographies related to the history of "gospel" can be found in, e.g., Harnack, "Gospel in the Early Church," 275–349; Burrows, "Origin of the Term 'Gospel,'" 21–33; Deissmann, *Religion of Jesus*, 102–4; Friedrich, "εὐαγγελίζομαι, κτλ," 707 (bibliography); Stuhlmacher, "Theme," 1–25; Strecker, "εὐαγγέλιον," 70 (bibliography); Dickson, "Gospel as News," 212–30; Horbury, "'Gospel' in Herodian Judaea," 7–30; Pokorný, *From the Gospel to the Gospels*; Silva, "εὐαγγέλιον," 306–13 (bibliography, 313).
13. Homer, *Od.* 14.152–53.
14. Homer, *Od.* 14.166.
15. Aeschylus, *Ag.* 21, cf. 475.
16. Aeschylus, *Ag.* 262.
17. Aeschylus, *Ag.* 264.
18. See the Appendix below.
19. Poole, *Synopsis Criticorum*, 4:3–4, followed by, e.g., Harnack, "Gospel in the Early Church," 275, and LSJ, "εὐαγγέλ-ιον," 705a. See the brief comments by Horbury, "'Gospel' in Herodian Judaea," 9.
20. Plutarch, *Demetr.*17 (first to second century CE). Cf LSJ, "εὐαγγέλ-ιον," 705.

for making a thank-offering for good-tidings (εὐαγγέλια θύειν),[21] which can presume good news,[22] and, as we are about to see, for good news itself.[23]

Before Paul, in the handful of times Greek writers used some form of the word "gospel," it generally referred to political news or reports of military success,[24] but also of the birth of a son,[25] of recovering health,[26] or of a relationship.[27] In Greek literature the word had no particular religious association. (Though as we will see below, in an inscription there was an indirect religious association through the plural noun—εὐανγελίων, "good news"—which was connected with the emperor.) Indeed, most Greek writers did not use the word.[28] Instead, they talked of, for example, messengers of "good"[29] or of "the blesseds,"[30] and even, in separate words, of "good" "news."[31] The only surviving example of the rather inelegant, compound word ἀγαθάγελος, "bearer of good news," is provided by Nicolaus of Damascus,[32] friend and advisor to Herod the Great.[33] It is unlikely, then,

---

21. Aristophanes, *Eq.* 656; Plutarch, *Phoc.* 16.8.1; *Cat. Min.* 51.1.4; *Demetr.* 11.4.5; *Praec. ger. rei publ.* 799.F.6; Philostratus, *Vit. Apoll.* 5.8.3. Cf. LSJ, "εὐαγγέλ-ιον," 705.

22. Aristophanes, *Eq.* 656; cf. Friedrich, "εὐαγγελίζομαι, κτλ," 722.

23. Aristophanes, *Eq.* 647; Plutarch, *Sert.* 11; cf. LSJ, "εὐαγγέλ-ιον," 705.

24. Lycurgus, *Leocr.* 18.2 (εὐαγγελιζόμενος, noun); Diogenes of Sinope, *Epistulae* 23.1.1 (εὐαγγελίζω verb); Diodorus Siculus, *Bibliotheca historica* 15.74.2.2 (εὐαγγέλια, plural noun); Nicolaus, *Fragmenta* 9.33 (εὐαγγελίζομαι, verb).

25. Theophrastus, *Char.* 17.7.1 (εὐαγγελιζόμενος, noun).

26. Menander, *Georg.* 83 (εὐαγγελίσασθαι, infinitive).

27. Menander, *Perik.* 993 [or 874] (εὐαγγέλια, plural noun). It is, then, puzzling that Friedrich, "εὐαγγελίζομαι, κτλ," 722, supposes that "The sense of 'good news' is attested only from the time of Cicero, *Att.* 2.3.1."

28. In the Hellenistic perod the "gospel" word group is not found in, e.g., Theocritus, Manetho, Pseudo-Lycophron, Aristarchus, Herodas, Callimachus, Aratus, Apollonius Rhodius, Corinna, Polybius, Bion, Moschus, Parthenius, Dionysius of Halicarnassus, Demetrius of Laconia, or Strabo.

29. E.g., Homer, *Il.* 24.173 (ἀγαθός).

30. *Hom. Hymn.* 29.9 (τῶν μακάρων); cf. Theognis, *Elegiae* 1.574.

31. Euripides, *El.* 230 (τἀγάθἀγγέλλειν); Euripides, *Orest.* 1276 (ἀγγελίαν ἀγαθάν); Aristophanes, *Eq.* 655-66 (ἀγαθαῖσιν εἰσηγγελμέναις εὐαγγέλια); cf. Theognis, *Eleg.* 1.573-74.

32. Nicolaus, *Fragmenta* 66.103.

33. Nicolaus, *Fragmenta* 134-39; Josephus, *Ant.* 16.29. On the uncertain nationality of Nicolaus, see Toher, "'Bios Kaisaros,'" 16n21. Schürer, *History of the Jewish People*, 1:28, is confident "he came from a distinguished non-Jewish family." Nicolaus was probably born in 64 BCE for he is said to be 60 years old at the death of Herod in 4 BCE (Nicolaus, *Fragmenta* 136.8).

that the (non-Jewish) Greek[34] literary world was the source of Paul's use of "gospel."

The Romans also shaped Paul's world. Using its Latin vernacular, Rome had long been a decisive influence in the cities where Paul spent most of his time.[35] In the past it has been argued that Paul spoke Latin,[36] which might open up the possibility that he borrowed the term "gospel" from the Latin world. However, this is highly improbable. First, there is very little direct evidence in his letters that Paul used Latin. The grammatical Latinisms that may point to a knowledge of Latin[37] can generally be explained on the basis of existing Greek usage.[38] Further, Paul uses only three Latin loan words,[39] hardly evidence that the language was part of his means of communication.[40] In any case, second, the earliest and only occurrence of the word "gospel" in a Latin writer before Paul is by Cicero (106–43 BCE). However, he uses not the Latin, but three times directly borrows the word in Greek lettering, εὐαγγέλια, using it to refer to good news.[41] The word was, then, clearly not established in Latin literature. Even if Cicero was expressing a widely held view, which he may be in that he mentions it twice, it was not the habit of the Romans to take up Greek words.[42]

---

34. It is tempting to use the term "secular Greek world" to distinguish between the Jewish and non-Jewish Greek world. However, the term "secular" would be misleading in that there was not then the modern boundary between the religious and the secular.

35. E.g., see Wright, *Paul and the Faithfulness of God*, 279–347, esp. 312.

36. E.g., Ramsay, *Pauline and Other Studies*, 65; Ramsay, "Tarsus XIV," 135–60; Moulton et al., *Grammar of New Testament Greek*, 1:21n2; Souter, "Did St. Paul Speak Latin?," 337–42; Bruce, *Paul*, 315–16. See the discussion by Porter, "Did Paul Speak Latin?" 289–308.

37. E.g., beginning a sentence with a relative pronoun (Gal 2:10; 4:24), and the use of πρό ("before") to specify time (2 Cor 12:2). See the lists and discussions of grammatical Latinisms in Thayer, "Language of the New Testament," 40; Buttmann, *Grammar of the New Testament Greek*, see Index of Subjects, "Latinisms"; Green, *Handbook to the Grammar of the Greek New Testament*, 158–59; Robertson, *Grammar of the Greek New Testament*, 108–11; Moulton et al., *Grammar of New Testament Greek*, vol. 3, see the index, "Latinisms (alleged)"; BDF §5.

38. Porter, "Did Paul Speak Latin?," 303–5, esp. 305.

39. Θριαμβεύω (*triumphare*, "lead in a triumphal procession," 2 Cor 2:14; also in the NT at Col 2:15); μάκελλον (*macellum*, "meat market," 1 Cor 10:25); and πραιτώριον (*praetorium*, "praetorium," Phil 1:13; also in the NT at Matt 27:27; Mark 15:16; John 18:28 (2x), 33; 19:9; Acts 23:35). For a list of lexical Latinisms in the New Testament, see Thayer, "Language of the New Testament," 40; cf. Moulton et al., *Grammar of New Testament Greek*, 2:155.

40. Cf. Porter, "Did Paul Speak Latin?," 308.

41. Cicero, *Att.* 2.3.1; 2.12.1; 3.40.1.

42. Cicero *Off.* 1.31.111; cf. *De or.* 2.36.153. See the discussion by Higbie, "Cicero

While non-Jewish Greek writers had shown little interest in it, in the second century BCE the "gospel" word group burst into the literature through the work of the Greek-speaking translators of the Hebrew Scriptures. The word is not used in the Pentateuch, the first part of the Hebrew Scriptures, translated[43] probably in the early- to mid-third century BCE.[44] However, "gospel" is taken up with relative enthusiasm in the translations of the remainder of the Jewish Scriptures.[45] Though there is no consensus, and any conclusions remain tentative, these translations were likely made a century later as they reflect, for example, Maccabean and Hasmonean events, and the literature of the period.[46] Equally debated is where these translations were undertaken, Egypt or Palestine or, less likely, Babylonia.[47] Notwithstanding, the Greek translations of the Hebrew Scriptures show that it was in second-century Jewish circles that "gospel" found a secure place in Greek literature.

It was primarily as a verb that "gospel" (εὐαγγελίζω) was used in the Greek translations of Scripture.[48] The verb is used twenty-three times to translate "bring news" (בשר),[49] a word that, from its Ugaritic background,

---

the Homerist," 380.

43. *Letter of Aristeas*; Josephus, *Ant.* 1.10–12; Jerome, *Orig. Jer. Ezech.* 5 (see Scheck, *St. Jerome*, 63); cf. Jerome, *Qu. hebr. Gen.* 31; *Comm. Mich.* 2, and the discussion by Swete, *Introduction to the Old Testament in Greek*, 23.

44. In light of serious, though not confounding, questions about the historical value of the *Letter of Aristeas*, it is only with caution that it can be used to establish details of the translation of the Hebrew Scriptures into Greek. See Rappaport, "Letter of Aristeas Again," 285–303. Nevertheless, it is generally said that the Pentateuch was translated by Alexandrian Jews in the time of Ptolemy, and the remainder of the Scriptures followed in the next century. See Swete, *Introduction to the Old Testament in Greek*, 1–23 (esp. 23); Marcos, *Septuagint in Context*, 40, 50; Dines, *Septuagint*, 28–33.

45. Εὐαγγελίζω (verb): 1 Kgdms 31:9; 2 Kgdms 1:20; 4:10; 18:19, 20 (2x), 26, 31; 3 Kgdms 1:42; 1 Chr 10:9; Ps 39:10 (MT 40:10); Ps 67:12 (MT 68:11); Ps 95:2 (MT 96:2); Pss Sol 11:1; Joel 3:5 (MT 2:32); Nah 2:1 (EV 1:15); Isa 40:9 (2x); 52:7 (2x); 60:6; 61:1; Jer 20:15; εὐαγγελία (feminine singular noun): 2 Kgdms 4:10; 18:20, 22, 25, 27; 3 Kgdms 7:9.

46. See Swete, *Introduction to the Old Testament, in Greek* 1–28 and 369–70, and the brief discussion by Dines, *Septuagint*, 41–42.

47. For a survey of views, see Jellicoe, *Septuagint and Modern Study*, 59–73, and the brief discussion by Dines, *Septuagint*, 45–46.

48. Εὐαγγελίζω (verb): 1 Kgdms 31:9; 2 Kgdms 1:20; 4:10; 18:19, 20 (2x), 26, 31; 3 Kgdms 1:42; 1 Chr 10:9; Ps 39:10 (MT 40:10); Ps 67:12 (MT 68:11); Ps 95:2 (MT 96:2); Pss Sol 11:1; Joel 3:5 (MT 2:32); Nah 2:1 (EV 1:15); Isa 40:9 (2x); 52:7 (2x); 60:6; 61:1; Jer 20:15.

49. 1 Kgdms 31:9; 2 Kgdms 1:20; 4:10; 18:19, 20 (x2), 26, 31; 3 Kgdms 1:42; 1 Chr 10:9; Ps 39:10 (MT 40:9); Ps 67:12 (MT 68:11); Ps 95:2 (MT 96:2); Joel 3:5; Nah 2:1; Isa 40:9 (x2); 52:7 (x2); 60:6; 61:1; Jer 20:15; Pss Sol 11:1.

inherently denoted good or joyful news.⁵⁰ As a noun the Greek translators of the Scriptures used "gospel" (εὐαγγελία, feminine singular) only six times — never with any religious significance⁵¹ — both for "good news"⁵² and also its reward.⁵³ Given that a bearer of bad news is punished (2 Kgdms 1:15; 4:10), the message is equated with what is reported,⁵⁴ a point that will become important for understanding Paul.⁵⁵

As did their gentile counterparts, these Jewish translators of Scripture used "gospel" (noun and verb) when referring to military victory.⁵⁶ Not surprisingly they also used the term, mainly as a verb, for news of the birth of a son,⁵⁷ the accession of a king,⁵⁸ eulogizing a king and his son,⁵⁹ and for the welcome news of the death of a king.⁶⁰

Two aspects stand out in the scriptural use of the verb. First, twelve of the occurrences, over half the number, refer to some form of God's saving activity:⁶¹ his military victory,⁶² deliverance (Ps 39:10 [MT 40:9]), mercy (Pss Sol 11:1), promise of peace (Nah 2:1 [MT 1:15]), and his salvation.⁶³ The psalmist, for example, says, "Sing to the Lord, bless his name; tell (εὐαγγελίζεσθε) of his salvation from day to day" (Ps 95:2 [MT 96:2]).

---

50. Friedrich, "εὐαγγελίζομαι, κτλ," 707: "In all Semitic languages, in Accadian, Ethiopic and Arabic, the sense of "joy" is contained in the stem," citing Schniewind, *Euangelion*, 30. Cf. the discussion by Schilling, "בשׂר," 313-15. The exception (1 Kgdms 4:17), in which bad news is conveyed, does not mean that בשׂר is a neutral word, as Koehler and Baumgartner, *Hebräisches und aramäisches Lexikon zum*, 163, suppose, or outweighs the inherently positive meaning of the word, inherited from its Ugaritic background.

51. Cf. Friedrich, "εὐαγγελίζομαι, κτλ," 721.

52. 2 Kgdms 18:20, 25, 27; 4 Kgdms 7:9.

53. 2 Kgdms 4:10; 18:22.

54. Friedrich, "εὐαγγελίζομαι, κτλ," 721.

55. See §5.5 below.

56. Εὐαγγελίζω (verb): 1 Kgdms 31:9; 2 Kgdms 18:19, 20 (2x), 26, 31; 1 Chr 10:9; Ps 67:12 (MT 68:11); εὐαγγελία (noun): 2 Kgdms 18:20, 22, 25, 27; 4 Kgdms 7:9. Cf. p. 28n24 above.

57. Εὐαγγελίζω (verb): Jer 20:15.

58. Εὐαγγελίζω (verb): 1 Kgdms 1:42.

59. Εὐαγγελίζω (verb): 1 Kgdms 31:9; 2 Kgdms 1:20.

60. Εὐαγγελίζω (verb) and εὐαγγέλιον (noun): 2 Kgdms 4:10.

61. 2 Kgdms 18:19, 20 (x2), 26, 31; Ps 39:10 (MT 40:9); Ps 95:2 (MT 96:2); Joel 3:5; Nah 2:1; Isa 52:7; 61:1; Pss Sol 11:1. As the Hebrew of Joel 2:32 has בשׂרידים ("survivors"), to use εὐαγγελιζόμενοι ("messengers," LXX Joel 3:5) the Greek translators likely had בשׂרים ("messengers") in their *Vorlage*. See Stuart, *Hosea-Jonah*, 257n5b.

62. 2 Kgdms 18:19, 20 (2x), 26, 31.

63. Ps 95:2 (MT 96:2); Joel 3:5 (MT 2:32).

Notable, second, is the concentration of the verb "gospel" in Isaiah, all related to Isaiah announcing God's presence (Isa 40:9), particularly in salvation.[64] The herald of good news (εὐαγγελιζόμενος) comforts the people, for God himself is coming to rule them with compassion like a shepherd (40:9). Also, it is said that God will restore his people, which provokes the comment, "How timely upon the mountains are the feet of the messenger who announces (εὐαγγελιζομένου) peace, who brings good news (εὐαγγελιζομένος ἀγαθά), who announces salvation, who says to Zion, 'Your God reigns'" (52:7). Further, in describing the restoration of Jerusalem it is said the gentiles will be attracted to the city, bringing gold and frankincense, and they "shall proclaim (εὐαγγελιοῦνται) the praise of the Lord" (60:6). Then, an anonymous voice declares that the Spirit of the Lord is upon him for "he has sent me to bring good news (εὐαγγελίσασθαι) to the oppressed" (61:1).

Whether or not the Greek Scriptures were influential in Paul's use of "gospel" remains to be determined.[65] For in his period it is not immediately apparent that the Greek Scriptures were important in shaping Jewish thinking about "gospel." Indeed, Gerhard Friedrich put the point strongly: "The NT use of εὐαγγέλιον does not derive from the LXX.... The prior history of the NT concept is not to be sought in the LXX."[66] In line with this assertion, it is clear from the work of Philo (c.20 BCE—c.50 CE),[67] that by Paul's time the word was used among Alexandrian Jews beyond its connection with Scripture. Philo, who uses "gospel" thirteen times, though only as a verb,[68] is obviously well acquainted with the term. Significantly, however, though the Septuagint was important in the Jewish community in Alexandria and was a basis for his writings,[69] Philo's use of the term

---

64. Isa 52:7 (2x); 60:6; 61:1.

65. See §2.4 below.

66. Friedrich, "εὐαγγελίζομαι, κτλ.," 725. More broadly, Schweitzer, *Paul and His Interpreters*, 44–45, made the sweeping statement that Paul "takes no ideas from the Old Testament with a view to giving them a new development, but uses only what he can take from it ready formed.... On the essential nature of the distinctively Pauline world of thought the Old Testament ... throws no light."

67. These dates are extrapolated from the only certain date we have in Philo's life. See *Embassy* 370; cf. 178–79, 357, and the discussions by Morris, "Jewish Philosopher Philo," 3.2.814–16, and Borgen, *Philo of Alexandria*, 14–15.

68. For εὐαγγελίζω ("bring good news") in Philo, see *Creation* 115.5 (also *frag.* 54.4); *Dreams* 2.28; *Joseph* 245.4; 250.4; *Moses* 2.186.3; *Virtues* 41.1; *Rewards* 161.4; *Embassy* 18.4; 99.6; 232.1; *QG* 4.144.4. Προευαγγελίζομαι ("proclaim good news in advance") is known to us first through Philo. See Philo, *Creation* 34.2; *Names* 158.4; *Abraham* 153.2.

69. Borgen, *Philo of Alexandria*, 38–41. For Philo's quotations of Scripture, see Pick, "Philo's Canon of Old Testament," 3 (131–42); Ryle, *Philo and Holy Scripture*. Cf. Cohen, *Philo's Scriptures*.

"gospel" is not determined by his Scriptures. For example, he cites none of the scriptural references to "gospel." For Philo, "gospel" (εὐαγγελίζω, verb) was used for "good news" in general,[70] for political news,[71] for sarcastic news of apostasy,[72] for finding a person,[73] and the recovery of health.[74] He also used it for the experience of hope announcing the coming of joy.[75] He uses the compound "proclaim good news in advance" (προευαγγελίζομαι) for the approach of a friend heralding kindly inner feelings,[76] as does the dawn anticipating sunrise[77] and the flutter of wings foreshadowing the flight of a fledgling.[78] In the same vein he uses "gospel" for stars announcing reaping time[79] and blossoms the coming of fruit.[80] But the political or military use of "gospel," which we have noted in his Scriptures,[81] is not well represented in Philo,[82] and there is no reflection of the use of good news for God's deliverance or salvation. This dissonance between the use of "gospel" in Philo and his Scriptures suggests that for him, and, by inference, readers in Paul's world, the word had become well established in the language apart from its scriptural associations.

In Rome, on the other side of the Mediterranean from Alexandria, writing just after Paul, Josephus (b. 37 or 38 CE),[83] another Jew, also made considerable use of "gospel."[84] As with Philo, his use of the term is not dependent on his Scriptures. On the one hand, when retelling stories from Scripture, five times Josephus introduces the word "gospel."[85] On the other

70. Philo, *Embassy* 99.6; *QG* 4.144.4.
71. Philo, *Dreams* 2.281; *Embassy* 232.1.
72. Philo, *Virtues* 41.1.
73. Philo, *Joseph* 245.4; 250.4.
74. Philo, *Embassy* 18.4.
75. Philo, *Rewards* 161.4.
76. Προευαγγελίζομαι: Philo, *Abraham* 153.2.
77. Προευαγγελίζομαι: Philo, *Creation* 34.2.
78. Προευαγγελίζομαι: Philo, *Names* 158.4.
79. Εὐαγγελίζω: Philo, *Creation* 115.5 (also *frag.* 54.4).
80. Εὐαγγελίζω: Philo, *Moses* 2.186.3.
81. Cf. p. 31nn56 to 60 above.
82. Εὐαγγελίζω: Philo, *Embassy* 99.6; *QG* 4.144.4.
83. Josephus, *Life* 5, 7. On dating Josephus, see Mason, *Josephus and the New Testament*, 51; Rajak, *Josephus*, 11n2, 195n23, 237-38.
84. Εὐαγγελίζω (verb: "bring good news"): Josephus, *Ant.* 5.24, 277, 282; 6.56; 7.245, 250; 11.65; 15.209; 18.228; *J.W.* 1.607; 3.143, 503; εὐαγγελία (noun: "good news"): *Ant.* 18.229; εὐαγγέλιον (noun: "good news"): *J.W.* 2.420; 4.618-19, 656.
85. Josephus, *Ant.* 5.24 (εὐαγγελίζω, verb)/Josh 6:1-27; *Ant.* 5.277 (εὐαγγελίζω)/Judg 13:1-5; Josephus, *Ant.* 5.282 (εὐαγγελίζω)/Judg 13:6-7; Josephus, *Ant.* 6.56

hand, when the word appears in a text from Scripture he is following, twice he takes up the word;[86] on one occasion he uses another word.[87] As both a noun and a verb, Josephus uses "gospel" in military and political contexts, often in relation to the emperor,[88] perhaps in line with its contemporary connotations. There is, then, no suggestion in the way Josephus uses the term that he saw "gospel" as having any particular theological or scriptural significance.

While the use of "gospel" in Hellenistic literature was limited, and largely confined to the Jewish community, inscriptions show that the word group probably had wide use, particularly in connection with the emperor.[89] As we have seen, the word already had strong political associations, and it fell easily into use in relation to the emperor. For example, the political association of "gospel" that we have noted reflected in Josephus is also found in the famous inscription from about 9 BCE, discovered by two German archaeologists at Priene,[90] a town across the Aegean Sea from Athens on the west coast of Asia, about six miles (ten kilometers) inland. Fragments of copies of the inscription have also been found not only in other larger cities—Apameia, Eumeneia, and Dorylaion—but also in the less-populated Maeonia, showing that the text was most probably widely displayed and known.[91] Two lines of the inscription decreeing that the new year is to coincide with the birthday of Augustus contain the statement: "The birthday

(εὐαγγελίζω)/1 Sam 9:26—10:13; Josephus, *Ant.* 11.65 (εὐαγγελίζω)/1 Esd 4:58.

86. Josephus, *Ant.* 7.245 (εὐαγγελίζω, verb)/2 Sam 18:19 (εὐαγγελίζω); Josephus, *Ant.* 7.250 (εὐαγγελίζω)/2 Sam 18:26 (εὐαγγελίζω) and 27 (εὐαγγελία, noun).

87. 2 Sam 18:31 (εὐαγγελίζω)/Josephus, *Ant.* 7.251 (σημαίνω, "report" or "communicate"; in the NT only at Acts 25:27 and Rev 1:1. As "foretell" or "indicate," σημαίνω also appears in the NT in John 12:33, 18:32, 21:19, and Acts 11:28).

88. For the noun, see Josephus, *Ant.* 18.229 (εὐαγγελία, of the death of Tiberius); *J.W.* 2.420 (εὐαγγέλιον, of a request for troops to crush a revolt); 4.618 (εὐαγγέλιον, of the cause of cities celebrating a new emperor); and 4.656 (εὐαγγέλιον, of embassies greeting Vespasian from every quarter). For the verb (εὐαγγελίζω), see 1.607 (to describe Antipater writing of his activities); 3.143 (of the intelligence of Vespasian's military success as God's provision); 3.503 (of news of what Titus has done); Josephus, *Ant.* 5.24 (of Joshua announcing the imminent capture of Jericho); 5.277, 282 (of an angel announcing the birth of a son who will afflict the Philistines); 6.56 (of news of the safety of Saul's assess); 7.245, 250 (of news from David's troops); 11.65 (that Jerusalem and the temple will be restored); 15.209 (news of Caesar's good will); and 18.228 (news of the death of Tiberius).

89. Cf. Porter, "Paul Confronts Caesar," esp. 170-72.

90. See the report by Mommsen and Wiliamowitz-Moellendorff, "Die Einführungen des Asianischen Kalenders," 275-93, and the brief discussion by Deissmann, *Light from the Ancient East*, 370-71.

91. For a discussion of the fragments see Laffi, "Le iscrizioni relative all'introduzione," 9-18; Sherk and Viereck, *Roman Documents*, 328-37. Cf. Lewis and Reinhold, *Roman Civilization*, 1:624-25.

of the god was for the world the beginning of good news."⁹² As we would expect from what we have seen of its use so far, the plural noun (εὐανγελίων) is used for this "good news." In that the inscriptions were intended to be widely read and understood, it can be assumed that εὐανγελίων was a part of the vocabulary of at least the literate populace. These lines come in the context of praising Augustus, a savior, for being filled with divine power for the benefit of humanity, and who is expected to put everything in peaceful order.⁹³ The lines have what Graham Stanton called "an unmistakable whiff of eschatology and soteriology."⁹⁴ Other inscriptions point in a similar direction: the plural noun was used through the Hellenistic period of good news, particularly in relation to the ruler's victories, benefactions, and resulting celebrations.⁹⁵ There is no need, then, to dissent from the view that the word "gospel," in both Paul's tradition and world, connoted at least announcing news.⁹⁶

What is notable for our understanding of the origin of Paul's use of "gospel" is the explicit and elaborate comparison the inscription makes between the emperor and the gods, which has no earlier parallel—marking a change in the imperial cult.⁹⁷ Also of note, this change was widely advertised using the plural noun "gospel."

Given the widespread public placement of the inscription, the use of "gospel" in relation to the emperor is undoubtedly at least part of the background to Paul's use of the term⁹⁸ and the way it would have been read.⁹⁹ That reading would have brought with it an association with a savior figure filled with divine power for the benefit of people, putting everything in peaceful order. However, in using the singular (εὐαγγέλιον) Paul clearly did

---

92. *OGIS* 458 II 40-41: ἦρξεν δὲ τῶι κόσμωι τῶν δι᾽ αὐτὸν εὐανγελί[ων ἡ γενέθλιος] | τοῦ θεοῦ. A translation is also available in Sherk, *Rome and the Greek East*, 125.

93. See also Johnson et al., *Ancient Roman Statutes*, 119 (Document 142=*OGIS* 458 II).

94. Stanton, *Jesus and Gospel*, 32.

95. E.g., *OGIS* (1970) 1.4.41-42; *SEG* (1923) 1.362.7-8; *IG* XII Suppl. (1939), 168; *IG* II2 (1974) 12224; *IG* VII (1892), 417.68; *IGRR* (1964), 860, cited by *NewDocs*, 3.13.

96. Dickson, "Gospel as News," esp. 212, 230.

97. Price, *Rituals and Power*, 55-57.

98. Cf. Stanton, *Jesus and Gospel*, 32.

99. It is possible that Paul's use of "gospel" to promote Jesus as Lord may have caused him to be open to the charge or was charged with treason or *maiestas minuta*, defined by Cicero as "a lessening of the dignity or high estate or authority of the people or of those to whom the people have given authority" (*Inv.* 2.17.53). In brief, see "maiestas," in Hornblower et al., *Oxford Classical Dictionary*, 888–89. In relation to Paul, e.g., Cassidy, *Paul in Chains*, esp. 55–67, 144–62.

not directly borrow the noun "gospel" (εὐανγέλιων, plural) from its use in relation to the emperor cult.

Though we find resonance in the word group between Paul and the emperor cult, the origin of Paul's use of "gospel" remains a puzzle. While the plural noun (εὐανγελίων) was used to convey "good news" relating to the emperor, and his Scriptures used primarily the verb (εὐαγγελίζω, though also the plural noun εὐαγγελία),[100] three-quarters of Paul's use was of the singular noun,[101] which, as we noted at the beginning of this section, is not attested between Homer and his own use.[102] Nevertheless, the ordinary non-Jewish Greek use of the singular noun "gospel" soon after the time of Paul[103] suggests that the word may have been in general, if not wide, spoken use in his period. And we have seen in the use Philo and Josephus made of other forms of the word that there is confirmation of this point. Given the remaining puzzle, we turn to enquire if there was a use of "gospel" among the early followers of Jesus that could explain Paul's interest in, and use of, the term.

§2.2 THE "GOSPEL" AMONG EARLY CHRISTIANS

As we have no earlier Christian writings than Paul's, we are largely dependent on him to tell us about influences on his thinking and work in relation to his use of "gospel." Nevertheless, before we take account of Paul's testimony, we can note the use of "gospel" in the literature arising from or circulating in Judea around the time of Jesus and his earliest followers to show that the word group would have been available to them. Also, we can take into account early traditions in the Gospels that can be considered a source for his use of "gospel." Further, used with care, the book of Acts may also be a source of information on the influence of earlier believers on him.

(a) "Gospel" in Herodian Judea. There is more than sufficient evidence to show that the "gospel" word group would have been familiar to Jesus and his earliest followers who preceded Paul. Given that the Septuagint used the word group,[104] it is notable that there are among the Qumran documents at least fragmentary copies of the Septuagint, though mostly from the

---

100. See p. 30n45 above.

101. See p. 3n22 above. Cf. Barclay, "Why the Roman Empire was Insignificant to Paul," 376n48.

102. See TLG.

103. See Josephus, *J.W.* 2.420; Plutarch, *Ages.* 33.5.1; *Demetr.* 17.6.7; *Glor. Ath.*; Appian, *Bell. civ.* 3.13.93.12; 4.4.20.9; 4.15.113.17.

104. See §2.1 above and the Appendix below.

Pentateuch, where "gospel" is not used.¹⁰⁵ Nevertheless, as well as the probability that the "gospel" word group in Greek would have been familiar to Paul's predecessors in the faith in Judea, there is good evidence that the Aramaic "announcement" (בשורתא), the equivalent of "gospel" (εὐαγγέλιον), was part of the working vocabulary at the time.¹⁰⁶ In particular, the biblical passages relating to the bearer of news (e.g., Isa 40:9; 41:27), especially as the returning Elijah or messianic king (Isa 52:7),¹⁰⁷ bring the Jewish language close to that of the kingship cult reflected in the Augustus inscription.¹⁰⁸ In any case, Herod's temples and cities, and his own attention to a ruler cult in relation to his own reign, nourished the cult of Augustus in Judea.¹⁰⁹

Notably, Gerhard Friedrich points out that in Jewish literature the noun was not related to the eschatological good news, for a new message was not expected. It was the messenger and the act of proclaiming that was more important than the news itself.¹¹⁰ This, as we will see, becomes significant in understanding Paul's notion of "gospel" as much broader than a message. For the present what is to be noted is that the vocabulary of "good news" was available for use by Jesus and his earliest followers and that the interrelations of the verb (בשר) and noun (בשורה) for "good news"¹¹¹ suggests that while this is the fertile soil in which the Pauline notion of "good news" (εὐαγγέλιον) could take root,¹¹² the wider use of "gospel" (εὐαγγέλιον), notably in relation to the emperor, would unavoidably have given significant content to the word group for Paul and his readers.

(b) Gospel traditions. Though the Gospels were all written after Paul had penned his letters, it is possible that earlier traditions—oral or written— taken up by the gospel writers reflect something of the early history of

---

105. See 4Q119 (Lev 26); 4Q120 (Lev 1–5); 4Q121 (Num 3–4); 4Q122 (Deut 11); 4Q127 (Exod paraphrase); 7Q1 (Exod 28); 7Q2 (Bar 6); 8Ḥev 1 (minor prophets). Also, the fragmentary 7Q3–19 may be Greek biblical texts. See Tov, "Greek Biblical Texts," 101–22. Cf. Kraft, "'Textual Mechanics,'" 51–72.

106. Dalman, *Words of Jesus*, 102–3, citing Ber. R. 81; Meg. Taan. xii; Ech. R. i.31; j. Keth. 35a; Ber. ix.1; Shek. 47c; b. Sot. 11a. Also, see Friedrich, "εὐαγγελίζομαι, κτλ," 726–27; Horbury, "'Gospel' in Herodian Judaea," 12–13.

107. Horbury, "'Gospel' in Herodian Judaea," 15 and n19, citing Dalman, *Words of Jesus*, 102–4, and, e.g., Tg. Lam. 2.22; Rab. Song. on 2.13.

108. Horbury, "'Gospel' in Herodian Judaea," 14–15.

109. Horbury, *Jewish Messianism*, 68–77, 134–36; Collins, "Worship of Jesus," esp. 242, 255–57; Horbury, "'Gospel' in Herodian Judaea," 22.

110. Friedrich, "εὐαγγελίζομαι, κτλ," 726.

111. Friedrich, "εὐαγγελίζομαι, κτλ," 726 and n46, citing Gen. Rab. 50 on 19:1 (Michael declares a message) and Num. Rab. 14 on 7:48 (God is the proclaimer of glad tidings).

112. Friedrich, "εὐαγγελίζομαι, κτλ," 726.

"gospel" among followers of Jesus that may have influenced Paul. Mark, the first to write a gospel, uses the noun "gospel" (εὐαγγέλιον) eight times; however, all of them are generally agreed to be redactional.[113] He does not use the verb "gospel" (εὐαγγελίζομαι). In Matthew, all the occurrences of the noun "gospel" (εὐαγγέλιον) are either from his hand,[114] or, in one case, taken up from Mark (Matt 26:13/Mark 14:9). Matthew's only use of the verb is borrowed from Q (εὐαγγελίζομαι; Matt 11:5).[115] Luke also borrows this verb from Q (Luke 7:22), which we will discuss in a moment. In his Gospel, though he does not have the noun, Luke uses the verb "gospel" a further nine times,[116] one perhaps taken up from Mark,[117] the remainder coming from his own hand.[118] The Fourth Gospel uses neither the noun nor the verb "gospel."

---

113. Mark 1:1, 14, 15; 8:35; 10:29; 13:10; 14:9; cf. 16:15. For those who suppose this material to be redaction see Pryke, *Redactional Style*, 10–23. More recently, among those who see this material as redactional, e.g. see France, *Gospel of Mark*, 52, 91, 516, 555, 670; Beavis, *Mark*, 32 (stating the view of Willi Marxsen that Mark has introduced the Pauline term into the Synoptic tradition).

114. (a) On Matt 4:23 (cf. Mark 1:39) see Davies and Allison, *Gospel According to Matthew*, 1:414; Luz, *Matthew 1–7*, 203–5. (b) On Matt 9:35 (cf. Mark 6:6, 34; Luke 10:2) see Davies and Allison, *Gospel According to Matthew*, 2:143–44; Luz, *Matthew 8–20*, 51. (c) On Matt 24:14 (cf. Mark 13:9–10) see Davies and Allison, *Gospel According to Matthew*, 3:343–44; Luz, *Matthew 21–28*, 194–95; Nolland, *Gospel of Matthew*, 966.

115. The discussion of the relationship between the gospels continues unabated. In this project the prevailing view will be adopted that Matthew and Luke rely independently on both Mark and Q. A brief but thorough summary of the question of the relationship between the gospels is set out by Baum, "Synoptic Problem," 911–19. For a more detailed introduction to the problem and a defense of Q, e.g., see Catchpole, *Quest for Q*, 1–59; Tuckett, *Q and the History of Early Christianity*, 1–39; Kloppenborg, *Excavating Q*, 11–54. For an account of Synoptic interrelationships without Q, e.g., see Goulder, "Is Q a Juggernaut?," 667–81; Goodacre, *Case against Q*.

116. In Acts the verb "gospel" (εὐαγγελίζομαι) occurs fifteen times: Acts 5:42; 8:4, 12, 25, 35, 40; 10:36; 11:20; 13:32; 14:7, 15, 21; 15:35; 16:10, and 17:18.

117. The use of εὐαγγελίζομαι at Luke 4:43 may be influenced by Mark 1:15. See Marshall, *Gospel of Luke*, 198.

118. (a) On Luke 1:19 see Nolland, *Luke 1–9:20*, 32. (b) Luke 2:10. Luke's hand is evident through this section (Luke 2:1–21) in which the identification of sources is particularly difficult, suggesting that he is responsible for its composition. See Brown, *Birth of the Messiah*, 411; Nolland, *Luke 1–9:20*, 98. Though his conclusion does not help us trace "gospel" behind Luke's composition, Marshall, *Gospel of Luke*, 97, is more cautious in suggesting that Luke was restricted to stylistic revision of source material. (c) On Luke 3:18/Matt 3:11–12 see Nolland, *Luke 1–9:20*, 154; Bovon, *Luke I*, 127. (d) Luke 4:18. For a brief discussion of the origin of Luke 4:16–30, see Nolland, *Luke 1–9:20*, 192–94, and Fitzmyer, *Gospel According to Luke (I–IX)*, 526–27, who reasonably suggests that as 4:17–21 suit a distinctive Lukan concern they are probably his creation. (e) On Luke 4:43/Mark 1:38 see Marshall, *Gospel of Luke*, 197; also see Luke 4:18, which may be influencing Luke's word use; cf. Bock, *Luke 1:1–9:50*, 440. However, see the

It turns out that there is, then, just one place in the Gospels where we possibly catch a glimpse of the pre-Pauline use of "gospel" among early followers of Jesus. As we have just noted, Matthew and Luke take up the verb "gospel" (εὐαγγελίζω; Matt 11:5/Luke 7:22) from what is referred to as Q, an early Christian tradition they appear to share. Even if Q's history is complex,[119] it is reasonable to suppose that it was published in its final form as early as the 50s, and therefore potentially available to Paul.[120] Indeed, it has been convincingly argued that Paul knew and depended on Q,[121] particularly its mission discourse.[122] In turn, as Q appears to have been influential in Paul's thinking, we need to give attention to what he would have inherited from Q in relation to "gospel."

---

previous note. (f) The Lukan verbal and grammatical characteristics in Luke 8:1—καὶ ἐγένετο ἐν ("and it happened in," in the NT at Mark 1:9; 4:4; Luke 1:59; 5:12, 17; 7:11; 8:1; 9:18, 29, 33; 11:1; 14:1; 17:11, 14; 19:15; 20:1; 24:4, 15, 30, 51); καὶ ἐγένετο ἐν . . . καὶ αὐτός ("and it happened in . . . and he," in the NT at Luke 5:17; 8:1; 17:11; 24:15); καὶ ἐγένετο ("and it happened") in relation to a verb (in the NT at Matt 7:28; 9:10; 11:1; 13:53; 19:1; 26:1; Mark 1:9; 2:23; 4:4; 9:7; Luke 1:23, 41, 59, 65; 2:15, 42, 46; 4:36; 5:12, 17; 6:13; 7:11; 8:1; 9:18, 29, 33; 11:1; 14:1; 17:11; 19:15, 29; 20:1; 22:14, 66; 24:4, 15, 30, 51; Acts 2:2; 5:11; 10:13; Rev 16:18, 19); καθεξῆς ("afterwards," in the NT at Luke 1:3; 8:1; Acts 3:24; 11:4; 18:23); διοδεύω ("travel through," in the NT at Luke 8:1 and Acts 17:1); cf. Creed, *Gospel According to St. Luke*, 112-13; Nolland, *Luke 1-9:20*, 365—suggest Luke is responsible for the statement. Cf. Fitzmyer, *Gospel According to Luke (I-IX)*, 695. Alternatively, Luke has used Q material. Cf. Matt 4:23; 9:35; Marshall, *Gospel of Luke*, 315. (g) On Luke 9:6/Mark 6:12-13 see Marshall, *Gospel of Luke*, 349; Fitzmyer, *Gospel According to Luke (I-IX)*, 754. (h) Luke 16:16/Matt 11:12-13, an example in the NT of Luke's unique combination of εὐαγγελίζομαι with "the kingdom of God" (Luke 4:43; 8:1; Acts 8:13) see Marshall, *Gospel of Luke*, 629. (i) On Luke 20:1 (cf. Mark 11:27) see Marshall, *Gospel of Luke*, 724; Fitzmyer, *Gospel According to Luke (X-XXIV)*, 1271-72; Nolland, *Luke 18:35-24:53*, 943; Bock, *Luke 9:51-24:53*, 1584.

119. Cf., e.g., Kloppenborg, *Excavating Q*.

120. Cf. Catchpole, "Question of Q," 36-37. On the dating of Q, e.g., see Theissen, *Gospels in Context*, 206-34. Allison, *Jesus Tradition in Q*, 49-54. Dunn, *Jesus Remembered*, 159, remains doubtful about specifying a date.

121. The most frequently discussed parallels between Paul and Q include: (1) Luke 10:7/1 Cor 9:14; (2) Luke 16:18/1 Cor 7:10; (3) Luke 17:1-2/Rom 14:13; 1 Cor 8:13; (4) Luke 11:47-51; 13:34/1 Thess 2:14-16. See the discussions by, e.g., Allison, "Pauline Epistles and the Synoptic Gospels," 1-32; Tuckett, "1 Corinthians and Q," 607-19; Tuckett, "Synoptic Tradition in 1 Thessalonians," 160-82; Hiestermann, *Paul and the Synoptic Tradition*, 113-45; and the brief discussion in Twelftree, *Paul and the Miraculous*, 120-22.

122. Cf. 1 Cor 9 and Luke 10, and in particular 1 Cor 9:14 and Luke 10:7 (see the discussion below); 1 Cor 10:27 and Luke 10:8; 1 Thess 4:8 and Luke 10:16. See, e.g., Fjärstedt, *Synoptic Tradition in 1 Corinthians*, 67-77, and interchange between Allison, "Pauline Epistles and the Synoptic Gospels," 1-32, and Tuckett, "Paul and the Synoptic Mission Discourse," 376-81, and the response by Allison, "Paul and the Missionary Discourse," 369-75. Also, see Hollander, "Words of Jesus," 340-57.

Q's single use of the verb "gospel" is in the paragraph about Jesus' reply to John the Baptist. In answer to John's question whether or not Jesus was the One who is to come (Luke 7:20), Jesus is said to describe his ministry in two sets of three parallel phrases of two words each:

the blind receive their sight,	τυφλοὶ ἀναβλέπουσιν,
the lame walk,	χωλοὶ περιπατοῦσιν,
the lepers are cleansed,	λεπροὶ καθαρίζονται
and	καὶ
the deaf hear,	κωφοὶ ἀκούουσιν,
the dead are raised,	νεκροὶ ἐγείρονται,
the poor have good news brought to them.[123]	πτωχοὶ εὐαγγελίζονται[124]

As we will see, it is important to note that this is a place in Christian tradition where Paul would have seen the connection between Isaiah and the idea of gospel, and between the term "gospel" and Jesus the "gospeller."

In order to see what Paul would have gathered from the Q statement about what the "gospel" meant to his predecessors in the faith, we have to take into account three things. First, he would have been able to see that all but one of the parallel clauses in the passage—the one about the cleansing of lepers (cf. 2 Kgs 5)—echoed or were dependent on Isaiah.[125] From this, and Q's frequent allusion to Isaiah,[126] Paul could not but conclude that Isaiah was important in his predecessors' understanding of "gospel" and the ministry of Jesus. Notably, in using Isaiah to describe Jesus' ministry as comforting whose who mourn (Luke 6:21; cf. Isa 61:2) and as the poor being evangelized (Luke 7:22; cf. Isa 61:1), the Q Paul knew portrays Jesus as the evangelizing eschatological prophet of Isaiah.[127]

In turn, second, the resonance of Isaiah in this passage helps us see how Paul probably would have understood the two words πτωχοὶ εὐαγγελίζονται, which can be translated as "the poor have good news brought to them." Although the "poor" invariably included the economically disadvantaged

---

123. Luke 7:22, my translation.

124. Εὐαγγελίζονται: verb, third person, present passive, plural.

125. Cf. Isa 29:18; 42:18; 26:29; also see 35:5–6; 61:1.

126. Luke 3:22 (Isa 11:2; 42:1); Luke 6:20 (Isa 61:1); Luke 6:21 (Isa 61:2–3; 65:18–19); Luke 6:38 (Isa 65:7); Luke 6:29 (Isa 50:6); Luke 6:49 (Isa 28:17–19); Luke 7:22 (Isa 26:19; 29:18–19, cf. 28; 35:5–6; 42:18; 61:1); Luke 9:35 (Isa 42:1); Luke 10:2 (Isa 27:12); Luke 10:13 (Isa 58:8); Luke 10:15 (Isa 14:13–15); Luke 10:21 (Isa 29:14; 44:25); Luke 11:2 (Isa 5:16; 63:16; 64:7); Luke 4:12 (Isa 7:12); Luke 11:22 (Isa 49:24–25; 53:12); Luke 11:23 (Isa 40:11); Luke 13:29 (Isa 25:4; 43:5–6; 49:12; 59:19); Luke 13:34 (Isa 31:5).

127. Cf. Tuckett, "Isaiah in Q," 57.

and socially marginalized, along with his contemporaries, Paul would have taken the term as more widely applied. To begin with, its meaning here is controlled by Isaiah where three broad and interrelated portraits of the poor emerge.[128] In First Isaiah (chs. 1–39), the poor are those squeezed off their lands by the rich and powerful.[129] In Second Isaiah (chs. 40–55), the poor are the exiles in captivity.[130] In Third Isaiah (chs. 56–66), from where the Lukan quotations come, the poor are the whole nation awaiting salvation.[131]

From nearer Paul's time a similar portrait of the poor in Third Isaiah is shared by the Qumran scrolls. Those responsible for the scrolls describe their community—which they took to represent all Israel—as the poor waiting for salvation.[132] Also from around Paul's time, in the Psalms of Solomon, with the parallelism of Hebrew poetry still clear in the extant Greek translation, God's dependent people and the poor are synonymous.[133] In other words, not only under the influence of Third Isaiah in particular, but also from his contemporary culture, in a description of those receiving from God, Paul would have been inclined to take mention of the poor in Q to refer not (only) to a disadvantaged sector of society but primarily as a metaphor expressing the deep need all have of God's salvation and help, or, as defined by Q, to be "gospelled."

Further, third, in its final position in the list, and with its all-encompassing reference in the word "poor," evangelizing "all" effectively encapsulates and summarizes Jesus' ministry. What is notable is that the ministry of Jesus that Paul would have seen in Q is described primarily in terms of various healings and is encapsulated using the verb "gospel." The considerable significance of this use of the "gospel" will become clear and important when in chapters 3 and 4 below we turn to examine what Paul says about "gospel." For the present, we note in Q's use of "gospel" that the verb was in circulation among Paul's predecessors in the Jesus movement and

---

128. Cf. Seccombe, *Possessions and the Poor*, 23–43; Twelftree, *People of the Spirit*, 183–84. However, see the recent critique by Coleman, *Lukan Lens on Wealth and Possessions*.

129. See Isa 3:14-15; 10:1-2; cf. 5:8; See the discussion by Kaiser, *Isaiah 1–12*, 44–45, 70–71.

130. See Isa 25:1–5; 41:8–20; 42:22; 49:13.

131. See Isa 58:4–7; 59:2–15; 61:1; 62:4, 8. Cf. Pss 9:18; 68:10; Zech 11:7, 11. See Goldingay, *Isaiah*, 347.

132. E.g., 1QH^a 23.14–15; 1QM 11.8–15; 13.13–16; 4Q171 1.21; 2.9–12; CD 19.9–10.

133. E.g., Pss Sol 10:5–6; cf. 18:1–4; *1 En.* 108:7. Apart from lone voices, e.g., Hilgenfeld, *Messias Judaeorum*, it is agreed that the Pss Sol were written in Hebrew. See Denis, *Introduction aux pseudépigraphes*, 63, and the summary discussion in Wright, *Psalms of Solomon*, 11–13; and Wright, "Psalms of Solomon," 640.

that he would see in the term the importance of Isaiah in understanding it,[134] that all had a deep need for it, and that healing dominated its expression.

(c) Acts. There is the possibility that, along with Q, Acts lends support to a case that, before Paul, "gospel" as a noun, along with the verb, was also part of the written or spoken vocabulary of the early followers of Jesus who influenced Paul's thinking. In his report to the Jerusalem council—in Paul's presence (Acts 15:12)—Peter is reported as saying: "Men, brothers, you know that from early days God chose among you that through my mouth the Gentiles would hear the message of the gospel and believe" (15:7, my translation).[135]

Though Luke acknowledges the use of the accounts of others (Luke 1:1-4), few now consider any of his written sources to be recoverable.[136] Nevertheless, if as is reasonably concluded, Luke is reporting on the same conference as Paul (Gal 2:1-10),[137] we can be confident that such an event took place involving the same issue—the inclusion of the gentiles—and the same participants, notably including Peter and Paul.[138] Therefore, Luke's description is likely to be the result of more than his imaginative reconstruction.[139] From what he says about his dependence on others (Luke 1:1-4), it is likely that his account is the result of using written and oral sources, as well as his own creativity.[140] Just which parts of his report can be traced back to eyewitness accounts is a matter to be determined. If at least Peter's statement about his call can be established as historically reliable we will have evidence that "gospel" (noun) was part of the vocabulary of

---

134. Cf. Dunn, "Gospel According to St. Paul," 140.

135. Acts 15:7: Ἄνδρες ἀδελφοί, ὑμεῖς ἐπίστασθε ὅτι ἀφ' ἡμερῶν ἀρχαίων ἐν ὑμῖν ἐξελέξατο ὁ θεὸς διὰ τοῦ στόματός μου ἀκοῦσαι τὰ ἔθνη τὸν λόγον τοῦ εὐαγγελίου καὶ πιστεῦσαι.

136. Earlier confidence by e.g. Harnack, *Acts of the Apostles,* and Torrey, *Composition and Date of Acts* in recovering the sources in Acts was given pause by Haenchen, *Acts of the Apostles.* See Jervell, "Problem of Traditions in Acts" (1962), in his *Luke and the People of God,* 19-39 (esp. 20). Among those who have remained confident in identifying Luke's sources in Acts, e.g. see Hemer, *Book of Acts,* 335-64; Fitzmyer, *Acts of the Apostles,* 80-89, who followed Benoit, "La deuxième visite de Saint Paul," 778-92; Pervo, *Acts,* 12-14. For a survey of the discussion of sources from the eighteenth century to the early 1960s, see Dupont, *Sources of the Acts.* For a more recent survey, see Kea, "Source Theories for the Acts," 18-23, who gives special attention to Acts 15. Also, note the brief and balanced summary discussion by Keener, *Acts,* 1:178-83.

137. See the discussions by, e.g., Jewett, *Dating Paul's Life,* 63-87; Longenecker, *Galatians,* lxxii-lxxxviii; Tatum, "Galatians 2:1-14 / Acts 15," 70-81.

138. Lüdemann, *Early Christianity,* 171; Barrett, *Acts of the Apostles,* 2.711.

139. Hanson, *Acts,* 155; though he supposes the "decree" and the accompanying letter are not the result of Luke's imagination.

140. Cf. Barrett, *Acts of the Apostles,* 2:711.

followers of Jesus whom Paul knew. We may also be able to suggest what the term meant.

There is no doubt that, even if he found it in his sources, Luke has left his mark on Peter's speech. The introduction to Peter—he "rose ... said" (ἀναστὰς ... εἶπεν)[141]—and his opening words, "Men, brothers" ("Ανδρες ἀδελφοί, Acts 15:7), are almost uniquely Lukan.[142] Nevertheless, there are hints that Luke may be reflecting earlier tradition in what Peter says. Peter refers to the conversion of Cornelius (10:1—11:18)—the basis of his call— as "from days of old" (ἀφ' ἡμερῶν ἀρχαίων). This implies the episode is near forgotten, when in Luke's story it is recent and dominates the Acts narrative and should have obviated the need for the council.[143] The dissonance created by this phrase suggests that Luke is conveying traditional material. At first sight, the idiom "God made a choice among you" (ἐν ὑμῖν ἐξελέξατο ὁ θεός) may be a Hebraism and therefore point to the early origin of the idea.[144] However, at times adopting a deliberate biblical style, Hebraisms are a special characteristic of Luke's style.[145]

Perhaps more telling of the antiquity of at least one aspect of Peter's speech is the use of the noun "gospel" (εὐαγγέλιον) itself to describe what was being propagated by the early followers of Jesus. While Luke frequently uses the verb "gospel" (εὐαγγελίζομαι) in both of his works,[146] in his Gospel he has not used the noun, and in Acts it is found only one other time (Acts 20:24).[147] Further, introducing the word using one of his favorite phrases,

---

141. In the NT, see Matt 26:62; Acts 1:15; 13:16; 15:7. Cf. Schneider, *Die Apostelgeschichte*, 1:215n25.

142. Aside from Luke's use of the phrase Ἄνδρες ἀδελφοί in Acts 1:16; 2:29, 37; 7:2, 26; 13:15, 26, 38; 15:7, 13; 22:1; 23:1, 6; 28:17, it is known only in 4 Macc 8:19, from a writer sharing the same world as Luke. See de Silva, *4 Maccabees*, xiv–xviii; Van Henton, *Maccabean Martyrs as Saviors*, 73–81.

143. Rackham, *Acts of the Apostles*, 162; Dibelius, "Apostolic Council," 94–95; Pervo, *Acts*, 373.

144. Wilcox, *Semitism of Acts*, 92–93, 177. Torrey, *Composition and Date of Acts*, 21–22, argued that all of Acts 15:7 was a translation from the Aramaic. Bruce, *Acts of the Apostles*, 336, takes a more cautious approach. Barrett, *Acts of the Apostles*, 2:714, sees "no reason to think Luke is here translating with verbal literalness a Hebrew source" as the object of ἐξελέξατο can be taken as ἀκοῦσαι τὰ ἔθνη ... καὶ πιστεῦσαι, which is how the NRSV translates the phrase (quoted above).

145. Dalman, *Words of Jesus*, 38–40; Creed, *Gospel According to St. Luke*, lxxviii–lxxx; Fitzmyer, *Gospel According to Luke (I-IX)*, 118–23.

146. Luke 1:19; 2:10; 3:18; 4:18, 43; 7:22; 8:1; 9:6; 16:16; 20:1; Acts 5:42; 8:4, 12, 25, 35, 40; 10:36; 11:20; 13:32; 14:7, 15, 21; 15:35; 16:10; 17:18.

147. As Acts 20:24 contains key Pauline terms, διακονία ("ministry"), χάρις ("grace"), and εὐαγγέλιον ("gospel"), and appears deliberately to echo Paul, it is of little value in recovering pre-Pauline material. Cf. Fitzmyer, *Acts of the Apostles*, 87, 677–68; Pervo,

"the word of . . .," we could have expected Luke to have Peter say, "the Gentiles would hear the word of God," or "the Lord," from his mouth.[148] Against an apparent aversion to the noun and using "gospel" in the phrase "the word of the gospel"[149] both suggest "gospel" was probably part of his historical tradition, reflecting something Peter had said. In this is further evidence, slight though it be, that Paul did not introduce the noun into Christian vocabulary.[150] That is, though weakly attested, before Paul the noun was probably already in use by early Christians, even if in a limited way. We can note in passing that, even if Luke has introduced "word" (λόγος), in line with the view that a message was equated with its content,[151] the gospel is something to be heard and conveys salvation.

(d) Results. To begin with, we have seen that the Aramaic vocabulary of "gospel"—verb as well as noun—was available in Herodian Judea for Jesus and his earliest followers. Although Peter's speech in Acts has been heavily reworked by Luke, it is most likely that, in a conference in which Paul was participating, Peter used the noun "gospel" to describe or encapsulate the message of salvation of the followers of Jesus. Thus, until we have evidence to the contrary, it is reasonable to conclude that in their bilingual world, Aramaic enabled Paul's predecessors in the faith to bring the singular Greek noun "gospel" (εὐαγγέλιον) into their vocabulary.

When we also take into account what we have seen from Q—that "gospel" as a verb was clearly part of the vocabulary of the early Christians represented in that tradition—it is reasonable to conclude that among the followers of Jesus whom Paul knew, "gospel," as a verb and noun, was in current use. In Q, the verb conveyed to Paul what Jesus was doing—bringing salvation and help—particularly through healing. From Q Paul would also have concluded that Isaiah had made important contributions to what the

---

Acts, 522. However, this evidence supports the conclusion that Luke has little interest in the term.

148. The phrase "the word of God" (τὸν λόγον τοῦ θεοῦ) is particularly Lukan. In the NT the phrase occurs in Matt 15:6, Mark 7:13, Luke 5:1, 8:21, 11:28, Acts 4:31, 6:2, 8:14, 11:1, 13:5, 7, 44, 15:7, 18:11, 2 Cor 2:17, 4:2, Col 1:25, Heb 13:7, Rev 1:2, 9, 6:9, and 20:4. In the NT the phrase "the word of the Lord" (τὸν λόγον τοῦ κυρίου), uniquely Lukan, occurs only in Acts 8:25 (NA[28] citing ℵ B C D E L 38. 81 etc.), 13:44, 48, 15:35, 36, 16:32, and 19:10. Cf. Luke 22:61: τὸν ῥήματος (A D K N etc. have λόγον) τοῦ κυρίου ("the word of the Lord").

149. In Greek literature, the phrase τὸν λόγον τοῦ εὐαγγελίου ("the word of the gospel") only occurs here (Acts 15:7) and again from Origen, *Hom. Jer.* 10.8.27; *Hom. Luc.* 1.11.9; 27.157.5; *Fr. 1 Cor.* 15.57; 76.5; *Fr. Ps. 1-150* 38-2-4.28.

150. Contra Dunn, "Gospel and the Gospels," 293.

151. See §2.1 above.

early followers of Jesus understood by the "gospel."[152] Given that Q probably used the verb of Jesus' ministry dominated by healing, and that Peter used the noun of the message of salvation, it is reasonable to suppose that the early followers of Jesus applied the noun to their understanding of Jesus' ministry and their message about him.[153]

Notwithstanding, while Paul did not introduce the term—noun or verb—to the Christian tradition, finding so few uses of the term among these followers of Jesus, it cannot be concluded that the word group was very important to Paul's predecessors in the faith. While Q may have used the term "gospel" (as a verb), that our only evidence for this comes from a quotation from Isaiah (Luke 7:2; cf. Isa 61:1) suggests that it was not particularly important to this tradition. Taking into account the Jesus saying in Q, "If it is by the Spirit [Luke has "finger"] of God that I cast out demons then has come upon you the kingdom of God,"[154] it can hardly be doubted that "gospel" and the "kingdom of God" were brought into association at least by Q. We will now see from Paul's testimony that we have corroborating evidence that he did not introduce the noun "gospel" into Christian vocabulary.

§2.3 PAUL'S TESTIMONY

So far, we have identified a number of possible sources and influences on Paul's use of "gospel": his Hellenistic culture, his Greek Scriptures, a Christian tradition (Q) with which he was familiar, and from what we see in Acts, his interaction with earlier followers of Jesus. In the hope of identifying the nature and extent of these influences in determining Paul's use and understanding of "gospel" we turn to his letters. In doing so we also see the inherent nature of the "gospel" he took up.

(a) A revealed but shared gospel. In his enthusiasm for using the term "gospel" and what it implied for him it is not immediately apparent that Paul would admit to the influence of others. For example, conveying a strong sense of ownership, Paul talks about "my gospel,"[155] or, with the same

---

152. On the influence of Isaiah in general on the literature of early Christianity, see Moyise and Menken, *Isaiah in the New Testament*.

153. Cf. p. 26n11 above.

154. Matt 12:28/Luke 11:20, my translation.

155. Rom 2:16; 16:25. On the authorship of Rom 16:25 see p. 171n282 below. Cf. 2 Tim 2:8.

meaning, "our gospel."[156] He even stresses that his gospel was not of human origin (Gal 1:11).[157]

In defending himself before the Galatians he says that he did not consult people but that it was God who was pleased "to reveal his Son to (ἐν) me" (Gal 1:16).[158] That Paul uses "revealed" (ἀποκαλύψαι), and not a verb of seeing, shows that he understood the gospel to be divine disclosure or revelation from God.[159] In his earliest letter he says, "we have been approved by God to be entrusted with (πιστευθῆναι) the gospel" (1 Thess 2:4, my translation). The implication is that it was God who has revealed and entrusted him with the gospel (cf. 1 Cor 9:17). From the very beginning of Galatians—"Paul an apostle, sent neither by human commission nor from human authorities, but through Jesus Christ" (Gal 1:1)—and the remainder of the first chapter (cf. 1:16), what is at stake for Paul is that his call to the gentiles is divine and that his gospel is from God.[160]

However, even though he is adamant that his gospel and commission for mission came from God (Gal 1:12), at another level he readily acknowledges that he shares the gospel with other followers of Jesus. To begin with, though some English translations say Paul went to Jerusalem for fifteen days to "visit" Cephas (1:18),[161] using ἱστορέω, with its basic meaning of "inquire into or about,"[162] suggests Paul was gaining information from Peter. Not only did this exchange bring about no change to Paul's gospel, it was part of his case for the veracity of his gospel (1:13—2:14). Thus, in his discussion of the Jerusalem Council, Paul says that he "had been entrusted with (πεπίστευμαι) the gospel for the uncircumcised, just as Peter had been entrusted with the gospel for the circumcised" (2:7). Here the important point for us is that in James, Peter, and John offering him and Barnabas "the right hand of fellowship" (2:9) there is acknowledgment on both sides that they and the Jerusalem "pillars" all share the same gospel. In other words, Paul is not claiming the gospel is new in his ministry.[163] In that Paul implies

---

156. 2 Cor 4:3; 1 Thess 1:5; cf. 2 Thess 2:14. On the "literary plural" see BDF §280; Cranfield, "Changes of Person and Number," 280–89; Thrall, *II Corinthians*, 1:105–7.

157. Cf. Twelftree, *Paul and the Miraculous*, 107–9.

158. See §3.3 (c) below.

159. Cf. Michaelis, "ὁράω, κτλ," 358.

160. Cf. Dunn, "Relationship between Paul and Jerusalem," 112.

161. E.g., see ESV, NET, NJB ("meet"), NKJ ("see"), NRSV.

162. E.g., Polybius, *Hist.* 3.48.12; 3.61.3. Further, see LSJ, "ἱστορέω," 842; BDAG, "ἱστορέω," 483; *EDNT*, "ἱστορέω," 2.207; MGS, "ἱστορέω," 991. See the exchange between Dunn, "Relationship between Paul and Jerusalem," 108–25, Hofius, "Gal. 1.18," 73–85, then Dunn, "Once More—Gal. 1.18," 138–39.

163. Cf. Stuhlmacher, "Pauline Gospel," 157; Dunn, "How New Was Paul's Gospel?,"

that his gospel was the same as those in Jerusalem, the assumption is that they would also have understood what they preached as "the gospel." From what we have seen of Luke's report of the council, this shared gospel was something spoken, conveying salvation.[164]

In writing to the Philippians Paul describes the various motivations of his fellow missionaries. In highlighting that he has been assigned to "defend" (ἀπολογία) the gospel, some, he says, preach out of "envy and rivalry" (φθόνον καὶ ἔριν), others out of "selfish ambition" (ἐριθεία), and others out of "good will" or "pleasure" (εὐκοφία), that is "love" (ἀγάπη, Phil 1:15-17). Despite the various motivations of the missionaries, what is not in question, but assumed, is that all these, including Paul, share the same gospel. The gospel Paul describes as shared is something they "preach" (κηρύσσω, 1:15), "proclaim" (καταγγέλλω, 1:17, 18), or "defend" (ἀπολογία, 1:16), which in context here most obviously means to defend by speaking.

Sharing the same gospel, and the implied interchanges between Paul and other followers of Jesus in these statements, makes it difficult to conclude other than that Paul's reception and understanding of the gospel would have involved the influence of other believers and their traditions. The nature of that influence becomes clear as we take into account other aspects of his testimony.

(b) An inherited gospel. Not only does Paul acknowledge that others also preach the gospel, at another level, in a number of places a close reading of his writings shows that he was reliant for his gospel on earlier traditions, including about Jesus.[165] Probably one of the most significant points established in the twentieth century of Pauline studies is that Paul had Christian predecessors.[166]

In three places—Romans 1, 1 Corinthians 15, and 1 Thessalonians 1—Paul uses the noun "gospel" to describe what appear to be creedal or traditional statements he has received from earlier followers of Jesus. So important are these passages for our project that we will return to them in the next two chapters when we look more closely at what Paul means by "gospel." For the present our interest in these passages is in showing that Paul was dependent on earlier followers of Jesus for his gospel, at least as it is understood in terms of statements and ideas. We begin by noting a

369-74.

164. See §2.2 (c) above.

165. For a concise discussion of the criteria for isolating what he calls "performed creedal, confessional, liturgical, hymnic, and other kinds of tradition" in Paul, see Sumney, *Steward of God's Mysteries*, 15, and also 16-19.

166. So Meeks, "Christian Proteus," 440.

point where he is probably dependent on Q, not for the content, but for his understanding of aspects of the gospel.

(i) 1 Corinthians 9:14. Defending his apostleship, including the right to gain a living from his work, he says, "the Lord directed that those gospelling the gospel should live by the gospel" (1 Cor 9:14, my translation).[167] Paul most probably has in mind the saying of Jesus he knew from Q that was part of the mission charge: "the worker is worthy of reward" (Luke 10:7, my translation).[168]

Depending on the mission charge in Q to legitimize his work, and using the noun and verb "gospel" for what he has and does, we can see what Paul thought he inherited in what he calls "gospel." First, he is supposing that he is obeying the same call and doing the same work as the early followers of Jesus. Second, in that followers replicated the work of their masters,[169] and knowing at least from Q that Jesus' call was to replicate his ministry (cf. Luke 7:22 and 10:7), Paul is also implying that his gospel replicates Jesus' ministry. That is, his gospel was, fundamentally, more than words. Third, therefore, Paul is using the term "gospel" to describe a peripatetic work that involves curing the sick and saying the kingdom of God has come near (cf. 10:7). All these points will become increasingly important through this study.[170] We turn now to three places where Paul is arguably dependent on others for the ideation of his gospel.

(ii) 1 Thessalonians 1:9-10. It is likely that some material that Paul arguably inherited from previous followers of Jesus,[171] now in his earliest letter, would have been understood by him and his readers as "gospel." In the epistolary thanksgiving (1 Thess 1:2–10)[172] Paul reminds his readers of the coming of the gospel and their positive response to it (1:5). As evidence

---

167. 1 Cor 9:14: ὁ κύριος διέταξεν τοῖς τὸ εὐαγγέλιον καταγγέλλουσιν ἐκ τοῦ εὐαγγελίου ζῆν. Also, see the discussion of 1 Cor 9:14 at §4.1 (d) below.

168. See the summary discussion in Twelftree, *Paul and the Miraculous*, 123-24.

169. Cf. Luke 4:43; 8:1; 9:2, 60; 10:9. See Hengel, *Charismatic Leader and His Followers*.

170. Further, see §4.1 (d) below.

171. See the summary discussion by Sumney, *Steward of God's Mysteries*, 88–90, citing, e.g., Best, *Thessalonians*, 85–87; Richard, *First and Second Thessalonians*, 74–76; Bruce, *1 and 2 Thessalonians*, 17–18; Lüdemann, *Paul*, 219.

172. Although O'Brien, *Introductory Thanksgivings*, 143–46, considers Paul's Thanksgiving extends from 1 Thess 1:2 to 3:13, most agree it ends at 1:10. See the discussion by Hooker, "1 Thessalonians 1:9-10," 444.

he says: "For they report of us[173] the kind of welcome we had with you, that[174] ..." (1:9, my translation). It is not clear who is reporting to whom, but the reported lines can be set out in two, three-line strophes:

You turned to God from idols	ἐπεστρέψατε πρὸς τὸν θεὸν ἀπὸ τῶν εἰδώλων
to serve a living and true God	δουλεύειν θεῷ ζῶντι καὶ ἀληθινῷ
[10]and to await his Son out of heaven	[10]καὶ ἀναμένειν τὸν υἱὸν αὐτοῦ ἐκ τῶν οὐρανῶν,
Whom he raised from the dead	ὃν ἤγειρεν ἐκ [τῶν][176] νεκρῶν
Jesus who delivers us	Ἰησοῦν τὸν ῥυόμενον ἡμᾶς
from the coming wrath.[175]	ἐκ τῆς ὀργῆς τῆς ἐρχομένης.

Along with the structure, which suggests its creedal nature, there is considerable evidence (and agreement) that these statements are not of Paul's making, but inherited from earlier Christians:[177] The words "turn" (ἐπιστρέφω)[178] and "heaven" (οὐρανός)[179] are not common in Paul, and he

173. The reading "of you" (ὑμῶν, B 81, 323, 614, e.g.) is probably secondary. See NA[28]; Fee, *First and Second Letters*, 41–42n58.

174. On the cusp of the period in which πῶς will absorb the functions of ὅτι and ὡς, here πῶς can be translated either "that" or "how." See Moulton et al., *Grammar of New Testament Greek*, 3:137 and note 2, citing Matt 12:4; Mark 2:26; 12:26, 41; Luke 14:7; Acts 11:13, and 1 Thess 1:9. Cf. Best, *Thessalonians*, 81.

175. 1 Thess 1:9b–10, my translation. On the structure of the text, see Best, *Thessalonians*, 86; and Richard, *First and Second Thessalonians*, 75.

176. Evidence for the omission of τῶν is not strong. See NA[28] and Best, *Thessalonians*, 85.

177. See the brief essay by Collins, *Thessalonians*, 20–23. Also, for those who consider 1 Thess 1:9–10 pre-Pauline, Munck, "1 Thess 1:9–10," 101 lists W. Lueken, Albrecht Oepke, William Neil, L.-M. Dewaily and B. Rigaux, B. Rigauz, Leon Morris, and Charles Masson, to which can be added, e.g., Best, *Thessalonians*, 81–87. Munck, "1 Thess 1:9–10," 101 also notes dissenters: G. Wohlenberg, George Milligan, James Everett Frame, and Alfred Plummer, to which can be added, e.g., Richard, *First and Second Thessalonians*, 75; Hooker, "1 Thessalonians 1:9-10," 439, who finds the evidence "insufficient to justify labelling the passage as non-Pauline"; and Kim, "Jesus the Son of God as the Gospel," 118n6.

178. Only three of the thirty-five occurrences of ἐπιστρέφω in the NT are in Paul's letters: 2 Cor 3:16; Gal 4:9 (where Paul is reminding the Galatians of their conversation and urging them not to turn back to idols), and here in 1 Thess 1:9 (where Paul is recalling his urging the Thessalonians to turn from idols). In the remainder of the NT see: Matt 10:13; 12:44; 13:15; 24:18; Mark 4:12; 5:30; 8:33; 13:16; Luke 1:16, 17; 2:39; 8:55; 17:4, 31; 22:32; John 21:20; Acts 3:19; 9:35, 40; 11:21; 14:15; 15:19, 36; 16:18; 26:18, 20; 28:27; Jas 5:19, 20; 1 Pet 2:25; 2 Pet 2:22; Rev 1:12. Also, see Milligan, *St Paul's Epistles to the Thessalonians*, 13. Dobschütz, *Die Thessalonicher-Briefe*, 77, notes that we could expect Paul to mention idols before God.

179. Of the 272 occurrences of οὐρανός in the NT, only eleven are from Paul's hand:

usually describes conversion using "believe" (πιστεύω);[180] this is his only use of "true" (ἀληθινός)[181] and "wait" (ἀναμένειν) in his letters.[182] Infrequently in his letters, and only here in this letter, does he refer to "the Son" (ὁ υἱός).[183] We would expect Paul to write of serving Jesus[184] rather than God.[185] Elsewhere Paul says "from dead" (ἐκ [τῶν][186] νεκρῶν), without using the article,[187] and we could expect "save" (σῴζειν)[188] rather than "deliver" (ῥύεσθαι), which is not otherwise used eschatologically by Paul.[189] Further, Ernest Best is right in noting that the only particularly Pauline word in this statement is "idol" (εἴδωλον).[190]

Rom 1:18; 10:6; 1 Cor 8:5; 15:47; 2 Cor 5:1, 2; 12:2; Gal 1:8; Phil 3:20; 1 Thess 1:10; 4:16; cf. Eph 1:10; 3:15; 4:10; 6:9; Col 1:5, 16, 20, 23; 4:1; 2 Thess 1:7.

180. Typically, Paul uses the aorist of πιστεύω to describe conversion. Cf. Rom 13:11; 1 Cor 3:5; 15:2, 11; Gal 2:16. See Best, *Thessalonians*, 82. In noting that the "verb seems to be precisely what is required in the present context" (1 Thess 1:9), the point is missed by Hooker, "1 Thessalonians 1:9–10," 437.

181. 1 Thess 1:9 is the only place Paul uses the adjective ἀληθινός ("true, dependable, genuine, real"), though it is well used in the Johannine literature: John 1:9; 4:23, 37; 6:32; 7:28; 8:16; 15:1; 17:3; 19:35; 1 John 2:8; 5:20; Rev 3:7, 14; 6:10; 15:3; 16:7; 19:2, 9, 11; 21:5; 22:6. Otherwise in the NT ἀληθινός appears in Luke 16:11; Heb 8:2; 9:24; 10:22. In Rom 3:4, God is called "true" (ἀληθής), not in terms of his nature or character but in relation to what he speaks. Cf. Bruce, *1 and 2 Thessalonians*, 18.

182. Paul only uses ἀναμένω ("wait") here in 1 Thess 1:9. Instead of ἀναμένειν we would expect Paul to use a compound of δέχομαι. E.g. ἀπεκδέχομαι ("await eagerly"): Rom 8:19, 23, 25; 1 Cor 1:7; Gal 5:5; Phil 3:20; or ἐκδέχομαι ("wait," "expect"): 1 Cor 11:33; 16:11. Cf. Best, *Thessalonians*, 85.

183. In the NT υἱός (referring to the "son" of God) occurs seventy-eight times (including Mark 1:1). Although Paul uses υἱός ("son" of God) for Jesus fourteen times— Rom 1:3, 4, 9; 5:10; 8:3, 29, 32; 1 Cor 1:9; 2 Cor 1:19; Gal 1:16; 2:20; 4:4, 6; and only once at 1 Thess 1:10; (cf. Eph 4:13; Col 1:13)—this is surprisingly infrequent (cf. Dunn, *Theology of Paul the Apostle*, 224) given his strategic use of the word, particularly in Romans. In any case, this is the only time in this letter that Jesus is designated God's Son (1 Thess 1:10). Cf. Fee, *Thessalonians*, 48–49 and n83.

184. Cf. Rom 12:11; 14:18; 16:18.

185. The injunction in Rom 12:11 is ambiguous. See Hooker, "1 Thessalonians 1:9–10," 437.

186. On the status of τῶν ("the") see p. 49n176 above.

187. See Rom 4:24; 6:4, 9, 13; 7:4; 8:11 (2x); 10:7, 9; 11:15; 1 Cor 15:12, 20; Gal 1:1; Phil 3:11. In the NT, "from the dead" (ἐκ τῶν νεκρῶν) is found only in Eph 5:14 and Col 1:18.

188. E.g. see Rom 5:9, 10; 11:26; 1 Cor 3:15; 5:5. Cf. Best, *Thessalonians*, 85.

189. For "deliver" (ῥύομαι) in Paul: Rom 7:24; 11:26; 15:31; 2 Cor 1:10 (3x); 1 Thess 1:10. Cf. Col 1:13; 2 Thess 3:2; 2 Tim 3:11; 4:17, 18. Elsewhere in the NT, ῥύομαι occurs at Matt 6:13; 27:43; Luke 1:74; and 2 Pet 2:7, 9.

190. Best, *Thessalonians*, 85. Paul dominates the use of εἴδωλον ("idol") in the NT. See Rom 2:22; 1 Cor 8:4, 7; 10:19; 12:2; 2 Cor 6:16; 1 Thess 1:9, and in the remainder of

It is true that the phrase "whom he raised from the dead" (1 Thess 1:10) interrupts the description of Jesus, suggesting Paul may have introduced it.[191] However, as we have just noted in the phrase "from the dead" (ἐκ [τῶν] νεκρῶν), this interruption is not expressed in the way we would expect from Paul. It is reasonable, therefore, to maintain the view that Paul is rehearsing traditional material, untidy though that rehearsal may be. Or, perhaps, Paul is assembling the statements from a reservoir of traditional ideas. Moreover, in the context of this thanksgiving (1:2–10) in which Paul's relationship with his readers is being recalled and reestablished, the description of their conversion using traditional material is more likely to be in terms they shared than for Paul to use the report of a third party.[192] It is not that Paul is reciting an entire creed or rehearsing a complete proclamation of the gospel,[193] but setting out—sufficient of their common belief and memory—for his readers to recall the content of their interaction.[194]

In short, it is reasonable to suppose that in these lines early in his letter to the Thessalonians, Paul is rehearsing memorable (probably oral) tradition he and his readers held in common. Although this pre-Pauline material is not in close proximity to his term "gospel" (1 Thess 1:5), so wedded is the material to his description of the Thessalonians' response to the gospel that it would most probably have been understood by the writer and the recipients as part of their shared understanding of "the gospel."[195] In other words, Paul's use of the noun "gospel" describes traditional material he inherited from earlier Christians. In the next two passages, the association between a creedal statement and "the gospel" is more obvious.

(iii) 1 Corinthians 15:3–5. When he begins to make his case for the resurrection of the dead (1 Cor 15:1–58), Paul reminds his readers of "the gospel" (τό εὐαγγέλιον, noun) he brought to them (15:1), describing it as "a

---

the NT, see Acts 7:41; 15:20; 1 John 5:21; Rev 9:20.

191. Richard, *First and Second Thessalonians*, 57.

192. Contra Richard, *First and Second Thessalonians*, 75. Cf. the brief discussion by Munck, "1 Thess 1:9–10," 102.

193. Contrast Hooker, "1 Thessalonians 1:9–10," 442, who requires 1 Thessalonians 1:9–10 to be a more complete creedal statement in order for this material to be pre-Pauline. However, as Hooker goes on to note (444n33), Paul is no slave to schematic patterns, citing Lambrecht, "Thanksgivings in 1 Thessalonians 1–3," 192.

194. This does not obviate the view that these verses (also) serve as a summary of what is to follow in the letter. See Munck, "1 Thess 1:9–10," 95–110; Hooker, "1 Thessalonians 1:9–10," 435–48.

195. Cf. Dibelius, *An die Thessalonicher I, II, An die Philipper*, 6–7, followed by Neil, *Epistle of Paul to the Thessalonians*, 26.

word" (λόγος, 15:2). The translation difficulties[196] and the range of meanings of λόγος[197] do not obscure Paul's assuming the propositional substance of the gospel in what he goes on to say. For, identifying the gospel and mentioning their reception of it, he proceeds to remind the Corinthians of the information handed on to them:

| that Christ died for our sins
    according to the Scriptures,
    and that he was buried,
[4]and that he was raised on the third day
    according to the Scriptures,
    [5]and that he appeared to Cephas,
then to the twelve.[198] | ὅτι Χριστὸς ἀπέθανεν ὑπὲρ τῶν ἁμαρτιῶν ἡμῶν
    κατὰ τὰς γραφὰς
    καὶ ὅτι ἐτάφη
[4]καὶ ὅτι ἐγήγερται τῇ ἡμέρᾳ τῇ τρίτῃ
    κατὰ τὰς γραφὰς
    [5]καὶ ὅτι ὤφθη Κηφᾷ
εἶτα τοῖς δώδεκα· |

The evidence is strong that these propositions, which he is saying constitute "the gospel," are not his own creation.[199] Paul uses the technical language for receiving and handing on religious instruction,[200] there is the exact and unnecessary repetition of the reference to Scripture suggesting a memorable and established form,[201] and there are hints of a Semitic origin

---

196. See the discussions by Barrett, *First Epistle to the Corinthians*, 336-37; Conzelmann, *1 Corinthians*, 248n4; Thiselton, *First Epistle to the Corinthians*, 1185.

197. BDAG, "λόγος," 598-601.

198. 1 Cor 15:3-5. Cf. Kelly, *Early Christian Creeds*, 17.

199. See the summary discussion by Sumney, *Steward of God's Mysteries*, 20-23. There is considerable discussion on the extent of the material Paul is quoting. See the discussions by Murphy-O'Connor, "Tradition and Redaction in 1 Cor 15:3-7," 583-84, and Bates, *Hermeneutics of the Apostolic Proclamation*, 62n10. E.g., Conzelmann, *1 Corinthians*, 251, suggests that the grammatical construction begins anew in 1 Cor 15:6. However, with 15:5b beginning with εἶτα (or επειτα; ℵ A K 33. 81. 614. 1175) reference to the twelve may be from a different tradition, even if it is pre-Pauline. Cf. p. 53n202 (3) below.

200. 1 Cor 15:1, 3. On the use of the verbs παραλαμβάνω ("receive"; "take to oneself," see Mark 7:4; 1 Cor 11:23; 15:1; Gal 1:9, 12; Col 2:6; 1 Thess 2:13; 4:1; 2 Thess 3:6) and παραδίδωμι ("pass on," "give," "transmit"; see Mark 7:13; Luke 1:2; Acts 6:14; 16:4; 1 Cor 11:2, 23; 2 Pet 2:21; Jude 3) for the transmission of tradition see 1 Cor 11:23 and the discussions by Büchsel, "παραδίδωμι," 172-73; Delling, "παραλαμβάνω," 11-14; and also, Gerhardsson, *Memory and Manuscript*, 288-306; Schrage, *Der erste Brief an die Korinther*, 3:29-31; Fee, *First Epistle to the Corinthians*, 548n12.

201. 1 Cor 15:3-4 (κατὰ τὰς γραφάς). Cf. Kramer, *Christ, Lord, Son of God*, 19.

THE GOSPEL PAUL INHERITED   53

of the material.²⁰² Though there is some dissent,²⁰³ not only is this received material, it is most probable that Paul is citing creedal material that he had received as a unit. The thrice-repeated καὶ ὅτι ("and that"), which Paul uses elsewhere in quoting from a single source (1 Cor 8:4), suggests he is doing the same here.²⁰⁴

Once again we can see that traditional material Paul received from earlier followers of Jesus and then handed on to the Corinthians is something known to him as "the gospel." This "gospel" is statements that constitute a very brief narrative about Jesus dying for sins and, three days after burial, being raised to appear to his closest followers.

However, in the penultimate proposition, "and that he appeared to Cephas," and in the last proposition, "then to the twelve"—likely part of his inheritance²⁰⁵—Paul is demonstrating that he understood he was inheriting a gospel that was more than propositions. Involved in the gospel was not only remarkable information about Christ's death, and his resurrection brought about by God obvious in the use of the passive (ἐργήγερται, "was raised," 1 Cor 15:4), but also the encounter of the risen Christ with Paul's predecessors. Paul considered that he had inherited from his predecessors a gospel in which there was an inextricable link between what was proclaimed and what was experienced.²⁰⁶

(iv) Romans 1:3-4a. Another place where we can see that Paul was reliant on earlier traditions about Jesus, which he calls "gospel," is in Romans. In the opening section of his letter there is a concentrated use of

---

202. If not a translation of a Semitic original, as argued by Jeremias, *Eucharistic Words of Jesus*, 102-3, though criticized by Conzelmann, *1 Corinthians*, 251-54, the Semitisms in 1 Cor 15:3-5 suggest at least a reliance on older material. E.g., (1) there is an absence of particles except καί. (2) The text is dependent on Hebrew rather than Greek Scriptures, for in LXX Isa 53:5, 12 ὑπέρ is not found. (3) In word choice Paul could be expected to use "apostle" (cf. 1 Cor 9:5; 2 Cor 11:5; 12:11; Gal 1:17, 19) rather than "twelve," which only appears here in his letters (1 Cor 15:5). On the use of ὁράω (1 Cor 15:5, 6, 7, 8), instead of the more natural φαίνω, see Jeremias, *Eucharistic Words of Jesus*, 102; cf. 103. (4) The word order in which the ordinal number is placed after the noun in τῇ ἡμέρᾳ τῇ τρίτῃ ("day three") is the only order used in Semitic. See Jeremias, *Eucharistic Words of Jesus*, 103. (5) Paul is using ideas found in other Christian writers. See Mark 8:31; 9:31; 10:32-34; Acts 10:42; 2 Tim 2:8; 1 Pet 2:21-22; 3:18-20. Cf. Conzelmann, *1 Corinthians*, 251n26.

203. Murphy-O'Connor, "Tradition and Redaction in 1 Cor 15:3-7," 582, cites Jean Héring, Paul Winter, Ernst Bammel, and Hans-Werner Bartsch.

204. Murphy-O'Connor, "Tradition and Redaction in 1 Cor 15:3-7," 583-84, followed by Bates, *Hermeneutics of the Apostolic Proclamation*, 62-64.

205. See p. 52n199 above.

206. Note the clear and important discussion by Thiselton, *First Epistle to the Corinthians*, 1187-88.

the word "gospel."[207] Having introduced himself as "set apart" (ἀφορίζω)[208] for the "gospel" (εὐαγγέλιον, noun; Rom 1:1; cf. Gal 1:15) of God, and that he is eager "to gospel" (εὐαγγελίσασθαι, verb; Rom 1:15),[209] he goes on to say what the gospel was about (περί, 1:3):

his Son	τοῦ υἱοῦ αὐτοῦ
came	τοῦ γενομένου
from the seed of David	ἐκ σπέρματος Δαυὶδ
according flesh	κατὰ σάρκα
[4]designated Son of God	[4]τοῦ ὁρισθέντος υἱοῦ θεοῦ
in power	ἐν δυνάμει
according to the spirit of holiness	κατὰ πνεῦμα ἁγιωσύνης
from the resurrection of the dead[210]	ἐξ ἀναστάσεως νεκρῶν

Although the exact limits[211] and precise content[212] are not clear, there is general agreement that Paul is quoting material he has inherited.[213] This is

207. Paul uses the noun εὐαγγέλιον three times (Rom 1:1, 9, 16) and the verb εὐαγγελίζω once (1:15). He also uses the verb καταγγέλλω ("publish or proclaim abroad," 1:8). See the discussion §4.4 below.

208. See BDAG, "ἀφορίζω," 158; Allen, "Old Testament Background, of προ ὁρίζειν in the New Testament," 104–8; and the discussion by Cranfield, *Epistle to the Romans*, 1:53–54.

209. Beaudean, *Paul's Theology of Preaching*, 24, 70, 71, 92, 153, 174, 193, uses "gospelize" to translate the verb εὐαγγελίζω.

210. Rom 1:3–4a, my translation. On the structure of the text, cf. Jewett, "Redaction and Use," 100; Jewett, *Romans*, 97.

211. Compared with the body of the material the distinctive Pauline phrase, "Jesus Christ our Lord" that immediately follows is probably from his hand. In the NT the exact phrase only occurs in Rom 1:4; 5:21; 7:25; 1 Cor 1:9; and Jude 25. Variations of the phrase that include the first-person plural pronoun (ἡμῶν, "our") are also distinctively Pauline: Rom 5:1, 11; 6:23; 8:39; 15:6, 39; 1 Cor 1:2, 3, 7, 8 (?), 10; 15:31, 57; 2 Cor 1:2, 3; 8:9; Gal 1:3; 6:14, 18; Phil 1:2; 1 Thess 1:3; 5:9, 23, 28; Phlm 1, 2, 3. Otherwise, in the NT, see Acts 15:26; Eph 1:3, 17; 3:11, 14; 5:20; 6:24; Col 1:3; 2 Thess 1:2 (?), 12; 2:1, 14, 16; 3:6 (?), 18; 1 Tim 1:2; 6:3, 14; 2 Tim 1:2; Jas 2:1; 1 Pet 1:3; 2 Pet 1:8, 14, 16; 2:20 (?); Jude 4, 17, 21, 25. Cf. Rom 1:7; 1 Cor 6:11; Phlm 25; Eph 1:2; 2 Thess 1:1; 2 Pet 1:11; 3:18.

212. In that ἐν δυνάμαι ("in power") and ἁγιωσύνης ("of holiness") disturb the neat pattern of the text, and that in the NT ἐν δυνάμει is overwhelmingly Pauline (Rom 1:4; 15:13, 19 (x2); 1 Cor 2:5; 4:20; 15:43; 2 Cor 6:7; 1 Thess 1:5; also, Mark 9:1; Col 1:29; 2 Thess 1:11; 1 Pet 1:5) and ἁγιωσύνη ("holiness") is only by Paul in the NT (Rom 1:4; 2 Cor 7:1; 1 Thess 3:13), he is likely to be responsible for their appearance here. See Linnemann, "Tradition und Interpretation in Röm 1:3f," 274–75; Dunn, "Jesus–Flesh and Spirit," 40–42; Jewett, "Redaction and Use," and more briefly in Jewett, *Romans*, 103–8.

213. E.g., see Dunn, "Jesus–Flesh and Spirit," 40n2; Jewett, "Redaction and Use," 99–122; Bates, *Hermeneutics of the Apostolic Proclamation*, 80–83, and Sumney, *Steward*

most apparent in, for example: introducing the gospel in terms of a "promise beforehand" (προεπαγγέλλω, Rom 1:2) so that the reader could expect traditional material;[214] the parallelism typical of shared and memorable texts;[215] the participles at the beginning of subordinate clauses found in other creedal material among early Christians;[216] the Davidic descent of Jesus not otherwise of interest to Paul;[217] and the adoptionist language of ὁρισθέντος ("appointed," "declared," or "designated") found in other formulations of the Christian *kerygma* in the New Testament.[218]

Again, Paul has used the noun "gospel" for a set of propositions describing the Christian message, this time not resulting in a narrative about Jesus culminating in the resurrection (cf. 1 Cor 15:3-5), but in a description of Jesus dependent on the resurrection. The words ἐν δυνάμει ("in power") and ἁγιωσύνης ("of holiness," Rom 1:4), probably coming from Paul's hand, point to something significant about his understanding of the gospel, a point to which we will return.[219]

(c) Results. Although the association of "gospel" with the emperor would have been an unavoidable backdrop to Paul's use of the word, from his testimony we have no hint that Paul's Greek or Latin cultures took an identifiable part in providing the source of his "gospel," or in shaping his understanding of it. Instead, his gospel was revealed (ἀποκαλύψαι) to him by God, and the content of that revealed gospel is the Son, Jesus Christ (Gal 1:11-16).

Yet, despite the claim that his gospel and call came from God, Paul readily acknowledged—and it was agreed by his peers—that he shared the same gospel as other followers of Jesus. Moreover, Paul signals to his readers that propositions forming brief narratives, which he called "the gospel," were handed on to him from others. Using the noun "gospel" for this traditional material suggests the noun was also part of his inheritance in what he spoke

---

of God's Mysteries, 53-56. For dissenting voices, e.g., see Poythress, "Is Romans 1:3-4 a Pauline Confession?," 180-83; Whitsett, "Son of God," 661-62.

214. Jewett, *Romans*, 98.

215. Neufeld, *Earliest Christian Confessions*, 50, 120.

216. Cf. 1 Tim 3:16; 1 Pet 3:18; and the discussion by Kramer, *Christ, Lord, Son of God*, 108 and n356. Cf. Norden, *Agnostos Theos*, 166-68, 202-3, 380-82; Hahn, *Titles of Jesus in Christology*, 247; Wengst, *Christologische Formeln*, 112; Jewett, "Redaction and Use," 100; Jewett, *Romans*, 98.

217. Other than here in Rom 1:3, "David" is only mentioned by Paul in Rom 4:6 and 11:9. However, Paul's interest in David is in relation to his scriptural voice not Jesus' ancestry.

218. See Acts 2:36, 10:42, 13:33, 17:31, and Heb 1:5, cited by Dunn, "Jesus-Flesh and Spirit," 40n2.

219. See §4.4 (a) below.

or preached. Earlier followers of Jesus were, therefore, clearly influential, at least to some extent, in Paul taking up and defining his gospel.[220] Broadly, the gospel in this traditional material is a narrative about God and especially about the salvific significance of the death and resurrection of his Son, Jesus. In assessing the nature and degree of the influence of earlier traditions and followers of Jesus on Paul we also have to take into account his Scriptures, another influence on his thinking.

§2.4 A SCRIPTURAL GOSPEL?

One of the principal sources of raw material for the theological workshop of early Christianity was Scripture. The impact of Scripture on the formation of early Christianity,[221] including Paul's thinking is not open to doubt, nor is his use of Scripture to express his thinking.[222] In particular, Dietrich-Alex Koch's analysis of the themes in which Paul most frequently uses Scripture showed that the focus of his use of Scripture lies in two issues, the righteousness of God and the law on the one hand, and on the other, the common vocation (*Berufung*) of Jews and gentiles.[223] Indeed, given the explosion of the use of "gospel" in the Greek translations of Paul's Scriptures, and that his encounter with "gospel" in the Q tradition came in a description of Jesus' ministry that depended entirely on concepts from Scripture, it could be expected that knowledge of these ancient texts also shaped his understanding of the term.

We have already noted that over half of the occurrences of the verb "gospel" in the Greek translations of the Scriptures refer to God's salvation,[224]

---

220. Cf. Stuhlmacher, "Pauline Gospel," 165.

221. The literature on the early Christians' use of their Scriptures in their own literature, notably in the New Testament texts, is vast. Classic discussions include Dodd, *According to the Scriptures*, and Lindars, *New Testament Apologetic*. Introductory discussions include Hanson, *Living Utterances of God*; Moody Smith, "Use of the Old Testament," 3–65; Snodgrass, "Use of the Old Testament" 407–34; Longenecker, *Biblical Exegesis*; Evans, "Old Testament in the New," 130–45. Also, see Beale and Carson, *Commentary on the New Testament*.

222. Most notably, including for surveys of research on Paul's use of Scripture, see Koch, *Die Schrift als Zeuge des Evangeliums*, 1–11; Hays, *Echoes of Scripture*, 5–14; Stanley, *Paul and the Language of Scripture*, 3–28; Litwak, "Echoes of Scripture?," 260–88; Wagner, *Heralds of the Good News*, 5–13; Bates, *Hermeneutics of the Apostolic Proclamation*.

223. Koch, *Die Schrift als Zeuge des Evangeliums*, 341.

224. 2 Kgdms 18:19, 20 (x2), 26, 31; Pss 39:10 [MT 40:9]; 95:2 [MT 96:2]; Joel 3:5; Nah 2:1; Isa 52:7; 61:1; Pss Sol 11:1. Cf. p. 31n61 above.

and that there is a concentration of the verb in Isaiah.²²⁵ This is notable for we have already seen the importance of Isaiah in informing Jesus and his early followers. That, in his turn, Paul is highly likely to have been influenced by Isaiah is easily demonstrated.

To begin with, in the Judaisms of Paul's time the book of Isaiah was already deeply influential. Isaiah is among the most frequently attested books of Scripture found at Qumran.²²⁶ The Psalms of Solomon²²⁷ is laden with allusions to, and quotations from, Isaiah.²²⁸ As well, the Similitudes of Enoch, also from Paul's time,²²⁹ frequently alludes to Isaiah.²³⁰ Second, not only were the Judaisms of Paul's world greatly influenced by Isaiah, in particular, the Christianity Paul inherited had also been shaped by the book. A point at which this can be most easily seen is in the Q material, a late redaction of which Paul most likely knew.²³¹ Third, not only does Paul make considerable use of Isaiah,²³² his only use of "gospel" from his Scriptures is from Isaiah (see [a] below).

225. Isa 40:9 (x2); 52:7 (x2); 60:6; 61:1.

226. Tov, "Text of Isaiah at Qumran," 491n1, 492; Tov and Pfann, "Lists of the Texts," 27–89; Tov, *Revised Lists of the Texts*, 5–110. On dating the Qumran material, see Doudna, "Dating the Scrolls," 430–65.

227. Some of the Psalms of Solomon were written before Pompey (Pss Sol 4, 7, 12, 15), some in the wake of the first conquest of Jerusalem in 63 BCE (Pss Sol 8) by Pompey and his later death in Egypt in 48 BCE (Pss Sol 2:25; cf. 2:26). See the discussion by Seager, *Pompey the Great*, esp. 168. For the dating of Pss Sol, e.g., see Collins, *Scepter and the Star*, 52–54. Other Psalms of Solomon were written following Herod's extermination of the Hasmoneans in 30 BCE (Pss Sol 17). See Atkinson, "Herod the Great," 313–22, and Wright, *Psalms of Solomon*, 1–7.

228. Wright, "Psalms of Solomon," 639–70, see the marginalia. Cf. Hannah, "Isaiah within Judaism," 15–16.

229. Though difficult to date, the Similitudes of Enoch are agreed to come from between the first century BCE and the first century CE. See the brief discussion in Hannah, "Isaiah within Judaism," 17n45. Cf. Suter, "Enoch in Sheol," 441–42; Stone, "Enoch's Date in Limbo," 444–49; Charlesworth, "Can We Discern the Composition," 450–68.

230. E.g., *1 En.* 38:2; cf. Isa 58:8, 10; 59:9; 60:1, 3; *1 En.* 39:3–14; cf. Isa 6:3; 39:12; *1 En.* 45:3–4; cf. Isa 42:1; *1 En.* 45:4b–5a; cf. Isa 65:17; 66:22; *1 En.* 46:1, 3; Cf. Isa 9:7 (MT 9:6); 11:4–5; *1 En.* 46:4–8; cf. Isa 14:3–23; *1 En.* 48:2–6; cf. Isa 49:1–7; 61:1–3; and *1 En.* 49:1–4; cf. Isa 11:1–9. There also appears to be a form-critical relationship between the fourth servant song of Isaiah (Isa 52:13—53:12) and *1 En.* 62–63. See *1 En.* 62:1; cf. Isa 42:1; *1 En.* 62:1–2a; cf. Isa 52:13; *1 En.* 62:2–3; cf. Isa 11:1–9; *1 En.* 62:3–5; cf. Isa 52:14; *1 En.* 62:4–5; cf. Isa 13:3; 21:3; 26:17; 62:5; cf. 13:8; *1 En.* 62:6, 9; 63:1–11; cf. Isa 53:1–6; *1 En.* 62:11–12; cf. Isa 34:5–6. See the discussion by Knibb, "Isaianic Traditions," 218–25; Hannah, "Isaiah within Judaism," 16–18.

231. See §2.2 (b) above.

232. See the table by Moody Smith, "Pauline Literature," 268–72 and the lists by Wilk, *Die Bedeutung des Jesajabuches für Paulus*, 443–46.

What is in question here, then, is how far Scripture was a source for his "gospel" and his understanding of it. Did Paul find his gospel (or at least aspects of it) in his Scriptures, or was it shaped by them, or were they of no significance in his understanding of "gospel"? If Scripture was important in Paul's understanding of the gospel, was that understanding mediated to him by earlier members of the Jesus movement or was it his own construction from reading Scripture? There are a number of places in his letters where we see the potential contribution of Scripture to Paul's understanding of "gospel." They are places where he is echoing[233] or quoting Scripture in relation to the gospel.

Initial caution is advised in supposing that Paul found his gospel, or his understanding of it, either directly or entirely from Scripture. For on the one hand, though he cites Scripture explicitly about 100 times,[234] only once does a citation involve "gospel." On the other hand, in his discussion of "gospel" he only occasionally uses Scripture to contribute to his definition.[235] Yet, even from this limited data important answers to our questions emerge as we take into account not only where Paul cites "gospel" from his Scriptures, but also where he engages his Scriptures—either in quotations or allusions—when he is talking about "gospel." We begin with a section of his letter to the Romans, the only place where Paul takes up the word "gospel" from his Scriptures, both in an allusion and a quotation.

(a) Romans 10:5–15. Part of Paul's argument in Romans is establishing that Israel's guilt is obvious.[236] At the point where "gospel" in his Scriptures is significant for his case, he says the law, which had been given, and had become important, to Israel (10:2), pointed to faith in Christ (10:4). But, he says, despite ample opportunity for everyone to call on the name of the Lord and be saved (10:13), Israel remained disobedient (10:21). In making his case Paul first alludes to and then cites from Joel in his Scriptures.

Apart from the addition of the conjunction "for" (γάρ), Paul cites Joel exactly in order to show that Israel was without excuse: "[for] everyone who calls on the name of the Lord shall be saved."[237] The sentence in Joel continues: "because in Mount Zion and in Jerusalem there shall be one who escapes, as the Lord has said, and those who receive good news

---

233. On detecting or "hearing echoes," see Hays, *Echoes of Scripture,* 29–32.

234. Cf. Moody Smith, "Pauline Literature," 268–72; Moyise, *Old Testament in the New,* 117. Koch, *Die Schrift als Zeuge des Evangeliums,* 21–24, gives a figure of eighty-nine; Ellis, *Paul's Use of the Old Testament,* 150–52, gives a figure of ninety-three.

235. Rom 1:1–2, 16–17; 11:25–28; 15:20–21; 1 Cor 9:16; 2 Cor 10:16.

236. E.g., Rom 2:17—3:20; 9:30—10:21.

237. Rom 10:13; cf. LXX Joel 3:5; (2:32 MT).

(εὐαγγελιζόμενοι), whom the Lord has called" (LXX Joel 3:5 [MT 2:32]; my translation).

Even though Paul does not reproduce this entire statement we can reasonably presume that the context of his Joel quotation that uses "gospel" informed his thinking.[238] The importance of the whole passage to him is suggested not only in noting that other early Christians used this section of Scripture (Joel 2:18—3:5) to understand their experience of God's activity,[239] but also in that Paul himself echoes another part of it elsewhere.[240] In particular, one of the cornerstones of Paul's argument so far in this section of his letter (Rom 9:6-29) has been based on taking up the prophetic principle that "only a remnant will be saved" (9:27; cf. Isa 10:22), which is also taken up in the remainder of the Joel passage (Joel 2:32). Also, although Paul is making a christological statement in referring to "the Lord" as Christ, his main interest is in establishing that everyone (Rom 10:4), Jew and Greek (10:12), can be saved, the same point made in the remainder of Joel's statement.

What this passage would establish for Paul in relation to "gospel" is that receiving God's call to be saved is equivalent to receiving the gospel. In this context the passive verb "receive gospel" (εὐαγγελιζόμενοι) is naturally understood as receiving a spoken message. Also, in line with what we have already noted, the Joel passage is used to reinforce Paul's point that the gospel is universally available and applicable.

To carry his argument, immediately following the citation of Joel, Paul continues to use quotations from Scripture, particularly from Isaiah.[241] His precise point is that, despite ongoing opportunities, Israel has not obeyed God's call inherent in the gospel (Rom 10:14-21).[242] Leading to his quotations from Isaiah, Paul uses a set of progressive rhetorical questions

---

238. Cf. Dunn, *Romans 9-16*, 611.

239. Cf. Matt 3:11 and Joel 3:1-5; Matt 9:2 and Joel 2:21-22; Matt 11:22 and Joel 3:4; Matt 24:29 and Joel 3:4; Mark 6:50 and Joel 2:12-22; Mark 13:24 and Joel 3:1; Mark 13:34 and Joel 3:4; Luke 12:51 and Joel 2:31; Luke 21:25 and Joel 3:3-4; Acts 2:17-21 and Joel 2:28-32; Acts 2:39 and Joel 3:5; Titus 3:6 and Joel 3:1; Rev 6:12 and Joel 3:4; Rev 8:7 and Joel 3:3; Rev 14:1 and Joel 3:5. See the brief discussion in Wolff, *Joel and Amos*, 69-70.

240. Cf. Rom 5:5 and Joel 2:28; and see Behm, "ἐκχέω, ἐκχύν(ν)ω," 468-69; Cranfield, *Epistle to the Romans*, 1:262-63; Dunn, *Jesus and the Spirit*, 142; Cosby, "Paul's Persuasive Language in Romans 5," 215. Cf. 1 Cor 1:2 and Joel 3:5; and see Fee, *First Epistle to the Corinthians*, 34n26.

241. See Rom 10:15 and Isa 52:7; Nah 2:1; Rom 10:16 and Isa 53:1; Rom 10:18 and Ps 18:5; Rom 10:19 and Deut 32:21; Rom 10:20 and Isa 65:1; Rom 10:21 and Isa 65:2.

242. Cf. Dunn, *Romans 9-16*, 619; Ziesler, *Paul's Letter to the Romans*, 265.

(10:14-15a), each one picking up on the last motif in the previous one—a *gradatio*:[243]

¹⁴How then shall they call on the one in whom they have not believed?	¹⁴Πῶς οὖν ἐπικαλέσωνται εἰς ὃν οὐκ ἐπίστευσαν;
And how can they believe in one of whom they have not heard?	πῶς δὲ πιστεύσωσιν οὗ οὐκ ἤκουσαν;
And how can they hear without someone preaching?	πῶς δὲ ἀκούσωσιν χωρὶς κηρύσσοντος;
¹⁵And how can they preach unless they are sent?[244]	¹⁵πῶς δὲ κηρύξωσιν ἐὰν μὴ ἀποσταλῶσιν;

With the formula "As it is written" (καθὼς γέγραπται)[245]—equivalent to saying "God said"[246]—Paul then draws attention to his first scriptural quotation, his only direct quotation of "gospel" from his Scriptures (Rom 10:15b). At first glance it is not clear whether he has taken the quotation from Nahum or Isaiah. However, setting out the options in parallel with the similarities underlined it is clear both that his source is Isaiah and that he has made what turns out to be significant changes to Scripture. Those changes tell us about the contribution of Scripture to his understanding of "gospel."

<u>ὡς ὡραῖοι</u> <u>οἱ πόδες</u> τῶν <u>εὐαγγελιζομένων</u> [τὰ][247] <u>ἀγαθά</u>

243. Building an argumentative chain was variously described: ἐπιπλοκή (*cateman* ["chain"], e.g., Publius Rutilius Lupus, *de Figuris sententiarum et elocutionis* 1.13); κλῖμαξ ("ladder," e.g., Demetrius, *Eloc.* 270) and *gradatio* ("climax," e.g. Cicero, *De or.* 3.207; *Rhet. Her.* 4.25.34; Quintilian, *Inst.* 9.3.54-57; Augustine, *Doctr. chr.* 4.32). For other examples in Paul, see Rom 5:3-5; 8:29-30. Cf. Tobin, *Paul's Rhetoric in its Contexts*, 349; Anderson, *Glossary of Greek Rhetorical Terms*, 57-58.

244. Rom 10:14-15a, my translation.

245. The precise formula "As it is written" (καθὼς γέγραπται) is particularly Pauline. In the NT, see Matt 26:24; Mark 1:2; 9:13; 14:21; Luke 2:23; Acts 7:42; 15:15; Rom 1:17; 2:24; 3:4, 10; 4:17; 8:36; 9:13, 33; 10:15; 11:8, 26; 15:3, 9, 21; 1 Cor 1:31; 2:9; 2 Cor 8:15; 9:9. Paul also uses variations of the formula involving Scripture as a noun (γραφή, "writing"; Rom 4:3; 9:17; 10:11; 11:2; Gal 3:8; cf. 1 Tim 5:18) or verb (γράφω, "write"; Rom 12:19; 14:11; 1 Cor 1:19; 3:19; 9:9, 10; 10:7; 14:21; 15:45, 54; 2 Cor 4:13; Gal 3:10, 13; 4:27). Ellis, *Paul's Use of the Old Testament*, 22-25, 48-49. For a list of the introductory formulae Paul uses to begin a quotation of Scripture, see Moody Smith, "Pauline Literature," 268-72.

246. At Rom 9:25; 11:4; 12:19; 15:10-11; 1 Cor 6:16; 2 Cor 6:2, 16, Paul equates Scripture with God's speech.

247. On the status of τά ("the") in the text, which should probably be read as its omission appears to be an assimilation to the LXX, see Zuntz, *Text of the Epistles*, 173n4; cf. Jewett, *Romans*, 634-35. Reading τά ("the") would more clearly identify τὰ ἀγαθά

How beautiful[248] are the feet of those messengers of [the] good things. (Rom 10:15b)[249]

ὡς ὥρα ἐπὶ τῶν ὀρέων ὡς πόδες εὐαγγελιζομένου ἀκοὴν εἰρήνης ὡς εὐαγγελιζόμενος ἀγαθά

How timely upon the mountains are the feet of the messenger announcing peace, a messenger of good things. (Isa 52:7a)

ἰδοὺ ἐπὶ τὰ ὄρη οἱ πόδες εὐαγγελιζομένου καὶ ἀπαγγέλλοντος εἰρήνην

Behold upon the mountains the feet of him who brings good news and announces peace. (Nah 2:1 [MT 1:15])[250]

With other Jews of the period finding promise of eschatological salvation in this statement (Pss Sol 11:1-2)[251] and even of the anointed Messiah (11Q13 2.15-18),[252] it is not surprising that Paul also turns to it. Leaving out the localizing phrase "upon the mountains" Paul universalizes the message, a point he will make again (Rom 15:21), also using Isaiah 52.[253] Similarly, he changes the singular "message" to the plural "messengers." As they are not the focus of his concern here, he is probably not alluding to the apostles in particular.[254] Rather, in line with his universalizing Scripture, and perhaps cognizant of the end-time expectation of the period of many heralds,[255] Paul is underlining the wide appeal God has made to Israel.[256] Achieving the same ends, Paul

---

("the good things") as the gospel about which Paul is interested here. Cf. Cranfield, *Epistle to the Romans*, 2:535n1.

248. Given Isa 52:7 (ὡς ὥρα, "How timely"), Paul's ὡς ὡραῖοι might be translated "how timely." See Käsemann, *Commentary on Romans*, 294; Dunn, *Romans 9–16*, 621–22; Fitzmyer, *Romans*, 597; BDAG, "ὡς," 1103; cited by Jewett, *Romans*, 640n44.

249. Cf. Isa 52:7; Nah 2:1.

250. The existence of a widely shared stock of tradition probably explains the similarity between Nah 2:1 (MT 1:15) and Isa 52:7. See Coggins and Re'emi, *Israel among the Nations*, 33. Cf. Achtemeier, *Nahum—Malachi*, 17.

251. Lev. Rab. 9.9; Deut. Rab. 5.15. See the discussion by Seifrid, "Romans," 661–62. Further, see Str-B 3:282–83; Stuhlmacher, *Das paulinische Evangelium*, 148–50; Wilk, *Die Bedeutung des Jesajabuches für Paulus*, 173–75.

252. See Fitzmyer, "Further Light on Melchizedek," 252–54, and de Jonge and van der Woude, "11Q Melchizedek and the New Testament," 301–26; Wilk, *Die Bedeutung des Jesajabuches für Paulus*, 174. Also, e.g., see Lev. Rab. 9.9; Rab. Song 2.33, noted by Seifrid, "Romans," 662.

253. Seifrid, "Romans," 661.

254. As supposed by Stuhlmacher, "Pauline Gospel," 163.

255. See Tg. Isa. 40:9. Cf. Schniewind, *Euangelion*, 70–71; Stuhlmacher, "Pauline Gospel," 163.

256. Wagner, "Isaiah in Romans and Galatians," 123–24; Seifrid, "Romans," 661, also noting that Paul may have omitted mention of "the messenger announcing peace"

removes from Isaiah mention of "announcing peace" (ἀκοὴν εἰρήνης). In the context of Isaiah the peace relates to the restoration of Jerusalem as the center of salvation (Isa 52:1-6), a centripetal model of salvation that would run against the centrifugal model with which Paul works.[257]

These changes show that in using Scripture Paul's attention is not particularly focused on the word "gospel" and how it is to be understood so much as on God having sent messengers of salvation (cf. Rom 10:13). Indeed, in the introduction to this citation using variations of the phrase "call on" (ἐπικαλέω),[258] which appears to have been used among early Christians as a confessional response to the message of salvation,[259] Paul is implying this good news relates salvation. Also, having used "hear" or "listen" (ἀκούω) and "preach" (κηρύσσω) leading up to mention of the gospel, the gospel is assumed to be a spoken message. (This is one of the few times Paul uses "preach" or "proclaim" in relation to the gospel. We will find the solution to this puzzle[260] as we increase our understanding of Paul's notion of "gospel.") Further, in leading up to his quotation of Isaiah he uses ἀποστέλλω ("send"). With its ambassadorial overtones[261] and obvious strong connections with his own self-consciousness as an apostle of Jesus Christ,[262] the term reinforces the motif in Isaiah that the good news to which Paul is dedicated is from God.[263]

However, after the quotation from Isaiah, Paul goes on to say, "Yet not all have obeyed the gospel" (εὐαγγέλιον, Rom 10:16a). "For"—he continues in an exact quotation of his Greek Scriptures—"as Isaiah says, 'Lord, who has believed our report?'" (10:16b; cf. Isa 53:1). Using Isaiah to place "believe" (πιστεύω) parallel to "obey" (ὑπακούω), along with its word play on "hear" (ἀκουή),[264] shows Paul considers hearing or obeying and believing

---

to use the idea a few lines later (Rom 10:16).

257. Cf. Jewett, *Romans*, 640: "The concept of 'peace' in the Isaiah citation has the same structure as the Pax Romana, resulting from the subordination of all potential enemies under the imperial capitol in Jerusalem."

258. See Rom 10:12, 13, 14.

259. See Acts 22:16 and the discussion by Jewett, *Romans*, 637 and n21.

260. Noted by Dunn, *Romans 9–16*, 621, citing Michel, *Der Brief an die Römer*, and Zeller, *Der Brief an die Römer*.

261. Rengstorf, "ἀποστέλλω, κτλ," esp. 398n4, citing Luke 19:32; Josephus, *J.W.* 4.32; 1 Clem. 65.1.

262. See Rom 1:1; 1 Cor 1:1; 4:9; 9:1, 2, 5; 15:2; 2 Cor 1:1; 11:5; 12:11, 12; Gal 1:1, 17; 1 Thess 2:7.

263. Cf. Wagner, "Isaiah in Romans and Galatians," 124.

264. Jewett, *Romans*, 641.

to be synonymous, and that Scripture requires this response for the gospel to become salvation (cf. Rom 1:5; 16:26).

It could be that Paul is answering an objection that the message was not believed by Israel because the messengers were not commissioned by God. More likely, as it is the simplest reading of him, Paul uses Isaiah as scriptural prophecy and confirmation of the reality of some not obeying or believing the gospel.[265] As the gospel is inextricably and closely tied to Jesus (e.g., Rom 1:9), it is not that Isaiah is, with Paul, a fellow preacher of the gospel.[266] Rather, the gospel is prefigured or announced (cf. 1:2) and its response explained by Isaiah.

In short, Scripture, which for Paul is God speaking,[267] informs Paul about the gospel: it both prefigures the proclamation of the gospel and prophesies its rejection by some. Throughout this paragraph in Romans, reinforced by two quotations from his Scriptures, the gospel is a call to everyone from God—a message to be believed—which is proclaimed by those whom God sends. From this single allusion and one citation of "gospel" from his Scriptures, we turn to a number of places where, though he does not cite the word from his Scriptures, Paul uses Scripture in relation to his discussion of "gospel." They are all in Romans and Corinthians, his later correspondence.

(b) Romans 1:1-2. His letter to the Romans begins: "Paul, a slave of Christ Jesus, called to be an apostle set apart for the gospel of God, which he previously promised through his prophets in holy Scripture" (my translation). In the opening or prescript of a letter, ancient writers set out to establish their credentials and authority.[268] Going well beyond the few words that might be expected—for example, "Paul to those in Rome, greetings"[269]— to over forty words, Paul is likely attempting to counter suspicion of himself and his gospel.[270] On a few occasions Paul has referred to himself as a slave of Jesus Christ.[271] For Paul's reader in Rome, slavery to such a figure as Jesus would likely have brought to mind Caesar's household slaves, of which there were thousands, according to grave inscriptions.[272] Michael Brown helps in

---

265. Cranfield, *Epistle to the Romans*, 2:536-37; cf. Fitzmyer, *Romans*, 598; Wagner, "Isaiah in Romans and Galatians," 124.

266. As supposed by Wagner, "Isaiah in Romans and Galatians," 124.

267. See p. 61n246 above.

268. Cf. Bryskog, "Epistolography, Rhetoric and Letter Prescript," 37, 40.

269. In the NT see Acts 15:23; 23:26; Jas 1:1. Cf. Dionysius of Halicarnassus, *Ant. rom.* 19.10.1; Plutarch, *Pyrrh.* 6.7.4; 21.3.3; Philo, *Embassy* 315.2; Josephus, *Ant.* 12.51, 148; 14.225, 235. See Chan-Hie, *Form and Structure*, 10-11 and Jewett, *Romans*, 96.

270. Cf. Dunn, *Romans 1-8*, 5.

271. Rom 1:1; Gal 1:10; Phil 1:1

272. Weaver, *Familia Caesaris*, 8-9, 17, 75-76.

understanding the impact of the imagery on Paul's readers in noting that "a slave of the emperor garnered power in a way that almost no other type of slave could. He could speak only on behalf of his master, but, given that his master was the son of a god and his word was backed by the full power of the Roman military establishment, the slave's word would be a powerful medium indeed."[273] Thus, in Paul's self-designation as a "slave of Christ Jesus" his Roman readers are likely to have understood him claiming to speak for his master, Christ Jesus.[274] Consistent with this apparent claim, unlike in his Corinthian correspondence, where the gospel he describes has been handed on to him by other followers of Jesus (1 Cor 15:1-7), here his gospel is introduced as "of God" (θεοῦ).[275]

The divine origin of his "gospel" (εὐαγγέλιον) is then reinforced using the middle voice and the same root word to say God "previously promised" (προεπηγγείλατο)[276] it "through his prophets in holy Scripture."[277] Given this is the only time Paul calls on prophets and holy Scripture to describe or defend his gospel, that he uses the rare expressions "his prophets"[278] and the Jewish "holy Scriptures"[279] (he prefers the simple "Scripture"),[280] and that

---

273. Brown, "Paul's Use of Δουλος Χριστου Ιησου," 733, also cited, in part, by Jewett, *Romans*, 100. Cf. Weaver, "Social Mobility in the Early Roman Empire," 123, 135-36.

274. Cf. the discussion by Weaver, "Social Mobility in the Early Roman Empire."

275. Rom 1:1; cf. Gal 1:11-12.

276. §§3.3 (e) and 4.4 (a) below.

277. Cf. Dunn, *Romans 1-8*, 10; Jewett, *Romans*, 103.

278. Before Paul the phrase προφητῶν αὐτοῦ ("his prophets") is used in Isa 29:10, and in the NT it only occurs in Luke 1:70. Thereafter, the phrase is found only in Eusebius, *Comm. Isa.* 1.96.25 and Origen, *Comm. Matt.* 11.11.15. The only other example cited by TLG is Procopius of Gaza (c.475-c.538), *Comm. Isa.* (PG 87.2253, line 34).

279. Paul's particularly Jewish term, "holy Scriptures" (γραφαῖς ἁγίαις, cf. הקדש כתבי; see the discussion by Schrenk, "γράφω, κτλ," 751n4, citing, e.g., *t. Shab.* 13.1) is only used here in the NT, and thereafter appears in Eusebius, *Dem. ev.* 7.2.53.3; *Marc.* 1.2.17.4, and the spurious work, Athanasius, [*Apoll.*] 26.1161.40. The singular, γραφῇ ἁγίᾳ, not in the NT, is found in *T. Naph.* 4.1; 5.8.

A similar phrase "sacred Scriptures" is used by 1 Clem. 45.2 (ἱερὰς γραφάς); Philo, *Heir* 106, 159, 286; *Flight* 4; *Abraham* 121; *Decalogue* 37; *Spec. Laws* 1.214; 2.104 (ἱεραῖς γραφαῖς); and Josephus, *Ag. Ap.* 2.45 (ἱερῶν γραφῶν), but not by NT or other early Christian writers. The phrase "sacred writings" (ἱερὰ γράμματα) is used by 2 Tim 3:15. Various forms of "sacred writings" are also used by Philo, *Unchangeable* 6; *Migration* 139; *Moses* 1.23; 2.290, 292; *Spec. Laws* 2.159, 238; *Rewards* 79; *Contempl. Life* 28, 75, 78; *Embassy* 195; *QE* 1.6; 2.19; *Decalogue* 1.8. Cf. Plutarch *Is. Os.* 353.B.5; Diogenes Laertius, *Lives* 9.49.3; and Plutarch *Is. Os.* 383.E.8; *De facie* 942.B.10. The singular, referring to an inscription, ἱερῷ [ἐπι]γραφῇ ("sacred text") is found in Dionysius of Halicarnassus, *Ant. rom.* 1.51.3.

280. Γραφή ("Scripture"): Rom 4:3; 9:17; 10:11; 11:2; 15:4; 1 Cor 15:3, 4; Gal 3:8, 22; 4:30; cf. 1 Tim 5:18.

he is about to continue by taking up more obviously creedal material (Rom 1:3-4), it is probable he is already echoing his Jewish tradition in this phrase.[281] Therefore, aligning himself with earlier Jewish followers of Jesus, Paul uses Scripture as part of establishing the credibility and trustworthiness of his gospel.[282] As we will see when we look more closely at Paul's understanding of the gospel, in appealing to Scripture[283] he is proposing that the gospel was not a mere novelty but at least adumbrated in God's promise.[284]

At first sight it may not appear that Scripture is called upon to give content or explain the nature of the gospel. In line with the idea that Scripture is God speaking,[285] it seems that Paul is doing no more than further reinforcing his point that his gospel is of divine origin. However, as readers will see as this letter unfolds, for Paul the "previous promise" (προεπαγγελία) in Scripture shaped his "gospel" (εὐαγγέλιον) in that he took the promise to be a prototype of the gospel.[286] For example, Paul uses the statement that "Abraham believed God, and it was reckoned to him as righteousness"[287] to explain the fundamental core of his gospel.[288] Already, then, from Scripture Paul is asserting that according to his gospel the way God dealt with people in the past is how God deals with all who believe in him (Rom 4:9-12). We will see a similar view below when we note the way he relates Scripture and the gospel in Galatians.[289]

(c) *Romans 1:16-17.* In setting out what is generally agreed to be the theme of his letter to the Romans,[290] Paul says the gospel "is the power of God for salvation to all who have faith, to the Jew first and to the Gentile. For in it God's righteousness is revealed from faith to faith, as it has been written, 'the

---

281. Michel, *Der Brief an die Römer*, 70; Minde, *Schrift und Tradition bei Paulus*, 39; followed by Jewett, *Romans*, 103.

282. Cf. Cranfield, *Epistle to the Romans*, 1:56. Also, see Hays, *Echoes of Scripture*, 34: "Paul is seeking to ground his exposition of the gospel in Israel's sacred texts."

283. On Paul's echo of God (through the prophet Nathan) telling David that he would raise up his offspring saying, "I will be a father to him, and he shall be a son to me" (2 Sam 7:14), see Hays, *Echoes of Scripture*, 85.

284. Also, Schlatter, *Romans*, 7; Grayston, *Epistle to the Romans*, 1; cf. Dunn, "How New Was Paul's Gospel?" 367-88.

285. See p. 61n246 above.

286. Käsemann, *Commentary on Romans*, 9. Cf. Keck, *Romans*, 42.

287. Rom 4:3; cf. 4:9; Gen 15:6.

288. Cf. Achtemeier, *Romans*, 28.

289. See §3.3 below.

290. E.g., see Cranfield, *Epistle to the Romans*, 1:87; Esler, *Conflict and Identity in Romans*, 139; Keck, *Romans*, 50.

righteous one by faith shall live'" (Rom 1:16-17, my translation).[291] When, in chapter 4, we come to set out what Paul understands by his gospel we will return to examine this statement in more detail. For the present we only need to ascertain what he says here about the part Scripture plays in his understanding of his gospel.

Echoing Scripture at all the key points of his vocabulary, Paul states that in the gospel "God's righteousness is revealed from faith to faith" (Rom 1:17).[292] Then he quotes a line from Habakkuk: "The righteous one by faith shall live" (1:17).[293] The introduction to this quotation—"as it has been written" (καθὼς γέγραπται)—well used in the period,[294] is something Paul has also picked up from Scripture[295] and made his own.[296] From what we can see of his use of the phrase in other places he signals that the text will establish the point he has made.[297]

The line Paul quotes from Habakkuk is known to us in three other forms, none of which he follows.[298] One form is known to us from the Alexandrinus (A) and Ephraemi (C) codices of LXX: "My [God's] righteous one by faith (or faithfulness) shall live" (Hab 2:4). As this was taken up by other early Christians, including the writer to the Hebrews,[299] this text was

291. Rom 1:16-17 is generally taken as the thesis or *propositio* of the letter. E.g., see Käsemann, *Commentary on Romans*, 21; Cranfield, *Epistle to the Romans*, 1:87; Jewett, *Romans*, 135.

292. Notably, Ps 97:2 (MT)/98:2 (LXX)—"The Lord has made known his salvation (σωτήριον) before the nations (τῶν ἐθνῶν, Paul has "Judeans . . . and Greeks," Ἕλληνι); he has revealed (ἀπεκάλυψεν) his righteousness (δικαιοσύνην αὐτοῦ)"—is echoed in Paul's programmatic statement (Rom 1:16-17). Cf. Hays, *Echoes of Scripture*, 37, who also cites and discusses Ps 98:3 (MT)/97:3 (LXX); Isa 50:7-8; 51:4-5; 52:10.

293. Rom 1:17: ὁ δὲ δίκαιος ἐκ πίστεως ζήσεται. Cf. Hab 2:4.

294. See 1QS 5.17; 8.14; CD 7.19; 4Q174 1-2 I, 12; 4Q163 4-7 II, 18; 4Q177 10-11.1; 4Q178 3.2, cited by Fitzmyer, *Essays on the Semitic Background*, 8-10, and Fitzmyer, *Romans*, 264.

295. The precise phrase, "as it has been written" (καθὼς γέγραπται), occurs in extant Greek literature before Paul only in LXX: 4 Kgdms 14:6; 23:21; 2 Chr 23:18; 25:4; 1 Esd 3:9; Tob 1:6; Tob (S/)) 1:6; Dan (Th) 9:13.

296. In the NT the precise phrase, "as it has been written" (καθὼς γέγραπται), occurs twenty-five times, eighteen of them in Paul's letters: Matt 26:24; Mark 1:2; 9:13; 14:21; Luke 2:23; Acts 7:42; 15:15; Rom 1:17; 2:24; 3:4, 10; 4:17; 8:36; 9:13, 33; 10:15; 11:8, 26; 15:3, 9, 21; 1 Cor 1:31; 2:9; 2 Cor 8:15; 9:9.

297. See the brief discussion by Ellis, *Paul's Use of the Old Testament*, 23. Cf. Dunn, *Romans 1-8*, 44; Jewett, *Romans*, 145.

298. For a discussion of the issues involved in Paul's use of Habakkuk 2:4 see Moody Smith, "Ο ΔΕ ΔΙΚΑΟΣ ΕΚ ΠΙΣΤΕΩΣ ΖΗΣΕΤΑΙ," 13-25. More recently, see Dockery, "Use of Hab 2:4 in Rom 1:17," 24-36; Harrington, "Paul's Use of the Old Testament in Romans."

299. Heb 10:38/Hab 2:4 (LXX: A, C): ὁ δὲ δίκαιος ἐκ πίστως ζήσεται μου ἐκ πίστως

probably available to Paul.³⁰⁰ However, Paul is not following this text, for he does not take up the personal adjective ("my," μου). Another form of the Greek, known from the Sinaiticus (S/)) and Parisiensis (W) codices of LXX, can be translated: "The righteous one by my [God's] faith (or faithfulness) shall live" (Hab 2:4).³⁰¹ It is not clear, however, that this text was available to Paul.³⁰² In any case, Paul is not following this text for he does not have the personal adjective ("my," μου). The other form of the text, the Hebrew of Hab 2:4, probably known to Paul,³⁰³ can be translated: "The righteous one by his faith (or faithfulness) shall live."³⁰⁴ Yet again, in not using the personal adjective ("his faith," אֱמוּנָתוֹ), Paul does not take up this text either. Instead, therefore, so far as we know from the texts likely available to him, Paul provides his own reworking of Habakkuk: "The righteous one by faith shall live" (Rom 1:17). In this rendering Paul avoids specifying the subject of faith—God or the person. Characteristic of Jewish exegesis, which sought to find as much meaning as possible in a text,³⁰⁵ he is able to imply the importance of the faith or faithfulness of both God as well as the person.

That in Galatians Paul has already quoted Habakkuk in this way shows that his reworking was considered and settled rather than accidental or ad hoc.³⁰⁶ Further, in that he is not following any of the texts he is likely to know, but bending the text to suit his established view, shows that Scripture is not the source of his thinking about the gospel but brought in to corroborate what he had already concluded on other grounds.

ζήσεται. Of the earliest citations, see also, e.g., Clement, *Strom.* 2.2.8.2.2 (ὁ δὲ δίκαιός μου ἐκ πίστεως ζήσεται); 4.16.101.3.5 (ὁ δὲ δίκαιός μου ἐκ πίστεως ζήσεται); Eusebius, *Dem. ev.* 6.14.8.5 (ὁ δὲ δίκαιός μου ἐκ πίστεως ζήσεται); Theodoret, *Ep.* 122.32 (ὁ δὲ δίκαιός μου ἐκ πίστεως ζήσεται); *Int. xii proph.* 81.1820.18 (ὁ δὲ δίκαιός μου ἐκ πίστεως ζήσεται), all citing Sinaiticus (S/)) and Parisiensis (W) codices.

300. Cf. Dodd, *According to the Scriptures*, 51, 57, who supposed Hab 2:4 was part of a collection of Old Testament passages seen as "testimonies" to aspects of the gospel.

301. Hab 2:4 (LXX: (S/), W): ὁ δὲ δίκαιος ἐκ πίστως μου ζήσεται.

302. The earliest known citations of Hab 2:4 ((S/) and W codices) are by Eusebius, *Dem. ev.* 6.14.1.6; 6.14.3.9; 6.15.2.4 (cited above), in the early fourth century. See Sirinelli and des Places, *Eusèbe de Césarée. La Préparation évangélique*, 8–15.

303. Habakkuk was well known at Qumran. See 1QpHab; 4Q82, frag 102 [Hab 2:4?]; Mur 88, XVII–XVIII [Hab 1:3–13, 15; 2:2–3, 5–11, 18–20; 3:1–19]; 8Ḥev 1, 16–19 [Hab 1:5–11, 14–17; 2:1–8, 13–20; 3:9–15]. See Ulrich, "Index of the Passages," 97; Fabry, "Reception of Nahum and Habakkuk," 241–56.

304. Hab 2:4 (MT): יִחְיֶה בֶּאֱמוּנָתוֹ וְצַדִּיק.

305. On the seven "rules" (*middoth*) of interpretation collected by Hillel see *t. Sanh.* 7.11, and the discussion by Strack and Stemberger, *Introduction to the Talmud*, 19–23; cf. Dunn, *Romans 1–8*, 45.

306. Rom 1:17: ὁ δὲ δίκαιος ἐκ πίστεως μου ζήσεται. Gal 3:11: ὁ δὲ δίκαιος ἐκ πίστεως μου ζήσεται.

(d) Romans 11:25-28. In this section of his letter Paul has been dealing with the problem of God's apparent rejection of his people.[307] Paul's conclusion (Rom 11:25-32)—a "mystery" now disclosed (11:25)—is that the divine plan is being carried out in three stages: a divine hardening of "part of Israel" (11:25b); the coming in "of the Gentiles" (11:25c); and then "all Israel will be saved" (11:26a).[308] To support his third point, that "all Israel will be saved," he quotes Isaiah as: "Out of Zion will come the Deliverer; he will banish ungodliness from Jacob. And this is my covenant with them, [Isa 59:20-21a] when I take away their sins [27:9]."[309] Notably, Paul's substituting the LXX's "for the sake of" (ἕνεκεν)[310] for "out of" (ἐκ) Zion,[311] has God's deliverer coming from Zion rather than to, or for the sake of, Zion.[312] This is not an apparently irrelevant change;[313] it is not only less offensive to his Jewish readers, but it also does not detract from his point that there is "no distinction between Jew and Greek" (Rom 10:11).[314] Though the prophet likely meant God would deliver Zion—that is remove ungodliness from his people (Jacob)—as does a rabbinic reading (*b. Sanh.* 98a),[315] Paul most probably takes Isaiah to refer to the Messiah.[316] For Paul, Zion could refer to heaven,[317] and the deliverer was most often Christ.[318]

There is a break (an asyndeton) between Paul's scriptural quotations and his ensuing statement: "Regarding the gospel they are enemies because

---

307. Rom 9:30—11:25; cf. 9:6; 11:1.

308. Cranfield, *Epistle to the Romans*, 2.572.

309. Isa 59:20-21a (LXX): καὶ ἥξει ἕνεκεν Σιων ὁ ῥυόμενος καὶ ἀποστρέψει ἀσεβείας ἀπὸ Ιακωβ καὶ αὕτη αὐτοῖς ἡ παρ᾿ ἐμοῦ διαθήκη. Isa 27:9: ὅταν ἀφέλωμαι αὐτοῦ τὴν ἁμαρτίαν.
Rom 11:26b-27a: ἥξει ἐκ Σιὼν ὁ'ῥυόμενος, ἀποστρέψει ἀσείας ἀπὸ Ἰακώβ. καὶ αὕτη αὐτοῖς ἡ παρ' ἐμοῦ διαθήκη. Rom 11:27b: ὅταν ἀφέλωμαι τὰς ἁμαρτίας αὐτῶν. See also Ps 14:7; Jer 31:33.

310. Isa 59:20 (MT): לְצִיּוֹן ("to Zion"). On the rendering of ἕνεκεν ("for the same of") for לְ ("to"), unique in LXX, see Stanley, *Paul and the Language of Scripture*, 166-68.

311. That Paul is following a hitherto undiscovered form of Isaiah, see Jewett, *Romans*, 703.

312. That texts reflecting Paul's reading—22c-93 564* 407 534 Bohairic; Epiphanius; Hilary; Jerome; see Ziegler, *Isaias*, 343—are likely dependent on him, see the discussion by Wagner, *Heralds of the Good News*, 284 and n204.

313. See Stanley, "'Redeemer Will Come ἐκ Σιων,'" 125.

314. Jewett, *Romans*, 703. Cf. Shum, *Paul's Use of Isaiah in Romans*, 236-45.

315. See the discussion by Cranfield, *Epistle to the Romans*, 2:578 and note 1.

316. Stuhlmacher, *Paul's Letter to the Romans*, 172.

317. Cf. Gal 4:26. Also, see Heb 12:22, Rev 3:12; 21, and the discussion by Cranfield, *Epistle to the Romans*, 2:578 and note 2.

318. See Rom 7:24-25; 1 Thess 1:10. In 2 Cor 1:10, God is the deliverer.

of you" (Rom 11:28, my translation). Yet, it is clear he is summarizing his point that the Jews are a "disobedient and contrary people" (11:21/Isa 65:2).[319] The break also reinforces what is obvious: he is not concerned with attempting to define the gospel in terms available from Scripture.

Later we will attempt to determine what Paul means here by "gospel."[320] For the moment what is to be noted is that, again, not only from the immediate quotations, but also from this section of Romans as a whole, in which his view that the entiles are to be saved first goes beyond what has been shown from Scripture,[321] Paul has begun with his conclusion and moved to Scripture to support his assertion. It is, then, not that his understanding of the gospel is shaped by Scripture, but that Scripture is read out of his already established understanding of the gospel.[322]

From what we have seen so far in this chapter it is tempting to conclude that it is the creedal material about Jesus he has inherited that is Paul's interpretive lens for Scripture.[323] However, as we will see, this conclusion is premature and does not take into account all the evidence in statements by Paul.

(e) Romans 15:20-21 and 2 Corinthians 10:16. What we are seeing in Paul's use of Scripture is seen again in these two passages: he cites Scripture in support of a point about the gospel he has otherwise already settled. In writing to the Romans Paul here notes his principle not "to gospel" (εὐαγγελίζεσθαι) where Christ has already been named or build on the foundation of others (Rom 15:20). The strategy of not building on the work of another had been well established among Paul and his peers. He had an agreement with the Jerusalem leaders that they would go to the Jews and he to the gentiles (Gal 2:6-10).

In the passage of interest to us, introducing to the Romans the idea that he intends to go to Spain, Paul appeals to the same long-established principle of distinct areas of work, this time finding the point made in

---

319. Cranfield, *Epistle to the Romans*, 2:579; Dunn, *Romans 9-16*, 648; Keck, *Romans*, 277.

320. See §4.4 (g) below.

321. Cf. Käsemann, *Commentary on Romans*, 314.

322. Käsemann, *Commentary on Romans*, 314-15: "Paul read Scripture in the light of his doctrine of justification." Cf. Grayston, *Epistle to the Romans*, 101.

323. So Bates, *Hermeneutics of the Apostolic Proclamation*, e.g., 56-57, 329.

Scripture: "Those who have never been told of him shall see, and those who have never heard of him shall understand" (Rom 15:21/Isa 52:15).[324]

In his Corinthian correspondence, defending himself against opponents who had transgressed his territory, he also writes assuming there are established boundaries within which he and others worked (2 Cor 10:12-18) and that he had not crossed them (10:14, 16). One of those boundaries was that "we had arrived first" (ἐφθάσαμεν).[325] That is, he had staked his claim on the Corinthians, and his opponents had no right to interfere.[326] In support of his adherence to the policy of not encroaching on the territory of other missionaries and taking credit for their work, Paul cites Scripture: "Let the one who boasts boast in the Lord" (2 Cor 10:17; Jer 9:24/LXX 9:23).

In writing to the Corinthians to support his point Paul uses Jeremiah (Jer 9:24/2 Cor 10:16), which he also uses for other purposes early in this correspondence (1 Cor 1:31). In both places he uses his own consistent rendering of Jeremiah.[327] This suggests it is not the text that is governing Paul's thinking about the gospel. Once again, it is other contingencies

---

324. Isa 52:15b:

οἷς οὐκ ἀνηγγέλη περὶ αὐτοῦ ὄψονται καὶ οἳ οὐκ ἀκηκόασιν συνήσουσιν,
"those who were not told about him shall see and those who have not heard shall understand."

Rom 15:21:

οἷς οὐκ ἀνηγγέλη περὶ αὐτοῦ   καὶ οἳ οὐκ ἀκηκόασιν συνήσουσιν,
"those who were not told about him   and those who have not heard shall understand."

325. Although like others of his period (e.g., Philo, *Creation* 5; 8; *Moses* 1.2; cf. Fitzer, "φθάνω, προφθάνω," 88–92) Paul can use φθάνω to mean "arrive" or "come" (Rom 9:31; Phil 3:16; 1 Thess 2:16), consistent with a classical use (LSJ, "φθάνω," 1926–27 [1926], citing, e.g., Hesiod, *Op.* 554, 570; Herodotus, *Hist.* 7.161; Euripedes, *Phoen.* 975; Xenophon, *Anab.* 6.1.18), and also occasionally with others in his period (e.g., Philo, *Embassy* 3.215; Josephus, *Ant.* 7.247), the term can mean "precede" or "come before" (1 Thess 4:15), which best suits the context in 2 Cor 10:14–15. See Barrett, *Second Epistle to the Corinthians*, 266–67; Thrall, *II Corinthians*, 2:648–49; Martin, *2 Corinthians*, 505.

326. Barrett, *Second Epistle to the Corinthians*, 267. Cf., e.g. Hughes, *Paul's Second Epistle*, 367–70; Barnett, *Second Epistle to the Corinthians*, 491–92.

327. Jer 9:24/LXX 9:23:

ἀλλ᾽ ἢ ἐν τούτῳ καυχάσθω ὁ καυχώμενος συνίειν καὶ γινώσκειν ὅτι ἐγώ εἰμι κύριος
"but let the one who boasts boast in this, that he understand and know that I am the Lord."

1 Cor 1:31:

ὁ καυχώμενος ἐν κυρίῳ καυχάσθω
"the one boasting, in the Lord boast."

2 Cor 10:17:

ὁ δὲ καυχώμενος ἐν κυρίῳ καυχάσθω.
"but the one boasting, in the Lord boast."

that have shaped his understanding of Scripture: Scripture gives voice to, rather than composes or provides the score for, his theology. Scripture is not so much the basis of his understanding of the gospel as a confirming expression.

(f) 1 Corinthians 9:16. At this point in his correspondence with the Corinthians Paul is defending himself, including his right to obtain his living by the gospel (1 Cor 9:13–14). But, through broken sentences,[328] he says he has given up this right. Not only does he not want to hinder the gospel (9:12), but, in any case, he is also under an obligation "to gospel" (9:16). He expresses this obligation in saying, "woe to me if I do not gospel!" (9:16, my translation).

As this is Paul's only use of "woe" or "alas" (οὐαί), a word characteristic of the prophets,[329] and as he saw himself in their tradition,[330] it is reasonable to suppose he is echoing Jeremiah's inability to remain silent (Jer 20:9).[331] Yet, in this passage Paul's "necessity" or "compulsion" (ἀνάγκη, 1 Cor 9:15) to gospel has been established on other grounds: he has a commission (from God) to make the gospel freely available (9:17–18). Indeed, in other correspondence he makes it clear that his obligation to gospel arose from his commission or conversion (Gal 1:15–16), and Christ's ownership of him (Phil 3:12), which from time to time he expressed in terms of his slavery to Christ.[332] Thus, again, in his Scripture Paul finds echoes and expression of his existing thinking rather than its source.

(g) Galatians 3:6–8. In Galatians Paul is also defending his gospel (Gal 1:6–9). As we have seen, he begins by asserting that the gospel he proclaimed was given to him directly by God (1:11–24).[333] He then appeals

---

328. See the discussion by, e.g. Orr and Walther, *1 Corinthians*, 239; and Fee, *First Epistle to the Corinthians*, 415–17.

329. Of the sixty-five occurrences of οὐαί ("woe") in the LXX, all but twelve are in the prophets, and most of those (thirty-one occurrences) are in Isaiah and Jeremiah. See Num 21:29; 1 Kgdms 4:7, 8, 21; 3 Kgdms 12:24; 13:30; Jdt 16:17; Tob (S) 10:5; Odes Sol 10:8; Prov 23:29; Eccl 4:10; 10:16; Sir 2:12, 13, 14; 41:8; Hos 7:13; 9:12; Amos 5:16 (x2), 18; 6:1; Mic 7:4 (x2); Nah 3:17; Hab 2:6, 12, 19; Zeph 2:5; 3:18; Isa 1:4, 24; 3:9, 11; 5:8, 11, 18, 20, 21, 22; 10:1, 5; 17:12; 18:1; 24:16; 28:1; 29:1, 15 (x2); 30:1; 31:1; 33:1; Jer 4:13; 6:4; 10:19; 13:27; 22:18; 26:19; 27:27; 28:2; 31:1; Lam 5:16; Ezek 2:10; 7:26 (x2); 13:3, 18.

330. E.g., see Rom 1:1–2 (cf. 16:25–26); 11:1–6, 13; Gal 1:15–16; and Isa 49:1–6; Jer 1:5, 10, along with the discussion in Twelftree, *Paul and the Miraculous*, 61–66.

331. E.g., see Barrett, *Second Epistle to the Corinthians*, 209; Collins, *First Corinthians*, 348.

332. See Rom 1:1 (cf. 6:1–23); 1 Cor 7:23; Gal 1:10; Phil 1:1. Cf. Lindemann, *Erste Korintherbrief*, 208.

333. See §2.3 (a) above.

to the approval he has received from the leadership in Jerusalem (2:1–10). Next, in addressing the readers directly, Paul appeals to the experience of the Galatians (3:1–5). He asks, for example, if they received the Spirit and if God worked miracles among them by doing the works of the law or by believing what they heard (3:2, 5). Paul's fourth line of argument is an appeal to Scripture (3:6—4:31).

Notably, however, having appealed to the experience of the Galatians, Paul comes to Scripture not appealing directly to the text—even if he sees it as living and speaking[334]—but to the experience of Abraham (3:6), the greatest Jewish exemplar of faith.[335] Paul appeals directly to Abraham in two ways. First, he begins the quotation not with one of his usual phrases, "as it has been written" (καθὼς γέγραπται),[336] but with "as Abraham" (καθὼς Ἀβραάμ), the only absolute use of καθώς by Paul.[337] This odd introduction to Paul's quotation is probably to be understood as, "Just as I have said,"[338] or "As in your experience, so also in Abraham's."[339] In this way Paul links the discussion of the experience of the Galatians with that of Abraham.[340] In other words, Paul is expecting his readers to interpret Scripture through the lens of their experience.[341]

Then, second, in his quotation of Genesis Paul transposes "believed" and "Abraham" to bring Abraham's name to a position of emphasis.[342] Otherwise, Paul then quotes exactly a passage from Genesis often cited at the time: "As Abraham believed God, and it was reckoned to him as righteousness."[343] Confirming that he wishes the Galatians to see a parallel

334. Hays, *Echoes of Scripture*, 106.

335. Cf. Sir 44:19–21; 1 Macc 2:52; *Jub.* 12; 23:10; *Apoc. Ab.* 1–8; CD 3.2; Philo, *Abraham* 60–88; Josephus, *Ant.* 1.155–57; Betz, *Galatians*, 139–41; Lightfoot, *Saint Paul's Epistle to the Galatians*, 158–64; Hansen, *Abraham in Galatians*, 179–99; Dunn, *Epistle to the Galatians*, 160.

336. See p. 67n296 above.

337. Cf. Longenecker, *Galatians*, 112.

338. Barrett, *Freedom and Obligation*, 22–23. Cf. Guthrie, *Galatians*, 94; Stanley, *Paul and the Language of Scripture*, 235.

339. Cf. Lightfoot, *Saint Paul's Epistle to the Galatians*, 136; Stanley, *Paul and the Language of Scripture*, 235.

340. Cf. Ridderbos, *Epistle of Paul*, 117–18; Betz, *Galatians*, 141; Bruce, *Galatians*, 152.

341. Cf. Hays, *Echoes of Scripture*, 104: Paul uses "Christian experience in the church as a hermeneutical paradigm for reading Scripture."

342. Stanley, *Paul and the Language of Scripture*, 235. Paul's deliberation on this point is clear in noting that his other quotation of Gen 15:6 in Rom 4:3 follows the word order of LXX.

343. Gal 3:6: καθὼς Ἀβραὰμ ἐπίστευσεν τῷ θεῷ, καὶ ἐλογίσθη αὐτῷ εἰς δικαιοσύνην

between their experience and that of Abraham, Paul concludes: "You see then [γινώσκετε ἄρα], those who believe, they are the descendants of Abraham" (Gal 3:7, my translation).

Paul then appeals directly to Scripture: "And the Scripture, foreseeing that God would justify the Gentiles by faith, declared the gospel beforehand to Abraham, saying, 'All the Gentiles shall be blessed in you'" (Gal 3:8).[344] Attention to two of Paul's words helps us understand more clearly how he saw the relationship between his gospel and Scripture. The word προευαγγελίζομαι ("pre-announce"), sharing the ἀγγελι- ("angeli-") root with "gospel," was a rare and new word in Paul's world.[345] He says God's "previous promise" (προευηγγελίσατο, aorist middle) to Abraham that "All the Gentiles shall be blessed in you"[346] is a "foreseeing" (προϊδοῦσα, aorist participle)[347] of the gospel. To "foresee" (προοράω) something was, for Paul's readers, not to see or experience it, but to anticipate, know in advance, or prepare for it.[348] Here the gospel is not righteousness through faith (Abraham's unique experience),[349] but righteousness through faith for all nations in Abraham. The promise is that what one has experienced, all shall know. Therefore, Paul is certainly not suggesting the gospel for all nations was found in Scripture, but that it was adumbrated or anticipated in these ancient texts.[350] Likewise, for Paul, what God says to Abraham—"All the Gentiles shall be blessed in you"—was to "proclaim the gospel in advance" (προευηγγελίζομαι). Thus, in his citation, Paul maintains the future tense,

---

/ Gen 15:6 (LXX): καὶ ἐπίστευσεν Αβραμ τῷ θεῷ καὶ ἐλογίσθη αὐτῷ εἰς δικαιοσύνην, a passage also quoted in Rom 4:3, 9; Jas 2:23; Barn. 13.7; 1 Clem. 10.6; Justin, *Dial.* 119.6. Gen 15:6 is also cited by, e.g. Philo, *Embassy* 3.228; *Unchangeable* 4; *Migration* 44; *Heir* 90; *Names* 186; *Virtues* 216, but not by Josephus. Cf. Watson, *Paul and the Hermeneutics of Faith*, 229–31.

344. The blessing of Abraham takes a number of forms in Scripture (LXX): Gen 12:3; 18:18; 22:18; 26:4; 28:14; Ps 71:17; Sir 44:21. See Betz, *Galatians*, 142n32. Paul has used primarily Gen 12:3 (ἐνευλογηθήσονται ἐν σοὶ πάντα τὰ ἔθνη), but to suit his purpose of including the gentiles, substituting αἱ φυλαί ("the tribes") for τὰ ἔθνη ("the nations" or "the Gentiles"), found in Gen 18:18; 22:18; and 26:4.

345. Before Paul, in Greek literature, προευαγγελίζομαι only appears in Philo, *Abraham* 153.2; *Creation* 34.2; *Names* 158.4.

346. Cf. Gen 12:3; 18:18; 22:18.

347. In the NT προοράω is found in Acts 2:25, 31; 21:29; and Gal 3:8.

348. Cf., e.g. Homer, *Od.* 5.393; Xenophon, *Hell.* 4.3.23; Philo, *Rewards* 72; *Drunkenness* 1.160; *Spec. Laws* 1.99; *Dreams* 1.27; Josephus, *Ant.* 2.245; 13.189; *Ag. Ap.* 1.77; *J.W.* 1.42; 2.649; 5.271, 273; *Life* 19; and Michaelis, "ὁράω, κτλ," 381–82; BDAG, "προοράω," 873; MGS, "προοράω," 1780.

349. Cf. Betz, *Galatians*, 142–43.

350. Contra Dunn, *Epistle to the Galatians*, 166.

"shall be blessed" (ἐνευλογηθήσονται, Gal 3:8).³⁵¹ Though not found in Scripture, the gospel—Abraham's experience available for all nations—is promised and foreshadowed there.³⁵²

(h) Results. In this section we have been trying to discover the part Scripture likely played in Paul's understanding of the gospel. Given the considerable influence of Isaiah on earlier followers of Jesus and on the Judaisms of his time, and that Paul was a person thoroughly immersed in Scripture, it could hardly be doubted that the connection we noted between "gospel" and God's eschatological or end-time salvation in Isaiah would have been part of his basic theological raw material.

We have seen that in the only place he takes up the word "gospel" from his Scriptures,³⁵³ Paul is able to make the point that both its proclamation and its rejection (by some) have been prefigured (cf. Isa 52:7). From the passage in Joel that he cites³⁵⁴ we noted that he could have seen the connection between receiving the call of God and receiving the gospel ([a] above). In other places where he uses Scripture in his discussion we learn that it is not that Paul found his gospel in Scripture, but that what one (Abraham) experienced is now available to all (Gal 3:6-8). Not surprisingly, then, we also learn not only that the gospel is of divine origin (Rom 1:1), but that God's way of dealing with people who believe in him remains the same (4:9-12). Yet, Paul so bends the texts he quotes that it is clear Scripture is not the source but the support he needed for views of the gospel otherwise already established.³⁵⁵ Indeed, we have just seen in one place (Gal 3:6-8) that it is the experience of the gospel that is the lens through which Paul read Scripture. However, we have also seen that the creedal material he has inherited from the Jesus movement is an element of what becomes a multielement lens through which Paul reads his Scripture.

For Paul, the gospel is not scripturally mediated;³⁵⁶ rather it is Scripture that is mediated by the gospel. Also, even though exegesis is important to Paul, it is not for him the way to normative saving truth, as Francis Watson supposes.³⁵⁷ Instead, Paul approaches his exegesis with his established

---

351. Ἐνευλογηθήσονται is found in all the scriptural (LXX) representations of the blessing of Abraham: Gen 12:3; 18:18; 22:18; 26:4; 28:14; Ps 71:17; Sir 44:21.

352. In turn, as Hays, *Echoes of Scripture*, 107, suggests, for Paul, Scripture's "true meaning can be discerned only retrospectively."

353. Rom 10:13/Joel 3:5, NRSV 2:32.

354. See the previous note.

355. Rom 1:16-17; 11:25-28; 15:20-21 (cf. 2 Cor 10:16); 1 Cor 9:16.

356. As supposed by Watson, "Law in Romans," 102.

357. Watson, *Paul and the Hermeneutics of Faith*, 24. See the critique of the first edition in Eastman, Review of *Paul and the Hermenutics*, 610-14.

normative saving truth of the gospel.³⁵⁸ At least as far as Paul is concerned, we can agree with Gerhard Friedrich that "The NT use of εὐαγγέλιον does not derive from the LXX."³⁵⁹

In using Scripture to convey his understanding of gospel Paul appears to be ploughing his own furrow. In light of him encountering "gospel" in early Christian traditions about Jesus' ministry that were utterly dependent on scriptural concepts,³⁶⁰ it is to be expected that in his turn Paul would rely in some way on the ancient texts. However, while they invariably influenced his broader thinking, evident in his association of "gospel" and salvation, they did not supply, but instead supported, his views already established in his revelatory experience³⁶¹ and also in his received traditions.

§2.5 CONCLUSION: THE GOSPEL BEFORE PAUL

Only a few generations before Paul, "gospel" burst into the Greek language in the second century BCE through the work of those translating parts of the Hebrew Scriptures, and it had found its way into Greek literature, especially among Jews. From the information we have of the use of the εὐαγγελ- ("gospel") word group,³⁶² the irreversible hold the term appears to have taken in the early Christian movement took place in Paul's ministry and letters. Therefore, two questions have driven this chapter: Where did Paul get the term "gospel" and what did it mean when he took it up? Answers to these questions are important for they will help us see more clearly why the word "gospel" was so significant to him and what meaning he brought to it.

Inscriptions show that the word was also familiar to the general population of his time, not least in its association with the emperor as savior figure, filled with divine power for the benefit of the people, putting

---

358. Drawing attention to Harnack, "Das Alte Testament in den paulinischen Briefen un in den paulinischen Gemeinden," 124–41, observing that there are many weighty scriptural citations in Galatians, 1 and 2 Corinthians, and Romans, but few or none in 1 Thessalonians and Philippians (Martyn, "Article Review," 437, cf. 438), rightly questioned that if Paul saw the reading of Scripture to be the way to normative truth, "why should he leave it essentially aside as he composed some of his letters, while giving it a truly weighty role in others?"

359. Friedrich, "εὐαγγελίζομαι, κτλ," 725. However, the sweeping statement by Schweitzer, *Paul and His Interpreters*, 44–45, that Paul "uses only what he can take from it [the OT] ready formed" is not supported by what we have seen in the evidence.

360. Matt 11:3/Luke 7:22. Cf. Isa 29:18; 42:18; 26:29; also see 35:5–6; 61:1.

361. Cf. Koch, *Die Schrift als Zeuge des Evangeliums*, 347: "Paul reads Scripture in the knowledge of and in view of the present revelation of God, his divine acting in Christ."

362. See p. 3n22 and §2.1 above; cf. §3.2 below.

everything in peaceful order. Though Paul makes no allusion to this common knowledge—he did not need to—it will have been an unavoidable part of his received notion of the gospel and part of the background against which he was read.

The evidence is not strong, but in light of the verb "gospel" already being in circulation among those responsible for Q (Luke 7:22)—a tradition which influenced his thinking—and the noun probably having currency among very early followers of Jesus in Jerusalem (Acts 15:7), Paul probably did not need to introduce either the verb or the noun into Christian vocabulary. Notwithstanding, we have seen that a form of the term "gospel" was widely used in the non-Jewish Greek world and would have carried connotations from its association with the emperor that made it useful to him to maintain and develop. (It is very unlikely Paul's knowledge of Latin played any part in his use of the term.) It is not surprising, then, that Paul should use the term freely from his earliest letter, 1 Thessalonians.[363] In both, verb and noun already having some currency among his predecessors in the faith, there is corroborating evidence for Paul using the noun not in,[364] but as a description of, three pieces of creedal material passed on to him by earlier Christians.[365] That is, as had earlier followers of Jesus, Paul uses the noun "gospel" to describe the Christian message or its key ideas.

From his testimony, pivotal in understanding the gospel Paul received is his strong assertion that, although he shared it with his peers and predecessors, it was God who revealed it to him. He says, "I want you to know . . . that the gospel that was gospelled by me is not of human origin . . . God revealed his Son to me, so that I might proclaim him among the Gentiles" (Gal 1:11, 15–16). In this revelation Paul, in his turn (cf. 1 Cor 15:8), receives the Son as the gospel.

Given the importance of Scripture to Paul, and that the "gospel" was described in scriptural terms in Q, we have asked how far Scripture was a source for his understanding of the "gospel." Only once does Paul take up the word "gospel" (εὐαγγελίζω, verb) from his Scriptures (Rom 10:15b/Isa 52:7a). However, his attention was not on the word but on God sending messengers of salvation. For Paul "the gospel"—in this context God's salvation for all—is not found in Scripture but promised and prefigured in

---

363. See 1 Thess 1:5; 2:2, 4, 8, 9; 3:2. The verb "gospel" appears in 3:6. Cf. Tasmuth, "Paul's *Gospel* to the Romans," 312n7.

364. Dunn, "Gospel and the Gospels," 293, makes this point against Pokorný, *From the Gospel to the Gospels*, chapter 2, to support his view that Paul introduced the noun "gospel" into Christian vocabulary.

365. 1 Thess 1:9–10; 1 Cor 15:3b–5; Rom 1:3–4a.

it. That is, the way God dealt with Abraham is now the way God is dealing with all people (Rom 4:9–12).

The manner in which Paul is continually happy to alter texts he quotes shows that he comes to them with settled ideas. Scripture, though important to him, is not the source of his understanding of the gospel.[366] As we have noted a number of times, his understanding of the gospel was not shaped by Scripture. Rather, his established understanding of the gospel was the new lens through which he read—and shaped—Scripture. Scripture is brought in to corroborate rather than create his understanding of the gospel.

An important answer to our question regarding the origin and meaning of "gospel" when he took up the word is that, though it was well understood in society and was part of his Scriptures, Paul inherited the term from earlier followers of Jesus. As he took it up, "gospel" referred both to Jesus' ministry, including healing, and also traditions about that ministry remembered in the form of creedal-like statements.

Along the way we have caught glimpses of his understanding of the gospel: when he applies a description to received traditions about Jesus he uses the noun "the gospel"; when he speaks of his compulsion "to gospel" he points to his call-conversion experience; when he recalls for his readers the nature of the gospel it is to their experience he first draws attention; and when he uses Scripture to corroborate what has otherwise already been established. We turn, then, to explore further and set out in detail Paul's understanding of the gospel.

---

366. Käsemann, *Commentary on Romans*, 7, was right to resist the idea that Paul derived his "gospel" from Isaiah. Also noted by Elliott, *Arrogance of Nations*, 188n18.

3

The Gospel Paul Promoted
Thessalonians, Galatians, and Philippians

IN THE INITIAL CHAPTER we set out how in modern research Paul's gospel is taken to be his message. Yet, even a superficial look across his writings raises doubts that he would recognize his gospel in those descriptions. In the second chapter we saw that, although the word "gospel" was well used in his society and familiar to him from his Scriptures, Paul probably inherited the term from his predecessors in the Jesus movement where it referred to Jesus' ministry as well as to creedal-like traditions about him.

In passing we have already picked up hints of how Paul understood the gospel and the range of its meaning for him. Now we take up a close and detailed examination of the gospel he promoted. The question to be answered is: What was Paul's understanding of the gospel? In particular, even our setting out a list of Paul's use of "gospel" in chapter 1 suggests we should ask: Did he understand the gospel to be his message about Jesus, perhaps embodying God's transforming power, or was it something else?

Debate continues on which of the Pauline letters in the New Testament canon come from his pen and should therefore be taken into account in an enquiry such as this. As it is generally agreed that Romans, 1 and 2 Corinthians, Galatians, Philippians, 1 Thessalonians, and Philemon are his direct responsibility, we will use them to recover Paul's understanding of the gospel.[1]

---

1. Discussions of the authorship of the Pauline corpus can be found in, e.g., Brown, *Introduction to the New Testament*, Part III, and Hagner, *New Testament*.

In order to be as open as possible to the subtleties of Paul's thinking on the gospel, including of change or development (or both), we will examine his writings in the order in which they were likely written. Although it is far from agreed how his letters and Acts are to be interpreted in order to untangle the chronology of Paul's life, the order 1 Thessalonians, Galatians, Philippians, the Corinthian correspondence, Philemon, and Romans, has considerable support and will be assumed here.[2] As there is so much material to cover, the first three of these—1 Thessalonians, Galatians, and Philippians—will be the focus of attention in this chapter. Of these letters Thessalonians provides such a rich seam of material for our project that it will take some time to mine its riches. The remaining letters—Corinthians, Philemon, and Romans—will be examined in the next chapter.

The nature of Paul's writings, occasional letters written to address a variety of different, particular issues in relation to a variety of different people rather than doctrinal treatises, means that his basic theological views have been interpreted by him in a variety of different ways. Therefore, given the contingent nature of Paul's writing, our attempt to recover his understanding of the gospel requires taking into account the way he has applied his fundamental convictions to particular situations.[3] In practice, for us to understand what Paul means by "gospel" we will have to interpret what he says in light of the particular people and situation he is addressing.

§3.1 THE VOCABULARY OF THE "GOSPEL"

This project revolves around the use of a word. Although to understand the word "gospel" and what Paul promoted will require more than an attention to his vocabulary; that vocabulary is inherently important in understanding his ideas (cf. the Appendix below). As well as gathering up some data that has already been noted and taken into account, the broad historical distribution of the vocabulary will require our attention.

Almost immediately a number of aspects of Paul's use of these terms stand out from this table. To begin with, not only (as we saw in the last chapter) is Paul the first Greek writer since Homer to use the singular neuter noun, "gospel" (εὐαγγέλιον);[4] Paul is also the first Greek writer to make significant

---

2. On the chronology of the letters see, e.g., Riesner, *Paul's Early Period*, 26.

3. See Beker, *Paul the Apostle*, 11–36; Beker, "Paul the Theologian," 352–65, and the discussion by Campbell, "Determining the Gospel," 316–18.

4. Homer, *Od.* 14.152, 166. 2 Kgdms 4:10 uses the neuter noun, εὐαγγέλιον, but in the accusative plural common form, εὐαγγέλια.

use of "gospel" as a verb (εὐαγγελίζω).[5] Second, given the relative brevity of his earlier letters and the greater length of his later ones, it is in his earlier letters that he makes most use of "gospel" as a noun (εὐαγγέλιον).[6] The verb is clustered in Galatians and 1 Corinthians. In light of our discussions in this and the next chapter we may be able to explain this varying use of the vocabulary.[7] Third, in that he does not use the whole range of αγγελ- words,[8] it is also clear that Paul's interest in "gospel" is in the particular words he uses rather than a semantic predilection for the word group. Our close examination of what Paul means by "gospel" begins with his earliest letter.

§3.2 FIRST THESSALONIANS

Perhaps in 50 or 51 CE, two years after the establishment of the church in Thessalonica, Paul was in Corinth.[9] Timothy, perhaps bringing a letter with him,[10] had arrived (Acts 18:1–5) with long-awaited news from the believers that turned out to be positive (1 Thess 3:6–10). With evident delight Paul is able to write to urge them on (3:12; 4:1, 10).

In this letter we have the first use of "gospel" in Christian literature; Paul uses the noun (εὐαγγέλιον) six times[11] and the verb once (εὐαγγελίζω, 1 Thess 3:6). This use of the verb for Timothy "bringing good news" of the Thessalonians shows that, for Paul, the "gospel" word group was not restricted to describing the core of his identity and mission (e.g., Rom 1:1–6) but could be applied to others and their work. Compared to Romans, his last letter, Paul uses "gospel" three times more frequently here in 1 Thessalonians.[12] In that at least the majority of the members of the church to whom Paul is

---

5. However, Luke went on to use εὐαγγελίζω twenty-five times, Paul having used it nineteen times. See the Appendix below.

6. Εὐαγγέλιον occurs in Phil 1 in every 181 words; 1 Thess 1 in 247; Gal 1 in 319; Phlm 1 in 335; 2 Cor 1 in 560; Rom 1 in 790; 1 Cor 1 in 854.

7. See §5.4 below.

8. E.g., the following αγγελ- words are not used by Paul, but are found in other NT writings: ἀγγελία ("good news," 1 John 1:5; 3:11); ἀγγέλλω ("announce," John 4:51 in e.g., ℵ D b); ἐξαγγέλλω ("proclaim," 1 Pet 2:9; Mark 16:8 [shorter conclusion]); ἐπάγγελμα ("a promise," 2 Pet 1:4; 3:13); καταγγελεύς ("a proclaimer," Acts 17:18); and προκαταγγέλλω ("announce beforehand," Acts 3:18; 7:52).

9. E.g., Jewett, *Dating Paul's Life*, esp. "Graphs of Dates and Time-Spans," 161–65. For an earlier dating of 1 Thess, see Donfried and Marshall, *Theology of the Shorter Pauline Letters*, 9–12.

10. Best, *Thessalonians*, 14.

11. 1 Thess 1:5; 2:2, 4, 8, 9; 3:2.

12. See note 6 above.

writing appear to be gentiles,[13] we will see how Paul understood, described, and promoted the gospel for a gentile audience.

(a) Word, power, Holy Spirit, and much fullness (1 Thess 1:4–5). Part of Paul's delight and thankfulness (1:2) in relation to the Thessalonians is his recalling the establishment of the gospel among them. He says (my translation):

> [4]We know . . . he chose you, [5]because our gospel was not established among you in word only but also in power and in Holy Spirit and in much fullness
>
> [4]εἰδότες τὴν ἐκλογὴν ὑμῶν, [5]ὅτι τὸ εὐαγγέλιον ἡμῶν οὐκ ἐγενήθη εἰς[14] ὑμᾶς ἐν λόγῳ μόνον ἀλλὰ καὶ ἐν δυνάμει καὶ ἐν πνεύματι ἁγίῳ καὶ [ἐν][15] πληροφορίᾳ πολλῇ (1:4–5)[16]

Paul's point is that the evidence that God has chosen his readers (1:4) is that the gospel began among them in power, Holy Spirit, and much fullness, as well as by word. Although Paul is not describing the gospel per se, but its beginning among the readers, this description tells us a great deal about his understanding of it.

He begins by referring to the gospel as "ours" (ἡμῶν).[17] Although some copyists had trouble with Paul's expression, "our gospel" is very well established in the textual witnesses.[18] In writing to the Corinthians, Paul will use the phrase one other time (2 Cor 4:3)[19] where it comes in the context of Paul making a case over against his Corinthian opponents that God is the source of his ministry (2:14—4:6). The question is raised, therefore, as to whether or not in writing to the Thessalonians Paul is also dealing with opponents of his gospel (cf. 1 Thess 2:1–12).[20] However, even if there is no

---

13. 1 Thess 1:9; cf. 2:14. Luke says that "some of them [the Judeans] were persuaded and joined Paul and Silas" (Acts 17:4).

14. The NA[28] apparatus is witness to the difficulty copyists had with εἰς. See the discussion below.

15. Though not accepted in NA[25], thereafter NA[26], NA[27], and NA[28] conjecture ἐν is, with A C D F G Ψ, e.g., to be taken as Paul's text.

16. See the discussion in Twelftree, *Paul and the Miraculous*, 180–87.

17. In the NT, the phrase τὸ εὐαγγέλιον ὑμῶν occurs only in the Pauline corpus: 1 Thess 1:5 and 2 Cor 4:3. Cf. 2 Thess 2:14 (εὐαγγελίου ἡμῶν). For "my gospel" (τὸ εὐαγγέλιόν μου) see Rom 2:16; (16:25). Cf. §4.4 (e) below.

18. See GNT[4] and NA[28]. ℵ* has του θεου ημων; ℵc and C have του θεου. Cf. Metzger, *Textual Commentary*, 561.

19. The copyists appear not to have stumbled over this. See NA[28].

20. Cf., e.g., Still, *Conflict at Thessalonica*; Kim, "Paul's Entry (εἴσοδος)," 519–42.

reference to an attack on Paul or his character,[21] his mention of speaking the gospel in spite of great opposition (2:2) and not using "deceit or impure motives or trickery" (2:3) or flattery (2:5), for example, suggest that the rhetorical intent of his term "our gospel"—in contrast to other gospels—is to draw attention not to himself, but, as this statement goes on to make clear, to God as the source of the gospel he champions.

While the usual English translation, "our gospel did not come to you" (τὸ εὐαγγέλιον ἡμῶν οὐκ ἐγενήθη εἰς ὑμᾶς, 1 Thess 1:5),[22] is credible, it probably does not convey what Paul had in mind. Rather than ἔρχομαι ("come") or προσέρχομαι ("come to"), which an English reader could assume lay behind this translation, Paul uses γίνομαι. The word γίνομαι has a range of meanings that includes "come" or "reach,"[23] as in Paul saying that the blessing of Abraham comes to the gentiles (Gal 3:14). However, γίνομαι is used primarily to convey the idea of becoming, originating, or being created,[24] as it does the three other times Paul used it in this introductory thanksgiving (1 Thess 1:5, 6, 7).[25] Doubts about using "came" to translate γίνομαι in the statement under investigation are confirmed when we take into account that Paul follows it with εἰς ("into") rather than πρός ("to"),[26] as some early copyists assumed.[27] Again, it is credible to use "to" in translating εἰς,[28] but its more usual meaning in relation to place or proximity is conveyed by the English "into" or "among."[29]

Thus, reading Paul carefully he is not saying that he brought the gospel to the readers. Rather, he is reminding the Thessalonians that the gospel took place or was established among them or was even created among

---

21. Cf. Sanders, *Paul*, 183.

22. E.g., ASV, ERV, ESV, KJV, NAB, NAS, NET, NIB, NIV, NIRV, NJB, NKJ, NRSV, RSV, RWB, TNIV, and TNT.

23. BAGD, "γίνομαι," 158–60 (159) (I.4.c); MGS, "γίγνομαι...," 429–30 (B).

24. BDAG, "γίνομαι," 196–99; MGS, "γίγνομαι...," 430 (C–E).

25. 1 Thess 2:5 (οὔτε γάρ ποτε ἐν λόγῳ κολακείας ἐγενήθημεν) can also be translated taking γίνομαι as "come": "For we never came with words of flattery" (cf. ESV, NAB, NAS, NAU, NET, and NRSV). However, taking into account the broader use of γίνομαι, it can be more credibly translated, "For we never used words of flattery" (cf. ERV, GNV, KJV, MIT, NET, NIRV, NIV, NJB, NKJ, NLT, RSV, RWB, TNIV, and WEB).

26. On the relationship of εἰς to πρός, see Harris, *Prepositions and Theology in Greek*, 83–84.

27. See p. 81n14 above.

28. In 1 Thess see 2:9. Cf. BAGD, "εἰς," 228–30 (228) 1.a–c. BDAG "εἰς," 288–91 (288–89) (1).

29. See BAGD, "εἰς," 228–30 (228) (1); MGS "1. εἰς," 610–11 (610). On the relationship between εἰς and ἐν see O'Rourke, "ΕΙΣ and EN in John," 139–42; Harris, *Prepositions and Theology in Greek*, 83–86.

them. In other words, for Paul the gospel was more than something he brought, but something that took place among the readers.³⁰ This reading is congruent with him going on to say that the gospel took place or was established among them "not . . . in word only but also in power and in Holy Spirit and in much fullness" (1 Thess 1:5).

The first aspect or component involved in the establishment of the gospel is its being established "in word" (ἐν λόγῳ). Paul uses "word" (λόγος) across the range of its meanings³¹ so that its use here needs to be settled. Using the construction "not . . . only but also" (οὐκ . . . μόνον ἀλλὰ καί, 1 Thess 1:5) contrasts λόγος with the more obviously supranatural or divine categories suggesting λόγος refers to the mundane. In turn, in this context of his relationship with the Thessalonians and the origin of the gospel among them, it is reasonable to take him to be referring to his own speech or message.³² Indeed, it was typical to use the singular "word" (λόγος) to refer to what was spoken: a speech, message, declaration, or narrative, for example.³³ Yet notably in this letter, a number of times λόγος applies to the word of God as Paul's message.³⁴ In particular, he says, "when you received the word of God that you heard from us, you accepted it not as a human word but as what it truly is, God's word, which is also at work in you the believers" (1 Thess 2:13). Here, with an emphasis on "the word of *God*,"³⁵ he equates his message with that word. It is not, as Denys Whiteley supposed, that Paul's "preached word was an hypostasis independent of God. Grammatically, it is distinct from God, but it is still the word which he utters."³⁶ Paul goes on to

---

30. Contrast Best, *Thessalonians*, 111, who equates the gospel and Paul's message.

31. Paul uses λόγος for a spoken word (1 Cor 1:5), a statement (2:1), an assertion (1 Thess 4:15), a speech (1 Cor 2:4b), written words (15:54), reckoning (Rom 14:12), God's word (9:6), promise (9:9) or law (13:9), and God's revelation in Christ (Phil 1:14). See BDAG, "λόγος," 598–607.

32. Paul uses λόγος for his message or speech in, e.g., Rom 15:18; 1 Cor 1:18; 2:1, 4, 13; 5:19; 15:2; 2 Cor 1:18; 2:17; 10:10; 11:6. Cf. 2 Cor 5:19; 6:7; 10:11; Phil 1:14; 1 Thess 1:8; 2:5, 13 (x2); 4:15. Cf. the following note.

33. For the use of λόγος as "narrative" or "speech" after the age of the ancient epic, see the discussion in Debrunner, "λέγω, κτλ," 69–77. Cf. MGS, "λόγος," 1249–51. For the NT use, e.g., see Matt 19:22; Mark 7:29; Luke 1:29; John 2:22; 6:60; Acts 7:29; 13:15; 14:12. Examples in Paul include Rom 15:18; 1 Cor 1:5, 17, 18; 2:1, 4; 4:19, 20; 14:9; 15:2, 54; 2 Cor 1:18; 5:19; 6:7; 8:7; 10:10, 11; 11:6; 1 Thess 2:5. Cf. the previous note; also see Abbott-Smith, *Manual Greek Lexicon*, 270–71.

34. 1 Thess 1:8 ("the word of the Lord," otherwise only at 2 Thess 3:1); 2:13 (x2, quoted above); 4:15 ("the word of the Lord"). Cf. 2 Cor 2:17; 4:2.

35. My emphasis. Cf. Bruce, *1 and 2 Thessalonians*, 44: "τοῦ θεοῦ ['of God'] occupies an emphatic position after παρ' ἡμῶν ['from us'] and perhaps in contrast to it."

36. Whiteley, *Thessalonians*, 46.

say that this word was at "work in" (ἐνεργεῖται) or energizing the believers,[37] a strong term that implies a supernatural source of power at work in—even possessing—believers.[38]

Although from what he says in this letter we will have good cause to modify this conclusion, insofar as the gospel is Paul's message, it is an empowered or energizing word from God that changes the believer.[39] That is, in accepting Paul's word as God's word, the message changes the believers, the evidence being that they became imitators of Paul (2:14).[40] Also, equating his message (λόγος) with the word (λόγος) of God brings together all the elements for the establishment of salvation in what we will see as divine action.

Using ἐν ("in") with λόγος, the most used and versatile of prepositions,[41] Paul's meaning is not immediately obvious. As the instrumental use of ἐν[42] was, under Semitic influence,[43] its most frequent use in biblical Greek,[44] readers are likely—at least initially—to take Paul as recalling that the gospel came "by means of" his message, power, Holy Spirit, and much fullness. However, this would imply a distinction between these entities and the gospel, and we know from his letter to the Romans that "power" (δύναμις) is in some way fundamentally constitutive of the gospel for Paul.[45] Therefore, it is more reasonable to take ἐν as also descriptive. That is, Paul also means that the gospel consisted not of any one but of all these elements. Indeed, Paul has another similar statement in which (using ἀλλά, "but") word and power are also contrasted, and in which ἐν is used in the same way. In deprecating the "talk" or "message" (λόγος) of his arrogant opponents (1 Cor 4:19) he says to the Corinthians that "the kingdom of God is not in (ἐν) word but (ἀλλά) in (ἐν) power" (4:20). For this contrast between Paul

---

37. Milligan, *St Paul's Epistles to the Thessalonians*, 28–29.

38. Cf. Matt 14:2; Mark 6:4; 1 Cor 12:6, 11; 2 Cor 4:12; Gal 3:5; Eph 1:11, 20; 3:20; Phil 2:13; Col 1:29; Clark, "Meaning of ἐνεργέω and καταργέω," esp. 95, 98, 101).

39. Cf. Bourke, "Holy Spirit as the Controlling Dynamic," 149–50. Best, *Thessalonians*, 112, incorrectly takes the faith or trust to be what changes the believer, rather than the received word.

40. Best, *Thessalonians*, 112.

41. Bortone, *Greek Prepositions from Antiquity*, 193. Also, see Moulton et al., *Grammar of New Testament Greek*, 1:98; Harris, *Prepositions and Theology in Greek*, 32, 115–36, esp. 118–22. MM 209, call ἐν the "maid-of-all-work."

42. Moule, *Idiom-Book of New Testament Greek*, 77.

43. Bortone, *Greek Prepositions from Antiquity*, 193.

44. Bortone, *Greek Prepositions from Antiquity*, 192; Harris, *Prepositions and Theology in Greek*, 119.

45. Rom 1:16; see §4.4 (d) below.

and his opponents to be understood ἐν needs to be taken as descriptive, that is, meaning "consisting of."[46] Therefore, in the similar statement we are considering (1 Thess 1:4–5), Paul is probably intending to convey the idea that the gospel came in or by means of, as well as also consisted of, his message, power, Holy Spirit, and much fullness. In turn, understanding Paul's gospel will depend considerably on understanding these elements.

Word. We have just noted that "word" (λόγος), one of the elements of which Paul uses to describe the gospel, as well as its means of establishment, most probably refers to Paul's message, which he equates with God's word energizing the Thessalonians. It is recognized as notoriously difficult to distill from Paul's letters his initial preaching to a group of people as distinct from his subsequent teaching of them.[47] In this letter, for example, some of what Paul appears to have said when he was with the readers was probably not part of his initial message, but articulates implications of that message and gospel. For instance, the setting of Paul saying that he was "urging and encouraging you and pleading that you lead a life worthy of God" (1 Thess 2:12) is logically and theologically[48] more likely to be an implication of the coming or experience of the gospel. Thus Paul is recalling what he said after, rather than before, the Thessalonians became believers (cf. 3:4; 4:1–8).[49]

There are, nevertheless, a number of places in Paul's letters where it is suggested his initial preaching appears to be reflected in what he writes.[50] It is not our intention, however, to trawl Paul's letters in order to reconstruct his initial message. Instead, we will concentrate on this letter to the Thessalonians. For it is the one place in his writings where he appears to allude most clearly to his initial message, notably in the context of talking about the gospel.

In the same opening thanksgiving (1 Thess 1:2–10) in which Paul is recalling the establishment of the gospel among them (1:5), a few lines later he goes on to recall how the Thessalonians turned to God from idols (1:9). He says: "you turned to God from idols, to serve a God living and true,

---

46. Cf. Moule, *Idiom-Book of New Testament Greek*, 79.

47. Cf. Still, "'Since We Believe,'" 7–18; Sanders, *Paul*, 189–90.

48. Note that in Romans Paul's encouragement to live in a particular way (Rom 12:1) follows his presentation of his gospel.

49. To the contrary, Dibelius, *An die Thessalonicher I, II, An die Philipper*, 9, takes Paul to be using formulas from his missionary preaching in 1 Thess 2:1–12.

50. For an attempt at reconstructing Paul's missionary proclamation from other parts of Paul's letters, e.g., see Belleville, "Gospel and Kerygma," 156–62. For a discussion of points in Paul where the content of his preaching can be identified, see Campbell, *Deliverance of God*, 158–64, who identifies, e.g., the frame of Rom, esp. 1:1–16; 15:15–24; 16:4, 17–20, as well as 1 Thess 1:4–10.

and to await his Son out of heaven, whom he raised from the dead—Jesus, who delivers us from the coming wrath" (1:9–10). In line with one of the ways "turn" (ἐπιστρέφω) was used, on two other occasions Paul uses the word in a religio-moral sense[51] to refer to conversion or coming to faith.[52] Therefore, in that this statement is part of the same paragraph that recalls their coming to faith and contains vocabulary used to describe conversion, this statement most probably reflects something of the content of Paul's initial preaching to the Thessalonians.[53] It is going beyond our fragmentary evidence to suggest that this is Paul's missionary preaching to gentiles in a nutshell[54] or the summary of his missionary preaching.[55] Nevertheless, we have seen that Paul's language is not only consistent with him sharing traditional material,[56] but also with him recalling an initial message or set of messages that he used repeatedly as he traveled to speak to new audiences.[57] From this description of the conversion of these gentiles at Thessalonica we have seen that it is possible to recover a number of aspects of Paul's initial preaching, if not his overall message.

We have just noted that from the Thessalonians, Paul's initial preaching elicited the response of them turning from idols to serve a God who was living and true (1 Thess 1:9). For Paul, idols were of no account or significance[58] and were considered lifeless and mute (1 Cor 12:2) human creations, as did streams of his Jewish tradition[59] and other early Christians after him (Rev 9:20; Did. 6.3). It is not surprising, then, that in his missionary preaching to the gentile Thessalonians—considered to be serving lifeless,

---

51. Bertram, "ἐπιστρέφω," 722–29; BDAG, "ἐπιστρέφω" (1a), 382; MGS, "ἐπιστρέφω," 793.

52. 2 Cor 3:16; Gal 4:9. Cf. Acts 3:19; 9:35; 11:21; 14:15; 15:19; 26:18, 20, 27.

53. E.g., so also Munck, "1 Thess 1:9–10," 100.

54. So Harnack, *Mission and Expansion of Christianity*, 1:89.

55. Milligan, *St Paul's Epistles to the Thessalonians*, xlii–xliii; Munck, "1 Thess 1:9–10," 101, lists Louis-Marie Dewailly, Martin Dibelius, Wilhelm Lueken, Charles Masson, Leon Morris, William Neil, Albrecht Oepke, and Béda Rigaux as holding this view. More recently, e.g., see Wanamaker, *Epistles to the Thessalonians*, 84; Kim, "Jesus the Son of God as the Gospel," 118–21, 137.

56. See §2.3 (b) (ii) above.

57. Cf. Munck, "1 Thess 1:9–10," 95–96.

58. See 1 Cor 8:4 (οἴδαμεν ὅτι οὐδὲν εἴδωλον ἐν κόσμῳ; "we know that idols are nothing in the world"); 10:19 (Τί οὖν φημι; ὅτι εἰδωλόθυτόν τί ἐστιν ἢ ὅτι εἴδωλόν τί ἐστιν; "What then do I say? That meat offered to idols is anything, or that an idol is anything?"). Cf. Isa 37:19.

59. Note Wis 15:15; Sir 30:19. Also, see Lev 26:30; Num 33:52; Deut 29:17; Pss 115:4; 135:15; Hab 2:18; Isa 37:19; 41:28; Dan 5:4, 23; Bel 1:4 (LXX, 1:5).

mute idols—he should inform them of a living[60] and true God (1 Thess 1:9),[61] two descriptions of God consistent with his Jewish heritage[62] and later Christians.[63]

Others have noted that, contrary to what might be expected in relation to missionary preaching, God is mentioned before the idols[64] and that this suggests that in his missionary preaching Paul directed the attention of the Thessalonians to the living God so that they naturally abandoned the idols.[65] There is considerable merit in this suggestion in that, otherwise, when Paul describes or alludes to his message in this letter he does not mention the idols. Rather, his attention is on, for example, "the gospel of God" (1 Thess 2:2, 8, 9). Also, Paul's subsequent pleading is not for the Thessalonians to remain turned from the idols. Rather, put positively, they are to live a life worthy of God (2:12). Further, Paul's ongoing interest is not that the Thessalonians have left the idols but that they have received the word of God (2:13).

The book of Acts gives corroborating evidence not only that the response among gentiles to Paul's missionary preaching could involve turning from idols to the living God but also that the emphasis in the preaching was on the living God. Luke has Paul and Barnabas say to the gentile crowd at Lystra, "We bring you good news, that you should turn from these worthless things to the living God" (Acts 14:15). Then, in what

---

60. Paul also describes God as "live" or "living" (ζάω) in Rom 9:26; 2 Cor 3:3; 6:16; cf. 1 Tim 3:15; 4:10. In 2 Cor 6:16 Paul also contrasts idols with the living God.

61. Paul also describes God as "true" (ἀληθής) in Rom 3:4.

62. Although an approximation of Paul's expression is found in the MT in Jer 10:10 ("But the LORD is the true God; he is the living God," NRSV), this text does not appear in the LXX, his Scriptures. However, a Qumran fragment (4Q71) shows that the LXX text had a Hebrew *Vorlage*. See the discussion by Lundbom, *Jeremiah 1–20*, 580–82. Given that no quotation or allusion to Jer 10:10 (MT) is cited in Lange and Weigold, *Biblical Qutations and Allusions*, it is not possible to establish that Paul would have known it. In any case, in the LXX God is separately described as true (LXX: e.g., 2 Chr 15:3; 3 Macc 6:18; Wis 12:27; 15.1) and living (e.g., Deut 4:33; 5:26; Josh 3:10; 1 Kgdms 13:26; 4 Kgdms 19:6; Esth 6:13; Pss 42:2; 84:2; Isa 37:17; Dan 6:21; Hos 1:10; Bel 1:5, 6, 24, 25; 2 Macc 7:33 ["living Lord"]; 3 Macc 6:28).

Even if not using the same vocabulary, the same sentiment is thoroughly shared by Philo. See *Embassy* 3.177, 188; *Cherubim* 1.27; *Prelim. Studies* 1.103; *Abraham* 1.80, 143; *Moses* 2.67, 100; *Decalogue* 1.59, 81; *Spec. Laws* 1.65, 176, 309, 313, 332, 345; 2.255; 3.125, 127; 4.192; *Virtues* 1.34, 64, 102; *Embassy* 1.347. Again, with different vocabulary, for Josephus God is also true (*Ant.* 8.335, 337, 338, 343, 402; 9.256; 10.263; 11.55; *J.W.* 7.323) and gives life (*Ant.* 1.152; 8.326–27; 10.26–27).

63. God is described as "true" in John 3:33 (ἀληθής); 17:3 (ἀληθινός); Rev 6:10 (ἀληθινός), and as "live" or "living" (ζάω) in Matt 16:16; 26:63; Acts 14:15; Heb 3:12; 9:14; 10:31; 12:22; and Rev 7:2.

64. E. von Dobschütz, cited by Munck, "1 Thess 1:9–10," 101n2.

65. Munck, "1 Thess 1:9–10," 101n2.

follows in the speech, the attention is placed entirely on the greatness and generosity of God (14:15–17).

With Paul's considered description of his gospel early in Romans focused on the Son,[66] it is not surprising that in his initial preaching to the Thessalonians Jesus is referred to as God's Son (1 Thess 1:9–10). This missional preaching also conveyed the view that he is in heaven and that God raised him from the dead. The implication is that the Son is in heaven as a result of, or by means of, the resurrection. In contrast to what we find in his latter correspondence, Paul makes no connection between the death of Jesus and his salvific efficacy.[67] Even though his death may be assumed, it is only the resurrection and his being in heaven that identifies Jesus as "the one rescuing us" (1:10).

Beyond his basic identity as the Son, the emphasis here in Paul's preaching is not on the identity of Jesus but on believers waiting for the Son from heaven (1 Thess 1:10). In this eschatological context Paul could be expected to use ἀπεκδέχομαι ("await eagerly").[68] Instead, he uses ἀναμένω ("wait"), its only occurrence in his letters. This supports the view proposed here that in this reminder Paul is recalling not only traditional material but his initial message, a well-used message that he would have reused or mined when he spoke to successive audiences for the first time.

The impression left is that this waiting is a dominant feature of the believer's life perspective.[69] Using ἀναμένω ("wait"), with its aspect of expectancy,[70] for Paul the waiting is an active, expectant waiting.[71] As he explains later, waiting is living a life worthy of God because "God calls you into his own kingdom and glory" (1 Thess 2:12).

In that here the call is ongoing[72] and elsewhere Paul relates God's call to the beginning of the Christian life,[73] it is most probable that Paul's

---

66. Rom 1:2; see §4.4 (a) and (b) below; Phil 1:27—2:11; see §3.4 (c) below. Also see p. 50n183 above.

67. E.g., see Rom 3:25; 8:3; 1 Cor 5:7; 2 Cor 5:21.

68. For ἀπεκδέχομαι in Paul see: Rom 8:19, 23, 25; 1 Cor 1:7; Gal 5:5; Phil 3:20.

69. The theme of waiting remained important beyond Paul's visit to play an important part in this letter. See 1 Thess 2:19; 4:13–18; 5:1–11.

70. LXX: Job 2:9; 7:2; Sir 2.7; 6.19; Jud 8.17; also, 2 Clem. 19.4; Ign. *Phld.* 5.2; Cf. BDAG, "ἀναμένω," 68; MGS, "ἀναμένω," 144.

71. Langevin, "Le Seigneur Jésus selon un texte prépaulinien, 1 Th 1:9–10."

72. Paul uses the present participle, "calling" (καλοῦντος). See 1 Thess 5:24: ὁ καλῶν ὑμᾶς ("the one calling you"). Cf. Rom 8:30; 9:24; 1 Cor 1:9; 7:15, 17, 18, 20, 21, 22, 24; Gal 1:6, 15; 5:13; Bruce, *1 and 2 Thessalonians*, 37.

73. Rom 4:17; 8:30; 9:7, 12, 24; 1 Cor 1:9; 7:15, 17, 18, 20, 21, 22, 24; Gal 1:6, 15; 5:13; 1 Thess 2:12; 4:7. Cf. Best, *Thessalonians*, 108.

initial message to the Thessalonians included the theme of God's call into his kingdom and glory.[74] For Paul the kingdom was the powerful manifestation of God's active reign experienced in the present (Rom 14:17; 1 Cor 4:20) and also to be inherited in the future.[75] If not immediately, given the emphasis in this letter, soon after Paul would have explained the ethical implications of this call.

The impression is also left that the waiting will be rewarded in the near future, at least in the life of the Thessalonians. Hence the trauma for the Thessalonians when some of them died (1 Thess 4:13). Also consistent with the initial urging that the Thessalonians wait for the Son (1:10) is the way the theme is picked up again nearer the end of the letter. Paul says, clearly reminding them of what he had told them: "For you yourselves know very well that the day of the Lord will come like a thief in the night" (5:2, cf. 9, 23), when least expected. Paul's initial message, then, involved being ready for the unknown timing of "the day," which, if not in his initial preaching, he immediately goes on to associate with sudden, painful destruction (5:3-4; cf. 1 Cor 3:13-15).

The importance of this waiting for the Son is seen in Paul, later in this letter, picking up the theme with considerable and colorful elaboration (1 Thess 4:15-17). However, this elaboration that involves the archangel's cry, the sound of God's trumpet and those living being caught up in the clouds with the Lord, is not likely to have been part of the initial preaching.[76] For Paul is addressing the new problem of believers dying before the coming of the Lord. Also, he does not give the impression he is reminding his readers of these ideas as he does of other ideas in other places.[77] Further, there is some inconsistency between this material and what we are taking to be indicative of his preaching (1:9-10) in that it is now the Lord not the Son who descends and the dead are to rise (4:15-17; cf. 1:10).

From what we know of Paul's great interest in the resurrection of Jesus expressed across his letters,[78] it is no surprise that this motif was part of his initial message to the Thessalonians (1 Thess 1:10). The importance of the

---

74. "Kingdom" and "glory" are probably not, as supposed by Milligan, *St Paul's Epistles to the Thessalonians*, 27, to be taken to refer to two manifestations of God's power. Rather both terms are used to refer to the manifestation of God's presence. Cf. Whiteley, *Thessalonians*, 45.

75. 1 Cor 6:9, 10; Gal 5:21. Further, e.g., see Bauckham, "Kingdom and Church," 1–26.

76. To the contrary, see Sanders, *Paul*, 118–19.

77. Cf. e.g., 1 Cor 11 and 15.

78. E.g., see Rom 1:4; 6:1-11; 8:11; 1 Cor 15:1-58; 2 Cor 3:16-17; 5:15; Gal 2:20; Phil 2:9; 3:10-11; 1 Thess 1:10.

resurrection both in his initial preaching, and in his estimation of Jesus, is clear in that it is the only feature of Jesus' earthly life that Paul includes here. Although he otherwise always attributes Jesus' resurrection to God,[79] later in the letter, in the statement "we believe that Jesus died and rose again" (4:14), Jesus appears to do so in his own power.[80] Perhaps in his early ministry Paul's mind had not settled on the source of power for the resurrection, God, or Jesus (cf. 1:10). More likely, Paul is citing early creedal material he has inherited from a time before the convictions about God's particular involvement in the resurrection had solidified.

The statement, "we believe that Jesus died and rose again" (1 Thess 4:14), is almost certainly creedal. To begin with, the words "we believe that" (πιστεύομεν ὅτι) are likely to be a typical introduction to a creed.[81] Also, as we have just seen above, unique in his correspondence, Paul does not credit God with Jesus' resurrection. Further, Paul does not often use the name "Jesus" alone, as here and, notably, in a traditional statement earlier in this letter (1 Thess 1:10),[82] reflecting a time in early Christianity before Christology had developed more complex names for him.[83] Telling, furthermore, is Paul not using his usual word for "raise" (ἐγείρω).[84] Instead, he uses another word (ἀνίστημι), which is widely used by later New Testament writers, but not often by Paul and, again notably, only in quotations.[85]

Given that the phrase is creedal and dealing with a fundamental tenet of early Christianity, it is probably something Paul included in his initial message or messages to the Thessalonians that we are attempting

---

79. See Rom 4:24; 6:4; 8:11; 10:9; 1 Cor 6:14; 15:15; 2 Cor 4:14; 13:4; Gal 1:1; cf. Eph 1:20; Col 2:12.

80. Fitzmyer, *Paul and His Theology*, 55.

81. Cf. John 4:42; Acts 15:11; Rom 6:8; 10:9. Havener, "Pre-Pauline Christological Credal Formulae of 1 Thessalonians," 111, is more confident.

82. Paul uses the name "Jesus" (Ἰησοῦς) 143 times, but only on its own at Rom 3:26; 8:11; 1 Cor 12:3; 2 Cor 4:10 (x2), 11, 14; 11:4; Gal 6:17; Phil 2:10; 1 Thess 1:10; 4:14 (x2).

83. Cf. Havener, "Pre-Pauline Christological Credal Formulae of 1 Thessalonians," 111–12; Best, *Thessalonians*, 187.

84. Paul uses ἐγείρω thirty-seven times: Rom 4:24, 25; 6:4, 9; 7:4; 8:11 (x2), 34; 10:9; 13:11; 1 Cor 6:14; 15:4, 12, 13, 14, 15 (x3), 16 (x2), 17, 20, 29, 32, 35, 42, 43 (x2), 44, 52; 2 Cor 1:9; 4:14 (x2); 5:15; Gal 1:1; Phil 1:17; 1 Thess 1:10.

85. Paul uses ἀνίστημι four times: in Rom 15:12 (quoting Isa 11:10); 1 Cor 10:7 (quoting Exod 32:6); and 1 Thess 4:16, which is either influenced by his use of the word in 4:14, or, more likely, used in a quotation of "the word of the Lord" (4:15). Cf. Best, *Thessalonians*, 187. In the remainder of the NT ἀνίστημι occurs: Luke seventy-one times (including forty-five in Acts); Matthew four times; Mark seventeen; John eight; Hebrews two; and Ephesians one.

to recreate.⁸⁶ In any case, the statement "we believe" signals a shared idea. For the statement to have rhetorical force, it will be a statement shared at least by Paul and the Thessalonians, therefore something he has already communicated while he was with them.

There is no mention of the ascension of Jesus in the recollection by Paul of his initial preaching (1 Thess 1:9-10) or in the brief creedal statement (4:14). Indeed, Paul never mentions the ascension; that is a Lukan construct.⁸⁷ Rather, in the passage of interest to us the collection and progression of the main ideas—Son coming from heaven (whom God raised from the dead) and Jesus rescuing from the coming wrath—the implication is that the resurrection was Jesus' entry into heaven (1 Thess 1:10).⁸⁸ Writing to the Philippians Paul is more explicit. In his *Carmen Christi* (Phil 2:6-11) Paul immediately moves the ideas from "death on a cross" (2:8) to "therefore God also highly exalted him" (2:9). The framework that makes this thinking possible is clear in his statement to the Corinthians that, through the resurrection Jesus became a life-giving spirit, the second Adam, with a spiritual body (1 Cor 15:42-47). On this model, which fits well with his scheme in 1 Thessalonians, we can assume that in his initial preaching Paul led his hearers to assume that Jesus' resurrection was his exaltation.

The theme of the wrath to come also appears to have been part of Paul's initial preaching. The Thessalonians are reminded that Jesus is "the one rescuing us (τὸν ῥυόμενον ἡμᾶς) from the wrath that is coming" (1 Thess 1:10). That Paul uses the "timeless" present participle "rescuing" (ῥυόμενον)⁸⁹ shows that he considered that the rescue was already taking place in the present before the Son appeared.⁹⁰

Consistent with this motif of wrath—hence a likely elaboration of what we can see of his preaching here—a little later Paul writes to them: "For God has destined us not for wrath but for obtaining salvation through our Lord Jesus Christ who died for us" (1 Thess 5:9-10). Though the death of Jesus is here linked to salvation—perhaps prompted by the motif of death

---

86. On the speculation that Paul may have truncated a creedal formula that continued with "for us" (ὑπὲρ ἡμῶν; cf. 1 Thess 5:10) see Havener, "Pre-Pauline Christological Credal Formulae of 1 Thessalonians," 112, and Wanamaker, *Epistles to the Thessalonians*, 168-69.

87. Dunn, *Theology of Paul the Apostle*, 265. Cf. Schlier, *Grundzüge einer paulinischen Theologie*, 144-47.

88. E.g., cf. Dunn, *Theology of Paul the Apostle*, 265.

89. Whiteley, *Thessalonians*, 40.

90. Best, *Thessalonians*, 84.

among believers (4:13—5:11)—we cannot be sure this was part of Paul's initial preaching.

From the closing remarks of Paul's opening thanksgiving, which we have been examining as a reflection of his initial preaching to gentiles at Thessalonica, we are able to reconstruct his "word," or message, that he lists as one of the elements of the gospel, as well as its means of establishment. It seems that in initially speaking to his audience Paul introduced them to God, encouraging these gentiles at Thessalonica to turn from lifeless idols "to serve a living and true God" (1 Thess 1:9). In this preaching Paul conveyed the idea that Jesus, God's Son, was in heaven by virtue of being raised from the dead by God, and that their lives were to be taken up with waiting for him from heaven, expecting him soon. This waiting was a life perspective of living a life worthy of God. Notwithstanding the waiting, Jesus the Son is the one who already rescues them from the coming wrath. He equates this message with God's word energizing the Thessalonians.

We cannot suppose that in this reconstruction we have been able to capture all that Paul would have said in his initial or missionary preaching. Indeed, there are probably a number of apparent lacunae in what we have reconstructed. Contrary to what we would expect from other letters,[91] nothing suggests that, in his missionary or initial message, Paul spoke about the death of Jesus as theologically significant, though the idea is mentioned later in the letter as a means of encouraging hope for those who have died (1 Thess 4:14) and vigilance in each other (5:9-11). Nor are we able to establish that in this initial preaching that Paul spoke of God's justifying grace.[92] Also, though it is an important theme in this letter (4:13-18), his preaching—initial or subsequent—did not appear to entail the subject of the resurrection of dead believers, for the Thessalonians seem to know nothing about the topic.[93]

In this reconstruction there are echoes of the story of Jesus and its connection with a larger one of the people of God and an even larger cosmic story. Yet, at least when considering Paul's message to the Thessalonians, it does not appear to be a story. There may be a narrative substructure to Paul's spoken gospel that we might reconstruct,[94] but from what we can see in this letter to the Thessalonians, for Paul, that narrative substructure was neither

---

91. Cf. e.g., Rom 3:25; 1 Cor 2:2; Gal 3:1; 6:14.
92. Cf. Bruce, *1 and 2 Thessalonians*, 18.
93. Cf. Schnelle, *Apostle Paul*, 183.
94. Campbell, "Story of Jesus in Romans and Galatians," esp. 108.

tight nor carefully presented to the readers. It seems reasonable to conclude that in his "gospelling" Paul was not fundamentally a storyteller.[95]

Along with his message, we are also able to recover something of the style or manner of Paul's initial preaching. Having recalled their conversion experience (1 Thess 1:9-10), Paul turns to defend himself, not so much in terms of what he said (though see 2:12), but in terms of his motives and approach or style (2:1-12). Leaving aside his motives,[96] which may not have been obvious to the listeners, we can note he reminds the Thessalonians that his message (λόγος) did not come out of "flattery" (κολακεία) or as a pretext for "greediness" (πλεοεξία, 2:5). Knowing what he says to the Corinthians about his poor showing as a speaker (1 Cor 2:1-5) and that he says in his message he did not seek human praise, it is reasonable to assume that his oratory among the Thessalonians would not have gained any praise (1 Thess 2:5-6). Paul also claims to have adopted a gentle approach to the Thessalonians (2:7). Yet, using the word "proclaim" or "announce" (κηρύσσω, 2:9), with its overtones of authority and confidence associated with speaking for a royal or divine figure,[97] suggests that his missionary preaching was carried out with confidence. Indeed, Paul uses the word "appeal" (παράκλησις) of his speaking the gospel to them (2:2-3). Ernest Best was right to say this appeal "is no neutral presentation of the facts about Jesus but an exhortation to accept what is presented."[98]

Besides his message, the other elements involved in the establishment of Paul's gospel—power, Holy Spirit, and much fullness—also need to be taken into account to understand his gospel. In another discussion of these items my interest was in establishing that separately and collectively they pointed to the experience of God's tangible action or, in shorthand, to the miraculous.[99] Here the interest is in establishing their role in filling out our understanding of Paul's gospel.

Power and Holy Spirit. On its own, the singular "power" (δύναμις) was used for the source or cause of miracles.[100] Luke, for example, says of Jesus

---

95. Watson, "Is There a Story," 232.

96. Paul mentions, e.g., πλάνης ("deception"), ἀκαθαρσία ("impurity"), and δόλος ("deceit," 1 Thess 2:3) as potential motives, on which see Best, *Thessalonians*, 93-94.

97. See MGS "κηρύσσω," 1125-26; *NIDNTTE*, "κηρύσσω," 2.674-82 (674-76). E.g., see Epictetus, *Diatr.* 3.13.12; Josephus, *Ant.* 10.117; Philo, *Agriculture* 112.

98. Best, *Thessalonians*, 92.

99. In more detail for what follows, see Twelftree, *Paul and the Miraculous*, 182-87.

100. In the NT, see Mark 5:30; 6:5; 9:39; Luke 5:17; 6:19; 8:46; 9:1; Acts 3:12; 4:7; 6:8; 10:38; Rom 15:19; 1 Cor 4:20; and 2 Thess 2:9. See Friedrich, "δύναμις," 357-58; BDAG, "δύναμις," 262-63, esp. (3). Cf. Grundmann, "δύναμαι/δύναμις," 311-12. Less frequently the singular δύναμις ("power") is used to refer to miracles. In the NT see Mark 6:5; 9:39.

that the "power (δύναμις) of the Lord was with him to heal" (Luke 5:17), and he later says that "power came out from him and he healed all of them" (6:19). In turn, Jesus is depicted as giving "power" to his followers to heal (9:1). Paul himself also uses "power," probably referring to this source as well to miracles themselves. In writing to the Corinthians he says that he is coming to visit them to "find out not the talk of these arrogant people but their power. For the kingdom of God depends not on talk but on power" (1 Cor 4:20). Given the strong connection in Jesus' ministry between the kingdom of God and miracles,[101] Paul would probably be assuming that his readers would take it that by his collocation of kingdom and power he was referring to both the miraculous and its source.[102]

In Paul's world, "power" and (Holy) "Spirit" could be synonyms.[103] For example, in hendyadic statements Luke says that John the Baptist is expected to have "the spirit and power of Elijah" (Luke 1:17), and an angel says to Mary, "The Holy Spirit will come upon you, and the power of the Most High will overshadow you."[104] In the Dead Sea Scrolls the Holy Spirit and power are also closely associated.[105] Paul not only occasionally used "power" and "Spirit" closely together,[106] but he can also use them as synonyms, notably when he says that his proclamation to the Corinthians came "with a demonstration of the Spirit and of power" (1 Cor 2:4). It is most likely, then, that in describing the establishment of the gospel among the Thessalonians, the phrase "in power and in Spirit" is to be taken as a hendiadys.[107] Using "Holy Spirit" without

---

The plural "powers" (δυνάμεις) could also be used for the source or power for miracles (Matt 6:14; 13:54; 14:2/Mark 6:14) though its overwhelming use was for the miracles. In the NT, see Matt 7:22; 11:20, 21, 23; 13:54, 58; 14:2; 24:29; Mark 6:2, 14; Luke 10:13; 19:37; Acts 2:22; 8:13; 19:11. Cf. 1 Cor 12:10, 28, 29; Gal 3:5; Heb 2:4. Also, e.g., see Justin, *1 Apol.* 26.2; *Dial.* 11.4; 35.8; 115.4; 132.1; Irenaeus, *ep. Flor.* (cited by Eusebius, *Hist. eccl.* 5.20.6); Hippolytus, *Haer.* 7.23; Origen, *Cels.* 1.46. Cf. Grundmann, "δύναμαι/δύναμις," 284–317; BAGD, "δύναμις," 208 (4); BDAG, "δύναμις," 262–63 (263 §3); MGS, "δύναμις," 558 (E).

101. See particularly the so-called Beelzebul controversy, which is found in Mark (Mark 3:22–27/Matt 9:32–34) and Q (Matt 12:22–30/Luke 11:14–23) and reflected in Matthew and Luke. See also Jesus' answer to John the Baptist (Matt 11:2–6/Luke 7:18–23), and the discussion by Twelftree, "Miracles of Jesus," 117–22.

102. Cf. Twelftree, *Paul and the Miraculous*, 203–4.

103. See Mic 3:8; Luke 1:17, 35; 4:14; Acts 1:8; 4:7; 8:19; 10:38; Eph 3:16. Cf. Twelftree, *Paul and the Miraculous*, 183.

104. Luke 1:35; cf. 4:14; Acts 1:8.

105. 1QH^a 4.28–29, 34–38; 7.25–26; 13.38; 15.9–10. Cf. Mansoor, *Thanksgiving Hymns*, 76–77.

106. Rom 1:4; 15:13, 19; 1 Cor 2:4; Gal 3:5; 1 Thess 1:5. See also Eph 3:16; 2 Tim 1:7.

107. Bultmann, *Theology of the New Testament*, 1:156; Bullmore, *St. Paul's Theology of Rhetorical Style*, 213–14.

an article enabled him to place it in parallel with "in power." This paralleling of synonyms is not in reference to the empowerment of his message,[108] but reinforces and heightens the reference to miracles.

Defining miracles.[109] We need to pause to clarify Paul's understanding of miracles. Since the Enlightenment of the eighteenth century a miracle has come broadly to refer to an unexpected occurrence caused by a god that violates a law of nature.[110] However, for the biblical writers a miracle involved no infringement of any laws. Rather, a miracle was simply a striking or surprising phenomenon that was humanly impossible, and was thought to be brought about by and reveal a god.[111] What could be called παράδοξοι ("strange," "wonderful," or "remarkable" things)[112] included a range of the inexplicable: genetic anomalies, strange natural phenomena, and reports of events bringing human health and safety.[113]

It is in Paul's lists of gifts or "charismata" (χαρίσματα)[114]—phenomena he took to be activated by and to express God[115]—that we probably gain access to his view of miracle. In one of his lists of gifts, "helps" (ἀντιλήμψεις) and "administration" (κυβερνήσεις), as well as "healings" (ἰάματα) and "powers" or "miracles" (δυνάμεις), are expected in his churches as the result of the activity of God (1 Cor 12:28-29). This eclectic but hardly entirely

---

108. This is the import of the reading by Bourke, "Holy Spirit as the Controlling Dynamic," 145-47.

109. For more detail on what follows in this section, see Twelftree, *Paul and the Miraculous*, 20-26.

110. Cf., e.g., Locke, "Discourse of Miracles," 79; Hume, *Enquiries Concerning Human Understanding*, 114-15; Brown, *Miracles and the Critical Mind*, 23-100.

111. Crossan, *Birth of Christianity*, 303; Eve, *Jewish Context of Jesus' Miracles*, 1-2.

112. In the NT: Luke 5:26. In the LXX: Jdt 13:13; 2 Macc 9:24; 4 Macc 2:14; Wis 16:17; 19:5. In Josephus: *Ant.* 2.91, 223, 267, 285, 295, 345, 347; 3.1, 14, 30; 5.28, 125; 6.171; 8.130; 9.60; 10.28; 12.87; 13.140, 282; 14.455; 16.343; *J.W.* 1.518; 4.354; 6.102; *Ag. Ap.* 1.53; 2.114. In Philo: *Creation* 1.124; *Sacrifices* 1.100; *Worse* 1.44, 48, 94, 153; *Posterity* 1.19, 50; *Unchangeable* 1.127; *Planting* 1.62, 69; *Drunkenness* 1.66, 178; *Confusion* 1.31, 59, 132; *Heir* 1.81, 95; *Prelim. Studies* 1.3; *Flight* 1.180; *Dreams* 2.23, 136, 185; *Abraham* 1.196; *Moses* 1.143, 202, 203; 2.125, 213; *Good Person* 1.58, 105; *Eternity* 1.48, 109; *Embassy* 1.80; *QG* 3.18. See also Kittel, "παράδοξος," 255; BDAG, "παράδοξος," 763.

113. For a concise discussion, see Cotter, *Miracles in Greco-Roman Antiquity*, 1-2; more broadly, see Remus, *Pagan-Christian Conflict*, 27-72.

114. Paul appears to be the first to use the word χαρίσματα (cf. TLG). In the NT it only appears in Paul's letters: Rom 11:29; 12:6; 1 Cor 12:9, 28, 30, 31. Cf. Conzelmann, "χάρισμα," 402-3; Berger, "χάρισμα," 460.

115. 1 Cor 12:4-7, 18, 24, 28.

supernatural list is consistent with the ancient view, well represented in the Old Testament, that the miraculous involved any activity of a god.[116]

However, earlier in Paul's discussion of *charismata*, there is a catalogue of more obviously supranatural activities: wisdom, knowledge, faith, healings, miracles, prophecy, discernment, tongues, and the interpretation of tongues (1 Cor 12:8–10). Various suggestions have been made regarding what the order of the items in this list might imply about Paul's thinking.[117] At least part of what Paul has in mind is probably reflected in his change of word for "other" (from ἄλλος to ἕτερος) when he mentions faith early in the list (12:9), and tongues later in the list (12:10). In classical Greek, ἕτερος signalled a definite division.[118] Even though by Paul's time the distinction between ἄλλος and ἕτερος had largely been lost (cf. Gal 1:6–7),[119] he can appear to use ἕτερος to indicate specific, qualitative differences,[120] as he probably does here, reflecting a deliberate arrangement of his list. His use of ἕτερος separates the initial two items (wisdom and knowledge), which were not only of great interest to the Corinthians,[121] but also related to the opening discussion on speaking by the Spirit of God (12:1–3). The last two gifts (tongues and their interpretation), which he considered overrated (e.g., 14:19), are separated off at the end of the list by the use of ἕτερος.[122] This, therefore, probably intentionally leaves together a set of five gifts—faith, healings, miracles, prophecy, and discernment of spirits.[123]

It is in this cluster of activities that we probably best see the meaning and compass of Paul's idea of "miracle." For, along with what to us are obviously

---

116. Cf. Eichrodt, *Theology of the Old Testament*, 2:162n4, citing Exod 34:10; Num 16:30; Isa 48:7; and Jer 31:22.

117. For various suggestions how Paul may have intended his list to be categorized see, e.g., Robertson and Plummer, *First Epistle of St. Paul to the Corinthians*, 265; Bittlinger, *Gifts and Graces*, 20–22; Bruce, *1 and 2 Corinthians*, 119; Findlay, *St. Paul's First Epistle to the Corinthians*, 2:888; MacGorman, *Gifts of the Spirit*, 34–35; Martin, *Spirit and the Congregation*, 11–14; Fee, *First Epistle to the Corinthians*, 662–63.

118. Moulton et al., *Grammar of New Testament Greek*, 3:197; LSJ, "ἕτερος," 702; cf. Matt 10:23; 12:45; Luke 4:43; 10:1; 23:32.

119. Moulton et al., *Grammar of New Testament Greek*, 3:197; Robertson, *Grammar of the Greek New Testament*, 749; BDF §306.

120. 1 Cor 15:39–41; 2 Cor 11:4, cited by Findlay, *St. Paul's First Epistle to the Corinthians*, 2:888.

121. Cf. 1 Cor 1:17—2:16; 8:1–3, 7; Dunn, *Jesus and the Spirit*, 217–21.

122. Robertson and Plummer, *First Epistle of St. Paul to the Corinthians*, 265; Fee, *First Epistle to the Corinthians*, 590–91.

123. For similar divisions of the list of gifts in 1 Cor 12: 8–10 see, e.g., Robertson and Plummer, *First Epistle of St. Paul to the Corinthians*, 265; Findlay, *St. Paul's First Epistle to the Corinthians*, 2:887–88; Fee, *First Epistle to the Corinthians*, 662–63.

THE GOSPEL PAUL PROMOTED   97

miraculous gifts—healings and powers or miracles (also kept together in another list, 1 Cor 12:28–29, suggesting their similarity)—he includes faith, prophecy, and discernment of spirits. Understanding the nature of each of these gifts, considered as a class, will help us see what Paul understood by the miraculous. First, "faith" (or "trust," πίστις) in this context (cf. 12:9) is not related to salvation.[124] Nor is faith a sovereign or overarching *charism*,[125] nor is it particularly associated with the operation of the gifts of healings or miracles.[126] The structure of the sentence—"to another faith, to another healings, to another powers" (12:9)—accords faith its own identity and function. Occurring in a list of activities or tangible expressions of the Spirit, faith probably involves more than an "invincible confidence . . . assured by a supernatural instinct."[127] Rather, as it emerges from the hyperbole of his argument for the necessity of love (13:1–3), containing his only other use of the word in this section, faith is the gift to remove mountains (13:2).[128] Since the removal of mountains was a proverbial expression for the impossible or improbable,[129] taking into account Paul's hyperbole (he uses "all," πᾶς, three times in 13:2 and 3), faith in a list of *charismata* probably referred to the ability to be instrumental in accomplishing the ordinarily difficult or impossible. Given that Paul's interest here is the corporate value of the gifts (12:7), the outcome of the faith is likely expected to relate at least to the health and wellbeing of the group and its members. We can only guess what they might be; perhaps it was perceived protection during travel or in a time of danger or persecution, or the provision of food or money, for example.

Second, as the singular "healing" (ἴαμα) would already carry the idea of repeated use, the plural gift "of healings" (ἰαμάτων) suggests Paul has in

---

124. Collins, *First Corinthians*, 454, speaks for most commentators: "the charismatic faith of which Paul writes is something different form the faith that characterizes all believers." See also Dunn, *Jesus and the Spirit*, 211–12; Fee, *God's Empowering Presence*, 168.

125. Gillespie, *First Theologian*, 112–13.

126. Thiselton, *First Epistle to the Corinthians*, 947, cites Lang, Kistemaker, Allo, and Senft as associating faith with the healing of 1 Cor 12:9. Similarly, see Conzelmann, *1 Corinthians*, 209; Dunn, *Jesus and the Spirit*, 211.

127. Dunn, *Jesus and the Spirit*, 211, depending in part on Prat, *Theology of Saint Paul*, 1:426.

128. The noun πίστις occurs in 1 Cor 2:5; 12:9; 13:13; 15:14, 17. The verb, πιστεύω, occurs in 1 Cor 1:21; 3:5; 9:17; 11:18; 13:7; 14:22 (x2); 15:2, 11.

129. See Davies and Allison, *Gospel According to Matthew*, 2:727 citing Isa 54:10; Josephus, *Ant.* 2.333; *T. Sol.* 23.1; *b. Sanh.* 24a; *b. Ber.* 64a; *b. B. Bat.* 3b; and Homer *Od.* 5.480–85; also, e.g., see Hooker, *Gospel According to St Mark*, 269, and the detailed discussion by Yeung, *Faith in Jesus and Paul*, 21–30.

mind different kinds of healing (1 Cor 12:9).[130] Third, in Paul's world, the plural "powers" (δυνάμεις) could refer to heavenly beings or bodies,[131] or, as the context requires here, to deeds that exhibited or expressed power, that is miracles.[132]

Fourth, "prophecy" (προφητεία, 1 Cor 12:10) is a revelatory gift, for Paul uses the word "revelation" (ἀποκάλυψις), referring to prophecy and knowledge, when he is dealing with disclosing divine mysteries (cf. 14:6 and 16). He also uses the term "revelation" for visionary experiences (2 Cor 12:1, 9) and the gospel (Gal 1:12), or God's will being revealed to him (2:2). In this we see that Paul takes revelation to be in the same orbit of the miraculous with healing and miracles.[133]

Fifth, the meaning of "discernment of spirits" (διακρίσεις πνευμάτων) is not immediately obvious (1 Cor 12:10).[134] It could refer to judging which spirit—holy or otherwise—is the source of some phenomena (cf. 1 John 4:1). More likely, here it is to be taken to relate to prophecy. For, further on in his discussion of the gifts, he pairs prophecy with the need to "judge" or "weigh" (διακρίνω) what is said. Also, in the only other place Paul discusses the use of prophecy among believers (1 Thess 5:20–21), he also mentions the need to "examine" or "test" (δοκιμάζω) everything. Further, the two pairs of tongues/interpretation and prophecy/testing also found later in this section (1 Cor 14:27–29) support the view that in the "discernment of spirits" following prophecy, Paul has the testing of prophecy in mind.[135] Thus, for Paul, discernment of spirits belongs with prophecy as a revelatory gift.

From this list of actions of God expressed in individuals for the benefit of the community (1 Cor 12:7), we are able to conclude that the close association of extraordinary faith, healings, and powers or miracles, with revelatory gifts, shows that Paul saw them as of the same order (12:9–10): healings and miracles, the accomplishment of the impossible, and the

---

130. Thiselton, *First Epistle to the Corinthians*, 946.

131. In the NT, see Matt 24:29; Mark 13:25; Luke 21:26; Rom 8:38; and Heb 6:5.

132. In the NT, see Matt 7:22; 11:20, 21, 23; 13:54, 58; 14:2; Mark 6:2, 14; Luke 10:13; Acts 8:13; 19:11; 1 Cor 12:28, 29; Gal 3:5.

133. It is notable that Grudem, *Gift of Prophecy*, 136–38 (esp. 137), resists the conclusion that prophecy is miraculous for Paul in that it would mean that all the gifts would have to be deemed miraculous, and that the term "miracle" would be void of value in distinguishing various activities. Not only does this conception of miracle appear to arise from a post-Enlightenment perspective, it is exactly the opposite to what Paul wishes to convey.

134. See the summary of the debates by Thiselton, *First Epistle to the Corinthians*, 965–70.

135. Note Fee, *God's Empowering Presence*, 171.

experience and assessment of revelation were of a piece for Paul. While this could be taken to be the core of Paul's understanding of miracles, his inclusion of helps and administration among the *charismata* (12:28-29) means that his notion of the miraculous was not governed by their impossibility but their activation by and expression of God's grace.[136] As the differences between his lists of *charismata* also suggest,[137] miracles could, then, include more than the items he has listed, perhaps miracles such as exorcism or provision and protection.[138] This is an important conclusion for, as we examine Paul's writings, we need to take into account that for him not only healings and works of power, but any tangible expression of God's grace (χάρις)[139] would have been judged miraculous. Having settled what Paul probably meant by the miraculous we can return to considering his statement about the gospel coming word, power, Holy Spirit, and much fullness (1 Thess 1:4-5).

Much fullness. Paul adds "fullness" or "certainty" (πληροφορία) in parallel with the previous two terms, power and Holy Spirit (1 Thess 1:5):

also in power	καὶ ἐν δυνάμει
also in Holy Spirit	καὶ ἐν πνεύματι ἁγίῳ
also in much fullness	καὶ [ἐν][140] πληροφορίᾳ πολλῇ

The noun πληροφορία is generally translated "certainty" or "assurance,"[141] which is consistent with the non-Christian use of the term[142] and with

---

136. See Twelftree, *Paul and the Miraculous*, 20-26, 313-14.

137. Cf. Rom 12:4-8; 1 Cor 12:8-10, 28-30.

138. Cf. Bultmann, *Theology of the New Testament*, 1:325.

139. See Rom 12:6; 1 Cor 12:4, 28, 30, 31; Käsemann, "Ministry and Community," 73, who defines charism "as the concretion and individuation of grace or of the Spirit."

140. Though not accepted in NT[25], more recently, NT[26], NT[27] and NT[28] conjecture ἐν is, with A C D F G Ψ 0278. 81. 104. 365. 630. 1175. 1241. 1505. 1739. 1881. 2464 M lat, to be read here.

141. Cf. MGS, "πληροφορία," 1683; ASV ("assurance"), BBE ("completely certain"), CSB ("assurance"), DBY ("assurance"), ERV ("assurance"), ESV ("conviction"), GWN ("certainty"), KJV ("certainty"), NAB ("conviction"), NAS ("conviction"), NAU ("conviction"), NET ("conviction"), NEB ("conviction"), NIRV ("He gave us complete faith in what we were preaching"), NIV ("conviction"), NKJ ("assurance"), NLT ("assurance"), NRSV ("conviction"), PNT ("certayntie"), RSV ("conviction"), RWB ("assurance"), TNIV ("conviction"), TNT ("certayntie"), WEB ("assurance"), YLT ("assurance").

142. E.g., *P. Giess.* 87.25-26; *Rhet. Gr.* VII.108.3; Delling, "πληροφορία," 310; BDAG, "πληροφορία," 827. BAGD "πληροφορία," 670, say that "at least in Col 2:2; Heb 6:11; 10:22; 1 Clem. 42:3 the meaning *fulness* is also possible. Likewise Rom 15:29."

Paul's use of the verb.[143] However, the three other uses of the noun in the New Testament clearly refer to fullness,[144] as do the earliest Christian uses outside the canon.[145] As Paul is describing something about the coming of the gospel rather than its reception (see 1 Thess 1:6), πληροφορία should also be translated "fullness"[146] or, as the New Jerusalem Bible has it, "with great effect." Paul is reminding his readers not so much that the gospel came or was established among them in a particular way. He is saying the gospel took place or was established among the Thessalonians not only by word, but also in power, Holy Spirit, and much fullness, that is, in a richness or breadth of experience, not least of the miraculous.[147]

For our project it is notable that Paul is not saying that the gospel was established by his message and three other supranatural items: power, Holy Spirit, and much fullness. In these three items Paul is describing a single reality—God's miraculous intervention and presence—viewed from three different perspectives: its miraculous dimension; from the perspective of God's presence; and its overwhelming richness. This, with his message, is the gospel that was established among the Thessalonians. The rich experiential aspect of the gospel is a point Paul will return to when he reminds the Galatians of the nature of the gospel.[148]

As Paul distinguishes between,[149] yet holds together, speech on the one hand, and power and Holy Spirit and much fullness on the other hand, he cannot have in mind the current well-established view[150] that God's speech was effective in these ways in accomplishing its intention. Rather, the coming or establishment of the gospel in word is one of a two-part gospel that, alongside word, is said also to involve power, the Holy Spirit, and much fullness. In Paul's mind no distinction existed between the establishment of the gospel and its nature: word, power, Holy Spirit, and much fullness.[151] It is not so much that the gospel (understood as words) in any way caused or

---

143. For πληροφορέω in Paul see Rom 4:21; 14:5, cf. Col 4:12; 2 Tim 4:5, 17. Elsewhere in the NT the verb occurs only at Luke 1:1.

144. Col 2:2; Heb 6:11; 10:22.

145. 1 Clem. 54.1; Ign. *Mag.* 11.1; *Phld.* 1.1; cf. *Smyrn.* 1.1.

146. Also, see DRA translating the Vulgate's "in plenitudine multa" (1 Thess 1:5).

147. Cf. Twelftree, *Paul and the Miraculous*, 186.

148. See §3.3 (d) below.

149. In 1 Thess 1:5 Paul uses the "not only but also" construction (οὐχ ... μόνον ἀλλὰ καί).

150. As supposed by Best, *Thessalonians*, 74, citing Gen 1:3; Ps 33:6, 9; and Isa 55:10–11.

151. Lightfoot, *Notes on Epistles of St Paul*, 12, cf. 120 (on 2 Thess 2:14), is not justified in translating 1 Thess 1:5, τὸ εὐαγγέλιον ὑμῶν as "the gospel we preach."

enabled the miracles any more than the gospel caused words. Rather, as the word expressed the gospel, so also the miraculous expressed the gospel for the recipients.

(b) Declared and preached (1 Thess 2:1-12). In this section of Paul's letter describing his initial activity among the readers, there is a considerable concentration of the use of "gospel."[152] In describing his coming to the Thessalonians he says it was not in vain for although Paul and his associates[153] suffered and were mistreated, they had freedom of speech or "courage in our God to declare to you the gospel of God" (1 Thess 2:2).[154] In this Paul tells his readers two things about his understanding of the gospel.

First, in a much more limited description than we have just seen earlier in this letter (1 Thess 1:5), Paul says the gospel is something "we spoke freely" (ἐπαρρησιασάμεθα) about "to declare" (λαλῆσαι) to the readers (2:2). Also, further on in this passage he will remind his readers "we preached" (ἐκηρύξαμεν) the gospel to them (2:9).

Notably, especially for our project, this is only one of two occasions when Paul writes of "preaching" the gospel.[155] Otherwise, using the verb, he simply says he "gospels." The focus on his speaking in this description,[156] and its contrast with the "flattery" (κολακεία), "pretext for greed" (προφάσει πλεονεξίας, 1 Thess 2:5), and "glory" (δόξαν, 2:2) associated with popular public discourse,[157] suggests that Paul is conscious of criticism of his oratory. It is understandable, then, that he should uncharacteristically specify his preaching of the gospel. In other words, in contrast to what we have seen earlier in this letter, there is no hint here that the gospel is other than what the readers would have heard Paul and his companions speak about to them. Paul is equating the gospel with his message. Indeed, when Paul returns to his theme of thanksgiving, instead of them receiving the gospel (cf. 1:5), he says they "received the word of God that you heard (ἀκος) from us" (2:13).

---

152. 1 Thess 2:2, 4, 8, 9, all nouns. In 1 Corinthians there is also a concentrated use of the noun "gospel": 1 Cor 9:12, 14 (x2), 18 (x2), on which see §4.1 (d) below.

153. The verbs of 1 Thess 2:2 are all in the plural, referring to Silvanus (the Latin for Silas) and Timothy (1 Thess 1:1) who were involved in Paul's ministry in relation to Thessalonica. See Acts 17:1-9; 1 Thess 3:2, 6; Bruce, *1 and 2 Thessalonians*, 6; and Richard, *First and Second Thessalonians*, 37-38.

154. 1 Thess 2:2: ἐπαρρησιασάμεθα ἐν τῷ θεῷ ἡμῶν λαλῆσαι πρὸς ὑμᾶς εὐαγγέλιον τοῦ θεοῦ.

155. 1 Thess 2:9. Cf. Gal 2:2, on which see §3.3 (c) below.

156. See παρρησιάζομαι ("speak freely," 1 Thess 2:2); λαλέω ("speak," 2:2, 4); παράκλησις ("appeal," 2:3); λογός ("word," 2:5); κολακεία ("flattery," 2:5, on which see MM 352); and κηρύσσω ("preach," 2:9).

157. See the discussion by Richard, *First and Second Thessalonians*, 97-98.

The second thing Paul says about the gospel is that it is God's. This precise phrase, "the gospel of God" (τὸ εὐαγγέλιον τοῦ θεοῦ) is used by Paul at two other points in this letter, both in this passage (1 Thess 2:8, 9), and also in Romans.[158] In 1 Thessalonians there is an unusually high frequency not only in Paul's use of "gospel," which we have noted, but also of the word "God" (θεός).[159] In talking about his work in the passage in question (2:1–12), he uses θεός nine times in only 212 words, or once every 17.7 words.[160] When we take into account that he not only claims that his gospel is of God (2:2, 8, 9), but also that his freedom or courage to speak came from God (2:2), that he was approved by God (2:4), that he sought to please God (2:4), and that God was his witness (2:3, 10), it becomes obvious that Paul is at pains to communicate to his readers that his work among them had divine origins, approval, and guidance. If not writing against a particular group of opponents, as he will later in his career, Paul is most likely writing against the general question of the legitimacy of his gospel.[161] What this means for our understanding of the gospel according to Paul is that he is saying his gospel has divine origins rather than that it is about God, true though that may be for him.

In this same passage in which he is describing his coming to the Thessalonians (1 Thess 2:1–12) Paul says "we have been approved by God to be entrusted with the gospel" (2:4, my translation).[162] Though it is not what Paul wrote, one English translation reads that Paul says God "accepted us to preach" (NIRV), and another translation reads that he was "entrusted with the message of the gospel" (NRSV). These translations too quickly equate the message and gospel, or the gospel and preaching. Even though we have seen Paul is able to equate his message with the gospel, we have also seen him describe the gospel as distinct and different from his preaching. Not being his particular interest, here Paul leaves open how the gospel is to be understood in relation to his preaching.

That God's approval had enabled him to be entrusted with the gospel could mean that Paul considered that God had approved him to receive

---

158. Rom 15:16. Otherwise, in the NT the phrase τὸ εὐαγγέλιον τοῦ θεοῦ occurs only in Mark 1:14 and 1 Pet 4:17. In Rom 1:1 Paul has εἰς εὐαγγέλιον θεοῦ ("for the gospel of God") and in 2 Cor 11:7 he has τοῦ θεοῦ εὐαγγέλιον ("God's gospel").

159. In 1,475 words in 1 Thess he uses θεός thirty-six times, or 1 in 40.9 words; Rom: 1 in 46.4; 1 Cor: 1 in 64.9; 2 Cor: 1 in 56.6; Gal: 1 in 71.9; Phi: 1 in 67.9; and Phlm: 1 in 167.5.

160. 1 Thess 2:2 (x2), 4 (x2), 5, 8, 9, 10, 12. Cf. Richard, *First and Second Thessalonians*, 78.

161. E.g., Best, *Thessalonians*, 16–22.

162. 1 Thess 2:4: δεδοκιμάσμεθα ὑπὸ τοῦ θεοῦ πιστευθῆναι τὸ εὐαγγέλιον. Cf., e.g., ESV, NAB, NAS, NAU, NET, NIB, and NLT.

the gospel from his predecessors in the faith.[163] However, each of the few times Paul uses πιστεύω ("believe") in the sense of "entrust" it is God who issues the trust.[164] Notably, this is also how the writer of 1 Timothy, an early interpreter of Paul, understood him in that he has Paul say: "the gospel of glory of the blessed God, which he entrusted to me" (1 Tim 1:11; cf. Titus 1:3). Returning to summarize what Paul says about the gospel we can note that it has divine origins, has been entrusted to Paul, and is equated with his message in that it is preached by Paul and his companions.

(c) The gospel of Christ (1 Thess 3:2). Having recalled the establishment of the gospel (1:4-10), defended his ministry (2:1-12), and expressed gratitude for its reception (2:13-16),[165] Paul writes of his concern for the Thessalonians (2:17—3:13). Paul was so eager for news that he says "we sent Timothy our brother and co-worker of God in the gospel of Christ" (3:2). Although many copyists tried various ways to avoid suggesting Paul and Timothy were God's co-workers, the phrase "co-worker of God" (συνεργὸν τοῦ θεοῦ) most probably came from Paul's hand rather than a later copyist.[166] Saying he and Timothy are God's co-workers is not a slip of his pen. Paul's readers at Corinth will come across the same idea (1 Cor 3:9; 2 Cor 6:1),[167] and other early Christian writers also used this or a similar idea.[168] The implication of this for our study is that Paul understood that the gospel and its propagation involved both his (and his companions') work, as well as God's.

Here Paul also uses the term "the gospel of Christ" (τῷ εὐαγγελίῳ τοῦ Χριστοῦ), as he will a number of times in his letters.[169] This phrase marks

163. Cf. Marshall, *1 and 2 Thessalonians*, 66, citing 1 Cor 15:1-5 and Gal 1:11-12.

164. Rom 3:2; 1 Cor 9:17; Gal 2:7.

165. Despite universal external attestation, not least because of the apparent anti-Semitism (1 Thess 2:14-15), and following Baur, *Paul the Apostle of Jesus Christ*, 1:87-88, 1 Thess 2:13-16 is taken to be a post-Pauline interpolation by, e.g., Pearson, "1 Thessalonians 2:13-16," 79-94; and Boers, "Form Critical Study of Paul's Letters," 140-58. See the discussion of research by Okeke, "1 Thessalonians 2:13-16," 127-30, and the discussion by Weatherly, "Authenticity of 1 Thessalonians 2:13-16," 79-98, who, on the basis of style, theology, formal consistency with its context, and the manuscript evidence, reasonably concludes that "The difficulties it presents cannot reasonably be addressed merely by expunging it from the text of the Epistle" (98). Coming to the same conclusion is Bell, *Irrevocable Call of God*, 57-62.

166. See NA[28] 625. See Metzger, *Textual Commentary*, 563, and Richard, *First and Second Thessalonians*, 140-41, for brief discussions of the problems in the text.

167. Cf. Ellis, *Prophecy and Hermeneutic*, 6; Marshall, *1 and 2 Thessalonians*, 90-91. Contrary to the protest of Fee, *First Epistle to the Corinthians*, 144, the context is not against this reading, but positively supports taking Paul to mean that he and Apollos are fellow workers with God (cf. 1 Cor 3:5-9). Cf. Bruce, *1 and 2 Thessalonians*, 61.

168. See Mark 16:20; cf. Heb 2:4; 3 John 8.

169. As well as here in 1 Thess 3:2, see 1 Cor 9:12; 2 Cor 2:12; 9:13; 10:14; Gal 1:7;

the first time Paul takes up this rare word, the singular noun εὐαγγέλιον, eventually making it distinctive in his thought and writing. We have already seen that, in the repeated use of the phrase "the gospel of God," the divine origins of the gospel are uppermost in Paul's mind. Therefore, his genitive phrase "the gospel of Christ" is probably intended not so much as subjective (that is, Christ's), putting it in slight conflict with the gospel being God's, but as objective (that is, about Christ). Indeed, when he comes to write to the Romans he will similarly express this idea, though more explicitly: "the gospel of God ... about (περί) his Son" (Rom 1:3). In view of what we have seen of Paul using the term "gospel" for creedal-like descriptions of Jesus, his coining the phrase "the gospel of Christ" should not surprise us, and here should probably be taken to be shorthand for all he communicates about Jesus Christ.

(d) *The gospel lived (1 Thess 3:6).* Paul writes that Timothy has "just now" (ἄρτι) returned from the Thessalonians "having gospelled" (εὐαγγελισαμένου) of their faith and love. Apart from the writer of Hebrews equating the Old Testament promises and the gospel (Heb 4:2, 6), at first sight this appears the only place in the New Testament where the verb "gospel" (εὐαγγελίζω) is used other than in relation to the propagation of the "gospel" of Jesus Christ.[170] Yet we will see that behavior or activity can express the gospel,[171] including even Paul's imprisonment.[172] We will also see that Jews and gentiles sharing the grace of God was, for Paul, a tangible realization of the gospel.[173] Moreover, Paul wrote of the faith of the believers as an effective proclamation.[174] Therefore, in using the verb "gospel" (εὐαγγελίζω), Timothy's report of the Thessalonians was not simply mundane news, but "gospel" in the sense that their lives realized, proclaimed, and further propagated the gospel.[175] It appears then that Paul did not simply equate the verb "gospel" (εὐαγγελίζω) with preaching.[176] For him it was a much richer concept, including a report of lives realizing the gospel.

Phil 1:27, all discussed below. Cf. 2 Thess 1:8.

170. Cf. Lightfoot, *Notes on Epistles of St Paul*, 44.

171. On Gal 2:14 and Phil 1:27 see §3.3 (c) and §3.4 (c), respectively, below.

172. 1 Thess 1:12-14; also, see §3.4 (b) below on Phil 1:12-26.

173. 1 Cor 9:23; see §4.1 (d) below.

174. Rom 1:8; 1 Thess 1:8-9. Also, note the discussion by Jervell, "Problem of Traditions in Acts," 19-39.

175. Cf. John Chrysostom, *Hom 1 Thess.* (homiliae 1-11), PG 62.417, lines 50-59. Jervell, "Problem of Traditions in Acts," 19-39; Marshall, *1 and 2 Thessalonians*, 94; Best, *Thessalonians*, 139-40.

176. Contra Lightfoot, *Notes on Epistles of St Paul*, 44, on εὐαγγελισαμένος (1 Thess 3:6): "This word is not elsewhere used by St Paul in any other sense than that of preaching the gospel."

(e) Results: The gospel in 1 Thessalonians. Compared to his longer letters only a few years later, there is a high concentration of the noun "gospel" (εὐαγγέλιον) in 1 Thessalonians; there is also an occurrence of the verb (εὐαγγελίζω), its first known use in Christian literature. We have seen that, for Paul, the gospel had divine origins—a most important point for Paul in the face of criticism of him—and was entrusted to him and his companions by God.

What was entrusted to Paul was more than words or a message; it was the responsibility for involvement in God choosing the Thessalonians. In turn, the gospel was more than something he brought; it was something that took place among and for them. Thus Paul does not say that the gospel came, but that it took place. So far as the gospel is Paul's message, it is, or becomes, an energizing word from God that changes behavior.

In an attempt to recover from the letter the content of this initial energized word—what Paul is likely to have said in his initial or missionary message—we cannot suppose that we have reconstructed his entire message. From what we can reconstruct through a close reading, in gentleness and without great oratory, yet with confidence, Paul introduced the Thessalonians to God. In doing so he encouraged them to turn from lifeless idols to serve a living and true God, a message clearly tailored to gentiles. They were also to wait expectantly—and probably not very long—for his Son who was in heaven by virtue of God raising him from the dead. In this the gospel is eschatological, an end-time gospel. This waiting was, we saw, an eschatalogical perspective on life that meant living worthy of God. Yet, while he was awaited, the Son, Jesus, was already the One who rescued them from the coming wrath.

Although Paul's message was God's energizing word, the gospel's coming and establishment also involved factors that might be thought more obviously divine: power, the Holy Spirit, and much fullness. In other words, the coming and establishment of the gospel was a rich experience that could be described as miraculous, God-present, and overwhelming. It is not that these things brought the gospel, though they did that, so much as they were and expressed—or realized—the gospel itself for and in the recipients.

§3.3 GALATIANS

In this letter, written in the early fifties CE[177] in the face of unidentified rival missionaries (cf. Gal 1:6–9; 5:12) proposing to the Galatians a "different

---

177. The date of writing and the identity of the readers—south or north Galatians—remain the subject of debates. Dating Galatians in the early 50s accepts the hypothesis

gospel" (1:6) involving observance of the Jewish law,[178] Paul considers that the "truth of the gospel" (2:5, 14) is at stake. He says he is "amazed" (θαυμάζω) they are deserting Christ and turning to a different gospel (1:6)—not that there is one (1:7). He asserts that his gospel does not have human origins (1:11) but was revealed to him (1:12) and has been authenticated by the pillars in Jerusalem (2:1–10). The Galatians are, then, able to trust the truth of the gospel (2:5, 7).

As his central concern in writing to the Galatians is the integrity of the gospel he promotes, it is not surprising that Paul provides a clear description of his gospel. In doing so he uses the word "gospel" as a verb six times[179] and the noun seven times.[180] All but one of these occurrences are in his initial rebuke of his readers' response to his work and his personal defense of that work (Gal 1:6—2:21). Even his use of "gospel" as a verb later in the letter relates to a description of his work (4:13).

After his greeting (Gal 1:1–5) Paul is so preoccupied with the issue at hand that, without the customary thanksgiving[181] that would contain some hint of, or easing into, his reason for writing,[182] he launches into his concern. In the space of two short paragraphs—one rebuking[183] his readers (1:6-9) and another making an initial summary defense (1:10-12)—there is a high concentration of "gospel," three times as a noun and four times as a verb.

(a) An initial rebuke (Galatians 1:6-9). Paul begins his rebuke: "I am astonished that you are so quickly deserting the one who called you in [Christ's][184] grace and are turning to a different (ἕτερος) gospel—not that there is another (ἄλλος) gospel, but there are some who are confusing you

---

that Paul was writing to readers in south Galatia after the Jerusalem Council (Acts 15). See the summary discussions by, e.g., Bruce, *Galatians*, 5–10; Longenecker, *Galatians*, lxxii–lxxxviii; Dunn, *Epistle to the Galatians*, 7–8, 12–19.

178. E.g., see Gal 2:12; 4:10, 17; 5:2-12; 6:12-13.

179. Gal 1:8, 9, 11, 16, 23; 4:13.

180. Gal 1:6, 7, 11; 2:2, 5, 7, 14.

181. See Rom 1:8-15; 1 Cor 1:4-9; Phil 1:3-11; 1 Thess 1:2-5; Phlm 4-7. Cf. Eph 1:15-23; Col 1:3-8; 2 Thess 1:3-10; 2 Tim 1:3-7.

182. Cf. Schubert, *Form and Function of the Pauline Thanksgivings*, 180; O'Brien, *Introductory Thanksgivings*, 262.

183. In using θαυμάζω ("I marvel") Paul is not expressing amazement, but reproach. See P. Mich. 8.479.4-5 (early second century CE); P. Mich. 3.209.6 (second or third century CE); P. Corn. 52 (third century CE); P. Oxy. 113.20 (second century CE); P. Oxy. 3063.11-16 (second century CE). See the discussions by Bertram, "θαῦμα, κτλ," 28; White, "Introductory Formulae," esp. 94, 96; Mullins, "Formulas in New Testament Epistles," 385–86, and Longenecker, *Galatians*, 14.

184. See Metzger, *Textual Commentary*, 520–21, on the difficulty of determining whether or not Χριστοῦ ("of Christ") is from Paul's hand.

and want to pervert the gospel of Christ" (1:6-7). Though the difference between the two words for "other"—ἕτερος (other of a different kind) and ἄλλος (other of the same kind)—had largely been lost,[185] and is not always important to him,[186] in using them here Paul appears to be denying that the Galatians' different (ἕτερος) gospel is a gospel.[187] Rather, it is something perverted, that is not a gospel.[188]

What the Galatians are said to be deserting is "the one who called you in [Christ's] grace" (Gal 1:6). A possible reading of this is that the Galatians are deserting Paul who brought the gospel, for he goes on to set out a solid personal defense (1:10—2:21). Or, if "Christ" is from Paul's hand, he could mean they were called by Christ.[189] More likely, "Christ" is not from Paul's hand. For in line with his going on to say that it was God who called him (1:15), and his habit of saying God—never himself or any other person[190]—called his readers,[191] Paul is accusing his readers of abandoning God's call.[192] The implication is that in essence Paul's gospel is, or can be summarized as, God's call "by means of grace,"[193] which he experienced (Gal 1:11-17).

This is his only specific and direct equation of the gospel with God's call (cf. 2 Tim 1:8-9). Elsewhere he can equate God's call with becoming a believer, as he does in relation to his own life (Gal 1:15) and those of the Thessalonians.[194] Relying on the scriptural concept of God calling things (Rom 4:17; cf. Gen 17:5), especially his people,[195] into existence he can say those called are justified and glorified (Rom 8:30; cf. 1 Thess 2:12). They

185. See p. 96n119 above.

186. A closer reading of Gal 1:6-7 has caused me to change my mind to seeing that Paul probably intends a distinction between ἕτερος and ἄλλος. Contrast Twelftree, *Paul and the Miraculous*, 23.

187. See the discussion by Silva, *Interpreting Galatians*, 126-27.

188. Cf. Burton, *Epistles to the Galatians*, 420-23; Longenecker, *Galatians*, 15. Even if Paul intends irony (cf. Nanos, *Irony of Galatians*) the point remains that a perverted gospel is no gospel for Paul.

189. As supposed by, e.g., Luther, Calvin, and Bengel, cited by Longenecker, *Galatians*, 15.

190. Martyn, *Galatians*, 108-9.

191. See Rom 8:30; 9:11-12, 22-25; 11:29; 1 Cor 1:9, 26-27; 7:15-24; Phil 3:14; 1 Thess 2:12; 4:7; 5:23-24. Cf. Gal 5:8, 13.

192. Burton, *Epistles to the Galatians*, 20; Guthrie, *Galatians*, 61; Martyn, *Galatians*, 108-9; Dunn, *Epistle to the Galatians*, 40-41.

193. Cf. Lightfoot, *Saint Paul's Epistle to the Galatians*, 75. In the phrase, ἐν χάριτι Χριστοῦ ("in the grace of Christ"), ἐν with the dative χάριτι is designating a personal agent. See BDF §219; Longenecker, *Galatians*, 15.

194. See 1 Thess 2:12. Also, see 1 Cor 1:9; 7:18, 20-22, 24.

195. Rom 9:24-26; cf. 9:7; Hos 2:1, 25.

are called to freedom (Gal 5:13) and into "association" (κοινωνία) with his Son (1 Cor 1:9), and into God's kingdom and glory (1 Thess 2:12). The ongoing life of the believer is also equated with God's call[196] so that being called has behavioral implications (1 Cor 7:17), including holiness rather than impurity (1 Thess 4:7), and also peace in relationships (1 Cor 7:15). In other words, responding to God's call—the gospel—is receiving from and responding to God to be involved in and reflecting his life, perhaps best summed up in Paul's statement: "you were called into association with his Son, Jesus Christ our Lord" (1:9).

Not only is the gospel equated with God's call in grace, it is then characterized as "the gospel of Christ" (τὸ εὐαγγέλιον τοῦ Χριστοῦ, Gal 1:7). In that Paul's attention is on his readers' deserting God, the genitive (τοῦ Χριστοῦ) is probably to be taken as objective: the gospel is about Christ.[197] Negatively, the "different gospel" to which the Galatians are turning their allegiance is no gospel (1:7). As we will see, the nature of this "different gospel" comes into focus when, following his extended personal defense (1:10—2:21),[198] his description of it provides the foil for a reiteration of his gospel (3:1–5).

Another part of Paul's initial rebuke that contributes to our understanding of his gospel is his saying that even if "an angel from heaven should gospel (εὐαγγελίζηται) you[199] contrary to what we gospelled (εὐηγγελισάμεθα) to you, anathema to that one" (Gal 1:8). Introducing a repetition of this curse with the redundant duplication—"As we have said before, so now I repeat" (1:9)—suggests that he is not simply repeating what he has just written[200] but pointing out something he had told them before, presumably when he was with them:[201] "if anyone gospels (εὐαγγελίζεται) you differently from what you received (παρελάβετε), anathema to that one" (1:9). Obviously, then, even when he was with the Galatians, Paul was well aware of the vulnerability of his gospel and of his readers' allegiance to it.

---

196. 1 Cor 7:17; Gal 5:8; 1 Thess 5:24.

197. That both the objective and subjective are intended by Paul, see Longenecker, *Galatians*, 16, who incorrectly cites Rom 1:1–3; 15:16; and 1 Thess 2:2, 8–9 as evidence that "the gospel of Christ" and "the gospel of God" are synonyms for Paul. On the objective genitive (τοῦ Χριστοῦ) in 1 Thess 3:2, see §3.2 (c) above.

198. See §3.3 (d) below.

199. On the status of ὑμῖν ("to you"), see Metzger, *Textual Commentary*, 521.

200. As supposed by Bruce, *Galatians*, 84.

201. So also Schmithals, *Paul and the Gnostics*, 18–19. Schlier, *Der Brief an die Galater*, 40, considers the statement is probably a restatement of Galatians 1:8, but that it is possible Paul is thinking of a previous statement he made of his second trip to Galatia.

It is to be noted that although English translators habitually use "preach the gospel" to render all three occurrences of the verb "gospel" (εὐαγγελίζω), here and again later in this letter (Gal 4:13),[202] this is not what Paul says. He simply uses "gospel" as a verb. In other words, he describes his work as "gospelling." Paul's intentionality in this expression is seen in noting that, when he obviously has his speaking in mind or is conveying an idea, his habit is not to use "gospel" (εὐαγγελίζω)[203] but "preach" (κηρύσσω)[204] or "proclaim" (καταγγέλλω).[205] Also, that in using "gospel" (εὐαγγελίζω) he probably has more in mind than listening is suggested by his saying not that the Galatians had "heard" (ἠκούσατε) but that they had "received" (παρελάβετε) the gospel (1:9). A rich term, with uses beyond listening to include "capturing" and "associating with,"[206] Paul uses "receive" (παραλαμβάνω) eight times, primarily to mean receiving a tradition, narrative, or set of ideas.[207] Notably for this project, he can also use the word for receiving all that was involved in the coming of the gospel, including the Spirit and miracles (1:9; 3:2-5).

It is important to pause here to note that, for Paul, the verbs "gospel" (εὐαγγελίζω), "preach" (κηρύσσω), and "proclaim" (καταγγέλλω), while sometimes having overlapping uses and meanings, are not synonyms. The terms "preach" and "proclaim," which can be synonyms,[208] refer to conveying verbal information. However, we are seeing that, for Paul, the word "gospel" has a much broader range of meanings that extends well beyond referring to the relaying of information. The breadth and content of that meaning remains the focus of this project and is becoming particularly clear in this letter to the Galatians.

(b) A summary defense (Galatians 1:10-12). In this initial summary defense Paul goes on to say that he wants the Galatians to know that "the gospel gospelled" (τὸ εὐαγγέλιον τὸ εὐαγγελισθέν) by him was not of human

---

202. E.g., NIV, ESV, NASB, and KJB all use "preached the gospel."

203. Of Paul's use of "gospel" (εὐαγγελίζω: Rom 1:15; 10:15; 15:20; 1 Cor 1:17; 9:16, 18; 15:1, 2; 2 Cor 10:16; 11:7; Gal 1:8, 9, 11, 16, 23; 4:13; 1 Thess 3:6) only Rom 10:15; 1 Cor 1:17; 15:2; and 1 Thess 3:6 are clearly about speaking.

204. Rom 2:21; 10:8, 14, 15; 1 Cor 1:23; 9:27; 15:11, 12; 2 Cor 1:19; 4:5; 11:4 (x2); Gal 2:2; 5:11; Phil 1:15; 1 Thess 2:9.

205. Rom 1:8; 1 Cor 2:1; 9:14; 11:26; Phil 1:17, 18.

206. Note Delling, "λαμβάνω, κτλ," 5-15; MGS, "παραλαμβάνω," 1555.

207. 1 Cor 11:23; 15:1, 3; Gal 1:9, 12; Phil 4:9; 1 Thess 2:13; 4:1. Cf. Silva, "παραλαμβάνω," 84 (g).

208. Cf. Phil 1:15 and 18; Broer, "καταγγέλλω," 256 (3). Bultmann, *Theology of the New Testament*, 87, takes εὐαγγλίζεσθαι and κηρύσσειν as synonyms. Collins, *First Corinthians*, 85, uses "evangelize" to translate εὐαγγελίζεσθαι, taking it as synonymous with "proclaim." Also, see p. 134n12 below.

origin (1:11). Again, even though English translations use "preached,"[209] beyond using the verb "gospel," Paul does not specify what this gospelling involved. We will have to test the perspective that is emerging here that, for Paul, there was more to conveying the gospel than speaking and there was more to receiving the gospel than listening.

(c) A personal defense (Galatians 1:13—2:21). In his statement that "God ... was pleased to reveal his Son to me so that I might gospel him among the Gentiles" (1:15–16), Paul gives a strong signal that the gospel is more than ideas or his speaking. In particular, saying that God revealed "his Son" (τὸν υἱὸν αὐτοῦ) to (ἐν, "in") him, it is clear not only that his gospel was in some sense a revelation,[210] but that it was the Son, not just about the Son. That the Son himself can be the gospel for Paul will be made crystal clear in his Letter to the Philippians.[211]

Nevertheless, in this longer personal defense (Gal 1:13—2:21) Paul says that "in order to make sure that I was not running in vain, or had not run in vain" (2:2; cf. 2:7), he laid before James, Cephas (i.e., Peter), and John (2:9) "the gospel that I preach" (τὸ εὐαγγέλιον ὃ κηρύσσω, 2:2). Against his habit, which we have just noted,[212] it is understandable that he should—though only a second time[213]—describe his work as preaching the gospel. For he goes on to mention ideas or intellectual positions that were important to his gospel and were agreed in Jerusalem: The gentiles not needing circumcision, remembering the poor, and table fellowship (2:3-14). Indeed, his reason for not submitting Titus to circumcision was to "maintain the truth of the gospel" (ἡ ἀλήθεια τοῦ εὐαγγελίου διαμείνῃ, 2:5). And, drawing attention to the altercation at Antioch, in which he challenged Peter's violation of the agreement that there was to be table fellowship between Jewish and gentile believers, Paul says Peter and associates of James (2:12) were not "acting consistently with[214] the truth of the gospel" (τὴν ἀλήθειαν τοῦ εὐαγγελίου, 2:14).

209. E.g., ESV, KJV, NAB, NAS, NAU, NET, NIB, NIRV, NIV, NJB, NKJ, NLT, NRSV ("proclaimed"), RSV, RWB, and TNIV.

210. See §2.3 (a) above.

211. See §3.4 (c) below on Phil 2:5-11.

212. See p. 109n204 above.

213. Cf. 1 Thess 2:9, on which see §3.2 (b) above.

214. The preposition πρός with the accusative, as here, refers to an orientation toward someone or something, and can be variously translated (to, near, at, during, for, for the purpose, toward, e.g., see BDAG "πρός," 874-75 3 a–g). In the context of ὀρθοποδέω ("walk straight," cf. BDAG "ὀρθοποδέω," 722; Lampe ὀρθοποδέω," 972) being used figuratively of moral conduct (MGS "ὀρθοποδέω," 1481) the whole phrase, ὀρθοποδοῦσιν˙ πρὸς τὴν ἀλήθειαν can be taken to mean "acting consistently with the truth" of the gospel (e.g., NRSV).

The truth of the gospel that is expressed in the Jerusalem agreement he is referring to is that a person is reckoned as righteous through faith in Jesus Christ not by works of the law (Gal 2:14-16). In this personal defense, using "truth"—a term used in relation to truthful ideas or reports[215]—as an adjective to describe the gospel, Paul is conceiving of the gospel as ideas that could be spoken or preached and reflected in behavior.[216]

However, from what he is saying, the truth of the gospel is not simply "the truth that the gospel generates,"[217] as if the truth was simply a body of knowledge. The gospel in and of itself is, and has, a truth that also generates truth that measures human words and actions. That the gospel is in and of itself truth—and demands embodied truth—is clear later in the letter when Paul uses truth for the gospel: "Who prevented you from obeying the truth? (Gal 5:7).

(d) Experiencing the gospel (Galatians 3:1-5). In his main challenge to the Galatians, Paul returns to characterize the different or perverted gospel his readers are tempted to adopt, which he has said is not a gospel (1:6-7). What is of interest to us is that in his main argument (3:1—5:12) Paul's first appeal for the truth of the gospel (2:5, 14)—ahead of two appeals to Scripture (3:6-9; 4:21-31) and a personal appeal (4:12-20)—is a call for the Galatians to remember their initial and ongoing experience of the Spirit. In other words, in Paul's mind there is a direct relationship between the Galatians' initial and ongoing experience of the Spirit (3:3) and the truth of the nature of the gospel. In his impassioned defense Paul starts by reminding the recalcitrant Galatians of the beginning of their experience of the Spirit (3:3), their Pentecost.[218]

> O foolish Galatians! Who has bewitched you, before whose eyes Jesus Christ was placarded as crucified? This one thing I want to learn from you: Did you receive the Spirit from works of the law or from believing what you heard? Are you this foolish to have begun spiritually now to end humanly? Did you experience so much for nothing?—if it really was for nothing. (Gal 3:1-4, my translation)

Then, using the present tense, Paul turns to ask the Galatians about their ongoing experience of the gospel: "Then, does he who supplies (ἐπιχορηγῶν)

---

215. For the ἀληθής word group in Paul, see Rom 1:18, 25; 2:2, 8, 20; 3:4, 7; 9:1; 15:8; 1 Cor 5:8; 13:6; 2 Cor 4:2; 6:7, 8; 7:14 (x2); 11:10; 12:6; 13:8 (x2); Gal 2:5, 14; 4:16; 5:7; Phil 1:18; 4:8; 1 Thess 1:9; 2:13. Cf. MGS "ἀλήθεια," 85-86.

216. See Mark 5:33; Acts 26:25; Rom 9:1; 2 Cor 6:7; 12:6; Eph 4:25; 1 Tim 2:7.

217. Silva, *Galatians*, 209n234.

218. Cf. Twelftree, *Paul and the Miraculous*, 189.

you the Spirit and works (ἐνεργῶν) miracles among you do so from works of the law, or by your believing what you heard?" (Gal 3:5).

In contrasting the reception of his gospel with how they would have received the "different gospel," Paul provides a rich description of his gospel. In broad terms, Paul's important point in relation to our project is that the truth of his gospel (that a person is reckoned as righteous by faith in Jesus Christ) is evident in justification being experienced in the reception and ongoing experience of the Spirit and miracles through believing what they heard, which is of Jesus Christ crucified.

On examination a number of features of Paul's gospel become apparent. He begins his case by saying that "before your eyes Jesus Christ was publicly placarded (προγράφη) as crucified" (Gal 3:1). There is no evidence to support the idea that Paul is thinking the placarding involves scriptural references to the death of Jesus. Indeed, the placarding is something that took place "before [your] eyes" (κατ᾽ ὀφθαλμούς).[219] Though "placard" (προγράφω) could refer, for example, to something written earlier in a text,[220] such as a heading,[221] this also is not what Paul has in mind, for he has not so far mentioned the crucifixion in this letter. Nor could Paul be thinking about a prediction in Scripture, for that would not have been written down before their eyes. An earlier writing of his is also not likely to be in Paul's mind for he uses the word in relation to his preaching.[222] Rather, as the word was also often used for public notices and announcements,[223] it is more reasonable to suppose that Paul is reminding the Galatians that the coming of the gospel involved him relating the crucifixion of Jesus for them in a way that was as clear or obvious as a public notice.[224]

Although Paul does not often use the word "crucify" (σταυρόω),[225] as three of his eight uses are in Galatians, the idea is clearly important to him in this correspondence. Not surprisingly, when he refers to the crucifixion of Jesus as a particular event in the past he uses the aorist indicative

---

219. So Lightfoot, *Saint Paul's Epistle to the Galatians*, 134.
220. E.g., see Thucydides, *Hist.* 1.23.5; Eph 3:3.
221. E.g., see Polybius, *Hist.* 11.1–5; BDAG, "προγράφω," 867.
222. For a discussion of these and other interpretations of "προγράφω": Davis, "Meaning of προεγράφη."
223. Aristophanes, *Av.* 450; Plutarch, *Cam.* 11.2; Josephus, *Ant.* 10.254; Epictetus, *Diatr.* 3.1.28–29. Further, see Schrenk, "προγράφω," 771; BDAG, "προγράφω," 867; Balz, "προγράφω," 3.154; MGS, "προγράφω," 1753.
224. Davis, "Meaning of προεγράφη," proposes Paul uses his own scars (Gal 6:17) to display the crucifixion of Jesus Christ.
225. 1 Cor 1:13, 23; 2:2, 8; 2 Cor 13:4; Gal 3:1; 5:24; 6:14.

tense.²²⁶ However, as here in his assertion to the Galatians, when he talks of proclaiming Christ crucified he uses the perfect participle.²²⁷ The significance of this for our project is that Paul's gospel involved not only a clear description of the crucifixion of Jesus but also consideration of its ongoing, permanent significance.²²⁸

Indeed, at least beyond his Letter to the Thessalonians,²²⁹ there is ample evidence that preaching of the crucifixion was central to and could even sum up Paul's work.²³⁰ Moreover, statements such as, "I decided to know nothing among you except Jesus Christ and him crucified" (1 Cor 2:2) suggest that the verbal placarding of the death of Jesus featured in his preaching beginning from his arrival among the Corinthians. Of course, to convey the significance Paul gave it, more was needed than a graphic description of the crucifixion, a common form of Roman execution for criminals.²³¹ We can expect he would have been giving its interpretation along the lines set out in his salutation, that Jesus Christ "gave himself for our sins to set us free from the present evil age" (Gal 1:4), an interpretation adumbrated in his earliest letter (1 Thess 5:9–10), which is developed here in him saying, for example, that "I have been crucified with Christ" so that the life he lives is Christ's (Gal 2:20).²³²

It was this preaching or placarding of the killing of Jesus, God's anointed Messiah (Gal 3:1), along with its interpretation we must assume, that should have been sufficient to put a stop to any temptation to take up "another gospel" (1:7). As the revelation of this to Paul had transformed his life,²³³ he could only expect the same for his readers.²³⁴

226. 1 Cor 1:13 (Paul denies he himself was crucified); 2:8; 2 Cor 13:4. In Gal 5:24 he also uses the aorist in saying, "those who belong to Christ Jesus have crucified (ἐσταύρωσαν) the flesh." On the debate about the aorist, e.g., see Beetham, "Aorist Indicative," 236.

227. Gal 3:1; 1 Cor 1:23; 2:2. In Gal 6:14 Paul also uses the perfect (indicative passive) in saying "the world has been crucified (ἐσταύρωται) to me and I to the world."

228. Cf. Thiselton, *First Epistle to the Corinthians*, 213.

229. See §3.2 above.

230. Notable are 1 Cor 1:18 ("the word (or message) of the cross"); 1 Cor 1:23 ("we proclaim Christ crucified"); and 1 Cor 2:2 ("I decided to know nothing among you except Jesus Christ and him crucified."). On 1 Cor 1:17 where "gospel" (εὐαγγελίζω, verb) and the cross are closely related, see below. See also 1 Cor 15:3; Gal 5:11; 6:12; Phil 3:18. Cf. Longenecker, *Galatians*, 101; Dunn, *Epistle to the Galatians*, 152.

231. See Hengel, *Crucifixion in the Ancient World*, esp. 33–38.

232. These ideas find expression in other letters. E.g., see Rom 4:25; 8:32; 1 Cor 11:24.

233. Gal 2:20–21; cf. 3:13–14.

234. Cf. Dunn, *Epistle to the Galatians*, 152.

Then, in a series of questions Paul asks about the experience of the Galatians when the gospel came to them. Not only is its reception described, but the nature of the gospel also comes into view. At one point, separated by a short, sharp question, "Are you so foolish?" (Gal 3:3a), Paul asks the same question in two ways. He begins: "Did you receive the Spirit by doing the works of the law or by believing what you heard" (3:2)? It is clear that the coming of the gospel involved the reception of the Spirit, a reception about which they were expected to be well aware. Going on to ask the same question in another way—if the Galatians had begun with the Spirit (3:3)—shows the centrality of the reception of the Spirit in Paul's understanding of the coming of the gospel.[235]

From these two questions it is also clear that the reception of the Spirit was not possible "by doing the works of the law" (Gal 3:2), in other words, by the flesh (3:3). Instead, the Galatians received the Spirit by trusting what they heard (3:5). In turn, the assumption is that the gospel was something the Galatians had experienced as well as heard from Paul and had believed.

Further, asking if they had begun with the Spirit but were tempted to finish with the flesh (Gal 3:3) assumes that the reception of the Spirit also marked not only an initial experience but also the beginning of an ongoing "Spirit" way of life. Moreover, the nature of the initial and ongoing experience is recalled by a further two questions. First: "Did you experience so much (τοσαῦτα) for nothing?—if it really was for nothing" (3:4). "Therefore,"[236] second, he asks, "does the One who supplies (ἐπιχορηγῶν) to you the Spirit and works powers (δυνάμεις) among you do so on the basis of works of the law, or of faith from hearing?" (3:4–5, my translation). Twice Paul has used this exact adjectival genitive phrase, "of hearing faith" (ἐξ ἀκοῆς πίστεως, 3:2, 5), which may echo a Semitic idiom.[237] The similar phrase in Romans, "faith from hearing" (πίστις ἐξ ἀκοῆς, Rom 10:17), clarifies that Paul understands that through the Galatians' hearing the gospel there was elicited in them a response of trust in God and, in that event, their reception of the Spirit and miracles.[238]

---

235. Cf. Rom 8:15; 1 Cor 2:12; 2 Cor 11:4; Gal 3:14; Dunn, *Epistle to the Galatians*, 152–53.

236. In the postpositive οὖν ("then" or "therefore") Paul indicates that he is concluding his argument from experience. See Longenecker, *Galatians*, 105.

237. Moule, *Idiom-Book of New Testament Greek*, 175. Although the noun ἀκοή could mean either "a report" or "hearing" (cf. BDAG, "ἀκοή," 36–37), the context of Paul's use, notably put in antithesis to "works of the law" (ἔργων νόμου), a human activity, requires the meaning "hearing," not "proclamation," as Betz, *Galatians*, 113n50, and Martyn, *Galatians*, 285–89, suppose. Cf. the brief discussion by Longenecker, *Galatians*, 102–3.

238. Cf. Moule, *Idiom-Book of New Testament Greek*, 175; Guthrie, *Galatians*, 92–93; Dunn, *Romans 9–16*, 623; Dunn, *Epistle to the Galatians*, 154.

In this final question Paul is reminding his readers that in the coming of the gospel not only did God "give" or "supply" (ἐπιχορηγέω) the Spirit, but also "powers" (δυνάμεις) or miracles. Again, this question implies that God supplied the Spirit and the miracles by their believing what was heard (3:5). Again, the clear assumption is that Paul's gospel involved what he spoke to them. However, reminiscent of the gospel's establishment among the Thessalonians,[239] its coming and the experience of it, described as "so much" (τοσαῦτα), and therefore probably obvious to all, involved more than hearing, to include powers or miracles. Whether or not Paul thinks that the proclamation itself carried divine power[240] is not clear and will have to be determined after we have examined more of his writings.[241] Notwithstanding, what is important for our project is to note that, given that their misunderstanding of the reception of the gospel is their perversion of it (cf. 1:7 and 3:1–5), Paul must see the gospel not only as his message, but also the way it is received and what is experienced—the reception of the Spirit and miracles.[242] Just what those miracles might have been Paul does not say. We have already seen that, for Paul, the miraculous or "charismata" (χαρίσματα)—solidified expressions of God's grace (χάρις)—range from, for example, healing to helps (see §3.2. [a] 2 above). However, for his argument here, he and his readers would be recalling the more dramatic aspects or expressions of the miraculous.

(e) The antiquity of the gospel (Galatians 3:8). As proof that the gospel came to the Galatians not on the basis of works of the law but by believing what was heard, as we noted when discussing the scriptural origins of his gospel,[243] Paul points to Abraham (3:6–18). Paul says that Scripture "foreseeing" (προϊδοῦσα, 3:8) that the gentiles would be justified by faith, God "proclaimed in advance" (προευηγγελίσατο) to Abraham that, "In you will all nations be blessed" (3:8). Besides making the works-faith point, Paul is also making it clear not only that there is no other gospel (1:6–9), but that the gospel that he is propagating is the gospel that God has always

---

239. See 1 Thess 1:5 and §3.2 (a) above.

240. So Betz, *Galatians*, 113n50.

241. Cf. §5.2, esp. (e) below.

242. In this connection between good news and its reception there is, as John Nelson suggested to me, likely to be an echo of the early use of εὐαγγέλιον in which the news and its reward or response were intimately connected. See Homer, *Od.* 14.152–53, 166 and §2.1 above.

243. See §2.4 (g) above.

proclaimed.²⁴⁴ We will see that he makes a similar point in the opening of Romans.²⁴⁵

(f) Gospel as work (Galatians 4:13). In a statement that has generated considerable debate about the nature of Paul's illness and why he connects this with arriving among the Galatians, Paul says that "through physical sickness I gospelled to you first" (4:14).²⁴⁶ He is using "gospel" to encompass his entire activity among the Galatians. If Paul understood his work only or primarily in terms of preaching, we could have expected him to use "proclaim" (καταγγέλω) or "preach" (κηρύσσω). But he does not. Given what we have seen in his Letter to the Thessalonians,²⁴⁷ and his reminder to the Galatians of their initial and ongoing experience of the gospel,²⁴⁸ his use of "gospel" to describe his work probably arises out of his assumption that his work and the gospel involved more than his speaking.

(g) Results: The gospel in Galatians. Never is Paul more passionate about the gospel than in this letter to a group of believers at risk of deserting his gospel—not that there is another gospel in Paul's view. In defending himself and rebuking the readers his understanding of the gospel comes into sharp relief. It is a rich term. It is the revelation of the Son; it is the Son. The gospel is truth that can be articulated and responded to in its human reflection or embodiment.

In contrast to the "no gospel" of "works of the law" Paul says the gospel he gospelled was God's call of grace to them. Receiving this gospel is responding to God's call in grace to be involved in, and to reflect, or embody his life. In that the truth of the gospel includes a person being reckoned as righteous through faith in Jesus Christ, the gospel is a set of ideas that can be preached. One of these ideas is Jesus crucified—giving himself for our sins—and with whom we are crucified so that we can live in him by faith. But the truth of the gospel is also evident in this "rightwising" being experienced.

But there was more to the gospel than its articulation, more to bringing of the gospel than preaching, and more to receiving it than hearing it. The gospel came embodied and experienced in the miraculous, including the obvious reception of the Spirit. It was responded to in lives participating in, and embodying, the Son, and in behavior consistent with its truth.

---

244. Cf. Dunn, "How New Was Paul's Gospel?," 371–72.

245. On Rom 1:2 see §2.4 (b) above and §4.4 (a) below.

246. See the discussion in Dawson, *Healing, Weakness and Power*, 193–95; Twelftree, *Paul and the Miraculous*, 155–58.

247. On 1 Thess 1:5 see §3.2 (a) above.

248. See (a) above on Gal 3:1–5.

§3.4 PHILIPPIANS

The importance of the gospel to Paul is obvious in his Letter to the Philippians. He does not use the verb, but the noun "gospel" (εὐαγγέλιον) appears nine times,[249] more frequently than in any other of his letters.[250] Also, twice he uses a related verb "proclaim" (καταγγέλω, Phil 1:17, 18).

As Paul writes, he is in prison, perhaps in Caesarea Maritima[251] or Rome[252] or more likely Ephesus,[253] between 54 and 56 CE.[254] He is awaiting a trial that may lead to capital punishment.[255] From the hands of Epaphroditus, who had fallen ill on the journey from Philippi,[256] Paul has received from his loyal and concerned supporters there (1:5; 5:15-16) a financial gift for his support.[257] Epaphroditus, who also brought news to Paul, has recovered (2:27-28). In order to respond to the gift and news, and to allow the Philippians to see their messenger and fellow worker (2:25), who is a great concern to them (2:26, 28) and they to him (2:26), Paul is sending him and this letter back to them. Also, from what he has heard, Paul is concerned to address particular needs: opponents are intimidating the Philippians;[258] there is dissension among them;[259] and they need encouragement in light of the suffering of Paul (1:12-14, 19-26), Epaphroditus (2:25-30), and themselves (1:29-30). Not surprisingly, then, the letter is marked by mutual affection,[260] not least in Paul's generous use of "friendship" language,[261] as well as their praying for him (1:19), obedience to him (2:12), interest in the

---

249. Phil 1:5, 7, 12, 16, 27 (2x); 2:22; 4:3, 15.

250. See p. 3n22 and p. 80n6 above. Cf. Fee, *Paul's Letter to the Philippians*, 82.

251. See Acts 23:12—26:32.

252. See Phil 1:13 and 4:22 and the discussion by Holloway, *Philippians*, 21-24. Cf. 1 Clem. 5.7. For a summary discussion of the location of Paul's imprisonment, see Brown, *Introduction to the New Testament*, 494-96.

253. See the discussion by Trebilco, *Early Christians in Ephesus*, 83-87.

254. Brown, *Introduction to the New Testament*, 496: "There is no way to decide this issue; but the best arguments seem to be on the side of Ephesus, and the weakest on the side of Caesarea."

255. Phil 1:7, 12-14, 20; 2:17-18. Cf. 4:14.

256. Phil 2:25-27, 30; 4:18.

257. Phil 1:5; 2:25, 30; 4:10, 14, 18.

258. Phil 1:15-18, 28-30; 3:2-3, 17-19.

259. Phil 1:27; 2:2-4; 4:2-3.

260. Phil 1:3-11; 4:1, 10-20.

261. E.g., Paul mentions his "absence" (Phil 2:12); his desire his readers "cheer" him (2:19); and calling his readers "longed for ones" (4:1). In more detail, see Fee, *Paul's Letter to the Philippians*, 19, citing Phil 1:12, 27; 2:12, 19, 20, 23; 3:1; 4:1, 14, 15; and the recent summary discussion by Holloway, *Philippians*, 32-33.

welfare of his companions (2:22, 25–28), and in supporting him financially (e.g., 4:10–18).

Interpretation of this letter has long been overshadowed by discussions of its integrity or unity.[262] However, not only do we have no textual evidence to suppose that this letter was known in any other form,[263] none of the attempted reconstructions[264] of earlier letters or fragments has gained wide support.[265] Indeed, as it stands, the letter is rhetorically viable,[266] and its integrity widely supported.[267]

(a) Thanksgiving (Philippians 1:3–8). After the customary salutation (1:1–2),[268] Paul begins his thanksgiving saying he thanks God every time he remembers the Philippians,[269] always praying with joy because of "your

---

262. E.g., the "finally" (Τὸ λοιπόν, Phil 3:1a) in the middle of the letter, the apparent break between 4:9 and 10, the delayed gratitude (4:10–20), the "Amen" (ἀμήν, 4:20) followed by further greetings and a benediction (4:21–23), the apparent different attitudes to the opponents addressed (cf. 1:27—2:18 and 3:2, 18–19), and Polycarp saying in his letter to the Philippians that Paul ὑμῖν ἔγραψεν ἐπιστολάς ("to you he wrote letters," Pol. *Phil.* 3.2), have caused some to propose that the letter we have has been patched together from fragments or smaller letters. On the history of the problem, see Koperski, "Early History of the Dissection of Philippians," 599–603. For a list of those who divide this letter into a number of separate letters, see Garland, "Composition and Unity of Philippians," 141–43; Reed, *Discourse Analysis of Philippians*, esp. 124–52, 406–18. Also, see Dalton, "Integrity of Philippians," 97–102; Linko, "Paul's Two Letters to the Philippians?," 156–71; Ruemann, *Philippians*, 8–13; Holloway, *Philippians*, 10–19.

263. Cf. Fee, *Paul's Letter to the Philippians*, 23; Bockmuehl, *Philippians*, 24.

264. For a list of various proposals, see Garland, "Composition and Unity of Philippians," 155n50.

265. See the brief but thorough discussion by Martin, *Philippians*, 10–21; Bockmuehl, *Philippians*, 20–25. In more detail on the fluctuating fortunes of the unity of Philippians, see, e.g., Garland, "Composition and Unity of Philippians," 141–73.

266. Saunders, "Letter to the Philippians," 504.

267. See those cited by Garland, "Composition and Unity of Philippians," 142–43n5; and Bockmuehl, *Philippians*, 25. Also, see Reed, *Discourse Analysis of Philippians*, 406–18.

268. Cf. Alexander, "Hellenistic Letter-Forms," 88.

269. A storm has erupted over Paul's statement in Phil 1:3: Εὐχαριστῶ τῷ θεῷ μου ἐπὶ πάσῃ τῇ μνείᾳ ὑμῶν. E.g., the genitive (ὑμῶν) can be taken as subjective so that Paul is saying, "I thank my God for your every remembrance [of me]." This would mean Paul was already expressing his gratitude for the financial gift. Cf., e.g., O'Brien, "Gospel in Philippians," 217; Witherington, *Friendship and Finances in Philippi*, 37–38. However, as Bockmuehl, *Philippians*, 58, summarizes, Paul's other thanksgivings (in Romans, 1 Thessalonians and Philemon) having the readers as the object, and the grammar (the genitive pronoun with the verb of remembering denotes those remembered) support the Vulgate, early commentators, and most English translations interpreting Paul to mean, "I thank my God every time I remember you." For more detailed discussions see Hawthorne and Martin, *Philippians*, 19–20; and O'Brien, *Introductory Thanksgivings*, 41–46.

sharing in the gospel" (τῇ κοινωνίᾳ ὑμῶν εἰς τὸ εὐαγγέλιον, 1:5).[270] Without using any modifier, either here or in all but one (1:27) of his other uses of τὸ εὐαγγέλιον in this letter, there was clearly a shared understanding of "the gospel."[271] Taken in the passive, the phrase could refer to their acceptance of the gospel, or their faith.[272] However, in view of a similar expression and construction by Paul—"your confession of the gospel"[273]—and all the other uses of εὐαγγέλιον in this letter carrying a dynamic or active sense,[274] the phrase is to be read in the active sense, as something the Philippians do. Paul could have in mind their sharing or being partners in the preaching of the gospel.[275]

However, three observations call this reading into question. First, nowhere else in the letter is there any hint that the Philippians are or should be involved in the preaching of the gospel.[276] Second, although in the period there may have been an increasing interchange between εἰς ("into") and ἐν ("in"),[277] Paul was not in the habit of confusing them.[278] Therefore, Paul must have in mind not so much sharing "in," but the telic sense of sharing "for the purpose of" the gospel.[279] Third, using another κοινός ("common" or "shared") word, Paul immediately goes on to write of his confidence of God's[280] ongoing work in their lives (Phil 1:6) and of their being "partners (συγκοινωνούς) in grace" (1:7). This "grace" could refer to Paul's ministry,[281]

270. In the NT εἰς τὸ εὐαγγέλιον ("into," "to" or "toward the gospel") occurs only in Paul's writing: 2 Cor 2:12; 9:13; Phil 1:5; 2:22. Cf. BDAG, "εἰς," 288–91 (288); Fee, *Paul's Letter to the Philippians*, 83n50; Silva, "εἰς," esp. 121.

271. Cf. O'Brien, "Gospel in Philippians," 220; Hawthorne and Martin, *Philippians*, 23; Bockmuehl, *Philippians*, 61.

272. Seesemann, *Der Begriff KOINONIA im Neuen Testament*, 73–75, 79.

273. 2 Cor 9:13: τῆς ὁμολογίας ὑμῶν εἰς τὸ εὐαγγέλιον. O'Brien, "Gospel in Philippians," 217.

274. Panikulam, *Koinōnia in the New Testament*, 82.

275. Cf. NIRV ("spreading the gospel"), NLT ("spreading the Good News"); O'Brien, "Gospel in Philippians," 217, 218; Ruemann, *Philippians*, 108.

276. Pace O'Brien, *Epistle to the Philippians*, 63 and 148, on Phil 1:27.

277. See the examples in Moulton et al., *Grammar of New Testament Greek*, 3:255–56.

278. Moulton et al., *Grammar of New Testament Greek*, 3:256, are only able to cite Ephesians 3:16.

279. Cf. 2 Cor 2:12. Also, see Lightfoot, *Saint Paul's Epistle to the Philippians*, 83; Fee, *Paul's Letter to the Philippians*, 83n50.

280. Paul does not mention God, but says, ὁ ἐναρξάμενος ("the One beginning," Phil 1:6). Cf. Hawthorne and Martin, *Philippians*, 24.

281. Cf. Benoit, *Les épîtres de saint Paul*, 22; Caird, *Paul's Letters from Prison*, 108; Collange, *Epistle of Saint Paul to the Philippians*, 47; Hawthorne and Martin, *Philippians*,

as it can elsewhere in his letters.[282] However, the partnership in grace includes "my chains" (1:7). Although they are familiar with suffering (1:29) and struggles (1:30),[283] perhaps from the Jews (cf. 3:2–4) rather than city officials[284] perhaps causing their poverty,[285] imprisonment is something the Philippians probably do not generally, if at all, share with Paul. Therefore, consistent with his interest in God's ongoing work in their lives (1:6), in the phrase "your sharing in the gospel" (1:5), Paul means your "close association in the furtherance of the gospel,"[286] and probably has in mind their sharing in the breadth of common experience of God's grace or work in their lives (1:5) for the purpose of the gospel.

How their lives function to contribute to the gospel and, in turn, what Paul means by "the gospel" comes into focus when we take into account, first, that one of Paul's reasons for writing is to thank the Philippians for their financial gift (cf. Phil 4:10–20). The verbal connections—in such words as "joy," "share," "think," "increase," "fill," and "fruit"—between this general thanksgiving and his more specific note[287] suggest that what Paul means by sharing in the gospel includes their sharing their financial resources.[288]

Second, Paul's next use of "gospel" (Phil 1:7) also shows that it is their lives that share in or contribute to the gospel.[289] What he says can be translated: "Just as it is right for me to think about all of you because I have

---

27.

282. See Rom 1:5; 12:3; 1 Cor 3:10; Gal 2:9; cf. Eph 3:2.

283. In 1 Thess 1:6–7 Paul says the readers are examples to the Macedonians of receiving the word in spite of persecution. At this stage the only church in Macedonia was in Philippi. See Best, *Thessalonians*, 79. In 2 Cor 7:5 Paul draws attention to his affliction in Macedonia that involved the believers (8:2), and Luke maintains a tradition of both Paul and his companions, as well as the Philippians, being persecuted (Acts 17:5–8). That suffering is a significant aspect of the experience of the Philippians, and pervades Paul's letter to them, e.g., see Jewett, "Epistolary Thanksgiving," 51; Bloomquist, *Function of Suffering in Philippians*, esp. chs. 7–10; Oakes, *Philippians*, esp. 76–84.

284. Cf. 1 Thess 1:6–7 and 2:14.

285. Cf. 2 Cor 8:2. On the manner and cause of the poverty of the Philippians, see Thrall, *II Corinthians*, 2:522–23.

286. Vincent, *Epistles to the Philippians and to Philemon*, 7.

287. Note the discussions by Peterman, *Paul's Gift from Philippi*, 91–92; Fowl, "Know Your Context," 49 and note 7.

288. Cf. Rom 15:26; 2 Cor 9:13; Lightfoot, *Saint Paul's Epistle to the Philippians*, 83; Collange, *Epistle of Saint Paul to the Philippians*, 44. Note the nuanced discussion by Fee, *Paul's Letter to the Philippians*, 84.

289. Cf. Lightfoot, *Saint Paul's Epistle to the Philippians*, 83: "as the context denotes, it [κοινωνία] denotes cooperation in the widest sense, their participation with the Apostle whether in sympathy or in suffering or in active labor or in any other way."

you in my heart,²⁹⁰ in my chains and in the defense and confirmation of the gospel, you all share with me the grace" (1:7, my translation). Given his imprisonment and impending trial,²⁹¹ alluded to in his use of legal language—"defense" (ἀπολογία)²⁹² and "confirmation" (βεβαίωσις, 1:7)²⁹³— Paul is probably echoing his conviction that the Philippians' experience of God's grace can be taken as evidence to vindicate his ministry.²⁹⁴ Indeed, Paul says later that their "holding fast to the words of life" will show he has not run or labored in vain (2:16). That is, the breadth of the experience in the lives of the Philippians confirm the truth of what he is doing;²⁹⁵ his readers' sharing "in the gospel" (εἰς τὸ εὐαγγέλιον, 1:5) is both a participating in its experience and in its purpose, as well as the vindication of its truth.²⁹⁶ In other words, the gospel is described as both experienced grace and the subject of Paul's ministry. The gospel as the subject or nature of Paul's ministry we will see expressed similarly and more clearly in his note to Philemon.²⁹⁷

(b) Personal report (Philippians 1:12-26). In reporting on his imprisonment Paul says that "what has happened to me has actually helped to spread (εἰς προκοπήν) the gospel" (1:12). What Paul has in mind by "the gospel" is seen as his report continues. That is,²⁹⁸ he explains, his imprisonment has helped the spread of the gospel through "the entire

---

290. In light of the word order and context of gratefulness for the Philippians, Caird, *Paul's Letters from Prison*, 108, translates διὰ τὸ ἔχειν με ἐν τῇ καρδίᾳ ὑμᾶς "you have me in your heart" (Phil 1:7). However, in the construction in which an infinitive is followed by two accusatives it can be expected that an author intended the first accusative to be the subject (με, "I," that is, Paul) and the second (ὑμᾶς, "you," that is, the Philippians) the object. See Porter, "Word Order and Clause Structure," 197; cf. Reed, "Infinitive with Two Substantival Accusatives," 10; and the discussion by Fee, *Paul's Letter to the Philippians*, 90.

291. Martin, *Philippians*, 67; O'Brien, *Epistle to the Philippians*, 69.

292. Cf. Acts 22:1; 25:16; 2 Tim 4:16; Josephus, *J.W.* 1.621; Kellermann, "ἀπολογέομαι," 137; BDAG, "ἀπολογία," 117; on the judicial verb, ἀπολογέομαι, see MM, 66.

293. Deissmann, *Bible Studies*, 104-9; Schlier, "βέβαιος, κτλ.," 600-4.

294. Cf. Bockmuehl, *Philippians*, 64. There is no reason to think that Paul had in mind only his preaching, as supposed by O'Brien, "Gospel in Philippians," 219.

295. To suppose this partnership is their gifts and prayers—see Gnilka, *Philipperbrief*, 101-2; Beare, *Epistle to the Philippians*, 53; Caird, *Paul's Letters from Prison*, 115-16; Martin, *Philippians*, 63—is near to trivializing Paul's intentions.

296. Cf. Fee, *Paul's Letter to the Philippians*, 93.

297. See §4.3 below.

298. On ὥστε ("so that" or "therefore," Phil 1:13), see BDAG, "ὥστε," 1107, and the discussion by Moule, *Idiom-Book of New Testament Greek*, 142-46.

palace guard[299] and to everyone else," knowing that his imprisonment was "in Christ" (ἐν Χριστῷ, 1:13).

Initially, it is hardly convincing that news of Paul's imprisonment as a follower of Christ would have advanced the gospel.[300] The opposite may have been the general opinion.[301] Rather, taking "in Christ" to refer to the entire phrase, "the manifestation of my chains,"[302] Paul is saying that his imprisonment was a valid expression of life in Christ and as such advanced the gospel throughout the praetorian guard and beyond.[303] This understanding of Paul's expression is consistent with the theme of self-emptying and humiliating suffering that dominates the letter, especially the Christ hymn.[304]

In turn, understanding Paul's chains as an expression of the gospel,[305] believers had become confident "to speak the word" (τὸν λόγον λαλεῖν) more fearlessly (Phil 1:14). Since the spread of the gospel had been aided by Paul's imprisonment because it was an expression of life "in Christ" becoming known, and by people speaking the word, the gospel he has in mind is not so much the message, but its dynamic and personal subject, Christ.[306] Paul's concept of the gospel as the subject of his message is confirmed when he goes on to balance or parallel his imprisonment as a "defense of the gospel" (ἀπολογίαν τοῦ εὐαγγελίου, 1:16) with others who "preach" (κηρύσσω, 1:15) or "proclaim" (καταγγέλλω, 1:17, 18) Christ.

Paul also uses "spread" or "progress" (προκοπή)[307] at the end of his report where the word refers to the progress and joy "of the faith" of the readers (Phil 1:25). Though Paul probably does not intend to exclude the subjective meaning,[308] "the faith" (τῆς πίστεως, 1:25) is probably not primarily the Philippians' trust in Christ,[309] but the gospel itself. As we will

---

299. On πραιτώριον referring to a body of men rather than the building or place, see Lightfoot, *Saint Paul's Epistle to the Philippians*, 99–104 (esp. 101–2).

300. Jewett, "Conflicting Movements," 366–67; cf. Dibelius, *An die Thessalonicher I, II, An die Philipper*, 64.

301. Jewett, "Conflicting Movements," 366.

302. Dibelius, *An die Thessalonicher I, II, An die Philipper*, 64.

303. Neugebauer, *In Christus*, 121, followed by, e.g., Jewett, "Conflicting Movements," 367; O'Brien, "Gospel in Philippians," 221.

304. Phil 2:6–11; cf. 1:29; 3:8, 10; 4:11–13. Jewett, "Conflicting Movements," 367–68.

305. Cf. Fowl, *Philippians*, 40.

306. Cf. O'Brien, "Gospel in Philippians," 222.

307. In the NT the word προκοπή only appears here (Phil 1:25) and in 1 Tim 4:15.

308. Cf. Bockmuehl, *Philippians*, 94. On the alternative interpretations see Stählin, "προκοπή, προκόπτω," 715.

309. As supposed by, e.g., Vincent, *Epistles to the Philippians and to Philemon*, 30;

see, in a few lines he goes on to specify the faith as "the faith of the gospel" (1:27).³¹⁰ The faith is what is believed, or the object or content of faith,³¹¹ which, as we will see, he specifies as Christ (1:27). Indeed, "progress" (προκοπή) functioning as an *inclusio*³¹²—bracketing his report—helps see that Paul probably intends "the progress of the [that is, their] faith" (1:25) to be an echo of "the progress of the gospel" (1:12).³¹³ The progress of the gospel is not the preaching,³¹⁴ therefore, but Christ being known and expressed in the lives of believers, including in suffering. In short, the gospel is the subject of the message, Christ. It is not that in the proclamation itself that God was mightily at work in Christ,³¹⁵ but that the proclamation was about the mighty work of God in Christ.

*(c) The gospel of Christ (Philippians 1:27—2:11).*³¹⁶ Having reported on his personal affairs to satisfy his concerned readers, Paul turns more directly to express his pastoral concern for them, notably their attitudes and behavior (1:27; 2:2).³¹⁷ In doing so, what we have just seen in his use of "gospel" as referring to Christ (1:27) becomes clearer. For in calling for action on the basis of the gospel his understanding of the gospel is elaborated.

In appealing for particular attitudes and behavior among his readers Paul does not use his customary word "walk" or "conduct oneself" (περιπατέω).³¹⁸ Instead, he uses "live" (πολιτεύομαι), a term with political or civic origins and overtones, meaning to live as a loyal citizen.³¹⁹ Thus,

---

Michael, *Epistle of Paul to the Philippians*, 61; Müller, *Epistles of Paul*, 64-65. See the discussion by Fee, *Paul's Letter to the Philippians*, 153n16.

310. Fee, *Paul's Letter to the Philippians*, 153. For a detailed discussion of the alternative interpretations of τῇ πίστει τοῦ εὐαγγελίου, see Hawthorne and Martin, *Philippians*, 71.

311. Note Lightfoot, *Saint Paul's Epistle to the Philippians*, 106. Cf. Vincent, *Epistles to the Philippians and to Philemon*, 32; Silva, *Philippians*, 89; Witherington, *Friendship and Finances in Philippi*, 53.

312. Fee, *Paul's Letter to the Philippians*, 111n22.

313. Cf. Bockmuehl, *Philippians*, 74.

314. As supposed by O'Brien, "Gospel in Philippians," 223.

315. As supposed by O'Brien, "Gospel in Philippians," 223-24.

316. At least up to the date of publication (2004), key contributions to the mountainous volume of literature on Phil 2:6-11 are listed in the various bibliographies in Hawthorne and Martin, *Philippians*. More recently, see Fewster, "Philippians 'Christ Hymn.'"

317. Cf. Caird, *Paul's Letters from Prison*, 114.

318. Περιπατέω occurs ninety-five times in the NT, eighteen times in Paul: Rom 6:4; 8:4; 13:13; 14:15; 1 Cor 3:3; 7:17; 2 Cor 4:2; 5:7; 10:2, 3; 12:18; Gal 5:16; Phil 3:17, 18; 1 Thess 2:12; 4:1 (x2), 12.

319. In the NT πολιτεύομαι occurs only here in Phil 1:27 and Acts 23:1. Paul—and

Paul has in mind behavior that arises out of loyalty. In particular, although Paul's concern is with their loyalty to the gospel, rather than discharging political obligation[320] or even loyalty to each other,[321] that would be the result.[322] The use of πολιτεύομαι ("live"), playing on their dual citizenship,[323] most probably drew the attention of the readers to the political backdrop, ground, and implications of their loyalty.[324] Their allegiance was, and could only be, to Christ and no other (cf. Phil 3:7-11).

In developing his call to the readers to be loyal to or "live worthy of the gospel of [or about] Christ" by having "one mind [or "one spirit," μιᾷ ψυχῇ] for the faith of the gospel" (Phil 1:27), he provides content to that gospel. Consistent with his using Christ as the model for behavior in other places,[325] the object of their loyalty or the model for living worthy of the gospel is not—it must be noted—a message about Christ but Christ himself, as the *Carmen Christi*, the Song of Christ, makes clear. Put another way, the paradigm is not a message but a person. In sweeping, powerful broad-brush strokes, Paul graphically depicts the intertwining cosmic and earthly story of Christ (2:5-11),[326] focusing on Christ's humility, as the model for living.

Having described the manner of life they should be living—standing firm in one spirit, "striving side by side" (συναθλοῦντες, Phil 1:27),[327] not intimidated by opponents (1:28), and suffering for Christ (1:29)—Paul presumes[328] they will find this possible through "encouragement in

---

Polycarp after him (cf. Polycarp, *Phil.* 5.2, echoing Phil 1:27)—would have known the term had resonating power for the Philippians, citizens of a Roman colony. On the use of πολιτεύομαι in the period, see Strathmann, "πόλις, κτλ," 522–29. Cf. BDAG, "πολιτεύομαι," 846.

320. As argued by Brewer, "Meaning of *Politeuesthe* in Philippians 1:27," 83. See the brief discussion by Strathmann, "πόλις, κτλ," 534.

321. As supposed by Beare, *Epistle to the Philippians*, 66–67.

322. See Martin, *Philippians*, 82. Cf. Miller, "Πολιτεύεσθε in Philippians 1:27," 86–96; Hawthorne and Martin, *Philippians*, 69.

323. Cf. Fee, *Paul's Letter to the Philippians*, 161–62.

324. However, Ruemann, *Philippians*, 287, notes that there is no indication of the Philippians needing to choose between Christ and Caesar.

325. Rom 15:1-7; 1 Cor 10:31—11:1; 2 Cor 8:6-9; 1 Thess 1:6.

326. Despite, e.g., Käsemann, "Critical Analysis of Philippians 2:5-11," 45–88 (e.g., 87); and Martin, *Hymn of Christ*, esp. 83, 84–88, it is widely though not entirely taken that Paul presents Christ as a model for behavior. See, e.g., Marshall, "Christ-Hymn in Philippians 2:5-11," esp. 117–19; Hurtado, "Jesus as Lordly Example in Philippians 2:5-11," 122–26; Fowl, *Story of Christ*, 77–101; Hooker, "Philippians 2.6-11," 90–91, 93; and Oakes, *Philippians*, 188.

327. Pfitzner, *Paul and the Agon Motif*, 114–20; Krentz, "Military Language and Metaphors in Philippians," 122–23.

328. Phil 2:1: Εἴ τις οὖν ("If anyone then"). Bockmuehl, *Philippians*, 104: "The 'if'

Christ," consolation from (his)[329] love, sharing in the (Holy)[330] Spirit, and compassion and sympathy (2:1).[331] Continuing more obviously to anticipate the Christ hymn he is about to set out,[332] he further describes the manner in which they should be living: being of "the same mind" (τὸ αὐτὸ φρονῆτε), "the same love" (τὴν αὐτὴν ἀγάπην), "the same spirit" (σύμψυχη), and "one mind" (τὸ ἓν φρονοῦντες, 2:2), doing nothing, he says, "from selfish ambition or conceit, but in humility regard others as better than yourselves. Let each of you look not to your own interests, but to the interests of others" (2:3-4).

Then, linked back through this vocabulary—from μιᾷ ψυχῇ ("one mind," 1:27), σύμψυχη ("one mind"),[333] and ἓν φρονοῦντες ("one mind," 2:2), to τοῦτο φρονεῖτε ("this mind," 2:5)—to his call and description of living worthy of the gospel of Christ (1:27), he then describes "this mind" (τοῦτο φρονεῖτε, 2:5) or attitude of Christ Jesus in the *Carmen Christi*. The Christ hymn—his description of Christ—is, then, Paul's description of the gospel which his readers are to use to measure their lives. The repeated use of φρονεῖν ("to think" or "to understand"),[334] with its summons to an attitude that is to be put into practice,[335] undergirds and emphasizes his point.

(which occurs four times in the Greek of this verse) does not of course designate a doubtful proposition but one that is certain."

329. The love Paul has in mind is most likely that of Christ's in that he is the subject that dominates this paragraph (Phil 2:1-5).

330. In view of the focus of the sentence being on Christ's influence, the Holy Spirit rather than the human spirit is most likely intended. Cf. Fee, *Paul's Letter to the Philippians*, 181n38. On the debate on whether the genitive πνεύματος ("of the Spirit") is subjective, referring to sharing in what is created by the Spirit or objective, sharing in the Spirit see the brief discussion by Martin, *Philippians*, 87.

331. Without a qualifying genitive it is not clear whose "compassion" (σπλάγχνον) and "sympathy" or "pity" (οἰκτιρμός) is in mind. See Hawthorne and Martin, *Philippians*, 84-85; Fee, *Paul's Letter to the Philippians*, 182.

332. Though he has adapted the hymn against, e.g., Kim, *Origin of Paul's Gospel*, 147-49; O'Brien, *Epistle to the Philippians*, 198-202; Fee, "Philippians 2:5-11," 29-46, who take Paul to be the author, it is generally agreed that in Phil 2:6-11 Paul is using traditional or existing material. See Martin, *Hymn of Christ*, xxxiv, 42-62, 297-309. However, the origin of the material is far from agreed. See Hawthorne and Martin, *Philippians*, 104.

333. On Paul picking up μιᾷ ψυχῇ ("one mind," Phil 1:27), in σύμψυχη ("one mind," 2:1), see Fee, *Paul's Letter to the Philippians*, 185-86 and note 60.

334. There is a concentration of Paul's use of φρονεῖν in Philippians, and in this section, a distinctly Pauline word. In the NT see: Matt 16:23; Mark 8:33; Acts 28:22; Rom 8:5; 11:20; 12:3, 16; 14:6; 15:5; 1 Cor 13:11; 2 Cor 13:11; Gal 5:10; Phil 1:7; 2:2, 5; 3:15, 19; 4:2, 10; Col 3:2.

335. Note Rom 8:5 where attitude and action are closely associated in φρονεῖν. See Silva, "φρονέω," 619; Martin, *Philippians*, 90-91.

Moreover, this call of loyalty to Christ using a politically charged term—"live worthy"—and describing this loyalty in terms appropriate to loyalty to the emperor—Christ's authority being granted to him, his universal authority, his universal salvation, and the anticipated universal submission[336]—not only reflects Paul's view of Christ, but also his view of the gospel. The gospel is not about Christ; Christ is the gospel. What we saw adumbrated in Galatians is here made clearer.[337] Given both the space Paul devotes to Christ as the gospel and the measure of its expression, and its reverberations through the letter, the importance of this understanding of the gospel as Christ is not to be underestimated.

(d) Timothy (Philippians 2:22). Having urged the Philippians to have the same attitude that was in Christ (2:5) as a model for their behavior (1:27—2:18), including their source of joy (2:17–18), Paul says that he hopes to send Timothy in order to "be cheered by news of you" (2:19). He says of Timothy: "With me he served the gospel."[338] Again Paul uses the phrase "to" or "toward the gospel" (εἰς τὸ εὐαγγέλιον).[339] Again, and in line with his other uses of the phrase, Timothy's service was for the purpose of, or in the cause of, the gospel.[340] In that Paul introduces himself and Timothy as "slaves of Christ Jesus" (δοῦλοι Χριστοῦ Ἰησοῦ, 1:1), and here the service is to, or for, the cause of the gospel rather than self-interest (cf. 2:21), there is confirmation of our reading that Paul understands the gospel as more than the message about Christ; the gospel is identified with Christ and his cosmic story.

Though Paul does not spell out the nature of Timothy's service for the gospel it is certainly not simply functioning as Paul's servant.[341] Even if Timothy acts as a messenger and encourager (Phil 1:19), and Paul describes their intimate relationship in father-son terms (2:22; cf. 1 Cor 4:17), it is not in terms of subordination but of intimacy,[342] and Paul introduces himself and Timothy each as servants of Christ Jesus (1:1). And in the statement of interest to us here, Paul says Timothy is a servant "with me" (σὺν ἐμοί,

---

336. See the detailed discussion by Oakes, *Philippians*, 129-74.

337. On Gal 1:15–16 see §3.3 (c) above.

338. Phil 2:22: σύν ἐμοὶ ἐδούλευσεν εἰς τὸ εὐαγγέλιον.

339. See 2 Cor 2:12; (cf. §4.2 [a] below); 9:13; Phil 1:5.

340. Bockmuehl, *Philippians*, 163.

341. Long ago, Marius Victorinus (fourth century) noted: "He says he served with me, not he served me." See Edwards, *Galatians, Ephesians, Philippians*, 262.

342. Fee, *Paul's Letter to the Philippians*, 268n39, points out that Paul's use of "τέκνον . . . emphasizes the relationship involved, as over against υἱός, where the emphasis is more on the status of 'sonship' itself." Cf. BDAG, "τέκνον," 994-95 (§3); and the discussions by Caird, *Paul's Letters from Prison*, 129; Hawthorne and Martin, *Philippians*, 156.

2:22).³⁴³ Timothy's service in the cause of the gospel is, then, neither as Paul's servant nor as simply preaching,³⁴⁴ or the work of evangelism,³⁴⁵ but the much broader sharing in his overall work that serves the cause of the gospel. Expressed otherwise, the gospel is shorthand for Paul's work as a servant of Jesus Christ. In this point we continue to see the breadth of Paul's understanding of "the gospel."

(e) Struggling together (Philippians 4:1-3). In beginning his final appeals in this letter (4:1-9), Paul picks up two key verbs he has already used. He returns first to make specific his earlier general call (1:27) for the Philippians to "stand firm" (στήκετε, 4:1), and then for Euodia and Syntyche in particular to be of "the same mind."³⁴⁶ In his appeal for someone³⁴⁷ to help these two women, Paul describes them as: "in the gospel having struggled together with me" (ἐν τῷ εὐαγγελίῳ συνήθλησάν μοι, 4:3). What is of interest to us is whether Paul is recalling their involvement in his missionary tours or if, in the mention of "the gospel," he has something else in mind.

In relation to the gospel, we have seen that Paul has already used "striving side by side" (συναθλέω), a term with athletic and military connotations,³⁴⁸ for the Philippians' way of living rather than for their accompanying him on preaching journeys (Phil 1:27). We also saw in his thanksgiving (1:3-8) that Paul was thankful for the lives of the Philippians, which he described as sharing in the gospel (1:5). Further, Paul uses athletic imagery, not only of his ministry (2:16), but also for his own life (3:10-14; cf. 1 Cor 9:24-27). Then, although Paul's description of the women as "fellow workers" (συνεργοί, Phil 4:3) would usually mean they were Paul's fellow travelers,³⁴⁹ he also uses the word for fellow believers,³⁵⁰ as do the authors of one of the Johannine

---

343. Cf. Martin, *Philippians*, 118.

344. Collange, *Epistle of Saint Paul to the Philippians*, 117, limits the service to "the announcement of God's free and mighty intervention in history."

345. O'Brien, "Gospel in Philippians," 226-27.

346. Phil 4:2 (τὸ αὐτὸ φρονεῖν); cf. 2:2, 5; 3:15; and 1:27 (ἐν ἑνὶ πνεύματι μιᾷ ψυχῇ, "in one spirit, one mind"). Fee, *Paul's Letter to the Philippians*, 386-87.

347. For a discussion of who Paul has in mind when he says, ναὶ ἐρωτῶ καὶ σέ ("Yes, and I ask you" [singular]) to help these women (Phil 4:3), see Fee, *Paul's Letter to the Philippians*, 392-95.

348. See BDAG, "συναθλέω," 964, citing Malinowski, "Brave Women of Philippi," 60-64; and Krentz, "Military Language and Metaphors in Philippians," 122-23.

349. Of his fellow workers or travelers Paul uses συνεργός ("fellow worker") at Rom 16:3, 9, 21; 1 Cor 3:9; 2 Cor 8:23; Phil 2:25; 1 Thess 3:2; Phlm 1:1, 24. Otherwise, in the NT συνεργός occurs here in Phil 4:3; and Col 4:11; 3 John 1:8.

350. Cf. 2 Cor 1:24. See Plummer, *Critical and Exegetical Commentary*, 45; Barrett, *Second Epistle to the Corinthians*, 84-85; Furnish, *II Corinthians*, 152, though doubted by Bertram, "συνεργός, κτλ.," 874n2; Thrall, *II Corinthians*, 1:162.

Epistles[351] and the Pseudo Clementine Homilies.[352] Moreover, there is otherwise no suggestion these two women had accompanied Paul on his preaching tours.[353] Therefore, consistent with the general "lifestyle" thrust of this paragraph, the women contending or fighting with him for the gospel is also most probably intended as a description of their lives as his colleagues.[354] That is, in contending in the gospel with him the lives of these two women expressed and confirmed the gospel of Paul's ministry. The gospel is, then, for Paul, something that can—and should—be lived, embodied, or expressed in the life of the community as a whole and in its individual members.

(f) The beginning of the gospel (Philippians 4:15). Although Paul has alluded to their gift in his initial thanksgiving (1:5), and again when referring to Epaphroditus their messenger ministering to his needs,[355] not until the end of the letter does Paul focus on thanking his readers (4:17–18). However, Paul's thanks is only indirect, even vacillating (4:10–13).[356] If Paul had offered a direct "thank you" he would have been acknowledging a conventional, even mercantile, relationship of reciprocity.[357] This would have compromised his natural, cordial relationship with them.[358] Instead, as part of defining his relationship with the Philippians[359] as a mutual sharing in the gospel, not only is the thanks indirect, the gift is seen as an offering to God (4:18) who, echoing the conventions of gifts and relationships, will repay the readers (4:19).[360]

Consistent with a concern for his relationship with his readers he says: "You Philippians indeed know that in the beginning of the gospel (ἐν ἀρχῇ τοῦ εὐαγγελίου), when I left from Macedonia, no church shared with me

---

351. 3 John 8. See Brooke, *Johannine Epistles*, 187; Schnackenburg, *Johannine Epistles*, 296n126; Smalley, *1, 2, 3 John*, 338; Ellis, *Prophecy and Hermeneutic*, 6n15.

352. Ps.-Clem. *Hom.* 17.19.7.4 (ἡμῖν συνεργός, "a fellow worker with us"). Bultmann, *Johannine Epistles*, 99.

353. To the contrary, see O'Brien, "Gospel in Philippians," 227–28.

354. Cf. Malinowski, "Brave Women of Philippi," 62–63.

355. Phil 2:25; note 4:18. The gift may also be in view in Phil 2:17, 30. See Fee, *Paul's Letter to the Philippians*, 422.

356. Cf. Fowl, "Know Your Context," 49–50.

357. On Paul's response to the complexities of Greco-Roman social conventions regarding the giving and receiving of gifts see Peterman, *Paul's Gift from Philippi*, and the astute summary comments by Bockmuehl, *Philippians*, 257.

358. See P. Merton 12 and the discussion by Peterman, "'Thankless Thanks,'" 261–70; Peterman, *Paul's Gift from Philippi*, 73–83, of letters between friends dispensing with thanks to preserve a cordial relationship.

359. Cf. Bockmuehl, *Philippians*, 258.

360. Cf. Bockmuehl, *Philippians*, 266.

in the matter of giving and receiving, except you alone" (Phil 4:15). The puzzling phrase, "in the beginning of the gospel,"[361] cannot refer to the beginning of Paul's ministry.[362] He otherwise makes clear his work began in the East (Gal 1:11—2:14), which he is unlikely to discount.[363] Nor is Paul likely to be thinking in terms of the beginning of his full responsibility for the gospel,[364] for this places too much weight on the gospel as Paul's.[365] More likely, he is referring to the beginning of the gospel for the Philippians, that is, his arrival in Philippi. What he says here echoes what he has said earlier about the Philippians "sharing in the gospel from the first day" (Phil 1:5), by which he means the beginning of his relationship with them.[366] Also, we have already noted the verbal connections between this section on the financial gift and his earlier thanksgiving.

Although it may, then, be reasonable to understand Paul's phrase to mean, "from the beginning of the preaching of the gospel,"[367] this is unlikely what Paul had in mind. The perspective of the sentence is from that of the experience of the Philippians. Further, the emphasis of the statement is on the activity of the Philippians and on Paul's relationship with them, including while he is absent from them.[368] In light of already seeing that the gospel was something which the Philippians experienced and shared with Paul, it is most natural to understand the gospel here to mean what they had received in Paul's ministry and continued to experience and express, including in their financial sharing.

(g) Results: The gospel in Philippians. Though Paul is concerned for his readers and his relationship with them, it is probably not an exaggeration to say that the gospel is both a key theme and his overarching interest in

---

361. Fee, *Paul's Letter to the Philippians*, 440n12, notes the "unusual amount of speculation over this phrase."

362. As argued by Suggs, "Date of Paul's Macedonian Ministry," 60–68.

363. As suggested by Glombitza, "Der Dank des Apostels," 140.

364. As proposed by, e.g., Collange, *Epistle of Saint Paul to the Philippians*, 152. Vincent, *Epistles to the Philippians and to Philemon*, 147, is correct to regard as fanciful the view of Lightfoot, *Biblical Essays*, 237, that in this phrase Paul was saying "The faith of Christ had, as it were, made a fresh start."

365. O'Brien, "Gospel in Philippians," 228.

366. Cf. e.g., Vincent, *Epistles to the Philippians and to Philemon*, 147; O'Brien, *Epistle to the Philippians*, 63, 531–32; Lüdemann, *Paul, Apostle to the Gentiles*, 106; O'Brien, "Gospel in Philippians," 228; Fee, *Paul's Letter to the Philippians*, 440–41; Bockmuehl, *Philippians*, 263; Ruemann, *Philippians*, 660. Notably, 1 Clem. 47.1 also uses the same phrase, ἐν ἀρχῇ τοῦ εὐαγγελίου, to refer to the beginning of Paul's work at Corinth.

367. Lüdemann, *Paul, Apostle to the Gentiles*, 106.

368. Cf. Peterman, *Paul's Gift from Philippi*, 150; Fowl, "Know Your Context," 55.

this letter.[369] However, contrary to the generally received understanding of the gospel, it has become clear that for Paul the gospel can neither be understood simply as Christian teaching as a whole nor, in particular, as the message he preached.

In Philippians the gospel takes two forms. Fundamentally, the gospel is Christ (the cosmic Christ), his character, life, and work.[370] This Paul describes most clearly and elaborately in the Christ hymn.[371] The gospel here is not so much Paul's message as its subject, Christ. It is not that Christ is the core of the gospel;[372] Christ is the gospel. In turn, Jean-François Collange is correct to say that in Philippians Paul's "Gospel exhibits a 'glory' attributable not to itself but to Christ."[373] As Christ is described in terms reminiscent of the emperor—someone granted universal authority for universal salvation and obeisance[374]—the nature of Paul's gospel comes into clearer focus. As succinctly put by J. B. Lightfoot: "Though the Gospel is capable of doctrinal exposition, though it is eminently fertile in moral results, yet its substance is neither dogmatic system nor an ethical code, but a Person and a Life."[375] Yet, second, in that the *Carmen Christi* was the model and measure for his readers' lives,[376] the gospel is also to be lived, embodied, or expressed in the individual members and the shared life of the community.[377] The gospel as Christ, and him experienced and expressed, explains why it is both the subject of Paul's ministry and what he shares with his readers. The gospel as Christ also explains why the gospel is lived in a certain way (2:1–5), with Christ as the model for life before God (2:5–11) and as a life of suffering like Christ's (3:7–11).

This chapter and the one that follows form a unity in that they both give close attention to Paul's writings to answer the question: What was Paul's understanding of the gospel? In order not to conclude prematurely and prejudice our ongoing enquiry we will delay drawing conclusions on

---

369. Cf. Fee, *Paul's Letter to the Philippians*, 14, 47.

370. Cf. Fee, *Paul's Letter to the Philippians*, 82, comes close to this conclusion: "Above all, the gospel has to do with Christ, both his person and his work."

371. Contrast Fee, *Paul's Letter to the Philippians*, 47: "there is very little that is said in Philippians as to the *content* of the gospel" (emphasis original).

372. Ruemann, *Philippians*, 197.

373. Collange, *Epistle of Saint Paul to the Philippians*, 73–74.

374. Cf. Taylor, *Divinity of the Roman Emperor*, 239–46.

375. Lightfoot, *Saint Paul's Epistle to the Philippians*, x. The Preface is dated July 1, 1868.

376. Cf. Collange, *Epistle of Saint Paul to the Philippians*, 45.

377. Cf. Fee, *Paul's Letter to the Philippians*, 395.

what has been covered so far until the examination of all Paul's letters has been completed.

4

The Gospel Paul Promoted
Corinthians, Philemon, and Romans

So far in examining what Paul had to say about the gospel he promoted we have considered his three earliest letters: those to the Thessalonians, the Galatians, and the Philippians. From the first of these letters it was relatively easy to piece together what he said about the gospel in his initial preaching to the Thessalonians. In this chapter, considering his later correspondence—that to the Corinthians, to Philemon, and to the Roman believers—we will have the opportunity to see his more considered treatment of his gospel in Romans. We begin with Paul's most extensive correspondence.

§4.1 1 CORINTHIANS

In Acts, Luke offers a detailed story of Paul's arrival from Athens and activity then in Corinth that included working with Aquila and Priscilla (Acts 18:1–3). Every Sabbath, according to Luke, Paul would be in the synagogue arguing with the Jews (18:4), but "when they opposed and reviled him" (18:6) he was forced to move the discussion next door (18:7). After more than eighteen months (cf. 18:11 and 18) and further trouble (18:12–17), Paul, Priscilla, and Aquila left for Syria (18:18). Paul, however, says nothing of this. Yet, in telling of his coming to Corinth he provides the most we have about his approach to his work (1 Cor 2:1–5).[1] Although he does not use the

---

1. See the detailed discussion in Twelftree, *Paul and the Miraculous*, 192–201.

term "gospel" we will have cause to take into account what he says about his approach to ministry to help us understand his gospel.

Of the letters Paul wrote to the Corinthians—perhaps five, or even thirteen[2]—only two survive, and both of those are arguably compilations.[3] Here I will assume that 1 Corinthians is a single letter, the second he wrote (cf. 1 Cor 5:9), and that there was an intervening letter (2 Cor 2:4; 7:8) before writing the two letters that now form 2 Corinthians (2 Cor 1–9 and 10–13).

At least because the Corinthians misunderstood his first letter on fornication and idolatry (1 Cor 5:9–11), and him hearing of dissensions (1:10–12), scandals,[4] and their questions (7:1), as well as wishing to assure the Corinthians that Apollos would come when he was able (16:12), Paul wrote a second time (1 Corinthians).[5] In doing so he uses "gospel" as a noun (εὐαγγέλιον) eight times,[6] and as a verb (εὐαγγελίζομαι) six times.[7] Three times he also uses the related verb "proclaim" (καταγγέλω).[8] Our purpose in this discussion remains to understand what the gospel means to Paul.

(a) Paul's call and purpose (1 Corinthians 1:17–18). The first matter to which Paul gives attention are the cliques that have developed in Corinth, compromising the unity of the church (1:10—4:21). Over against the members rallying around different key figures in the life of the church—Paul, Apollos, Cephas, or Christ (1:12)—one of Paul's retorts is to ask if they were baptized into his name (1:13). He is thankful that he baptized so few of them for, he says, "Christ did not send me to baptize but to gospel (εὐαγγελίζεσθαι), and not in wisdom of word (ἐν σοφίᾳ λόγου), in order not to void the cross of Christ. For the word of the cross is foolishness to those perishing, but to those of us being saved it is the power of God" (1:17–18, my translation).

2. Schmithals, *Die Briefe des Paulus*, 19–85.

3. On the many theories regarding the unity of both 1 and 2 Corinthians, and the existence of other letters, e.g., see Schenk, "Der 1 Korintherbrief," 219–43; Schmithals, "Die Korintherbriefe," 263–88; Schmithals, *Die Briefe des Paulus*; De Boer, "Composition of 1 Corinthians," 229–45; Thrall, *II Corinthians*, 1:3–49; Hall, *Unity of the Corinthian Correspondence*; Martin, *2 Corinthians*, 39–70; and the salutary essay, Stewart-Sykes, "Ancient Editors and Copyists," 53–64.

In view of these competing theories, dating the Corinthian correspondence is not straightforward. See, e.g., Brown, *Introduction to the New Testament*, 512, 542, placing 1 Corinthians at late 56 CE or very early 57 CE from Ephesus, and 2 Corinthians at late summer or early autumn 57 from Macedonia.

4. 1 Cor 3:4–5; 5:1; 6:1–11; 8:1; 11:18–19; 12:1.

5. Cf. Fitzmyer, *First Corinthians*, 51–52.

6. 1 Cor 4:15; 9:12, 14 (x2), 18 (x2), 23; 15:1.

7. 1 Cor 1:17; 9:16 (x2), 18; 15:1, 2.

8. 1 Cor 2:1; 9:14; 11:26, all discussed below.

Two aspects of Paul's personal statement contribute to understanding what he means here by his "gospelling." The most striking point of what he says about himself is not that he was sent to "preach" (κηρύσσω) the gospel (cf. Gal 2:2; 1 Thess 2:9), but that he was sent "to gospel" (εὐαγγελίζεσθαι, 1 Cor 1:17). Whatever else this word does it draws attention to his work involving the gospel.[9] Given that "to gospel" is one of his preferred ways of speaking about his work,[10] even though it may have had overlapping meanings with, or involved, preaching,[11] in order not to miss what Paul has in mind, it is important to resist using "preach" or "proclaim" to translate εὐαγγελίζειν.[12] As we are repeatedly seeing, there was clearly something about his work that was not captured simply by saying that he preached or proclaimed the gospel.

In order to see clearly the second aspect of Paul's understanding of gospelling here, a preliminary matter has to be settled. It is not immediately clear whether the method or the content of his work is in mind when he says he was not sent to gospel "in wisdom of word" (1 Cor 1:17). In view of going on to say that his purpose was not to void or empty the cross of Christ, his concern was probably with the content of his gospelling. His gospelling was not characterized by wisdom—rhetoric or reason.[13] Instead—and here we come to the second aspect of what Paul says about his work—he directly implies that the word (or message) about the cross is the content of his gospelling, a point we have seen him make with other readers.[14]

What is notable here, however, is that he says in his gospelling "the word [his message] of the cross is ... the power of God" for those being saved (1 Cor 1:18). This is not quite as succinctly expressed as it will be early in Romans (see Rom 1:16-17). Yet, in a description of his work he has brought into a sequential relationship his gospelling, his message, the cross, the power of God, and salvation. It is tempting to conclude that Paul was equating the gospel with his message and that his message was the power of God for salvation. However, the stumbling block to such a conclusion

---

9. Schrage, *Der erste Brief an die Korinther*, 1:157; Thiselton, *First Epistle to the Corinthians*, 142.

10. See p. 109n204 above.

11. See §3.3 (a) above.

12. Paul's εὐαγγελίζειν is translated "preach" or "proclaim" by, e.g., Barrett, *First Epistle to the Corinthians*, 48-49; Robertson and Plummer, *First Epistle of St. Paul to the Corinthians*, 15; Reuf, *Paul's First Letter to Corinth*, 10; Morris, *1 Corinthians*, 42; Fitzmyer, *First Corinthians*, 147; Ciampa and Rosner, *First Letter to the Corinthians*, 86; Keener, *1-2 Corinthians*, 26. Also, see p. 109n208 above.

13. See Fee, *First Epistle to the Corinthians*, 66.

14. Phil 2:8; cf. §3.4 (c) above.

is his use of "gospelling" instead of preaching to describe his work. In this statement Paul is probably grappling with expressing the point that, while he has a message about the cross, something more than his message was involved in bringing salvation. Though we have not seen all the evidence for such a conclusion, Gordon Fee's view that, from Paul's perspective, the preaching of the gospel is effective when "it is accompanied by the effectual work of the Spirit"[15] may be close to the mark.

(b) Ministry strategy (1 Corinthians 2:1-5). Aspects of Paul's understanding of the gospel become clear in a recollection of his approach to his work. Echoing the personal statement we have just noted, in which he said he was not sent with or "in wisdom of word" (ἐν σοφία λόγου, 1:17), he says here that it was not with "eloquence or wisdom" (ὑπεροχὴν λόγου ἢ σοφίας) that he came "proclaiming" (καταγγέλλων) the mystery[16] of God" (2:1).

To describe his work, Paul's choice of the word "proclaim" (καταγγέλλω) is telling. In Paul's world, "proclaim," which for him could be a synonym for "preach" (κηρύσσω),[17] was used especially in the proclamation of sacred festivals.[18] Among New Testament writers, Paul has a predilection for the word "proclaim" (καταγγέλλω),[19] likely finding it valuable not only because of its sacral associations but also because of its auditory ties with εὐαγγέλλω; the word could readily evoke the gospel for him and his readers. Paul may also have found the word useful as it was already affiliated with proclaiming the power of God.[20] Notably, Paul's proclamation is making known Jesus Christ and him crucified (1 Cor 2:2), the theme we have already seen associated with the gospel,[21] confirming that the gospel is the subject of his work and discussion here.

Having evoked the gospel as the focus of his ministry, Paul goes on to remind readers of his "word" (ὁ λόγος) and "proclamation" (τὸ κήρυγμα, 1

---

15. Fee, *First Epistle to the Corinthians*, 66.

16. We do not need to be distracted by the question of whether Paul used the word "mystery" (μυστήριον), as read by NA²⁸, or "testimony" (μαρτύριον), as argued by, e.g., Wolff, *Der erste Brief des Paulus an die Korinther*, 47; and Fee, *First Epistle to the Corinthians*, 92n180, 96. See the discussions by Metzger, *Textual Commentary*, 480; Thiselton, *First Epistle to the Corinthians*, 207-8; Garland, *1 Corinthians*, 88; and comments by Twelftree, *Paul and the Miraculous*, 199n152.

17. See p. 109n208 above.

18. Schniewind, "ἀγγελία, κτλ," 70 and note 3.

19. Rom 1:8; 1 Cor 2:1; 9:14; 11:26; Phil 1:17, 18. Cf. Silva, "ἀγγέλλω, κτλ," 117.

20. 2 Macc 9:17; also see 8:36. Cf. Broer, "καταγγέλλω," 256.

21. See §3.3 (d) above.

Cor 2:4).²² As λόγος refers primarily to oral utterances,²³ as it does for Paul the last time he used it (1:18), "proclamation" (κήρυγμα, noun) paired with it also probably refers not to the manner or act of his speaking,²⁴ but to the content of his proclamation.²⁵ The balanced phrase "my word and my proclamation" (ὁ λόγος μου καὶ τὸ κήρυγμά μου) is, then, a hendiadys²⁶ referring to his message—what he said—about Jesus Christ and him crucified. Indeed, it is in his next statement that Paul talks about the style of his presentation. He says his message was "not in persuasive (πειθοῖς)²⁷ words²⁸ of wisdom" (2:3). Over against the persuasion of the spoken word²⁹—the purpose of rhetoric³⁰—Paul says his message and proclamation came in or "with a demonstration of Spirit and power" (ἐν ἀποδέξει πνεύματος καὶ δυνάμεως, 1 Cor 2:4).

In another place I have already offered a detailed discussion regarding Paul's intentions in his phrase "with a demonstration of Spirit and power," arguing that he is referring to miracles.³¹ He is not referring to the convicting power of the gospel,³² or he could be expected to say simply that his speech and proclamation were in Spirit and power. Nor does Paul see the response of the Corinthians as the proof of the gospel.³³ For he says this (prior) demonstration in Spirit and power was "in order that" (ἵνα) their (subsequent) faith might rest on the power of God (1 Cor 2:5). Rather, given

---

22. On the (at least) eleven variant readings of 1 Cor 2:4, see Thiselton, *First Epistle to the Corinthians*, 215–16; Perkins, *First Corinthians*, 52–53.

23. See §3.2 (a) above.

24. For κήρυγμα as the manner or act of speaking see Xenophon, *Ages.* 1.33; Barn. 12.6; Friedrich, "κῆρυξ, κτλ," 714 and note 2; BDAG "κήρυγμα," 543 §1.

25. For κήρυγμα as the content of the speaking, e.g., see Rom 16:25; 1 Cor 1:21; Friedrich, "κῆρυξ, κτλ," 714 and note 3; BDAG "κήρυγμα," 543 §2.

26. Conzelmann, *1 Corinthians*, 54; and the discussion by Thiselton, *First Epistle to the Corinthians*, 217–18.

27. The adjectival form πειθός ("persuasive") occurs only here in the NT and is otherwise unknown. See Conzelmann, *1 Corinthians*, 54–55; Pogoloff, *Logos and Sophia*, 137n25, who discusses the textual problems related to πειθός in 1 Cor 2:4; BDAG, "πειθός," 791.

28. On the status of λόγοις in 1 Cor 2.4, see Metzger, *Textual Commentary*, 481.

29. Cf. Quintilian, *Inst.* 2.15.3.

30. Pogoloff, *Logos and Sophia*, 137.

31. Twelftree, *Paul and the Miraculous*, 196–200, cf. 183.

32. As supposed by Polhill, "Wisdom of God and Factionalism," 331.

33. As supposed by Robertson and Plummer, *First Epistle of St. Paul to the Corinthians*, 33–34; Robinson, "Word and Power," 68–82; Ciampa and Rosner, *First Letter to the Corinthians*, 118; Fee, *First Epistle to the Corinthians*, 100.

that the word "power" by itself can mean a miracle,[34] and that Spirit and power are often used together in the context of the Spirit being responsible for unusual or miraculous activity,[35] Paul's expression "Spirit and power" (πνεύματος καὶ δυνάμεως, 2:4) refers to miracles. That he includes mention of the Spirit, rather than simply saying "powers" (δυνάμεις),[36] draws attention to the divine origin of the miracles.

How the miracles are related to his proclamation of Jesus Christ and him crucified is seen in him saying: "my message . . . in a demonstration of Spirit and of power" (ὁ λόγος μου . . . ἐν ἀποδείξει πνεύματος καὶ δυνάμεως). In rhetoric, a "demonstration" or "proof" (ἀπόδειξις)[37] was part of an argument,[38] "a method of proving what is not certain by means of what is certain," as Quintilian, the first century CE rhetorician put it.[39] For Paul the proof consists of the Spirit and power.[40] Therefore, Paul's gospel, which he has alluded to in his word "proclaim" (καταγγέλλω), and which is about a crucified figure, is convincing and acceptable not because of any expected orator's skill, but because of the miracles.[41] Or, put the other way, without the miracles Paul's message or gospel would be neither convincing nor acceptable. Therefore, though the assumption is that Paul's gospel is his message, it is dependent on the miraculous for its conviction, acceptance, and completion.

(c) Fathered through the gospel (1 Corinthians 4:14–21). So far, in this letter, the issue that has occupied Paul is his appeal for unity among the Corinthians (1:10—4:21). Part of Paul's solution is an attempt to reestablish his leadership, which appears in doubt.[42] What is of note for us is that, in part, he says, "though you might have countless guardians in Christ, you do

---

34. See p. 93n100 above.

35. See 1 Sam 11:6; Luke 1:17, 35; 4:14; Acts 1:8; 10:38; Rom 1:4; 15:19; 1 Thess 1:5.

36. See p. 93n100 above.

37. Though the noun ἀπόδειξις ("proof") is not otherwise found in the NT, the cognate verb, ἀποδείκνυμι ("to bring out" or "to show") occurs at Acts 2:22; 25:7; 1 Cor 4:9; 2 Thess 2:4.

38. E.g., see Aristotle, *Eth. nic.* 1.3; Quintilian, *Inst.* 5.10.7; Diogenes Laertius, *Lives* 7.45; Plato, *Tim.* 40e; *Phaed.* 77c.

39. Quintilian, *Inst.* 5.10.7.

40. Robertson and Plummer, *First Epistle of St. Paul to the Corinthians* 33: "The genitives are either subjective, 'demonstration proceeding from and wrought by the Spirit and power of God,' or qualifying, 'demonstration consisting in the spirit and power of God.'"

41. Cf. Fitzmyer, *First Corinthians*, 173.

42. See 1 Cor 1:1; 4:3; 9:1–3. Cf. Fee, *First Epistle to the Corinthians*, 199.

not have many fathers. For, in Christ Jesus, through the gospel, I fathered you" (4:15, my translation).

Paul might have been expected to use the verb "gospel" (εὐαγγελίζομαι) to describe the means of his fathering. Indeed, it is tempting to translate the noun in the verbal mode: "through proclaiming the gospel."[43] Instead, however, Paul uses the noun to say it was "through the gospel" (διὰ τοῦ εὐαγγελίου) he fathered them (1 Cor 4:15). This is the first time Paul has used the noun "gospel" in this letter. Unexplained, the key term was probably, therefore, part of their shared vocabulary. In any case, given his association of the verb—as the nature of his work—with his "message . . . of the cross" (ὁ λόγος . . . τοῦ σταυροῦ, 1:17), and that his message comes with authenticating miracles (2:1–5), the Corinthians are likely to take the noun "gospel" to refer to all that was involved in Paul's coming to them. In this is the explanation for why he uses the noun. In "the gospel" Paul is not referring simply to his message or preaching about past salvific acts,[44] but to all the Corinthians experienced in God's coming.[45]

(d) *All for the realization of the gospel (1 Corinthians 9:12–23).* Paul develops a number of themes in this letter. In particular, he gives attention to unity among the believers (1 Cor 1:10—4:21), sexual immorality (5:1–13; 6:12–20), lawsuits (6:1–11), marriage (7:1–40), food sacrificed to idols (8:1—11:1), spiritual gifts (12:1—15:40), and the resurrection (15:1–58). Yet, it is his apostleship that is the pedal note of this correspondence. From time to time the theme comes to the fore as it does here (9:1–27).[46] He has been urging an approach to eating meat sacrificed to idols that will not wound the conscience of the weak (8:12). As an example, he says he would never eat meat if it caused a believer to fall (8:13). This, Paul appears to assume, will play into the hands of the Corinthians for whom freedom of behavior was important.[47] They could, therefore, be expected to reply that if he was a true apostle he would not curb his freedom. Paul's defense is that, indeed, he is an apostle (9:1), including to the Corinthians (9:2), and that he has rights, including to food and drink (9:3–4), and to make a living from his work as an apostle (9:5–11). Yet, for the sake of not hindering the gospel, he does not make use of his freedom (9:12). In developing this idea

---

43. So Thiselton, *First Epistle to the Corinthians*, 370. Cf. Collins, *First Corinthians*, 195.

44. As suggested by Garland, *1 Corinthians*, 145.

45. There is no reason to take up the view of Oecumenius, *In Ep. I ad Cor.* 4.14 B (PG 118.693–94), that Paul has baptism in mind. See the discussion by Fitzmyer, *First Corinthians*, 222.

46. Also, e.g., see 1 Cor 1:10–17; 2:1–5; 3:5—4:21.

47. Barrett, *First Epistle to the Corinthians*, 200.

(9:12–23) Paul uses some form of the word "gospel" more than in any other section of his writings.[48] In doing so, fresh light is thrown on his notion of the gospel and his relation to it.

His opening statement on his rights in relation to the gospel is that he will "endure all things in order not to provide any obstacle to the gospel of Christ" (1 Cor 9:12, my translation). The noun "obstacle" (ἐγκοπή)—only used here in the New Testament[49]—referred to a hindrance, such as a road block, perhaps a temporary one.[50] Paul uses the verb "hinder" (ἐγκόπτω) of being prevented from visiting people.[51] But that is not his concern; neither is he suggesting his preaching would have been hindered.[52] Rather, he is echoing his major concern in the previous section on eating food offered to idols (8:1–13) that behavior can be a stumbling block (8:9) and cause others to fall away (8:13).[53] For him, Paul explains, to accept financial support from the Corinthians would be to put a stumbling block in the path of the gospel (9:12).[54] On this reading, the gospel seems to have an identity, force, or agency, and life independent of him.[55] The gospel is also something that can be misunderstood. Therefore, Paul seems to have in mind the cognitive and ethical dimension of the gospel. By the term "gospel of Christ," undoubtedly an objective genitive,[56] Paul would mean the gospel concerning Christ, as well as its ethical implications.

Developing the theme of his right to receive financial support for his work (1 Cor 9:3–12), Paul says that just as the temple priests share in what is sacrificed (9:13), "In the same way the Lord commanded that those who proclaim the gospel should get their living from the gospel" (9:14).[57]

48. In 1 Cor 9:12–23 the noun "gospel" (εὐαγγέλιον) occurs at 9:12, 14 (x2), 18 (x2), 23, that is six of the eight occurrences of the word in this letter. The verb "gospel" (εὐαγγελίζομαι) occurs at 9:16 (x2), 18, that is three of the six times the word occurs in this letter. The verb "proclaim" καταγγέλω occurs in 9:14, one of three occurrences in this letter.

49. However, Paul uses the verb ἐγκόπτω ("hinder") three times: Rom 15:22; Gal 5:7; 1 Thess 2:18. In the remainder of the NT, see Acts 24:4; 1 Pet 3:7.

50. Abbott-Smith, "ἐγκοπή," 155; Stählin, "ἐγκοπή, ἐγκόπτω," 855–56; BDAG, "ἐγκοπή," 274; Silva, "ἐγκόπτω; ἐγκοπή," 81–82.

51. Rom 15:22; 1 Thess 2:18. In the NT ἐγκόπτω also occurs at Acts 24:4; Gal 5:7; 1 Pet 3:7.

52. As implied by, e.g., Fee, *First Epistle to the Corinthians*, 454.

53. Cf. Hays, *First Corinthians* 152; Horsley, *1 Corinthians*, 127.

54. On the nature of the stumbling block see the helpful discussion by Garland, *1 Corinthians*, 419.

55. Cf. Schütz, *Paul and the Anatomy of Apostolic Authority*, 52.

56. Fitzmyer, *First Corinthians*, 365.

57. If asked, Paul would probably agree that he receives spiritual sustenance from

If Paul probably knew the saying about "the worker is worthy of reward"[58] and Jesus' mission charge from which it came, he will also have known the tradition about Jesus' instructions to them.[59] Thus, when Paul writes of those who "proclaim" (καταγγέλλω) the gospel (1 Cor 9:14), it is reasonable to assume his thinking will be informed by the tradition he received from Q that Jesus said to his followers: "cure the sick there and say the kingdom of God has come near to you" (Matt 10:7–8/Luke 10:9). Indeed, for Paul and his readers, the point we must not miss is that the force of his argument depends on Paul seeing his commission and work as the same as for those sent out by Jesus.[60] That is, what Paul describes as the gospel is not only a reference to the message, but, by association with the Lord's command, also alludes to the performing of healings and preaching the kingdom of God. Notwithstanding, while it is notable that the Lord's command, both to perform healings and to preach the kingdom of God, would be informing what he calls the gospel, from his use of "proclaim," his interest is focused more on the speaking or message of those sent out by Jesus (1 Cor 9:13).

Despite the Lord's command, which he saw gave him the right to make a living from his work, in less-than-clear sentences,[61] Paul explains why he has not accepted the Corinthians' financial support. One point that becomes clear is that he is, therefore, under no obligation except to Christ's will and the commission from him (1 Cor 9:17–18). Further clarity in his explanation of his motives comes when he says his working model is such that he can gospel "free of charge" (ἀδάπανος, 9:18). His model of working is, therefore, a model of the free nature of the gospel.[62]

Twice here Paul uses "gospel" as a verb to describe his work.[63] In light of him having just said "I proclaim" (καταγγέλλω, 1 Cor 9:14) the gospel, we might have expected him to repeat that here, but he does not. Instead, while his attention seems to be on proclamation (9:14), his vocabulary hints at the gospel being more than words.

Paul began this section saying he would endure anything rather than put an obstacle in the path of the gospel (1 Cor 9:12). In the same tone, at

---

the gospel. Cf. Garland, *1 Corinthians*, 416. But that is not the point of Paul's narrative.

58. Luke 10:7, my translation. See §2.3 (b) (i) above.

59. See Fjärstedt, *Synoptic Tradition in 1 Corinthians*, 66–77. Cf. Allison, "Paul and the Missionary Discourse," 371–72. See the more detailed discussion in Twelftree, *Paul and the Miraculous*, 120–22.

60. Cf. §2.2 (b) above.

61. For a discussion of the confusion and complexity of Paul's expression, see Fee, *First Epistle to the Corinthians*, 457–59.

62. Cf. Fee, *First Epistle to the Corinthians*, 459.

63. 1 Cor 9:16: εὐαγγελίζωμαι and εὐαγγελίσωμαι.

the end of his explanation signaled by his "now then" (δέ),[64] Paul concludes: "I do all for the sake of the gospel, in order that I may share in it" (9:23, my translation). In this statement the gospel is clearly his life's great passion.[65] As in the opening statement (9:12), he refers to the gospel not as if it was his message,[66] but of something larger and independent of him. Given his echo of the Jesus saying (9:14; cf. Luke 10:7) is pivotal and dominates this section (9:12–23), the most natural way to understand what Paul means by "gospel" is, according to the tradition he has received, as Jesus commanded to his followers, including himself, to cure the sick and preach that the kingdom of God has come near.[67]

Paul's final purpose clause—the reason he does all for the sake of the gospel—is "in order that I might share in it" (ἵνα συγκοινωνός αὐτοῦ γένωμαι, 1 Cor 9:23). On a first reading it could be that Paul's purpose is to secure his own personal salvation[68] or to have others share in the work[69] or to reap the benefits or blessings of the gospel.[70] But that is not the point of what he has been saying (9:12–23).

Paul's other two uses of "share with" (συγκοινωνός) provide the clue to what he probably has in mind. First, in writing to the Philippians—a church probably largely made up of gentiles (Phil 2:25; 4:2–3)[71]—Paul writes of them sharing God's grace with him (1:7). Then, second, in his metaphor of the olive tree, which he uses in Romans to describe the grafting of the gentiles into the people of God so they could "participate in" or "share" (συγκοινωνός) the rich root stock, Paul's focus is on the Jewish-gentile composite nature of the new people of God (Rom 11:17).[72] By extrapolation, writing to the Corinthians, Paul is passionate about the gospel not simply because the work is valuable,[73] but because he will be able to share in its realization of both Jews and gentiles having a place in God's people.[74] That

64. Fee, *First Epistle to the Corinthians*, 476n383.

65. Thiselton, *First Epistle to the Corinthians*, 707; Fee, *First Epistle to the Corinthians*, 476.

66. Cf. Fee, *First Epistle to the Corinthians*, 476.

67. Cf. §2.2 (b) above.

68. Conzelmann, *1 Corinthians*, 161; Martin, *Slavery as Salvation*, 132.

69. Parry, *First Epistle of Paul*, 143.

70. Fee, *First Epistle to the Corinthians*, 476.

71. Cf. Hawthorne and Martin, *Philippians*, xxxviii.

72. See the extensive discussion in Esler, *Conflict and Identity in Romans*.

73. Cf. Hooker, "Partner in the Gospel," 89; Volf, *Paul and Perseverance*, 248–51; Garland, *1 Corinthians*, 437.

74. Note the discussion by Thiselton, *First Epistle to the Corinthians*, 707.

is, the gospel, which Paul does not want to hinder and which is the Lord's command to him to cure the sick and preach the kingdom of God, is realized in all people—including Paul—sharing in it.

(e) The gospel of the Lord's death (1 Corinthians 11:26). In the context of reprimanding the Corinthians for the divisions among them, evident in the way they behave when they come together (11:17–34), Paul relates the tradition about the Lord's Supper that he has received (11:23–25). His purpose—clear in using "for" (γάρ)—is to show that their behavior when eating together should be governed by the words and actions of Jesus at the Last Supper.[75] What makes this passage important in helping understand Paul's gospel is that, at the conclusion of repeating the received tradition, he says, "For as often as you eat this bread and drink the cup, you proclaim (καταγγέλλετε) the Lord's death until he comes" (11:26).[76]

Paul may be alluding to a verbal proclamation of the death of Christ that took place during the meal.[77] However, Paul's concern is with the significance of the meal itself, and a proclamation could on occasion be an event or deed,[78] as it could be for Paul.[79] Moreover, "proclaim" (καταγγέλλω) may normally have been verbal,[80] but the plain sense of Paul's statement—"as often as you eat" (ὁσάκις γάρ ἐάν ἐσθίητε, 1 Cor 11:26)—and his focus on their behavior (11:27–29), point to the meal itself and participation in it as the proclamation.[81]

We have already seen that early in this letter Paul uses "proclaim" (καταγγέλλω) to evoke the gospel as the focus of his work.[82] And we have just seen him use καταγγέλλω in relation to the gospel. Moreover, the other

75. Barrett, *First Epistle to the Corinthians*, 264.

76. The amount of literature discussing 1 Cor 11:23–26 is, to say the least, enormous. A relatively recent bibliography is provided by Fitzmyer, *First Corinthians*, 448–53.

77. E.g., Käsemann, "Pauline Doctrine of the Lord's Supper," 120–21; Jeremias, *Eucharistic Words of Jesus*, 106–7, 253; Bornkamm, *Early Christian Experience*, 141; Neuenzeit, *Das Herrenmahl*, 132; Barrett, *First Epistle to the Corinthians*, 270; Fee, *First Epistle to the Corinthians*, 616.

78. See 2 Macc 8:36; Philo, *Creation* 106; *Eternity*, 68; Josephus, *Ant.* 2.15, 85, all discussed by Gaventa, "'You Proclaim the Lord's Death,'" 381–82.

79. Gaventa, "'You Proclaim the Lord's Death,'" 381–83, notes that in 1 Thess 1:4–5, 8, action and faith can proclaim the gospel.

80. Dahl, "Anamnesis," 85; Schniewind, "ἀγγελία," 72; Bornkamm, *Early Christian Experience*, 141; BDAG, "καταγγέλλω," 515.

81. E.g., also, see Weiss, *Der erste Korintherbrief*, 288; Lietzmann, *An die Korinther I/II*, 58; Lenski, *Corinthians*, 474; Héring, *First Epistle of Saint Paul*, 118–19; Thrall, *II Corinthians*, 84. Also, Gaventa, "'You Proclaim the Lord's Death,'" 381–83, notes 1 Thess 1:4–5, 8, that, for Paul, action and faith can proclaim the gospel.

82. 1 Cor 2:1; see §4.1 (b) above.

uses of καταγγέλλω in the New Testament generally refer to preaching the gospel or Christ.[83] So clearly, then, does καταγγέλλω evoke the gospel, and so closely does Paul otherwise associate the word with the gospel that his statement here shows that the Lord's death was part of his gospel.[84] In turn, three points of what Paul says about the death of Jesus show the part it played in his gospel. First, the context of his statement tells us how that death was interpreted. Notable is the line: "This is my body for you" (1 Cor 11:24). Given Paul's consistent use of "for" (ὑπέρ) in relation to Christ's death, he understands the death to be on "our behalf" or in "our place."[85]

Second, the line associated with the cup taken after supper, "This cup is the new covenant in my blood" (1 Cor 11:25), interprets Jesus' death as the ratification of the new covenant Jeremiah prophesied about (Jer 31:31). That is, Paul took his gospel to be proclaiming the heart-inscribed, eschatological covenant or relationship with God which the prophet anticipated (31:31–34). Paul's mention of blood also brings into play the imagery of the covenant of Mount Sinai (Exod 24:1–11). In Paul's thinking as well as his gospel, then, the death of Christ as the ratification of a covenant underlines God's gracious faithfulness to his people (cf. Rom 9–11; esp. 9:4) in providing for their redemption.[86]

Third, Paul says that in the shared meal the Corinthians are proclaiming the death of Christ "until he comes" (1 Cor 11:26). Whether this is the point at which observing the meal is to stop,[87] or it echoes the "*maranatha*" or "Our Lord, come!" prayer (15:22) reminding God of the unfulfilled work of salvation,[88] the gospel involving Christ's death points forward rather than back to its fulfillment.[89] Thus, as he encouraged the Thessalonians, their lives were to be ones of expectant waiting (1 Thess 1:10).

---

83. Acts 4:2; 13:5, 38; 15:36; 16:17, 21; 17:3, 13, 23; Rom 1:8; 1 Cor 2:1; 9:14; Phil 1:17, 18; Col 1:28. The exceptions are Acts 3:24, which refers to the proclamation of the prophets, and Acts 26:23, which refers to the proclamation of the risen Messiah. Cf. Schniewind, "ἀγγελία," 71–72: "in Paul, and in Acts καταγγέλλειν reflects directly the language of mission."

84. Cf. Hays, *First Corinthians*, 197.

85. See 1 Cor 15:3; Rom 5:6, 8; 2 Cor 5:21; Gal 3:13, and the brief discussion by Fee, *First Epistle to the Corinthians*, 610. Also, e.g., see Thiselton, *First Epistle to the Corinthians*, 877–78; Fitzmyer, *First Corinthians*, 439; Hays, *First Corinthians*, 198. More recently, among the great number of contributions to the discussion on the understanding of Jesus' death in Paul's language here, see Gathercole, *Defending Substitution*.

86. Cf. Thiselton, *First Epistle to the Corinthians*, 885.

87. E.g., see Lenski, *Corinthians*, 474.

88. Jeremias, *Eucharistic Words of Jesus*, 253.

89. Cf. Fee, *First Epistle to the Corinthians*, 616–17.

(f) The gospel gospelled (1 Corinthians 15:1-2). With our interests focused squarely on understanding Paul's idea of the gospel there are many issues in this well-ploughed section of the letter that we will not need to engage.⁹⁰ Though he does not signal with his usual "Now concerning...,"⁹¹ Paul begins a new topic: the resurrection of the dead. Paul has heard, perhaps through Stephanas, Fortunatus, and Achaicus,⁹² that "some of you say there is no resurrection of the dead."⁹³ In responding to this view, Paul starts his argument by reminding his readers of the importance of Christ's resurrection from the dead in his gospel.⁹⁴ He begins:

> Now I make known to you, brothers and sisters,⁹⁵ the gospel that I gospelled (εὐαγγέλιον ὃ εὐηγγελισάμην) to you, and which you received, in which also you stand, through which also you are being saved, if you hold firmly to the message (λόγῳ) that I gospelled (εὐηγγελισάμην) to you, unless you have come to believe in vain. (1 Cor 15:1-2)

Using the technical language for the preservation of material or tradition,⁹⁶ he goes on to set out what he had received and handed on to the Corinthians in that gospel:

> that Christ died for our sins in accordance with the scriptures, and that he was buried, and that he was raised on the third day in accordance with the scriptures, and that he appeared to Cephas, then to the twelve. (1 Cor 15:3b-5)

---

90. For a helpful selection from the enormous secondary literature on this section of 1 Corinthians see Thiselton, *First Epistle to the Corinthians*, 1178-82.

91. Περὶ δέ ("Now concerning"): 1 Cor 7:1, 25; 8:1; 12:1; 16:1, 12.

92. 1 Cor 16:17. On Paul hearing reports also see 5:1; 11:18.

93. 1 Cor 15:12, and echoed in 16, 29, and 32.

94. Cf. Barrett, *First Epistle to the Corinthians*, 335.

95. Although Paul uses the word ἀδελφοί ("brothers"), in such a general address he is referring to men and women. Notably, in Phil 4:1 he addresses his readers as ἀδελφοί, immediately proceeding to address two women. Cf. Fee, *First Epistle to the Corinthians*, 53n21.

96. Important treatments of the "receive" (παραλαμβάνω) and "hand on" (παραδίδωμι) language, in the technical sense of material or tradition being preserved (cf. 1 Cor 11:23), include Cullmann, "Tradition," 59-99; Hunter, *Paul and His Predecessors*, 15-35; Neufeld, *Earliest Christian Confessions*, 42-68; Cambier, "Paul and Tradition," 53-63; Kramer, *Christ, Lord, Son of God*, 19-44; Kloppenborg, "Analysis of the Pre-Pauline Formula."

Given that these lines are widely, if not entirely, agreed to be the extent of the tradition that concerns Paul,[97] the gospel is a miniature, part-biography of Christ that focuses on the end of his life—his death, burial, resurrection—as well as on his appearance to his inner-circle of followers. The gospel that Paul gospelled is, then, both the story of Jesus and, in mention of the appearances, the verification of that material. Further, Paul goes on to include himself in the verification—"Last of all, as to one untimely born, he appeared also to me" (15:8)—enabling him to vouch for, and therefore establish, the reliability of the gospel he gospelled to them, which, he says, saves them (15:2).[98] In more detail, from the creedal material that he has handed on to them, the Corinthians will know, and are being reminded, that this salvation is centered in the statement "that Christ died for our sins" (15:3).[99]

From the way he has begun this section—"Now I make known to you" (Γνωρίζω δὲ ὑμῖν, 1 Cor 15:1)—it appears that Paul is introducing the reader to ideas.[100] There is no doubt that γνωρίζω[101] means to "make known" new knowledge,[102] as it does otherwise for Paul[103] and other New Testament writers,[104] along with other writers of the period.[105] Nevertheless, Paul can use γνωρίζω with a meaning shading to "clarify, explain, or make explicit," as when he "explains" speaking in tongues (1 Cor 12:3),[106] something his

---

97. On the discussion see the succinct note by Fee, *First Epistle to the Corinthians*, 802n50.

98. "Saves" is in the present tense (σῴζεσθε), denoting what is being done for them in the present for the future. See Robertson and Plummer, *First Epistle of St. Paul to the Corinthians*, 331; Thiselton, *First Epistle to the Corinthians*, 1185; Fee, *First Epistle to the Corinthians*, 800.

99. On Paul's treatment of the sacrificial death of Jesus, e.g., see Dunn, *Theology of Paul the Apostle*, §9.2.

100. A succinct summary of the debate on how Paul is to be translated here is offered by Thiselton, *First Epistle to the Corinthians*, 1183.

101. Radl, "Der Sinn von γνωρίζω," 243–45.

102. E.g., MGS, "γνωρίζω," 437.

103. Paul uses γνωρίζω in Rom 9:22, 23; 16:26; 1 Cor 12:3; 15:1; 2 Cor 8:1; Gal 1:11; Phil 1:22; 4:6.

104. Luke 2:15, 17; John 15:15; 17:26 (x2); Acts 2:28; Eph 1:9; 3:3, 5, 10; 6:19, 21; Col 1:27; 4:7, 9; 2 Pet 1:16.

105. BDAG, "γνωρίζω," 203, citing, e.g., Diodorus Siculus, *Bibliotheca historica* 1.6.2; 10.3.1; Plutarch, *Cat. Maj.* 1.2; Josephus, *Ant.* 8.102.

106. Plutarch, *Fab.* 21.3, the example cited by Grimm and Thayer, *Greek-English Lexicon*, 119 (col. 2), does not, as they suggest, use γνωρίζω "to recall to one's mind as though what is made known had escaped him," but as "make known." Thus, BDAG, "γνωρίζω," 203 (1).

readers already know about. Indeed, in the passage of interest to us here, Paul goes on to make known to them what he has already handed on to them (1 Cor 15:3–7). Therefore, in using γνωρίζω, Paul is reminding his readers of the gospel he has handed on to them when he was with them.[107] Given the similarity of topics between this "gospel" and his initial or missionary message to the Thessalonians,[108] it is reasonable to conclude that for the Corinthians, and probably people in other cities such as Thessalonika, this was at least part of what they initially heard from Paul when the gospel was introduced to them.

However, it cannot be concluded, as did Hans Conzelmann, that the words or the tradition Paul received and handed on constitute the entirety of Paul's understanding of the gospel. Conzelmann supposed that when the propositions (the gospel) encounter a person, "they go into action, so to speak—and this, too, by their own very nature: they mediate the event of salvation."[109] However, from what Paul says, his gospel here is not in the words but what is represented by the words, the death, burial, resurrection, and appearance of Jesus to his followers.

(g) Results. The gospel in 1 Corinthians. As we have just seen from his close attention to traditions he had received and then handed on to his readers, Paul sees himself as dealing with ideas, and those ideas he can take to be the gospel. It is striking, then, that only twice does he refer to his work as preaching (Gal 2:2; 1 Thess 2:9). Instead, he commonly says he was sent "to gospel" (εὐαγγελίζεσθαι, e.g., 1 Cor 1:17). It could be that Paul wanted to convey the idea that his preaching was inherently what "gospel" (εὐαγγέλιον) implied: good news.

However, we have already seen that Paul so variously defines and describes the gospel, and has reminded his readers of its coming in such a way, that in his term "to gospel" he is more likely capturing the notion that there was more about the good news than good news. From other letters of his we have seen what is also clear in 1 Corinthians: his message and proclamation came in or "with a demonstration of Spirit and power" (1 Cor 2:4). This shows that his proclamation was dependent on the miraculous for its expression, acceptance, and results as gospel. This is not surprising in that Paul saw his commission as the same as those who were sent out by Jesus.[110] Indeed, by the term "gospel" he can refer to all that his readers experience in

---

107. Contra Radl, "Der Sinn von γνωρίζω," 243.

108. See §3.2 (a) 1 above.

109. Conzelmann, *1 Corinthians*, 249. Similarly, Wright, "Paul as Preacher," 137. See p. 14n105 above.

110. Cf.§2.2 (b) above.

God's coming to them (4:15), including its inherent ethical demands. Thus, he can bring his gospelling, his message, the cross, the power of God, and salvation into a symbiotic relationship. The gospel for Paul, then, has a life and force independent from him. The gospel is not, or not only, his words, but what they represent. As news is not the events reported, but reflects events, so Paul's good news is not the gospel but a verbal representation of it.

§4.2 2 CORINTHIANS

(a) The gospel of Christ (2 Corinthians 2:12). In writing this letter[111] Paul is aware that the recipients are critical of him, not least in him not visiting them (1:12—2:4). At one point in explaining his movements he says that in "Coming to Troas[112] for the gospel of Christ an opportunity for me opened in the Lord" (2:12).

In using the preposition "to" (εἰς) to indicate purpose,[113] the phrase εἰς τὸ εὐαγγέλιον τοῦ Χριστοῦ is to be understood as saying that Paul came to Troas "for [the purpose of] the gospel of Christ."[114] However, though it is assumed,[115] there is nothing in what Paul says to suggest that he is thinking particularly of preaching. Indeed, with Paul using the noun (εὐαγγέλιον) rather than a verb (εὐαγγελίζω) there is less reason than usual to supply the idea of preaching.[116]

The term "gospel of Christ" could be understood in a number of ways. As a subjective genitive it could be the gospel Christ brought. Since we have not so far seen this use by Paul, this is not likely what he had in mind. Alternatively, as an objective genitive it could be the gospel about

---

111. On the theories relating to the composition, unity, and dating of Paul's letters to the Corinthians, see p. 133n3 above.

112. The debate over whether the article should be read with Troas (τὴν Τρῳάδα), that is the region of Troas, or without the article, indicating Troas, need not detain us. See Thrall, *II Corinthians*, 2:182-83; Harris, *Second Epistle to the Corinthians*, 236-37. Cf. BDAG, "Τρῳάς," 1019.

113. See Robertson, *Grammar of the Greek New Testament*, 595; Harris, *Second Epistle to the Corinthians*, 237.

114. Cf. Harris, *Second Epistle to the Corinthians*, 237. Furnish, *II Corinthians*, 169, takes εἰς τὸ εὐαγγέλιον as a functional equivalent of διὰ τὸ εὐαγγέλιον ("on account of the gospel").

115. E.g., see Windisch, *Die zweite Korintherbrief*, 94; Schütz, *Apostolic Authority*, 41n1; Barrett, *Second Epistle to the Corinthians*, 94; Harris, *Second Epistle to the Corinthians*, 235; Martin, *2 Corinthians*, 179; NRSV.

116. Also Furnish, *II Corinthians*, 169.

Christ. From what we have seen so far this is most likely.[117] However, as a "comprehensive genitive"[118] it could be that Paul understood the gospel was both about Christ and was brought with Christ's presence.[119] There is some merit in this suggestion in that Paul goes on to say that a door or opportunity[120] remained open[121] "in the Lord" (ἐν κυρίῳ) clarifying that the Lord was making the gospel possible.[122] It should probably be concluded that Paul is saying that the Lord made it possible for the gospel about Christ to come to Troas.

(b) Our gospel (2 Corinthians 4:3-5). This is one of two occasions Paul uses the term "our gospel" (τὸ εὐαγγέλιον ἡμῶν).[123] The phrase comes in the context of the climax of his self-defense of his ministry (4:1-6). He began his defense by asserting that he does not peddle (καπηλεύω)[124] God's word as merchandise for profit like many others. Instead, he claims he is sincere, sent by and standing in the presence of God (2:17). So, in contrasting his ministry with others it is not surprising Paul should use the term "our gospel" (4:3). However, it is probably not the content of the gospel that is at issue but its propagation, for Paul's interest is particularly in his activity in relation to its propagation. He says, "We have renounced the shameful things that one hides; we refuse to practice cunning or to falsify God's word; but by the open statement of the truth we commend ourselves to the conscience of everyone in the sight of God" (4:2). Hence, when he goes straight on to talk positively about his work, he uses the term "to proclaim" (κηρύσσειν, 4:5) rather than the more encompassing term "to gospel" (εὐαγγελίζειν) that we are seeing in this project involves more than his speaking. In short, here, "our gospel" (4:3) is, in contrast to his opponents, Paul's open, sincere proclamation sent

---

117. See §3.4 (b) above.

118. The term is that of Spicq, *Theological Lexicon of the New Testament*, 2:89n35.

119. Zerwick, *Biblical Greek*, 13, §37; Harris, *Second Epistle to the Corinthians*, 237 and note 16.

120. For an open door as a metaphor for opportunity see 1 Cor 16:9; Col 4:3; Rev 3:8; 4:1; cf. Acts 14:27; 16:26, 27; Rev 3:20. For the closed door as the loss of an opportunity see Matt 25:10; Acts 21:30.

121. Paul uses the perfect passive participle, ἀνεῳγμένης ("opened"), an implied divine passive. Cf. Harris, *Second Epistle to the Corinthians*, 238; Martin, *2 Corinthians*, 179.

122. Cf. Harris, *Second Epistle to the Corinthians*, 237-38.

123. See p. 81n17 above.

124. The verb καπηλεύω ("peddle" or "huckster"), carrying the connotation of avarice (cf. Josephus, *Ag. Ap.* 1.61) and trickery (cf. Anthologia Palatina 9.229.1), is only used here in the NT, reminiscent of its use by Plato (*Prot.* 313c, d) in the polemic against opponents. See Windisch, "καπηλεύω," 603-5; BDAG, "καπηλεύω," 508; MGS, "καπηλεύω," 1033.

by God (2:17), which he says is "of the glory of Christ, who is the image of God" (4:4).

(c) The gospel lived (2 Corinthians 8:18). Paul's collection of money for the believers in Jerusalem was very important to him.[125] In order to head off potential criticism, not least in relation to this financial exercise (8:20–21), and also of arrangements for delivering the funds to Jerusalem (Rom 15:3–31), Paul commends three individuals who are traveling to Corinth for him.[126] One of them, Titus, is going on his own initiative (2 Cor 8:17). The other two are unnamed (8:18–22),[127] which is surprising as Paul generally names those he is commending to others.[128] Of one, Paul says, "With him [Titus] we are sending the brother who is famous in the gospel among all the churches" (8:18). The extent of the praise or fame (ἔπαινος) need not concern us[129] beyond noting that he is described as a person well known and regarded. Instead, what is of interest to us is the individual's reputation "in the gospel" (ἐν τῷ εὐαγγελίῳ). It could be Paul is referring to the person as a well-known evangelist[130] or preacher of the gospel.[131] This, however, would be a strained interpretation of the noun[132] where the verb "gospel" could be expected to express the idea. A more natural reading of what Paul has written becomes obvious in recalling that in writing to the Philippians he uses the same expression which was argued to refer to lives that expressed and confirmed the gospel of Paul's ministry.[133] In the same letter Paul uses a similar phrase (εἰς τὸ εὐαγγέλιον, Phil 1:5) to describe both experienced

---

125. Rom 15:25–32; 1 Cor 16:1–4; 2 Cor 8:1—9:15; Gal 2:10; cf. Acts 11:27–30; 24:17. Note the brief discussion, including a note by D. J. Downs, and extensive bibliography in Martin, *2 Corinthians*, 416–27.

126. Harris, *Second Epistle to the Corinthians*, 600.

127. See the discussion by Barrett, *Second Epistle to the Corinthians*, 228, on the possibility that one individual (2 Cor 8:18) is the brother of Titus on the grounds that the article (τὸν) with "brother" (τὸν ἀδελφόν) is equivalent to the possessive pronoun, citing Robertson, *Grammar of the Greek New Testament*, 770. However, Thrall, *II Corinthians*, 2:561, points out that in a discussion of the possible identity of the delegates, in such a sensitive situation Paul is unlikely to send two brothers, and "the ἀδελφοὶ ἡμῶν ['our brothers'] of v. 23 shows that the term ἀδελφός ['brother'] does not in the present context, refer to a blood relationship."

128. Thrall, *II Corinthians*, 2:557. Chan-Hie, *Form and Structure*, 120, notes that of the Pauline epistles only 2 Corinthians and Galatians lack recommendations.

129. See the discussions by Furnish, *II Corinthians*, 422, and Martin, *2 Corinthians*, 453.

130. Noted by Martin, *2 Corinthians*, 453, referring to Eph 4:11.

131. Thrall, *II Corinthians*, 2:548 citing, e.g., Chrysostom, PG 61.524; Lang, *2 Korinther 5,1–10*, 321; Wolff, *Der zweite Brief des Paulus an die Korinther*, 177.

132. Cf. also Furnish, *II Corinthians*, 422.

133. On Phil 4:3 see §3.4 (e) above.

grace and the subject of Paul's ministry.[134] In light of these uses of "in the gospel," here in 2 Corinthians, Paul is also probably using the expression to refer to a reputation for a life and work expressing, and consistent with, the subject of Paul's ministry. In other words, here "gospel" is something that can be lived and expressed in an individual's life.[135]

(d) Confession of and obedience to the gospel of Christ (2 Corinthians 9:13). With this section (9:1-15) we may be reading a separate and distinct letter from Paul.[136] Even if this is a letter sent at a different time than what is now chapter 8, the topic remains Paul's collection for the poor believers in Jerusalem. In encouraging his Corinthian readers to contribute, he says: "Through the approval of this ministry you are glorifying God by your obedience to the confession of the gospel of Christ and by the generosity of your sharing with them and with all others" (9:13, my translation).

According to Paul, it is the Jerusalem believers who will glorify God because of the obedience of the Corinthians believers, which will be evident both in their confession and their generosity.[137] Although Paul does not otherwise use this noun "confession" (ὁμολογία), given that its other uses by New Testament writers[138] and Paul's two uses of the verb "confess" (ὁμολογέω, Rom 10:9, 10) relate to confession in the religious sense, here he can be taken to refer to a confession of faith.[139] Thus, in his phrase "your confession of the gospel of Christ,"[140] the gospel of Christ is the complex of religious ideas about Christ[141] that is confessed. The obedience of their confession could be to God.[142] However, in view of the reason for Paul writing—to gain financial assistance for the poor—and his saying elsewhere

---

134. See §3.4 (a) above.

135. Cf. §3.4 (a) above.

136. See p. 133n3 above.

137. The distinctive view of Betz, *2 Corinthians 8 and 9*, 122-25, that "confession" (ὁμολογία) is used of a contractual agreement regulating the relationship between Jerusalem and those contributing to the collection, and the Corinthians' "obedience" (ὑποταγή) is their acknowledgment of that contract, is not widely shared. See the discussions by Thrall, *II Corinthians*, 2:589-90, and O'Mahony, *Pauline Persuasion*, 172-74.

138. 1 Tim 6:12-13; Heb 3:1; 4:14; 10:23.

139. See the insightful discussion by Thrall, *II Corinthians*, 2:589-90.

140. 2 Cor 9:13: Τῆς ὁμολογίας ὑμῶν εἰς τὸ εὐαγγέλιον τοῦ Χριστοῦ.

141. The genitive ("the gospel of Christ," τὸ εὐαγγέλιον τοῦ Χριστοῦ) is most reasonably objective (about Christ). Contrary to Harris, *Second Epistle to the Corinthians*, 654n42, it is unlikely to be an example of a comprehensive genitive (see p. 148n118 above) as Paul does not otherwise describe the gospel as brought by Christ, but frequently describes the gospel as being about Christ. See §5.2 below.

142. NEB, REB, noted by Harris, *Second Epistle to the Corinthians*, 654.

that believers are to contribute to the needs of other believers (12:13) and to bear each other's burdens (Gal 6:2), the obedience more likely refers to subjection to the requirements of the gospel.[143] That the gospel, as a complex of religious ideas, involves behavioral elements or has ethical implications is something that we came across when we attempted to reconstruct the gospel Paul initially communicated to his readers in Thesssalonica.[144]

(e) First with the gospel of Christ (2 Corinthians 10:14). Here in a digression Paul is explaining that his God-given authority legitimizes his work among the Corinthians (10:12–18). We have already noted that in carrying out his work Paul insists he has not encroached on the territory of other missionaries.[145] He says: "For we were not overstepping our limits when we reached you; for we were the first to come to you with the gospel of Christ" (10:14, my translation). Paul's phrase is "in (ἐν) the gospel of Christ." Here the preposition "in" (ἐν) is to be translated "with" as it designates the circumstances of Paul's coming "with the gospel of Christ."[146] Once again, though it is assumed,[147] Paul says nothing that would give the impression that he is referring to his preaching for he uses the noun (εὐαγγέλιον) rather than a verb (εὐαγγελίζω) for "gospel."[148] The term "gospel of Christ" is most likely an objective genitive—the gospel is about Christ—though it could be another example of a comprehensive genitive through which Paul expresses his view that the gospel was about Christ as well as brought with Christ's presence.[149]

(f) A different gospel—at a cost (2 Corinthians 11:4, 7). In his appeal to the Corinthians to bear with him (11:1–4) Paul says he has a divine jealousy for them. He also says that he is fearful of them being corrupted and led astray from their "sincerity" or "devotion" (ἁπλότης) to Christ (11:3). He goes on to say: "For if someone comes and preaches another Jesus whom we did not preach—or if you receive a different spirit from the one you received, or a different gospel from the one you accepted—you tolerate it readily enough" (11:4). In this conditional sentence ("If someone comes . . . you tolerate it") with its present tenses, "preach" (κηρύσσει) and "receive" or

---

143. BDAG, "ὁμολογία," 709, §2. Cf. Harris, *Second Epistle to the Corinthians*, 654.

144. See §3.2 (a) 1 above on 1 Thess 1:9–10.

145. See §2.4 (e) above.

146. BDAG "ἐν," 326–30 (328, §5, citing 2 Cor 10:14); Harris, *Second Epistle to the Corinthians*, 718.

147. E.g., Barrett, *Second Epistle to the Corinthians*, 266; Furnish, *II Corinthians*, 472; Martin, *2 Corinthians*, 505.

148. Cf. §4.2 (a) above on 2 Cor 2:12.

149. See §4.2 (a) above.

"grasp" (λαμβάνετε) a present reality rather than a hypothetical situation is being described.[150]

This much-discussed statement of Paul's, though primarily useful for what it tells us about his opponents,[151] is able to shed some light on the gospel according to Paul. From what we are seeing so far, it is surprising and notable that he uses the term "proclaim" or "preach" (κηρύσσω) to describe the activity of his opponent[152] and, by implication, his own. *Prima facie* it may seem reasonable to think that preaching was also involved in the reception of the Spirit and acceptance of the gospel. However, while Jesus is preached, the Corinthians "grasp" (λαμβάνετε) the Spirit, suggesting more is assumed than listening.

This conditional sentence ("If someone comes ... you submit") is focused on the preaching of another Jesus. Embedded in it are the parallel statements about the Spirit and the gospel that, through an initial disjunctive "or" (ἤ), are linked to, yet distinct from, the preaching. This suggests that Paul assumes that the preaching of another Jesus is distinct from, yet gave rise to, a different spirit and gospel.[153]

In light of what we have seen of Paul's description of the coming of the gospel to the Thessalonians,[154] the distinction between the preaching and the gospel is not a too-subtle one. Rather, the distinction turns out to be significant in understanding the gospel according to Paul. In any case, the use of the noun "gospel" (εὐαγγέλιον) in the present context enables us to add to our understanding of what Paul has in mind.

Paul also uses the term, "another gospel" (εὐαγγέλιον ἕτερον, 2 Cor 11:4) in Galatians, though with the two words reversed. In writing to the Galatians, Paul says he is astonished that his readers are so quickly turning to "another gospel" (ἕτερον εὐαγγέλιον, Gal 1:6), which we learn is a gospel of works of the law (3:2). However, this information is of little use to us here.[155] There is nothing in what Paul says here to suggest that a gospel of works is a problem at Corinth. Instead, the issue is the rejection of his authority and the associated infiltration of an opponent (2 Cor 11:4). However, there

---

150. Cf. Harris, *Second Epistle to the Corinthians*, 742, citing Zerwick, *Biblical Greek*, §311; and Martin, *2 Corinthians*, 520, drawing attention to 2 Cor 11:19–21.

151. Käsemann, "Die Legitimität des Apostels," 36–41.

152. Given the singular here (ὁ ἐρχόμενος, "the one coming," 2 Cor 11:4) and the plurals in, e.g., 11:13 (ψευδαπόστολοι ["false apostles"], ἐργάται δόλιοι ["deceitful workers"], ἀποστόλους ["apostles"]), the opponent referred to is probably to be taken as the leader. Cf. Martin, *2 Corinthians*, 520.

153. Wolff, *Der zweite Brief des Paulus an die Korinther*, 215.

154. On 1 Thess 1:4–5, see §3.2 (a) above.

155. Furnish, *II Corinthians*, 502.

is also nothing in what Paul says to suggest that this is motivating Paul's rhetoric.[156]

In that the preaching of another Jesus has given rise to the acceptance of a different gospel, an understanding of this other Jesus can be expected to help us understand the different gospel, which, in turn, can be expected to help us gain further insight into Paul's understanding of his gospel. Since Paul does not explain the difference between his Jesus and the Jesus of his opponent, we are left to read the text carefully and modestly for clues.[157]

The context of Paul's charge that we are examining (2 Cor 11:4) is the personal defense he makes in preparation for his third visit.[158] In this part of his correspondence that is now 2 Corinthians, even though the resurrection is a recurring motif,[159] the Jesus Paul promotes is one of meekness, gentleness (10:1), weakness (13:4), and even of one made to be sin (5:21). Indeed, the first description of Christ in 2 Corinthians is one of suffering (1:5). Not surprisingly, then, in that he sees believers as betrothed to this Christ (11:2), he also portrays himself as weak (esp. 12:1-10). Paul had already said that he is always carrying in his body the death of Jesus (4:10, cf. 11).

Paul's boasting in his weakness (2 Cor 1:21—12:10) strongly suggests that his opponents—he calls them super-apostles (11:5; 12:11)—were doing the opposite. He implies they are better public speakers (11:6) and that they were accomplished miracle workers (12:11-13). In the context of attacking his opponents, Paul's defensive statement that he brought the gospel without cost (11:7) and that he did not burden the Corinthians—but "robbed other churches by accepting support from them in order to serve you" (11:8)—implies that his opponents were charging for their services. It seems from what he has already said in his correspondence with the Corinthians that he saw it as a right for an apostle to be supported financially.[160] However, it seems that only after he had moved on from a church he had founded did he accept financial support from it. Hence, while among the Corinthians, he sought his support from other churches (11:8), a practice in this case that cost him dearly in terms of their respect of him,[161] even if it did allow the gospel to come freely.

In Paul's statement, "without cost I brought the gospel of God to you" (2 Cor 11:7), the emphasis is on "without cost" (δωρεάν), drawing attention

---

156. To the contrary, see Furnish, *II Corinthians*, 502.
157. Cf. Matera, *II Corinthians*, 243.
158. See 2 Cor 10:1—13:10; esp. 12:14; 13:1.
159. E.g., see 2 Cor 1:9; 2:14-17; 4:11, 14; 5:15.
160. On 1 Cor 9:4-18 see §4.1 (d) above.
161. Cf. Martin, *2 Corinthians*, 531.

to God's free offering of the gospel,[162] a point that was important to Paul.[163] Further, in the term "the gospel of God" (τὸ τοῦ θεοῦ εὐαγγέλιον, 11:7), by its position, "of God" (τοῦ θεοῦ) is emphasized,[164] implying that their gospel is not God's.[165] In this statement, Paul uses the verb "I gospelled" (εὐηγγελισάμην), again at a point where we could expect "preach" (κηρύσσω). We will need to attempt to explain this when we draw our conclusions about Paul's gospel.[166]

From what we have seen in this section of 2 Corinthians it is reasonable to suppose that the super-apostles Paul is opposing (2 Cor 11:5; 12:11) were wonder-working, self-confident preachers charging for their services. In turn, the Jesus they likely promoted was of the same mold: a triumphant wonder worker, obscuring the weakness and humility of the Jesus of Paul's gospel. The gospel of these super-apostles would be one focusing on the miracles performed by them, and a gospel that was triumphant, centered on power and present glory.[167] Coming at financial cost to the Corinthians the gospel was not obviously God's free gift, a point of first order and of profound importance to Paul.

(g) Results: The gospel in 2 Corinthians. The wide range of use to which Paul puts the word "gospel"—verb and noun—continues to be apparent in this letter. Again, the gospel is about Christ (2:12; 10:14), whom Paul portrays and expresses in his own life as weak and humble (cf. 11:5). The gospel is also the religious ideas about Christ that are confessed (9:13). But the gospel can—and should—also be lived, embodied, and expressed in the life of a believer (8:18). Paul's emphasis on the gospel coming without cost (11:7) draws attention to God's free gift in Paul's gospel. And again, Paul uses "to gospel" rather than "to preach" to describe his work (11:7).

In 2 Corinthians, Paul's use of the verb "gospel" (εὐαγγελίζω) is not constant even though the whole letter is about his ministry.[168] In this letter Paul only uses the verb twice (2 Cor 10:16 and 11: 7), slightly less than could be expected. Given that Paul is writing into a context that has become hostile to his ministry, it could be that Paul has exchanged talking about his "gospelling" to focus readers' attention on his leadership and "the

---

162. Cf. Plummer, *Critical and Exegetical Commentary*, 303.

163. Rom 3:24; 5:6–8, 15–17; 2 Cor 9:14–15.

164. When Paul uses the articles with the nouns he otherwise always has τὸ εὐαγγέλιον τοῦ θεοῦ. See Rom 15:16; 1 Thess 2:2, 8, 9.

165. Harris, *Second Epistle to the Corinthians*, 756.

166. See §5.3 below.

167. Cf. Fallon, *2 Corinthians*, 94; Martin, *2 Corinthians*, 526.

168. Brought to my attention by Jerry Sumney and one of the publisher's anonymous readers.

gospel," for he uses the noun (εὐαγγέλιον) eight times, about what could be expected.[169]

§4.3 PHILEMON

Paul is in prison while writing this brief and personal letter (Phlm 1, 9–10, 13, 22–23), though it is not certain where or when: Rome in the mid-fifties (the traditional view), or Caesarea (Acts 24:26-27), or perhaps Ephesus.[170] Paul intercedes with Philemon on behalf of Onesimus who has run away (Phlm 15–16) and stolen from Philemon in the process (18–19). Onesimus had somehow ended up in the company of Paul, who had led him to faith in Christ (10). In his appeal Paul says, "I wanted to keep him [Onesimus] with me so that for you he may be of service to me in the chains of the gospel" (13).

As for all the texts we are passing under review we are enquiring what Paul means by the word "gospel." There is only one use of the word in this short letter. It is used in the phrase, "the chains of the gospel."[171] In this phrase Paul implies that he is in prison because of the gospel, most naturally understood as his activity.[172] In other words, what we saw implied in Philippians[173] is explicit here, Paul's work is the gospel and the gospel is his work. At least from this reference to the gospel, more cannot be said. Nevertheless it is clear that the chains or imprisonment are the badge of office or honor awarded for that work.[174] In this we see a reflection of what was spelt out clearly in his letter to the Philippians: suffering was a sharing in the Christ (Phil 3:10) who himself had suffered (2:5-11) before being raised to a life (2:9; 3:10–11), a life which Paul expected to share (3:11).

---

169. 2 Cor 2:12; 4:3, 4; 8:18; 9:13; 10:14; 11:4, 7. See p. 3n22 above.

170. See the discussions by Dunn, *Colossians and Philemon*, 307-8; Wilson, *Colossians and Philemon*, 20–23.

171. Phlm 13: τοῖς δεσμοῖς τοῦ εὐαγγελίου. Whether the genitive is subjective ("the chains the gospel has brought me," cf. NJB) or of reference or relation ("during my imprisonment for the gospel," cf. ESV and most EVV)—see Harris, *Colossians and Philemon*, 228—the meaning of "gospel" is not altered.

172. Cf. Moule, *Epistles of Paul the Apostle to the Colossians and to Philemon*, 146. The writer of Col 4:3 expresses a similar view.

173. See §3.4 (d) above.

174. Bruce, *Epistles to the Colossians*, 1984; cf. Lightfoot, *Colossians and Philemon*, 339.

§4.4 ROMANS

Few other pieces of ancient literature have been studied as much, or had the impact on Western civilization, as has Paul's Letter to the Romans. As well as the stories of the place of Romans in the spiritual journeys of Augustine of Hippo, Martin Luther, and Karl Barth, which we noted at the beginning of chapter 1 above, more recently Ernst Käsemann, one of the most significant Pauline scholars of the mid-twentieth century,[175] said in the preface to his milestone commentary that, "No literary document has been more important for me."[176]

Romans is of particular interest to us in that it is a mature piece of writing, the last letter we have of Paul's, written in the winter of 57-58 CE[177] when he was in Corinth.[178] Despite the attention given to this letter, its purpose remains elusive.[179] Most likely, Paul had a number of reasons for writing: informing or perhaps reassuring (Rom 1:13) the Roman Christians of his visit (15:22-25), preparing for a Western mission (15:24, 28), seeking support for the collection of money for Jerusalem (15:14-33), and an exercise in diplomacy to bring about unity (10:14-21; 11:13-36),[180] for example.[181] He also had a desire to set out a sustained and reflective defense of his gospel (1:16-17).[182] Indeed, in this letter he comes closest to defining "gospel" (cf. 1:3-4, 16).

Douglas Campbell has reminded interpreters of this letter of what Werner Georg Kümmel called the "double character" of Romans.[183] That is, while the letter opens with the appearance of being addressed to gentile

---

175. Wojtkowiak, "Unter der Herrschaft Christi," 103-20; Wojtkowiak, "Unter der Herrschaft Christi: Teil 2," 83-99; Klaiber, "Ernst Käsemann as Theological Exegete," 26-56. For a biographical sketch of Käsemann, see Harrisville, "Life and Work of Ernst Käsemann," 294-99.

176. Käsemann, *Commentary on Romans*, vii.

177. See the concise discussion by Jewett, *Romans*, 18-20, esp. 18 and those cited in n87.

178. See esp. Rom 16:23; cf. Acts 18:7; 1 Cor 1:14, and the discussion by Jewett, *Romans*, 21-22.

179. Wedderburn, *Reasons for Romans*, 5; Klein, "Paul's Purpose," 29; Jervis and Richardson, *Purpose of Romans*, 11; Reichert, *Römerbrief als Gratwanderung*, 58.

180. Campbell, "Determining the Gospel," 334-35.

181. For a brief though thorough summary of the debate concerning the purpose of Paul writing Romans, see Jewett, *Romans*, 80-91.

182. Cf. Dunn, *Theology of Paul the Apostle*, 25.

183. Kümmel, *Introduction to the New Testament*, 309-11; cf. Campbell, "Determining the Gospel," 316-18.

believers,[184] the body of the letter engages in an abstract way with Jewish topics such as circumcision, observing the law, and the significance of Abraham.[185] The abstract nature of Paul's discussion has, Campbell suggests, tempted interpreters to assume that the body of Romans—taken as Paul's description of his deepest theological convictions about the gospel—can be lifted out of the letter and reinterpreted for the modern reader.[186] However, given that the letter is written to a specific group of believers, any interpretation must take into account its contingent nature: what Paul writes is being shaped by those he expects to read it. Not to take this into account, as Campbell rightly asserts, leads "to quite distorted representations of Paul's gospel."[187]

Given the argumentative dimension of the letter, the sense of urgency in Paul's tone, and its "double character" in being addressed primarily to gentiles but also dealing abstractly with Jewish topics, it is reasonable to follow Campbell in supposing that this letter was written with militant Jewish-Christian opponents in the background.[188] In turn, in the passages in Romans requiring our attention, we will have to take into account that Paul is writing in the context of Jewish-Christian opponents who oppose his particular understanding of the gospel. We turn to those passages, continuing with the specific task of enquiring about his meaning of the term "gospel."

(a) God's gospel concerning his Son (Romans 1:1–6). Paul begins this letter:

> Paul, a servant of Christ Jesus, called to be an apostle set apart for the gospel of God, which he promised beforehand through his prophets in the holy scriptures, the gospel concerning his Son, who was descended from David according to the flesh and was declared to be Son of God with power according to the spirit of holiness by resurrection from the dead, Jesus Christ our Lord, through whom we have received grace and apostleship to bring about the obedience of faith for the sake of his name among all the nations. (Rom 1:1–5)[189]

---

184. E.g., see Rom 1:5, 13; cf. 11:13; 15:15–18. However, in the discussion of unbelief among Jews (Rom 9–11), in the assertion that Jews and gentiles have the same responsibility before God (1:16; 2:9–11, 25–29; 3:29; 10:12) and the appeal for mutual acceptance (15:7–13), the letter assumes the presence of Jews. See the discussion by Kümmel, *Introduction to the New Testament*, 310.

185. Campbell, "Determining the Gospel," 316.

186. Campbell, "Determining the Gospel," 317.

187. Campbell, "Determining the Gospel," 317.

188. Campbell, "Determining the Gospel," 321.

189. Johnson, "Romans 1:3–4," 488, suggests that 2 Tim 2:8 is our earliest extant

We have already noted that Paul begins this letter more elaborately than the anticipated, "From x to y, greetings."[190] This, with little elaboration, is the way Paul begins his first letter: "Paul, Silvanus and Timothy, to the church of the Thessalonians in God the Father and the Lord Jesus Christ: Grace to you" (1 Thess 1:1). However, in writing to the Romans, his last letter, with his self-identification considerably longer than could be expected (and longer than in any of his other letters), his readers could not help but notice that the identification is primarily a description of the gospel and his—and their—relationship to it.

In fact, three things about Paul's description of the gospel would likely strike the first readers immediately. The first is that the gospel is the fundamental aspect of Paul's self-understanding, determining his life. In this introduction of himself Paul tells his readers: he is a servant of Jesus Christ; he is called to be an apostle; and he is "set apart to (the) gospel" (ἀφωρισμένος ἐις εὐαγγέλιον, Rom 1:1). Though mentioned last, being set apart for the gospel is the aspect of his identity on which he spends the most time (1:2–6). Mentioning being "set apart to the gospel" last also enables him to go straight on to develop what he understands by "the gospel."[191]

What Paul initially tells his readers about himself (being a servant) is a description frequently used in his Scriptures for leaders and prophets, as well as for the nation and God's people,[192] and the second thing he tells them (he is called) is also said of servants of God in the Scriptures.[193] Further, that he will immediately go on to use scriptural motifs to describe the gospel, it can be expected that he would also be drawing on his Scriptures in saying that he is set apart.[194] Indeed, in describing his call to the Galatians, including using "separate" (ἀφορίζω), the same word as here, he echoes both the call stories of biblical prophets[195] and God's call for his people to be separate or holy

---

reception of Rom 1:3–4, which calls the statement "Remember Jesus Christ, raised from the dead, from the seed of David" "my gospel," in turn suggesting that the set of ideas in these verses was taken to be Paul's gospel.

190. See 1 Thess 1:1 and p. 64n269 above.

191. The anarthrous εὐαγγέλιον—omitting the article—identifies the "gospel" as the predicate. See Zerwick, *Biblical Greek*, §§171–83, and below.

192. Abraham: Ps 105:42; Moses: Exod 14:31; Num 12:7; Deut 34:5; Josh 1:1, 15; 8:21, 23; 18:7; 1 Chr 6:49; 2 Chr 1:3; 24:6; Neh 1:7; 10:29; David: 2 Sam 7:5–8; 1 Kgs 8:66; 11:36; 2 Kgs 19:34. For other figures, see 2 Kgs 10:10; 21:10; Isa 20:3; 41:8–9; 41:1; 49:5; 52:13—53:12; Jer 7:25; 27:6; 43:10; Amos 3:7.

193. Sanday and Headlam, *Critical and Exegetical Commentary*, 4, cite Abraham (Gen 12:1–3), Moses (Exod 3:10), prophets (Isa 6:8; Jer 1:4, 5, etc.), and draw attention to Hos 11:1 (LXX) and 1 Kgs 1:41, 49 (LXX).

194. Cf. Longenecker, *Epistle to the Romans*, 58.

195. Gal 1:15–16; cf. Isa 49:1–6; Jer 1:5, 10. Also, e.g., see Stendahl, "Apostle Paul

to him (esp. Lev 20:26). In the preposition "to" (εἰς, also "for" or "toward") the purpose of his call or separation is specified: the gospel. In turn, if, as is credibly argued, the Hebrew "to separate" (פרש) stands behind the word "Pharisee,"[196] Paul, once a Pharisee himself (Phil 3:5),[197] is signaling to his readers that, whereas as a Pharisee he was once set apart to the law (3:5), he is now separated or consecrated to the gospel.[198] As the law once dominated and defined his life so now the gospel dominates and defines him and his life.[199] This play on the word "Pharisee" would not have been lost on his readers,[200] or at least not on any of his militant Jewish-Christian opponents.

The second thing that would strike Paul's readers about his reference to the gospel is that he does not, using the infinitive, say that he is set apart "to gospel" (εἰς εὐαγγελίζεσθαι), as could be expected.[201] Instead he says he is set apart "to" or "for God's gospel" (εἰς εὐαγγέλιον Θεοῦ, Rom 1:1; cf. 15:16). Although he is identifying himself in relation to the gospel, at this point his prime interest is not in himself or his work but in the nature of the gospel. With "gospel" having no article—it is anarthrous—his statement should be read as "God's gospel" rather than "the gospel of God."

Notably, Paul is not saying that he is set apart for the purpose of preaching the gospel.[202] Indeed, given that in other places he does say something along the lines that he is called to gospel,[203] here it cannot be missed that he makes a statement that, antecedent to any activity he may think is required of him in relation to the gospel, his view is that it is God's gospel to which he belongs: it is fundamentally not his but God's gospel, and is, therefore, more than anything he may say or do in relation to it.

---

and the Introspective Conscience," 204; Munck, *Paul and the Salvation of Mankind*, 11-35; Aune, *Prophecy in Early Christianity*, 202 (cf. 405n74); and those cited by Fisk, "Paul," 303n79.

196. E.g., see Saldarini, *Pharisees, Scribes, and Sadducees*, 220-25. The criticisms of this view by Weiss in Meyer and Weiss, "Φαρισαῖος," 46n211, and Betz, *Galatians*, 70n134, are not convincing. Cf. Jewett, *Romans*, 102n58.

197. Though he does not repudiate being a Pharisee or being "a member of the people of Israel, of the tribe of Benjamin" (Phil 3:5), in including a description of his persecution of the church (3:6) and saying that "whatever gains I had, these I have come to regard as loss because of Christ" (3:7), being a Pharisee is clearly no longer determinative for him.

198. Cf. Barrett, *Romans*, 17.

199. Cf. Dunn, *Romans 1-8*, 10.

200. As supposed by Dunn, *Romans 1-8*, 9.

201. Michel, *Der Brief an die Römer*, 68.

202. As supposed by Dunn, *Romans 1-8*, 10. Cf. Jewett, *Romans*, 102.

203. Rom 1:15; 15:20; 1 Cor 1:17; 9:16, 18; 15:1, 2; 2 Cor 10:16; 11:7; Gal 1:8, 9, 11, 16, 23; 4:13.

Not only from his precise phrase, "God's gospel" (εἰς εὐαγγέλιον Θεοῦ, Rom 1:1), but also from what immediately follows, Paul makes clear it is God's gospel: it is also something that God promised (1:2) and it is about his Son (1:3).[204] In another play on words, Paul draws attention to the continuity between God's "gospel" (εὐαγγέλιον, 1:1) and his "promise" (προεπηγγείλατο, 1:2) of it. That he says the gospel was promised through God's "prophets in the holy scriptures" is confirmation of what we have seen in Galatians, that Paul's reading of his Scriptures is shaped by his understanding of the gospel.[205] The gospel is also God's in the sense that it is not Paul's gospel or something he has devised. He has already had to make this point to other readers. In the face of Jewish-Christian opponents in Galatia he stressed to his readers—he says "for I want you to know" (Γνωρίζω γὰρ ὑμῖν, Gal 1:11)—that his gospel was not of or from humans but received "through revelation of Jesus Christ" (1:12). We have seen that Paul goes on to say that the gospel to which he is committed was "proclaimed in advance" (προευηγγελίσατο) to Abraham.[206] So here in Romans, with Jewish-Christian opponents in mind, Paul stresses that his gospel, which he anticipates they withstand, is God's not his.

The third thing that Paul's readers would likely notice in this statement of self-identification is his description of the gospel itself. He says the gospel "concerns his Son" (περὶ τοῦ υἱοῦ αὐτοῦ, Rom 1:3). The debate around this phrase and those that follow (1:3–4) being a pre-Pauline formulation or containing creedal elements rumbles on.[207] What can probably be agreed upon is that even if the whole would not have been recognized by his readers as a formal creedal statement so many elements would have been taken as creedal or traditional that they would have seen Paul's gospel as something predating him and shared by others, probably including themselves,[208] a point we will see that Paul picks up when referring to the readers (1:6).

Paul says of the gospel "concerning his Son"—"his Son, who was descended from David according to the flesh and was declared to be Son of God with power according to the spirit of holiness by resurrection from the dead, Jesus Christ our Lord" (Rom 1:3b–4). Here, in essence, the gospel concerns the Son, of whom Paul immediately goes on to give a very brief description. At least here Paul is not saying that the gospel is to be equated with the Son or with what he is about to say about him. Yet, there is clearly

---

204. Note Gal 1:11–16, where Paul, in talking about the origin of the gospel, says God has revealed his Son to him, on which see §3.3 (c) above.

205. On Gal 3:8 see §2.4 (g) above.

206. On Gal 3:8 see §3.3 (e) above.

207. E.g., Calhoun, *Paul's Definitions of the Gospel*, 92–106; and the discussion at §2.3 (b) above.

208. Cf. Dunn, *Romans 1–8*, 5.

in Paul's mind a relationship between the story of Jesus and the gospel. Notably, Paul does not seem to have in mind relating the gospel to the teaching of Jesus so much as his identity and life.[209]

Though not often, when Paul uses "son" (υἱός) for Jesus, he draws attention to the relationship between Jesus and God.[210] Here Paul's use of "Son" reinforces his point that although the gospel is about Jesus it is God's gospel. Given the high dependence on scriptural motifs in what Paul is saying about the gospel, and that Jewish Christians seem to have been particularly fond of the title,[211] the title would catch the attention of his Jewish-Christian readers who opposed his gospel. The elementary sketch of the Son that follows—a composite or whole creedal statement—draws attention to two things: his human Davidic descent ("according to the flesh," Rom 1:3) and his designation as Son of God, in which his resurrection is pivotal (1:4).

It was widely expected that the Messiah would be a descendent of David.[212] In picking up these hopes in his description of the gospel Paul signals to his readers that the gospel brings to fruition the messianic hopes of Scripture.[213] In adding that the Son was a descendent of David "according to the flesh" (κατὰ σάρκα, Rom 1:3) he conveys both that this descent was in relation to his earthly life or human nature (see also 9:5), and also that his description did not encompass all that was significant about him.[214]

---

209. Barrett, "I Am Not Ashamed of the Gospel," 31, supposes Paul is aware of a relationship between his gospel and the life as well as the teaching of Jesus.

210. Rom 1:3, 4, 9; 5:10; 8:3, 32; 1 Cor 1:9; 15:28; 2 Cor 1:19; Gal 1:16; 2:20; (cf. 3:26); 4:4, 6; 1 Thess 1:10. Also, see Eph 4:13; Col 1:13. Also, see p. 150n183 above. Cf. Dunn, *Romans 1–8*, 11.

211. E.g., Matthew uses υἱός eighty-nine times (1 in 206 words); and Hebrews uses υἱός twenty-four times (also 1 in 206 words). Mark uses υἱός thirty-four times (1:331); Luke seventy-seven times (1:252); John fifty-five times (1:280). Longenecker, *Epistle to the Romans*, 63, notes that the writer of Hebrews uses υἱός in the caption (Heb 1:2), in the following confessional statement (1:3–4), and in the first scriptural citation (1:5; cf. Ps 2:7).

212. 2 Sam 7:16; Ps 89:3–4, 19–21; Isa 11:1, 10; Jer 23:5–6; 30:9; 33:14–18; Ezek 34:23–24; 37: 24–25; Pss Sol 17:23(21); 4Q252; 4Q174. See Cranfield, *Epistle to the Romans*, 1.58.

213. Cf. Cranfield, *Epistle to the Romans*, 1:59. While readers may hear echoes of the Greco-Roman sociopolitical use of this term, expressed in phrases such as "things appointed by law" (τὰ ὑπὸ νόμου ὁρισθέντ', Plutarch, *De Fato* 570d9; cf. Appian, *Mithr.* 152.1; Dionysius Halicarnassus, *Ant. rom.* 44.22; and Jewett, *Romans*, 104 and n84), the probable shared knowledge of this early Christian (Aramaic) creedal material suggests that it is the scriptural motifs that would be operative for Paul and his readers.

214. Cf. Cranfield, *Epistle to the Romans*, 1:59.

Indeed, what was also significant about the Son is that he was "designated Son of God" (τοῦ ὁρισθέντος υἱοῦ Θεοῦ, Rom 1:4). Since we have no clear uses of this verb (ὁρίζω) meaning "declare" or "shown to be"[215] either before or at the time of the writing of the New Testament, and since other writers took it to mean "determine" or "appoint,"[216] as it always is in the New Testament,[217] it is clear that Paul means that the Son was "appointed" or "installed" as Son of God.[218] Given Paul otherwise emphasizes the power of Christ despite apparent weakness (e.g., 2 Cor 13:4), and that elsewhere in his letters "in power" means "invested with power,"[219] he probably means that he was "appointed Son-of-God-in-power."[220] This took place "according to the spirit of holiness (κατὰ πνεῦμα ἁγιωσύνης) from (ἐξ) the resurrection of the dead" (Rom 1:4).[221] Since Paul otherwise deliberately avoids attributing Jesus' resurrection to the Holy Spirit (see 6:4; 8:11),[222] Dunn is probably right that in this vague expression, "according to the spirit of holiness"—clearly a Semitic term[223]—Paul is saying that the post-resurrection phase of the Son's existence and role was characterized by the Spirit.[224] Whether Paul means the appointment was "after" (temporal) or "on the basis of" (causal), the resurrection was pivotal and preceded the Son's appointment.[225]

The mention of David, the name of Israel's great king, and the appointment or installation of the Son as part of Paul's understanding of the gospel would have brought regal connotations to the minds of readers. They—readers in Rome, the seat of the emperor—are likely to see Paul

---

215. Cranfield, *Epistle to the Romans*, 1:61. Cf. BDAG, "ὁρίζω," 723.

216. See Acts 17:31; Heb 4:7. Cf. BDAG, "ὁρίζω," 723

217. Luke 22:22; Acts 2:23; 10:42; 11:29; 17:26, 31; Heb 4:7. Cf. Cranfield, *Epistle to the Romans*, 1:61 and n61.

218. Allen, "Old Testament Background of προ ὁριζειν in the New Testament," esp. 104.

219. 1 Cor 15:43; 1 Thess 1:5; also, see Mark 9:1.

220. Cranfield, *Epistle to the Romans*, 1:62; cf. Barrett, *Epistle to the Romans*, 21–22.

221. While Paul says ἐξ ἀναστάσεως νεκρῶν ("from the resurrection of the dead"), which Dunn, *Romans 1–8*, 15 (depending on Anders Nygren), rightly points out "reflects the earliest Christian belief that Jesus' resurrection was not simply a 'one-off' event, but actually part of the beginning of the general resurrection prior to the last judgement" (cf. Matt 27:52–53; Acts 4:2; 23:6; 1 Cor 15:20, 23), the reference is still to the resurrection that so far only involved the Son.

222. Cf. Dunn, *Christology in the Making*, 144; Dunn, *Romans 1–8*, 15.

223. Ps 51:11; Isa 63:10–11; 1 QS 4.21; 8.16; 9.3; 1QH^a 7.6–7; 9.32; 12.12; Dunn, *Romans 1–8*, 15.

224. Dunn, *Romans 1–8*, 15.

225. Cf. Barrett, *Romans*, 21.

calling an allegiance to the Son as more worthy and more profound and more necessary than any other allegiance.[226]

Using his own distinctive vocabulary[227] to sum up this thumbnail sketch, Paul adds to the creedal material another and parallel name for the Son (cf. Rom 1:3): "Jesus Christ our Lord" (1:4b).[228] In placing "Son" (1:3) and "Jesus Christ our Lord" (1:4) in apposition or parallel,[229] Paul reinforces his point that the gospel concerns this figure, and in the ways he has just set out within this *inclusio* formed by the two names. The centrality of Jesus in Paul's understanding of the gospel would be even clearer to the readers in noting that he uses the name "Jesus Christ" four times in this introduction (1:1-7).[230]

Paul has described God's gospel concerning the Son (Jesus Christ our Lord) in traditional or creedal terms (Rom 1:3-4), most probably so that he could demonstrate his orthodoxy[231] and establish common ground,[232] especially with his Jewish-Christian readers. His gospel is not, as they might allege, a misrepresentation of Scripture or of God's intentions, or even something Paul has devised (cf. Gal 1:11-12; 3:8).[233] Paul then describes the impact and purpose of this gospel. He says it was through (δι' οὗ, "through whom") the Son, Jesus Christ our Lord, that "we have received grace and apostleship" (Rom 1:5a).

It is not immediately obvious why Paul uses the first-person plural in his claim, "we have received" (ἐλάβομεν, Rom 1:5a). From his personal introduction in the opening lines (1:1), and his using the first-person singular to describe his mission throughout the remainder of the letter,[234] we would expect him to say "I have received" (ἔλαβον) this grace and apostleship (cf. 15:15). It is clearly not the readers Paul has in mind, for they

---

226. The point is put strongly and, arguably excessively so, by, e.g., Wright, "Paul's Gospel and Caesar's Empire," esp. 171-72. See the discussion on §5.5 below.

227. Cf. Jewett, *Romans*, 107.

228. Along with other phrases, such as "in power" (ἐν δυνάμει, Rom 1:4b), it is generally agreed that "Jesus Christ our Lord" (Ἰησοῦ Χριστοῦ τοῦ κυρίου ἡμῶν, 1:4e) has been introduced into the traditional material by Paul. See the discussion by, e.g., Jewett, *Romans*, 103-8. Dunn, *Romans 1-8*, 5, however, takes the whole of Rom 1:3-4 as a pre-Pauline formulation. Also, see Dunn, "Jesus–Flesh and Spirit," 40-68.

229. E.g., Cranfield, *Epistle to the Romans*, 1:65.

230. Cf. Dunn, *Romans 1-8*, 6.

231. Dodd, *Epistle of Paul to the Romans*, 5; Neufeld, *Earliest Christian Confessions*, 51; Jewett, *Romans*, 108.

232. E.g., Dunn, *Romans 1-8*, 5; Jewett, *Romans*, 108.

233. Dodd, *Epistle of Paul to the Romans*, 4.

234. Jewett, *Romans*, 108, citing Rom 1:9-16; 11:13-34; 15:15, 17-20, 23-32.

are yet to be drawn into the narrative. When they are, they will be described as beneficiaries of this grace and apostleship (1:6). Given the creedal or traditional nature of his description of the gospel, and his recognition that he is dependent on others for the gospel,[235] as well as his concern to win the confidence of his readers, the plural ("we") is probably a reference to his predecessors and peers, some of whom will have brought the gospel to the readers.[236] This further reinforces Paul's point that his gospel is not something unique to him or devised by him.

The purpose of the gospel, Paul then says, is "to bring about the obedience of faith among all the Gentiles for the sake of his name" (Rom 1:5b-c). The "obedience of faith" (ὑπακοήν πίστεως) could mean, for example, the obedience which works faith or obedience to the faith or Christian religion.[237] However, given not only that "obey" (ὑπακούω) derives from "hear" (ἀκούω), but more importantly the close relationship between obedience and trust in Paul's mind (note 6:15-17), he probably means that the purpose of the gospel is to bring about the "response of faith."[238]

In this opening greeting (Rom 1:1-6) we have seen that Paul has identified himself as an apostle in relation to the gospel. Once he was dedicated to and determined by the law. Now Paul is dedicated to God's gospel concerning his Son who, as a human, fulfills the scriptural hopes of the Messiah and, from the resurrection, characterized by the Spirit, was appointed Son-of-God-in-power rather than weakness. It is through God's Son, Jesus Christ our Lord, that he and others, including those who brought the gospel to the Romans, have received grace as well as apostleship to bring about the response of faith among the gentiles, including the readers. In this creedal or traditional description of the gospel to which Paul is dedicated, his opponents and those of the readers sympathetic to them can see that he has undercut them by establishing common ground with them in the scriptural and traditional understanding of the gospel. Also, Paul has distanced himself from them in establishing why he is dedicated not to the law but to God's gospel about his Son, through whom both he and they also have received grace.

---

235. See §2.3 above.

236. Cf. Roller, *Das Formular der paulinischen Briefe*, 152-87, and the brief discussion by Jewett, *Romans*, 108-9.

237. Cranfield, *Epistle to the Romans*, 1:66, lists seven ways in which ὑπακοήν πίστεως ("obedience of faith") has been understood by interpreters of Paul.

238. Cranfield, *Epistle to the Romans*, 1:66, prefers "faith which consists in obedience." Cf. Barrett, *Romans*, 22. See the insightful discussion by Dunn, *Romans 1-8*, 17, drawing attention to the range of meanings of ὑπακούω listed by LSJ, including "give ear to, answer, heed."

(b) The gospel of his Son (Romans 1:9). We have just seen that the gospel is God's (1:1), "concerning his Son" (περὶ τοῦ υἱοῦ αὐτοῦ, 1:3). Using exactly the same form, here Paul says the gospel is the Son's (τοῦ υἱοῦ αὐτοῦ, 1:9): "For God is my witness, whom I serve in my spirit in the gospel of his Son" (1:9-10). In this ambiguous language Paul is able to lead his readers from seeing that while the gospel is God's, in that it has been promised by him and is about his Son (1:1-3), it is also the gospel of the Son in that he is its focus, and the one through whom it is experienced (1:3-5). The gospel is, then, for Paul, more than a message about the Son: the Son, as the gospel (1:3), is served (1:9), and the gospel is experienced through his Son (1:5).

(c) Eager to gospel (Romans 1:15). Having assured the readers of his prayers and concern for them (1:8-12), which involves imparting some spiritual gift to strengthen the readers—a gift that is to be mutually encouraged (1:11-12)—and another mention of his obligation to the gentiles (1:13-14, cf. 1:5), Paul says, "hence my eagerness to gospel to you also in Rome" (1:15). This is another example where, in translating Paul, the verb "gospel" (εὐαγγελίζω) is often augmented with the word "preach."[239] Already in this study doubt has been raised about the merits of consistently translating the verb "gospel" (εὐαγγελίζω) as "preach the gospel."

From the definition of the gospel that we will see Paul goes on to supply (see on Rom 1:16 below) it is unlikely he would see his "gospelling" as limited to speaking. There is some support for this in Paul using the verb "gospel" as an alternate way of saying that he wants to have some "fruit" (καρπός) among the Romans (1:13), readers who are already believers. Similarly, in writing to the Philippian believers he also uses the word "fruit" to the describe the entire scope of his work (Phil 1:22). In other words, his term "to gospel" here is another example of Paul using the verb "gospel" to describe not just his speaking but the whole breadth of his work,[240] which, also from what we are seeing in his letters in general, clearly encompassed much more than preaching, or even other activities aimed at conversion.

(d) The gospel is the power of God for salvation (Romans 1:16-17). Having expressed his eagerness "to gospel" (1:15), Paul immediately goes on to define the gospel and to explain his eagerness: "For I am not ashamed of the gospel; for it is the power of God to salvation for everyone who has faith" (1:16). "For," he goes on, "in it the righteousness of God is revealed through faith for faith" (1:17). Then, again using the link "for" (γάρ), these lines are tied to the next paragraph about God's wrath on unrighteousness

---

239. E.g., see Dunn, *Romans 1-8*, 33; Barrett, *Romans*, 27; Fitzmyer, *Romans*, 251.

240. See also the discussions (h) and (i) below, respectively, on Rom 15:16 and 15:19-20.

(1:18–32). In this structure, using "for" (γάρ) four times (1:16–18) to tie his ideas together, Paul is able to move logically and economically from his eagerness to gospel, to defining the gospel, then to what it does, and why it is needed. In this he provides the reason for his mission, both in the summary of these lines and the argument of the letter.[241] Thus, these oft-quoted lines by preachers and theologians are of strategic importance in understanding Paul's view of the gospel. However, it will become apparent that this is a point in the interpretation of Paul where he is generally profoundly misunderstood.

To begin with, Paul says he is not ashamed of the gospel (Rom 1:16). This is likely to be heard by his readers at a number of levels. At one level, for Paul and his readers, not being ashamed was not tied to any particular social encounter for it was a basic confidence associated with being a believer. It was a notion embedded in early Christian tradition, traceable to a statement that Jesus is likely to have uttered about him being ashamed of those ashamed of him and his words (Mark 8:38).[242] Given Paul's heavy dependence on traditional material in his introduction (Rom 1:1–7), which only has its intended force if understood as such, it could be expected that his readers would hear in his statement both his solidarity with his predecessors[243] and his commitment to the gospel. Indeed, from his use of the idea elsewhere, in Paul's mind not being ashamed is not tied to any particular situation, including, therefore, his visit to Rome. In writing to the Philippians from prison (Phil 1:7, 13, 19), he says that whatever happens to him subsequent to his trial—life or death (1:21)—he will not at all "be ashamed" (αἰσχύνομαι, 1:20). His confidence rests not on this particular situation but on his expectation that Christ will, whether by life or death, be honored in his body (1:20). In other words, not being ashamed or put to shame is Paul's general conviction as a believer, regardless of his situation. The same conclusion arises when taking into account other places where Paul picks up this motif.[244]

At a related (and crucial) level, that Paul could be expected to be ashamed is because, as he has just hinted at in his brief sketch of him, there is human weakness in the Son. Indeed, Paul's missionary message involved the story of the crucifixion which, as we learn in a parallel formulation in 1 Corinthians, may be "the power of God" to those being saved, but "is folly

241. Cf. Dunn, *Romans 1–8*, 46.
242. See the discussion by Barrett, "I Am Not Ashamed of the Gospel," 22–28.
243. Cf. Barrett, "I Am Not Ashamed of the Gospel," 28.
244. See καταισχύνεσθαι ("disappoint"); esp. Rom 5:5; 9:33; 10:11; αἰσχυνθήσομαι ("be ashamed"); 2 Cor 10:8; Phil 1:20. See the discussion by Barrett, "I Am Not Ashamed of the Gospel," 19–22.

to those who are perishing" (1 Cor 1:18; cf. 2:2). As Paul goes on to say, "we proclaim Christ crucified, a stumbling block to Jews and foolishness to Gentiles" (1:23, cf. 1:27–28).[245] However, Paul is not ashamed because in this gospel of apparent weakness God's eschatological vindication is available to those who trust him.[246] Indeed, his quotation of the line of Scripture, "The one who is righteous shall live by trust" (Hab 2:4/Rom 1:17), was widely used in Paul's time among Jews and Christians to explain the delay of God's eschatological justice.[247] Paul is, on the basis of his gospel, confident that God's just ways of dealing with all people is revealed.[248] It is not surprising, then, that when he next returns to the theme of his gospelling at the end of Romans he uses the word "ambitious" or "glory in" (φιλοτιμέομαι) rather than shame to describe his approach (15:20).[249]

At yet another level, in protesting that he is not ashamed of the gospel, Paul may also be countering a perceived or real criticism that he did not highly regard them or want to come to them (cf. Rom 1:9–10). In any case, no matter how he is understood or treated in relation to the gospel he will not be ashamed for he is in solidarity with his predecessors, confident in the gospel itself (1:1–6) and, as we have seen, that Christ will be honored in him (cf. Phil 1:22).

As we will see, there are exceptions, but the majority view on what Paul means by gospel is reasonably summed up by James Dunn who, commenting on what Paul says here, concludes that the power of God is embodied and mediated through the gospel.[250] In this reading, the gospel is associated with or equated with Paul's message. But this is not what Paul says. Paul's statement is clear: "for it is the power of God" (δύναμις γάρ θεοῦ ἐστιν, Rom 1:16). Notably, Paul does not say that the gospel "concerns" (περί) the power of God. Rather, the gospel "is" (ἐστιν) the power of God.[251]

---

245. On the shame associated with crucifixion, see Hengel, *Crucifixion in the Ancient World*, esp. 1–11, 84–90.

246. Hays, *Echoes of Scripture*, 39.

247. See Strobel, *Untersuchungen Zum Eschatologischen Verzögerungsproblem*, 7–170, cited by Hays, *Echoes of Scripture*, 40. On Paul's citation of Hab 2;4 see §2.4 (c) above.

248. Cf., and further, see Hays, *Echoes of Scripture*, 40.

249. Cf. Plutarch, *Alc.* 16.4; further, see MGS, "φιλοτιμέομαι," 2287. Also, see the discussion of the term in Paul's time by Jewett, *Romans*, 915.

250. Dunn, *Romans 1–8*, 39. See the discussion above at §1.4.

251. In his effusive review of Watson, *Paul and the Hermeneutics of Faith*, Martyn, "Article Review," 430, draws attention to one of the lessons of Watson's book which is that readings of Paul such as Rudolf Bultmann's rendering of Rom 1:16b taking the gospel as the offer or possibility of salvation is a mistake. Rather, the gospel "is for Paul no mere offer, no conditional promise. It is nothing less than God's rectifying *power*

Käsemann is nearer the mark in his understanding of Paul when he points out that, "the gospel and preaching should not simply be equated. What is confessed is neither the action of preaching nor its content. The gospel is more than the message actualized in the church."[252] However, Käsemann is mistaken to go on to say that the gospel is God's declaration of salvation.[253] What Paul says is that the gospel is God's power that leads "to salvation" (εἰς σωτηρίαν). Here a subtle but important point is to be noted. Paul does not say that the power of God is the gospel. For Paul to say, instead, that the gospel is the power of God enables him to express his conviction that the gospel is much broader and richer than God's power, which could be taken too narrowly as particular powerful acts of God. In that Paul would have diminished the gospel to the miraculous!

In Paul not making much of the word "salvation"—he only uses it in Romans here and in 10:1 and 10:10—readers could be expected to assume its general meaning of "deliverance" or "preservation" from danger or death.[254] Using "for" (γάρ) to tie this paragraph together, and it to the next one, Paul identifies the danger or threat as the wrath of God (Rom 1:18).[255] Thus, taking note of Paul's use of "for," the gospel is the power of God that leads to salvation or deliverance from the wrath of God because the righteousness of God is revealed in it.

The meaning of the term "the righteousness of God" is the focus of another ongoing battle between those who take the righteousness to be imputed or, on the other side, transformative.[256] Since in this paragraph God's power (Rom 1:16) and God's wrath (1:18) refer to God's activity, it is probable that the righteousness of God is an activity of God.[257] Also, for Paul, for whom Hebrew categories were fundamental to his mindset,[258] "righteousness" was essentially relational. Righteousness was something that someone had not alone but in relation to others.[259] For people to be

---

itself" (emphasis original).

252. Käsemann, *Commentary on Romans*, 22. Cf. Barrett, *Romans*, 28, says that the gospel is not merely an announcement but a divine activity or power.

253. Käsemann, *Commentary on Romans*, 22.

254. See BDAG, "σωτήριος," 986.

255. Cf. Calhoun, *Paul's Definitions of the Gospel*, 150.

256. See the summary of the debate by Cranfield, *Epistle to the Romans*, 1:95–99 and more recently, Soards, "Righteousness of God," 104–9; Soards, "Once Again 'Righteousness of God,'" 14–44; Burk, "Righteousness of God (*Dikaiosunē Theou*)," 346–60; Stevens, "Righteousness of God," 47–69.

257. Jewett, *Romans*, 142.

258. See the classic statement by Davies, *Paul and Rabbinic Judaism*.

259. E.g., see Job 29:14; Ps 85:13 [LXX 84:14]; Dunn, *Romans 1–8*, 40–41.

righteous is for them to have met the claims others have on them in their relationships.²⁶⁰ For God to be righteous is for him to fulfill his covenantal obligation to rescue his wayward and embattled people.²⁶¹ Or, as Dunn put it in his *The Theology of Paul the Apostle*, "Paul took it for granted that God's righteousness was to be understood as God's activity in drawing individuals into and sustaining them within the relationship, as 'the power of God for salvation.'"²⁶²

Although the debate involves much greater complexities and subtleties than suggested here, given that the term "righteousness" assumes a relationship in which God acts for his defective covenantal partner, it is reasonable to conclude with those who take Paul's term "the righteousness of God" to refer to both God making as well as considering people righteous.²⁶³ Thus, the word that Paul used for "righteousness" (δικαιοσύνη) had been used in the Septuagint not only to translate the Hebrew "righteousness" (צדק),²⁶⁴ but also "loving kindness" (חסד).²⁶⁵ This is what Paul is saying the gospel reveals. His grammatical parallelism in the passage under discussion reinforces this point, defining the gospel in terms of the power of God (Rom 1:16b–c) and the righteousness of God (1:17a–b),²⁶⁶ which highlights Paul's notion of the gospel as God's loving drawing of people into salvation.

In this statement (Rom 1:16–17), not only is Paul defining the gospel, it is agreed on almost all sides that he is also establishing the theme of his letter.²⁶⁷ However, even though the whole of Romans may have the gospel as its single theme,²⁶⁸ it is not agreed how much of Romans is a direct explication of this definition and how much is a further development of it and a setting out of its implications. Maximally, James Dunn takes the entire

---

260. Dunn, *Romans 1–8*, 41, relying on Cremer, *Die paulinische Rechtfertigungslehre*, 34–38.

261. Cf. Dunn, *Romans 1–8*, 41.

262. Dunn, *Theology of Paul the Apostle*, 344.

263. Dunn, *Romans 1–8*, 41–42.

264. Job 29:14; Pss 85:1 (LXX 84:14); 85:10 (LXX 84:11); 89:14 (LXX 88:15); 94:15 (LXX 93:15); 97:2 (LXX 96:2); Prov 1:3; 8:15; 12:17; 16:13; Isa 26:9; 51:1; 58:2; Jer 22:13; Hos 10:12.

265. Gen 19:19; 20:13; 21:23; 24:27; 32:10 (LXX 32:11); Pss 36:10 (MT 36:11; LXX 35:11); 85:10 (MT 85:11; LXX 84:11); 89:14 (MT 89:15; LXX 88:15); 103:17 (LXX 102:17); Prov 14:34; 20:28; 21:21; Isa 63:7; Jer 9:24 (MT, LXX 9:23); Hos 2:19 (MT, LXX 2:21); 10:12.

266. Jewett, *Romans*, 136.

267. See, e.g., Käsemann, *Commentary on Romans*, 21–32; Cranfield, *Epistle to the Romans*, 1.87; Byrne, *Romans*, 51. Exceptions include, e.g., Achtemeier, *Romans*, 35–36, on whom see the discussion by Dunn, *Romans 1–8*, 38.

268. Cf. Jewett, *Romans*, 135.

body of the letter (up to 15:33) to be covered by Paul's thematic statement.[269] Minimally, though he sees Paul as announcing the theme of the whole letter, Joseph Fitzmyer more reasonably takes the first four chapters of Romans as the basic development of the theme of God's gospel.[270] First, Paul explains that without the gospel God's wrath is manifested against gentiles (1:18–32) and Jews (2:1—3:9)—indeed, all humans (3:10–20). Second, Paul explains that God's righteousness is shown to all sinners so that all by faith, apart from the law, share, without distinction, in the justification, redemption, and expiation of Christ Jesus (3:21–31). Third, in that Abraham was justified by faith before he was circumcised, he is an example of the point that all are justified by faith, not by works (4:1–25).[271] Given this arrangement of Paul's argument and the "therefore" (οὖν) that heads his next section (5:1), it is reasonable to conclude that by the end of chapter 3 Paul has set out his basic understanding of the gospel, which he immediately illustrates in Abraham and goes on to explicate in the remainder of the letter.

Although we could not claim completeness in the results, when compared to our reconstruction from his first letter of what Paul is likely to have said in his initial or missionary preaching to the Thessalonians, it is clear that Paul's description of his gospel in Romans is, not surprisingly, much richer and more highly developed. Also, to be kept in mind, Paul is writing to established believers not recalling what he initially said to new believers at Thessalonica.[272]

Notwithstanding, still evident in his later development here in Romans is the fundamental importance of Jesus as "the Son"[273] and his resurrection (Rom 1:4; cf. 1 Thess 1:10) as the focus of the gospel. There is also the negative mention of idols in both discussions of the gospel (Rom 2:22; cf. 1 Thess 1:9). The wrath of God, which had a prominent part in Paul's gospel in Thessalonians,[274] is well represented in his explanation of the gospel in Romans.[275] Also, his initial call in Thessalonians "to serve a God living and true" (1 Thess 1:9) is now captured in a fundamental description of himself

---

269. Dunn, *Romans 1–8*, 37. Cf. Best, *Letter of Paul to the Romans*, 18; Edwards, *Romans*, 43–44.

270. Fitzmyer, *Romans*, 254.

271. Fitzmyer, *Romans*, 254.

272. See the discussion above at §3.2 (a) 1.

273. Rom 1:3, 9; 5:10; 8:3, 29, 32; cf. 1 Thess 1:10.

274. 1 Thess 1:10; cf. 2:16; 5:9.

275. Rom 1:18; 2:5, 8; 3:5; cf. 5:9. Notably, Paul only uses "wrath" (ὀργή) in Romans and 1 Thessalonians, the two letters where his gospel message is most clear. For ὀργή ("wrath") in Paul see Rom 1:18; 2:5, 8; 3:5; 4:15; 5:9; 9:22; 12:19; 13:4, 5; 1 Thess 1:10; 2:16; 5:9; cf. 1 Tim 2:8; Eph 2:3; 4:31; 5:6; Col 3:6, 8.

(Rom 1:1) and then is developed into major sections of Romans where Paul spells out the implications of the gospel.[276] However, eschatology, the motif of waiting for the Son from heaven, prominent in Paul's first letter (1 Thess 1:10), has dropped out of sight in his basic description of the gospel to take a place, after some hints,[277] in a later development of living in the Spirit (Rom 8:18-23). Even though it is still considered imminent,[278] no longer in Paul's explanation of the gospel is the *parousia* expected in the lifetime of the believers (14:8). Later in Romans (15:9-20) we will see how Paul relates his theoretical or verbal explication of the gospel to his fuller understanding of it.[279]

(e) "My gospel" (Romans 2:15-16). Paul has just concluded that, in terms of Jews and Greeks, God shows no partiality (2:1-11). Neither of them, he says, will be excused "in the day when God will judge the secret thoughts of people according to my gospel through Christ Jesus" (2:15-16).

Paul nowhere else uses the precise phrase "my gospel" (τὸ εὐαγγέλιόν μου), though it is arguably not out of character for him in that in other places he uses the phrase "our gospel" (εὐαγγέλιον ἡμῶν).[280] Using "my" to describe the gospel, Paul can hardly mean that this gospel is unique to him.[281] For elsewhere he resists the idea that his gospel is different; rather it is shared by others (e.g., Gal 1:1—2:11). We have clues to the probable meaning of the phrase "my gospel" in its use by two early interpretations of him.

First, in the doxology to this letter (Rom 16:25-27),[282] which in various manuscripts can be found various places toward the end of the letter, or missing altogether,[283] there is the phrase "my gospel" (τὸ εὐαγγέλιόν μου):

---

276. Note Paul's "therefore" (οὖν) at Rom 6:1 and 12:1; cf. 5.1.

277. Rom 4:17; 6:4-5; 8:11.

278. Rom 13:11-12; 16:20.

279. On Rom 15:19-20 see (i) below.

280. See 2 Cor 4:3 and 1 Thess 1:5, and the discussion above at §3.2 (a).

281. Cf. Cranfield, *Epistle to the Romans*, 2:810.

282. For an outline of the case for and against Paul being the author of Romans 16:25-27, see Moo, *Letter to the Romans*, 952-53n341. More likely than outright creation, following O'Neill, *Paul's Letter to the Romans*, 260, the present prolix doxology had, by the end of the second century, evolved from a Jewish doxology. See the detailed discussions by Jewett, *Romans*, 1002-5; cf. Dunn, *Romans 9-16*, 912-13, 916-17, who reports the consensus that this doxology was "first added to an abbreviated (Marcionite) version of the letter" (912).

283. See the discussions by Cranfield, *Epistle to the Romans*, 1:6-11 and Fitzmyer, *Romans*, 48.

> ²⁵Now to God who is able to strengthen you
>   according to my gospel
>   and the proclamation of Jesus Christ,
>   according to the revelation of the mystery
>   that was kept secret for long ages ²⁶but is now disclosed,
>   and through the prophetic writings is made known to all
>   the Gentiles,
>   according to the command of the eternal God,
>   to bring about the obedience of faith. (Rom 16:25–26)

From the three-part, parallel structure provided by the repetition of "according to" (κατά),²⁸⁴ two points become clear. First, in that the second and third parts (Rom 16:25d–26) reflect early Christian preaching rather than that of Jesus,²⁸⁵ it is reasonable to assume this is the subject of the first concerning "my gospel" and "proclamation" (16:25a–c). Second, reminiscent of Semitic poetry, the opening lines of each part are echoed and explicated by what follows. It is reasonable to assume, then, that "my gospel" is echoed and explicated by the statement "proclamation (κήρυγμα) of Jesus Christ."²⁸⁶ It is an objective genitive in that the proclamation is about Jesus rather than by him. In turn, this "proclamation" about Jesus is, for the author of this doxology, if not identical to "my gospel," very closely related to it and a legitimate expression of it.²⁸⁷ On this reading, the gospel is Paul's in the sense that it is what he and others have been propagating.²⁸⁸

The other early interpretation of Paul using the phrase "my gospel" (τὸ εὐαγγέλιόν μου) is provided by the author of 2 Timothy.²⁸⁹ As part of his appeal to Timothy the author exhorts him to "Remember Jesus Christ, raised from the dead, a descendant of David according to my gospel" (2 Tim 2:8). Here the gospel is, reminiscent of its description in the salutation of Romans (1:3–4), a fragmentary outline sketch of Jesus. Again, while it is very closely related to the proclamation it is not the proclamation.

---

284. Käsemann, *Commentary on Romans*, 424. E.g., Dunn, *Romans 9–16*, 913, suggests that the entire doxology is structured for easy liturgical use.

285. Cf. Cranfield, *Epistle to the Romans*, 2:810.

286. Cranfield, *Epistle to the Romans*, 2:810.

287. Cf. Käsemann, *Commentary on Romans*, 424.

288. Cranfield, *Epistle to the Romans*, 2:810. Cf. Molland, *Das paulinische Euangelion*, 97: "'Mein Evangelium' ist kein paulinisches Sonderevangelium" ("'My Gospel' is not a special Pauline gospel").

289. Brown, *Introduction to the New Testament*, 668, says that the majority of those who take the Pastorals to have been written after the lifetime of Paul date them between 80 and 100 CE. Cf. Marshall, *Pastoral Epistles*, 92.

Given that the authors of the doxology of Romans and of 2 Timothy were near in time to Paul, it is reasonable to suppose they are likely to be reasonably reliable interpreters of Paul's understanding of his term "my gospel."[290] They both suggest that, for Paul, the term would have meant his story about Jesus. Here that story includes God, through Jesus Christ, judging the secret thoughts of all (Rom 2:16). This is a rich and familiar motif Paul is echoing from his Scriptures,[291] here introducing the notion of God's omniscience and mercy[292] into his gospel.

In turning to the next reference to "gospel" in Romans it cannot but be noticed that, having introduced himself as "set apart for the gospel" (Rom 1:1), signaled its promise in holy Scriptures (1:2), described Jesus as its central concern (1:3-7, 9), established the theme of the letter on the basis of his definition of the gospel (1:16-17), and reiterated the centrality of Jesus in his gospel (2:16), Paul does not mention the gospel for many chapters (until 10:15-16).[293] It is not that Paul has abandoned his concern for the gospel. Rather, as Francis Watson noted, Paul goes on to speak of the gospel in terms of salvation, faith, and righteousness (cf. 1:3-4, 9).[294] In doing so, along the way, he is preoccupied with pointing to scriptural underpinnings for his understanding of the gospel he is explicating. It is in citing Scripture that the term "gospel" appears again in his argument.

(f) The feet of those gospelling (Romans 10:15-16). In trying to identify the origin of Paul's gospel we have already given attention to his statement: "But how are they to preach unless they are sent? As it is written, 'How beautiful are the feet of those gospelling [the] good things.' But they have not all obeyed the gospel" (10:15-16). We saw that, using Scripture to support his point, for Paul the gospel is a call to everyone from God—a message to be trusted or believed[295]—which is proclaimed by those whom God sends.[296] Notably, here, in the paralleling of the two verbs, "preach" (κηρύσσω) and

---

290. Cf. Dunn, *Romans 9-16*, 917, concludes "that the doxology has summarized well some of the basic concerns of the letter."

291. Cf. LXX: Exod 2:3; Deut 15:9; 29:8; Job 21:24; 34:22; Pss 69:5 (MT)/68:6 (LXX); Jer 16:17; 23:24; Ezek 8:12; Sir 1:30; 17:15, 20; 39:19; 42:20; Pss Sol 9:3; Sus (Th) 1:42.

292. Hays, *Echoes of Scripture*, 43.

293. Noted by, e.g., Watson, "Law in Romans," 95.

294. Watson, "Law in Romans," 95.

295. See the brief but creative discussion of faith (in relation to Rom 1:16-17) by Stowers, *Rereading of Romans*, 199, pointing out the importance of context is translating this word with a wide range or meanings in ancient usage. Stowers lists, "loyalty, honesty, good faith, faithfulness, trust, trustworthiness, belief, proof, and confidence."

296. See §2.4 (a) above.

"gospel" (εὐαγγελίζω) uncharacteristically become synonyms.[297] The gospel is clearly a message that is spoken.

(g) Enemies of the gospel (Romans 11:28). Here Paul is drawing to a close a long section on the mystery of God's actions (Rom 9–11). There is a mystery in that God is, and will be seen to be merciful to all (11:32).[298] This is not clear from an historical perspective for "a hardening has come on part of Israel" (11:25). Indeed, Paul says, "Regarding the gospel they are enemies of God for your sake" (11:28).

At first glance it could be concluded from his wording, "regarding the gospel" (κατὰ μὲν τὸ εὐαγγέλιον, Rom 11:28a), that Paul saw the hostility of Israel as an innate or essential part of the gospel.[299] However, as the present hostility is contrasted with their election (11:28b), Paul is using the term "gospel" to describe not the final[300] but the present phase of the story or history of God's action as Savior which is being resisted by a part of Israel. Therefore, the term "gospel" captures not simply Paul's proclamation (or message)[301] or ministry or even the narrative of what God is doing or the geographical progress of gospel[302] or "the sphere of the proclamation of salvation."[303] The gospel is the present action of God as Savior in Christ.[304]

(h) "Priestly service of the gospel of God" (Romans 15:16). Even though Paul has completed the thrust of his argument, conveying news of his personal plans remains caught up in his understanding of the divine plan. He says his rationale for writing is in part—he does not mention the other part—to remind the readers of what they already know. In this, he says, he is a "minister" (λειτουργός) of Christ Jesus acting in "priestly service of the gospel of God" (15:16).

Here the gospel is not a story of Jesus or the narrative of God's action, or even Paul's preaching.[305] The gospel is itself the act or saving drama of God in which the gentiles become acceptable as they are sanctified in the

297. See p. 109n208 above.

298. Cf. Barrett, *Romans*, 205; Dunn, *Romans 9–16*, 677.

299. Noted by Dunn, *Romans 9–16*, 685.

300. As supposed by Dunn, *Romans 9–16*, 685.

301. Jewett, *Romans*, 707.

302. Cf. Cranfield, *Epistle to the Romans*, 2:579. On the next page (580) Cranfield is probably too inclusive in what he takes to be the meaning of "gospel" here. Also noted by Jewett, *Romans*, 707n120.

303. Käsemann, *Commentary on Romans*, 315.

304. Cf. Dunn, *Romans 9–16*, 693: "'The gospel' is Paul's watchword for the phase introduced by Christ," misses Paul's emphasis on God's action.

305. As supposed by Cranfield, *Epistle to the Romans*, 2:756; Fitzmyer, *Romans*, 709, 711; Jewett, *Romans*, 907.

Holy Spirit (Rom 15:16).[306] Paul acts as priest, not literally in cultic or even a spiritualized activity.[307] Rather, Paul applies to himself his earlier appeal that his readers present their "bodies as living sacrifices" (12:1). The ambiguity in Paul's expression of his work, and the fluidity of his thinking in relation to the gospel, is seen again (see 1:1 and 9) in his easy movement between saying he is serving the gospel of God (15:16) and, as we are about to see, completing the gospel of Christ (11:19).

(i) Completing the gospel of Christ (Romans 15:19-20). Having described his activities as priestly in the general sense (15:15-17), Paul earths his work in a concrete description of his ministry. Clearly self-conscious, using a double negative in a complex statement, Paul awkwardly expresses himself:

> For I will not presume to speak about anything that Christ has not accomplished through me, to win obedience from the Gentiles, word and deed, in the power of signs and wonders, in the power of the Spirit of God, so that from Jerusalem and as far around to Illyricum I have fulfilled (or completed) the gospel of Christ. Thus I am eager to gospel where Christ has not been named. (15:18-20, my translation)[308]

Our interest is in understanding what Paul means, first, by the noun "gospel" (εὐαγγέλιον) and then by the verb "gospel" (εὐαγγελίζω). The noun comes in a result clause introduced by "so that" (ὥστε): "so that I have fulfilled the gospel of Christ" (Rom 15:19). What "so that" refers back to, or includes, is not clear. It could refer only to his specific description of his work (15:18)[309] or back to include the general description of his work in priestly terms (from 15:15). Given the inferential conjunction "for" (γάρ) that holds together both his general and specific statements of his work, fulfilling or completing the gospel of Christ is his entire work, though understood specifically as what "Christ has . . . accomplished through me, to win obedience from the Gentiles, word and deed, in the power of signs and wonders, in the power of the Spirit of [God]"[310] (15:18b-19a).

---

306. The argument here is not altered should the phrase "the offering of the Gentiles" (ἡ προσφορὰ τᾶν ἐθνᾶν, Rom 15:16) be taken as a subjective genitive referring to an offering or collection given by the gentiles, which Paul discusses in 15:25-32. See Downs, "'Offering of the Gentiles,'" 173-86.

307. Cf. Dunn, *Romans 9-16*, 859-60.

308. On this sentence, see Barrett, *Romans*, 253, and the discussion by Goulder, *Paul and the Competing Mission*, 252-53. Also, see the discussion in Twelftree, *Paul and the Miraculous*, 219.

309. Cranfield, *Epistle to the Romans*, 2:760.

310. On the textual difficulties at this point see Jewett, *Romans*, 901-2.

The "gospel" is, then, what Christ is accomplishing through Paul. Notably, the gospel is accomplished not only in word, but also in deed, which he explains means signs and wonders or miracles, accomplished by the Spirit. However, the ensuing "thus" (οὕτως) means that fulfilling the "gospel" (εὐαγγέλιον, noun) is not only what he describes as "word and deed . . . from Jerusalem around to Illyricum" but also "to gospel" (εὐαγγελίζεσθαι, verb) where Christ has not been named (15:20). Thus, in turn, "gospelling" is the activity through which the gospel comes in Paul's ministry. In other words, the noun and the verb refer to the same thing: what Christ is accomplishing through Paul.

What Paul means in saying he has "fulfilled" or "completed" (πεπληρωκέναι) the gospel is not immediately obvious. It could be, given the strong association of πληρόω ("fill" or "complete") with eschatological expectation, especially those related to Scripture,[311] and the heightened eschatological expectation of the early church, shared by Paul (Rom 13:11-14), as well as the tradition associated with Jesus that before the end "the gospel must first be preached to all the Gentiles" (Mark 13:10), that Paul means that he has completed all the work of the gospel necessary before the *parousia*.[312] Or, Paul could simply mean that he has preached in every province.[313] Since Paul goes straight on to say that his ambition is "to gospel" where Christ has not been named, he probably means both that he has completed or gospelled in all the areas available to him (cf. Rom 15:23) and that this is part of the essential preparation for the *parousia*.

We have seen that in Paul using the verb "gospel" he expresses his understanding that propagating the gospel involved more than his speaking. Nevertheless, using a quotation from Isaiah shows that he saw his role as primarily speaking. He says that he makes it his ambition "to gospel" (εὐαγγελίζεσθαι) where Christ has not been named (Rom 15:20). He finds justification for this in Isaiah, which he quotes exactly: "Those who have not been told about him shall see, and those who have not heard shall understand" (LXX Isa 52:15/Rom 15:21). Thus, "to gospel" may be more than preaching, but his role is primarily preaching.

---

311. See Matt 1:22; 2:15, 17, 23; 4:14; 8:17; 12:17; 13:35; 21:4; 26:54, 56; 27:9; Mark 1:15; 14:49; Luke 4:21; 21:24; 22:16; 24:44; John 7:8; 12:38; 13:18; 15:25; 17:12; 18:9, (cf. 32); 19:24, 36; Acts 1:16; 3:18; 13:27; Rom 8:4; Jas 2:23. For a more direct eschatological use of πληρόω ("fill" or "complete") see Mark 1:15; Luke 21:24; John 7:8; cf. Acts 2:2.

312. Cranfield, *Epistle to the Romans*, 2:762, also citing, e.g., Munck, *Paul and the Salvation of Mankind*, 48-55; Barrett, *Romans*, 276-77; Barrett, "New Testament Eschatology," 228.

313. So Bruce, *Romans*, 261, citing NEB.

(j) Results: The gospel in Romans. The results of our enquiry into the meaning of "gospel"—noun and verb—in Romans are particularly important. Even though the time between his first extant letter and this one is only a few years,[314] this letter is the most mature expression of his thinking we have and should, therefore, in the final analysis of Paul's understanding of the gospel, be given particularly careful consideration. From the *exordium*, Paul's introduction (Rom 1:1–6), it is clear that it was no longer the law that determined and dominated his life, but the gospel. Since he is set apart for it, and though it is fundamental to his self-understanding, the gospel is more than anything he could say or do in relation to it. Rather, the gospel is God's, promised by him, and concerns his Son. However, we have seen that the gospel is not the teaching by Jesus; it is his identity and life. Yet it is not simply that the gospel is equated with the Son but that he is its focus and the one through whom it is experienced.

Describing God's gospel concerning his Son in recognizably traditional terms, Paul asserted before readers less enamored with him that his gospel was not devised by him or unique to him but was long and widely shared. Thus, the term "gospel" can capture not only Paul's message or ministry, but the narrative or drama of God's action in Christ, including in the present (Rom 11:28), in which the gentiles—the non-Jews—become acceptable in that they are sanctified in the Spirit (15:16). In turn, then, the gospel can be what Christ is accomplishing through Paul (15:19) and, hence, the activity (εὐαγγελίζω) through which the gospel comes in his ministry (15:20). Consistent with this, in the first of only three uses of the verb in Romans (1:15; also 10:15; 15:20) the term describes not Paul's preaching but the whole breadth of his work. In another use of the verb, "gospel" (εὐαγγελίζω) is equated with his preaching (10:15). As we have just seen (15:19, 20), noun and verb can refer to the same thing: what Christ is accomplishing through Paul, obedience of the gentiles through a message and miracles. In saying that in the gospel "the righteousness of God is revealed" (1:17) readers are being pointed to the gospel as God's loving kindness in drawing them into salvation. These results are important in understanding the gospel according to Paul, which we can now summarize in light of our study.

---

314. See the brief discussion in §5.4 below.

5

The Gospel According to Paul

OVER AGAINST THE CONTINUING scholarly obsession with Paul's notions of the "law," "grace," and "justification by faith," this study has turned the spotlight on Paul's "gospel." If not at the center of his theological thinking, "gospel" (noun and verb) is of such significance for him that he uses the term often. He uses "gospel" to describe his work and in relation to his self-identity. Our understanding of "gospel" for Paul is, then, fundamental to our perception of him and his mission. Further, in Paul's work and writing the word "gospel" took firm root in Christianity from early times to the present. We would serve Christianity well by understanding what he understood by "the gospel."

An initial review of what Paul says about his gospel suggests that the present understanding of his "gospel" (as a noun) as empowered speech, and "gospel" (as a verb) as "preaching," are probably very different from his.[1] Thus, the purpose of this project has been to answer the question, what is the gospel according to Paul?

To answer our central question—What is the gospel according to Paul?—a number of subsidiary questions needed to be answered: What did the word—noun (εὐαγγέλιον) and verb (εὐαγγελίζω)—mean in Paul's world? Where did Paul get the term? Did he introduce the term to Christianity, or did he receive it from earlier followers of Jesus? What role did Paul's Scriptures play in his understanding of the gospel? Is the gospel, for Paul, his preached message? Is the gospel his empowered message, a message embodying God's transforming power? Or, is the gospel something else,

---

1. See §1.5 above.

or even a number of things? In turn, does Paul intend the verb "gospel," perhaps translated "gospelling," to be a synonym for "preaching?"

Answers to our question about Paul's gospel have followed a similar line. In the older work of C. H. Dodd, Adolf Deissmann, and Martin Dibelius, for example, Paul's gospel was seen as his message, something he preached. In more recent times Paul's gospel continues to be equated with his preached message. Even though E. P. Sanders broke rank in noting (without comment, unfortunately) that Paul "brought his gospel not only with the word but also with manifestations of the Spirit,"[2] little changed in the scholarly conversation. What changed, we noted, was that there have been hints in the literature that Paul's preaching did not quite capture what he meant by "gospel," so that in the current conversation there lingers an uncertainty that Paul's gospel can be summed up by saying that it is his message. Instead, it is suggested that Paul's gospel message embodies, becomes or mediates God's transforming power in response to faith.[3] Even these views, however, do not capture what Paul has in mind when he uses the noun "gospel." Given the questions around his use of the noun, we have also been examining what he means by the verb.

To draw together our conclusions, first we will summarize the results of our enquiry into the origin of Paul's gospel. Second, we will attend to the major question of what Paul means by the noun "gospel." Third, leading directly from the results of what we have seen about his use of the noun, we will turn to set out in summary how Paul uses the verb "gospel," that is, what he meant when he says he "gospels." Fourth, the question of possible change and development in Paul's understanding and representation of the gospel will be considered. Fifth, this chapter and the project close with a succinct answer to the question, what is the gospel according to Paul? This will be followed by a brief contemporary coda that suggests some of the implications of our conclusions.

§5.1 THE ORIGIN OF PAUL'S GOSPEL

Given Paul's letters are the earliest extant Christian writings, and before him "gospel"—noun and verb—is rare in Greek literature, the origin of his "gospel" requires investigation. Indeed, without evidence that anyone other than Homer[4] had used the noun εὐαγγέλιον ("good news," neuter singular)

---

2. Sanders, *Paul and Palestinian Judaism*, 450.
3. Cf., e.g., Wolter, *Paul*, 66–67.
4. Homer, *Od.* 14.152–53, 166.

before Paul, establishing its origin for him, and the meaning that came with it, is a challenge to us.

In attempting to discover where Paul found the word "gospel"—and hence the likely significant content or initial meaning for him and his readers—there are a number of options. He may have taken up the word from his Hellenistic Jewish world or from his non-Jewish Greek or Latin worlds or from his Scriptures. Or, perhaps he inherited the word and idea from earlier followers of Jesus. Or, again, perhaps there were a number of influences on his use of the "gospel" word group and ideas.

(a) A Jewish source? As a Jewish intellectual it would not be surprising if Paul's Hellenistic, Jewish world provided him with the word "gospel" and its related ideas. We took the work of Philo and Josephus as examples of the use made of "gospel" among Hellenists in Paul's Jewish world.[5]

Philo used only the verb (εὐαγγελίζω) and in relation to "good news" in general, and also in relation to politics and the recovery of health, for example. Notably, he used the word in connection with the experience of hope announcing the coming of joy, and the compound "proclaim good news in advance" (προευαγγελίζομαι) with regard to the approach of a friend.[6] There is limited political or military use of "gospel" in the writings of Philo, showing that any political connotations of the word at the time, suggested by its use in relation to the emperor, had by no means come to dominate the meaning and use of the word. Also, Philo does not use the word for God's deliverance or salvation.

Josephus, writing a generation after Paul, but with no evidence of knowing of or borrowing from him, three times takes up the neuter singular noun (εὐαγγέλιον) so important to Paul. Josephus uses "gospel" (verb and noun) in military and political contexts, often connected with the emperor. As with Philo, Josephus does not otherwise use the term "gospel" with any particular theological or scriptural significance.

It is clear that Paul's Hellenistic, Jewish world did not provide him with the neuter singular noun "gospel" (εὐαγγέλιον). However, given that Josephus soon after Paul was independently using εὐαγγέλιον suggests Paul's readers would likely have been familiar with it. The connections evident in the writings of Josephus between "gospel" and the emperor, which are in line with the use found in the Augustus inscription, suggest that in Paul's world the word was associated with significant news, even (as we have just noted) with a savior figure filled with divine power bringing peace. Though,

---

5. See §2.1 above.
6. Philo, *Abraham* 153.2.

to repeat, we have not found reason to suppose that imperial connotations had a particular hold on the word "gospel."

(b) A scriptural source? We saw that the "gospel" word group was established in Greek literature through the mid-second-century-BCE second phase of the translation of Jewish Scriptures into Greek.[7] The word, primarily as a verb and concentrated in Isaiah, was used to refer to God's saving activity, a use not inconsistent with that of the Augustus inscription.

In that the Scriptures were of fundamental importance to Paul—he could well be described as living with "texts-in-the-mind"[8]—it would be expected that at least part of the impetus for his use of "gospel," and its significance, would have come from them. However, insofar as they reflect their cultural peers, from the writings of Philo and Josephus it is immediately obvious that the Scriptures were not significant among Jewish writers at the time in their use of the word group.[9] Indeed, Paul only once takes up "gospel" in a quotation from Scripture,[10] and only then as a verb, not as a singular noun, his most distinctive use of the term. Yet, the implied gospel in this instance—God's salvation for all, an inclusive scope also reflected in the Augustus inscription—is not portrayed as found in Scripture. Instead, our examination of this text (Rom 10:15) showed that Paul considered the gospel was promised and prefigured in Scripture. In any case, Paul makes such changes to this quotation from Isaiah that show his attention is not on the notion of "gospel" but on God having sent messengers of salvation.[11] Since Paul is continually happy to alter texts he quotes confirms the conclusion that his Scriptures are not the prime source of his "gospel."

It is reasonable to conclude, then, that although Paul took the gospel to be promised and prefigured in his Scriptures it was not in them that he found it. Instead of his Scriptures being the source of his thinking they were brought in to corroborate what he had already concluded about the gospel.[12] What he had already concluded became a lens through which he read and shaped his reading of Scripture. That lens or gospel through which he was reading Scripture was the promised experience of righteousness through faith for all.[13] In short, Scripture is neither the origin of Paul's gospel nor does

---

7. See §2.1 above.

8. The phrase is from Fishbane, *Biblical Interpretation in Ancient Israel*, 435, describing earlier tradents of Israel's sacred texts. Also, see Wagner, *Heralds of the Good News*, 357n43.

9. See §2.1 above.

10. Rom 10:15b/Isa 52:7a; see §2.4 (a) above.

11. See §2.4 (a) above.

12. Rom 1:16–17/Gal 3:11/Hab 2:4.

13. Gal 3:6–8; see §2.4 (g) above.

it shape it beyond foreshadowing and promising that what one (Abraham) had was available to all (Gal 3:6–8). Instead, Paul reads Scripture out of an already-established view of the gospel, calling on Scripture to verify the credibility and trustworthiness of the gospel (Rom 1:1–2) and to give voice to his views rather than to contribute to their composition.[14]

Nevertheless, even if Paul did not derive his gospel from his Scriptures, so important were they to him and many of his readers that the scriptural use of any of the "gospel" word group, along with its connotations, would invariably form the backdrop to what they were reading. That is, on the basis of what we saw of the use of the words in the Scriptures, he and his readers would know that "gospel" (noun and verb) referred to military victory, and as a verb was used for news of the birth of a son, the accession of a king, eulogizing a king and his son, and for the welcome news of the death of a king. More significantly, often the verb "gospel" referred to God's saving activity of one kind or another, including healing. Also, the concentration of the verb in Isaiah related to the prophet announcing God's presence, particularly in salvation. This would most probably have caused Paul's readers familiar with the Scriptures to bring to "gospel" notions related to significant—including divine—news in relation particularly to God's presence, including in salvation. Once again, these connotations are quite understandable in light of the Augustus inscription alluding to a powerful divine savior bringing universal peace.[15]

(c) A non-Jewish source? It quickly became clear that it is unlikely that Paul inherited the term or idea of "gospel" from the non-Jewish literary world. Before Paul there are very few uses in Greek literature of any form of the word "gospel." As we have repeatedly noted, among the Greeks the singular neuter noun (εὐαγγέλιον), so important to Paul, is only used twice before him, both in Homer.[16] And in all extant Greek literature before him the verb "gospel" (εὐαγγελίζω), also important to Paul, is found only nineteen times.[17] Apart from Cicero, who borrows the term in the plural using Greek letters (εὐαγγέλια),[18] the Latin writers do not use the term. In any case the Latin language appears to have had little perceptible influence on Paul.

---

14. Rom 11:25–28; 15:20–21; 1 Cor 9:16; 2 Cor 10:16. See the discussions in §2.4 above.
15. See §2.1 above.
16. Homer, *Od.* 14.152–53, 166.
17. See the Appendix below.
18. Cicero, *Att.* 2.3.1; 2.12.1; 13.40.1.

Yet, a significant use of "gospel" from the non-Jewish world before Paul is that of the widely distributed inscription by and about Augustus saying that, "The birthday of the god was for the world the beginning of good news (εὐανγελίων, plural)."[19] This text, intended to be widely read and, therefore, using the language of the people, shows that while we cannot establish that Paul was directly borrowing his singular "gospel" (εὐαγγέλιον) from wider current use, he was using a term that would have been well understood. His readers would likely include associating "gospel" with a divine savior filled with divine power who was expected to put everything at peace.[20] Although its association with the emperor did not dominate the currency of "gospel," readers would likely draw the conclusion that Paul was advocating a gospel that was understood in some way similar to, but in contrast to, the gospel associated with the emperor, which we have just seen relates to its significance, divine presence, and salvation.

(d) A Christian source? Although the evidence is limited, from what we have been able to argue, Paul probably found the term "gospel" already in use among followers of Jesus before him. Among at least some of Paul's predecessors in the faith "gospel" was used for what Jesus was doing in bringing salvation, particularly through healing (Matt 11:5/Luke 7:22). In this Q tradition of Jesus' statement for John the Baptist about his identity, which Paul most probably knew, he would also have seen the significance of Isaiah in informing this view of the gospel he had received.

Paul would, further, have seen from his predecessors that the gospel was the preached message of the believers (cf. Acts 15:12). Paul's testimony points in the same direction. He acknowledges that Peter and others before him preached the gospel (esp. Gal 2:7, 9). In turn, there are a number of places in his letters where he describes traditional material handed down to him as "gospel."[21] As we noted and will also see in the next section, the number of times Paul uses the noun "gospel" for this traditional material suggests that the word "gospel" and at least these elementary ideas were part of what he inherited from earlier believers. In their world in which Greek and Aramaic were used, these bilingual believers are most likely to have been those who were able to bring the Aramaic (בשורתא) for "good news" into their Greek vocabulary for "good news" (εὐαγγέλιον).

In short, Paul inherited the word "gospel" from earlier followers of Jesus. For them the word described both Jesus' ministry that involved healing, as well as their own preached message about him. They, in turn,

---

19. *OGIS* 458 II 40–41.
20. See §2.1 above.
21. Rom 1:3–4a; 1 Cor 9:14; 15:3–5; 1 Thess 1:9–10.

are likely to have picked up the word from Jesus whom, we saw, probably uncharacteristically used it at least once of his work.[22] Therefore, with so little evidence of its use, we can reasonably speculate that the "gospel" word group was not particularly important to Jesus or his early followers. It was in Paul reflecting on his ministry and its dramatic impact on his readers that caused him to take up this subversive term in a way that moved it to the center of his thinking, dramatically widened and deepened its meaning, leading to the concept's irreversible hold in early and later Christianity.

Paul's hearers would already have been familiar with the word group, which was used for good news in general. From its use among Hellenistic Jewish writers and at a popular level the word would have carried particular connotations of, among other things, a divine savior putting everything at peace. The influence of Scripture on his readers, even if not directly identifiable, would have given the word group an overtone of God's prophetic promise of salvation and saving activity.

(e) A revelation. Although Paul most probably found the term "gospel" in the vocabulary of believers before him, and although he acknowledges he and they preached the same message, he is adamant that his gospel came in, and was, a revelation. Alongside and undergirding all the human tributaries that may have contributed to his gospel, Paul's testimony is that his gospel came in, and as, a revelation. Writing to the Galatians he says that he received his gospel "through a revelation of Jesus Christ" (Gal 1:12), which he goes on to put in other words: "God ... was pleased to reveal his Son to me" (1:16). Just as he would have seen in his Scriptures,[23] his experience confirmed that the revelation (of Jesus Christ, God's Son) was both the gospel for him and also, notably, his call to propagate that gospel. This emboldened him to speak of "my gospel" (Rom 2:16) or "our gospel" (2 Cor 4:3), even though he acknowledged it was shared by peers.

§5.2 PAUL'S "GOSPEL"

We are now in a position to draw together some conclusions to answer the driving question of this project: What is the gospel according to Paul? If anything is already clear it is that Paul's "gospel" cannot be described as his God-empowered message of salvation. Nor—I must correct myself—can the gospel be described simply or only in terms of message and miracle.[24] From the discussion in chapters 3 and 4, the heart of this study, it is clear

---

22. See §2.2 (a) above.
23. Rom 10:13/Joel 3:5 (NRSV 2:32), on which see §2.4 (a) above.
24. This is to correct Twelftree, *Paul and the Miraculous*, 315–17.

that the gospel according to Paul is not one thing. For Paul and his readers the "gospel" word group is a polyvalent set of terms. "Gospel" can mean a number of things, and certainly more—much more—than Paul's message, even his empowered message and, as will be summarized below, more than the message and miracle that characterize Paul's ministry.

(a) The gospel as tradition about Jesus. This is the place to begin in drawing together our understanding of Paul's gospel, for it was from earlier followers of Jesus that he received both his vocabulary and basic information in relation to the gospel. We have seen that there are three places in Paul's letters where he uses the noun "gospel" for or in relation to traditional or creedal material that he has inherited from earlier followers of Jesus.[25] Each block of this material is about Jesus. First, in his earliest extant letter he reminds the Thessalonians of the coming of the gospel to them and their response:

> You turned to God from idols
>   to serve a God living and true
> [10]and to await his Son out of heaven
> Whom he raised from the dead
>   Jesus who delivers us
>   from the coming wrath.[26]

Even though the word "gospel," which occurs a little earlier in the letter (1 Thess 1:5), is not used directly of this inherited material, it is so closely connected to the description of the Thessalonians' reception of the gospel that it would most probably have been understood as part of their shared understanding of it. The gospel is, then, a brief narrative initially about God and then primarily his Son (Jesus) who is waited for from heaven. Salvific significance is attributed to Jesus without specifying in what way he "delivers us from the coming wrath" (1:10). By association, readers would reasonably assume that it is his resurrection. No significance is given to the death of Jesus beyond being a precursor to his resurrection.

Again, second, that Paul saw the gospel as received traditional propositions primarily about Jesus is clear in 1 Corinthians, where he, in a reminder, describes the gospel that he brought to the readers (1 Cor 15:1). The information he handed on to them as gospel is:

---

25. See §2.3 (b) above.
26. 1 Thess 1:9b–10, my translation. See the discussion at §2.3 (b) (ii) above.

> that Christ died for our sins
>> according to the Scriptures,
> and that he was buried,
> and that he was raised on the third day
>> according to the Scriptures,
> and that he appeared to Cephas,
> then to the twelve.[27]

Here the gospel handed on in a series of propositions that take a narrative form is, yet again, centered on Jesus. This time, though, his death is not implied, as in the material in 1 Thessalonians, but is included and given salvific significance.[28] Again, the resurrection is mentioned, though with added material about appearances, but not given salvific significance. Both the death and resurrection are said to be according to Scripture.

The third set of creedal statements that Paul most probably inherited, and which is called gospel, is at the beginning of Romans. He quite directly says what the gospel is about (περί, Rom 1:3):

> his Son
> came
>> from the seed of David
>> according to flesh
> [4]designated Son of God
>> in power
>> according to the spirit of holiness
>> from the resurrection of the dead.[29]

Once again, the gospel is a number of propositions forming a description of Jesus. In this material the statements focus on the origin and status of Jesus. For the first time among these three collections of material the resurrection is given meaning, reflecting in some way that Jesus was designated Son of God in power. No immediate salvific significance is given to Jesus, though Paul himself goes on to do so in saying of "Jesus Christ our Lord" that it was him "through whom we have received grace and apostleship" (1:5).

In describing traditional, inherited material about Jesus, along with its significance, as the gospel, it has to be noted that the gospel is not simply or primarily Paul's message. From this material it is clear that, for Paul, the gospel is the traditional material that he has received from earlier followers of Jesus for whom this was the message they preached. The inherited

---

27. 1 Cor 15:3–5. See the discussion at §2.3 (b) (iii) above. Cf. Kelly, *Early Christian Creeds*, 17.

28. Cf. 1 Cor 11:24; §4.1 (e) above.

29. Rom 1:3–4a, my translation. See the discussion at §2.3 (b) (iv) above.

material focuses on a sketch of Jesus—though only his origin and the end of his life—which is given salvific significance. Obviously, though only secondarily, this material went on to become his message, or at least part of it. Thus, the conclusion to draw from this discussion so far is not only that Jesus' ministry can be described as gospel, but so also can a rudimentary sketch of his life. Further, we can note that it is gospel—good news—because of the salvific significance of the person described.

Given that mention of the death and resurrection in some form is common to all three sets of statements, the central importance of this motif in what the early Christians—as well as, in turn, Paul—understood as gospel is obvious. We also saw the importance of the death of Jesus in Paul's gospel when, in using "proclaim," a word intimately associated with the gospel,[30] he says of involvement in the Lord's supper (1 Cor 11:20), "you proclaim the Lord's death until he comes" (11:26).[31]

However, the considerable differences between these three sets of traditional material suggest that in these statements Paul is mining a larger reserve of material, assembled as he saw fit in light of the needs of his hearers or readers. That not all these inherited statements fit tidily together—as in the interruption of "whom he raised from the dead" in the material in 1 Thessalonians[32]—is probably further evidence Paul is assembling these statements from a reservoir of traditional ideas about Jesus described as gospel.

Having set out these three statements in what is probably chronological order, it becomes apparent that Paul's use of the traditional material for the description of Jesus increases in complexity. In 1 Thessalonians there is the simple statement that Jesus was raised from the dead and is expected from heaven in the lifetime of the readers (1 Thess 1:10). Then in 1 Corinthians Christ dies, is buried, is raised, and appears to Cephas and others (1 Cor 15:3–5). In the latest statement the complexity is not in increasing the length of the story of Jesus but in its theological richness, in the detail included on his origin and the repercussion or significance of the resurrection, not for others, but for himself (Rom 1:3–4a). Among other things, then, the gospel is also the tradition about the status, death, and resurrection of Jesus, along with its salvific significance which, following his predecessors, he took up as his message. With the gospel being described as the traditions or story of Jesus, it is easier to see how he also sees the gospel as Jesus Christ.

---

30. See 1 Cor 2:1 and on which see §4.1 (b) above.
31. See §4.1 (e) above.
32. 1 Thess 1:10; see §2.3 (b) (ii) above.

In addition to these three traditional statements a fourth is to be added that draws attention to the central place the interpretation of the death of Jesus took in Paul's gospel message.[33] In the traditional material Paul hands on about the Lord's Supper (1 Cor 11:23-26) we saw that Paul's gospel message interpreted Jesus' death as on "our behalf" (11:24); the ratification of a new covenant (11:25; cf. Jer 31:31); and as pointing to a future fulfillment (1 Cor 11:26). Therefore, for the readers, the present involved a life of expectant waiting (cf. 1 Thess 1:10).

(b) The gospel as Jesus Christ. As his received tradition about the gospel is dominated by the story of Jesus it is a small step to equating him with the gospel. Early in his letter to the Philippians this aspect of his understanding of the gospel becomes apparent. When he writes of his imprisonment as a "defense of the gospel" (ἀπολογίαν τοῦ εὐαγγελίου, Phil 1:16) in parallel with mentioning others who "preach" (κηρύσσω, 1:15) or "proclaim" (καταγγέλλω, 1:17, 18) Christ, it is not so much a message about Christ, but that it is Christ himself who is the gospel (1:12-26).[34] Then, in calling his readers to live in relation to the gospel, his definition of the gospel as Christ is even more obvious and clear. Having called his readers to have an attitude worthy of the gospel of Christ (1:27) he goes on to describe that attitude as the attitude of Christ Jesus (2:5). The hymn to Christ is, then, a description of the gospel: Jesus Christ (2:6-11). In line with this, biographical details of Jesus are brought into the service of Paul's theological enterprise: Jesus is descended from David (Rom 1:3-4); "born of a woman" (Gal 4:4); had brothers (1 Cor 9:5; Gal 1:19); was humble (Phil 2:8), gentle (2 Cor 10:1), and compassionate (Phil 1:8) in a life characterized by distress (2 Cor 4:10); before his death he hosted a Passover meal with others (1 Cor 11:23-26); and died (e.g., Phil 2:8) by crucifixion,[35] and was raised to life (e.g., Rom 6:4; 1 Thess 1:10).[36]

Thus, the gospel is not so much Paul's message as its subject: Christ and his character, life, and work in the context of his cosmic story. Yet, it must be emphasized, Paul's gospel is not simply the story of Jesus. The gospel Paul says was revealed to him by God was not a story or a message but a person, Jesus Christ, God's Son (1:12, 16).

33. See §4.1 (e) above.

34. Hofius, "'All Israel Will be Saved,'" 37, appears to come close to this conclusion: "When 'all Israel' encounters the *Kyrios* at the parousia, it encounters the *gospel!*" However, this encounter has been explained in terms of hearing "the gospel from the mouth of Christ himself at his return" (37).

35. E.g., 1 Cor 1:23; 13:4; Gal 3:1.

36. Cf. Belleville, "Gospel and Kerygma in 2 Corinthians," 140-42, 163; Dunn, *Theology of Paul the Apostle*, 183-85.

For Paul, Christ is both the gospel and the measure of its expression. Or, for Paul, the gospel is both Christ and him experienced and expressed; the gospel is Christ and is brought and experienced in Christ's presence.[37]

Readers understanding this point are likely to have nuanced their reception of at least Paul's message by their general knowledge of the word "gospel." Even if the readers were not directly familiar with the widely known Augustus inscription using "gospel" in relation to a figure surpassing others, the notions implicit in the inscription, necessarily widely understood, would readily help readers see that it was an appropriate word to use in relation to Jesus Christ, the Son of God, a divine figure, a Savior, bringing peace.[38]

(c) The gospel as the ministry of Jesus and its replication. When discussing Paul's testimony concerning the gospel he inherited we established that Paul saw himself as responding to the same call, and carrying out the same work, as earlier followers of Jesus.[39] When he was defending his right to make a living from his ministry he says that "the Lord directed that those gospelling the gospel should live by the gospel" (1 Cor 9:14, my translation). Paul is probably echoing Q in which there is the statement that "the worker is worthy of reward" (Luke 10:7). Notably, this is from the mission charge that Jesus' followers are to replicate his peripatetic ministry of preaching and healing.[40] In that Paul implies he is "gospelling the gospel" as Jesus did, he is describing Jesus' ministry as "gospelling the gospel." This clearly suggests that he assumes this was how Jesus' ministry could be described. However, we noted that, while the Lord's command to heal and to preach would be informing his gospel, using "proclaim" (1 Cor 9:14) shows that he can focus on the verbal rather than the miraculous work of those like himself obeying the call to be sent (9:13). If the gospel is Jesus Christ or, sometimes, also his ministry, it is a short step to the gospel as God's saving event.

(d) The gospel as God's salvific drama and saving event. In Romans, Paul says that he is a servant of Christ Jesus acting in "priestly service of the gospel of God."[41] The gospel here is not the story of Jesus or God's action or the preaching of Paul. Rather, in a development of the idea that the gospel is the story of the salvific aspects of the story of Jesus, and in association with his own experience and that of his churches, the gospel is the act or saving drama of God in which the people become acceptable in their sanctification by the Spirit. Or, seen from another perspective, the gospel as the power of

---

37. See §4.4 (b) above on Rom 1:9.
38. *OGIS* 458 II 38–41, on which see §2.1 above
39. See §2.3 (b) (i) above.
40. See §4.1 (d) above.
41. Rom 15:16, on which see §4.4 (h) above.

God for salvation—revealing the righteousness of God (Rom 1:16–17)—draws individuals into and sustains them within a relationship with him. In turn, this gospel as salvific drama is experienced as the gospel in a saving event.

That is, a careful reading of his letter to the Thessalonians noted that rather than using "come" (ἔρχομαι), for example, to describe the arrival or experience of the gospel, Paul uses "come about" or "become" (γίνομαι). This suggests that Paul considered not that the gospel arrived or came to the readers but that it took place or was established among them.[42] The gospel was more than a message that Paul brought to them. The gospel, rather, was something that took place among them. Or, as Paul reflects elsewhere, the gospel is what Christ accomplishes through him (Rom 15:19–20). It was a gospel that was inherently transformative.

In one of the statements that is key to Paul's understanding of the gospel, he says to the Thessalonians that, "We know ... he chose you, because our gospel was not established among you in word only but also in power and in Holy Spirit and in much fullness" (1 Thess 1:4–5, my translation). It is here that we see most clearly that Paul's gospel is more than an empowered or energized word from God that changes recipients. It is his view that the gospel came in or by mean of, and at the same time consisted of his message, power, Holy Spirit, and much fullness. From this it appears that, in Paul's mind, there was no line between the establishment of the gospel and its nature. It was word, power, Holy Spirit, and much fullness in both its essence and its experience.

However, this fulsome experience of the miraculous is more than healings and exorcism, for example. We have seen that the miraculous included a great range of God-empowered activity reflected in Paul's discussion of the charismata or solidified expressions of God's grace.[43]

It needs to be noted that it was not Paul's view that the gospel caused or enabled the miracles any more than the gospel caused words. Instead, as Paul's message expressed the gospel, so also the miraculous or God's powerful presence expressed the gospel. In turn, then, just as there was more to the conveying and coming of the gospel than speaking, so there was more to receiving it than listening (Gal 1:10–12). It was experienced.[44] In writing to the Corinthians, although it could be assumed that his gospel was his message, it was dependent on the miraculous for its conviction

---

42. See §3.2 (a) above.

43. See the discussion at §3.2 (3) above on 1 Cor 12:8–10.

44. Gal 3:1–5; cf. 1 Cor 1:14. On the experiential nature of the Christian faith see the insightful book by Louth, *Discerning the Mystery*, esp. 74.

and acceptance (2:1–5), and the gospel is described in terms of all the Corinthians experiencing it (4:14–21). In turn, the gospel appears to have an identity and force independent of Paul (9:12–23). It is obvious, then, that Paul considered the gospel a composite expression of the audible (his message) and the tangible (the miraculous). For Paul the gospel is the power of God not simply because he understood his words were empowered by God, but because the gospel was word and deed—message and miracle.[45]

In short, even if it is a richer term than I had initially supposed,[46] the gospel is, in its establishment and experience, not less than both Paul's message and God's coming in what can broadly be called the miraculous.[47] The point remains, as I set out clearly in another place: "For Paul, *no more could the gospel be proclaimed without words than it could come or be experienced without miracles. Without the miraculous Paul may have had a message, but he would not have had a gospel. Without the miraculous there was no gospel, only preaching.*"[48] It is this intimate relationship between Paul's message and God's miraculous action that is reflected in the one clear definition Paul gives of the gospel, which was discussed at length: "it is the power of God that leads to salvation" (Rom 1:16, my translation).[49] Or, as he supposes later in Romans, the gospel is the action of God as Savior.[50] In view of Paul seeing the coming of the gospel involving his message and God's miraculous action, it is no wonder that he can speak of being a "coworker of God in the gospel of Christ" (1 Thess 3:2).

(e) The gospel as a message. Although we are seeing that, for Paul, the term "gospel" can be used to describe much more than his message, it cannot be missed that there are places where it is clear that the gospel is his message. Paul was a proclaimer![51] He talks of declaring and speaking the gospel freely (1 Thess 2:2) and he reminds his readers of what he had preached to them (2:9). Indeed, "the gospel" can be shorthand for all that

---

45. Note particularly Rom 1:16; 15:18–19; 1 Cor 2:4, Gal 3:3–4 and 1 Thess 1:5.

46. Twelftree, *Paul and the Miraculous*, 315–17.

47. On Paul's understanding of the miraculous see the discussion in Twelftree, *Paul and the Miraculous*, 20–26, and more briefly §3.1 (a) 3 above.

48. Twelftree, *Paul and the Miraculous*, 317 (emphasis original). Again, Ashton, *Religion of Paul the Apostle*, 165, can be noted. Also, again, it can be noted that the notion that the Christian faith is primarily not a matter of words or ideas to be believed, but something to be and experience, is explored in a masterly book by Louth, *Discerning the Mystery*, e.g., 74.

49. See §4.4 (d) above.

50. On Rom 11:28, see the discussion at §4.4 (g) above.

51. Emphasized by Lietaert Peerbolte, *Paul the Missionary*, 254–55. Also, see Barnett, *Paul, Missionary of Jesus*; Schnabel, *Paul the Missionary*.

Paul communicates about Jesus Christ (3:2). Gerhard Friedrich put it succinctly: "If we were to sum up the content of the [Pauline] Gospel in a single word, it would be Jesus the Christ."[52] In turn, the gospel becomes and is equated with God's call in grace (Gal 1:6-9). In this, and in a message being equated with what is conveyed,[53] and a message and what is conveyed accompanying each other as "word and deed" (Rom 15:18; cf. 1 Thess 1:5), Paul's message is from God and is empowered (2:13).[54]

From his letter to the Thessalonians, where it appeared his spoken gospel was at least partially visible, we attempted to reconstruct what he said (1 Thess 1:2-10). The message we were attempting to recover was not all that he may have said to his readers, but his initial missional message to them. To begin with, in his missional message Paul introduced his audience to God, encouraging them to turn from lifeless idols "to serve a living and true God" (1:9). We saw that Paul included the idea that Jesus, God's Son, was in heaven by virtue of being raised from the dead by God, and with a life-perspective of living a life worthy of God, readers were to wait expectantly for him, the one who already rescues them from the coming wrath.

In Paul's much more highly developed articulation of his gospel in the first three chapters of Romans, still evident is the wrath of God,[55] the negative mention of idols (Rom 2:22), and the fundamental importance of Jesus as "the Son"[56] and his resurrection (1:4). The call "to serve a God living and true" (1 Thess 1:9) is now taken up in the description of himself (Rom 1:1) and then extensively developed where Paul goes on in a number of places to spell out the implications of the gospel.[57] There are only hints of the motif of waiting for the Son[58] ahead of a discourse on living in the Spirit (8:18-23). No longer is the expectation of the *parousia* in the lifetime of the believers (cf. 14:8) part of Paul's explanation of the gospel.

Even though Paul's gospel can be his missional message, when he says to the Corinthians that "My speech and my proclamation were not with plausible words of wisdom, but with a demonstration of the Spirit and of power" (1 Cor 2:4), the assumption, which he immediately spells out, is that his message is dependent not simply on being empowered,[59] but on

---

52. Friedrich, "εὐαγγελίζομαι, κτλ," 731.
53. E.g., see the LXX at 2 Kgdms 1:15; 4:10.
54. Cf. Bourke, "Holy Spirit as the Controlling Dynamic," 149-50.
55. Rom 1:18; 2:5, 8; 3:5; cf. 2:16; 5:9.
56. Rom 1:3, 9; 5:10; 8:3, 29, 32; cf. 1 Thess 1:10.
57. Note Paul's "therefore" (οὖν) at Rom 6:1 and 12:1; cf. 5.1.
58. Rom 4:17; 6:4-5; 8:11. Cf. 1 Thess 1:10.
59. So Bourke, "Holy Spirit as the Controlling Dynamic," 149-50.

the miraculous for its conviction and acceptance (2:5). It is not surprising, then, that, though the gospel could be taken to be his message, Paul gives the impression that the gospel had a life and agency independent of him.[60]

(f) The gospel as embodied and lived. When Paul drew his Galatian readers' attention to his altercation with Peter at Antioch, challenging him that he was not acting consistently with "the truth of the gospel" (Gal 2:14), Paul was conceiving of the gospel not only as ideas that could be spoken or preached, but as also reflected in ethical behavior or a life lived. We noted that the truth of the gospel is that a person is justified by faith in Jesus Christ (3:1–5). The relationship between the gospel and its response echoes its early use in which "gospel" and its reward or response were intrinsically connected.[61]

However, more than ethical behavior lived or expressed in the life of an individual or the community (Phil 4:1–3), Paul could use "gospel" to capture his entire work (Gal 4:13; Phil 2:22). Indeed, even his imprisonment is an expression and proclamation of the gospel (1:13). In the same vein, Paul writes of his readers sharing in the gospel as a shorthand way of referring to their sharing in the breadth of the common experience of God's grace or work in their lives (1:5) for the purpose of the gospel. Paul both embodied the gospel and expected his readers to *"become* the gospel," as Michael Gorman puts it.[62] However, Paul is not embodying the message as Gorman argues but embodying the gospel.

(g) Results: The polyvalance of "gospel." From what we have seen in this section, Paul uses the noun "gospel" (εὐαγγέλιον) for tradition about Jesus, Jesus Christ himself, the ministry of Jesus, the replication of the ministry of Jesus, God's salvific drama, the salvation experience of people, a message, and something that can (and should) be lived. It is not that the gospel is one thing described in many ways, but different things described with one word—gospel. Like other terms, such as "law" and "righteousness," that are critical in Paul's theological construct, there can be ambiguity, an oscillation of the meaning of "gospel" depending on the context. Not surprisingly, Paul's understanding of the gospel is so rich and multivalent that even his own definition of it for the Romans (Rom 1:16–17) is frequently burst by his own hand so that it can take on different meanings.

The question could reasonably be raised whether "gospel" (εὐαγγέλιον) should be translated variously with different English words to convey Paul's intentions more clearly and precisely. However, any gains in doing so would

---

60. See §4.1 (d) above.
61. Homer, *Od.* 14.152–53, 166 and §2.1 above.
62. Gorman, *Becoming the Gospel*, 45 (emphasis original).

be outweighed by considerable loss. It could not have escaped such a mind as Paul's that he was using a single word to describe different things. What is notable, therefore, is that in doing so all that he describes by this one word is inextricably linked—deeply related—and, to some extent, overlapping in meaning and significance. If "gospel" (εὐαγγέλιον) was variously translated, the overlapping meanings and echoes through Paul's text would be lost to us.

What had been for Paul and his readers a word used of a report of something positive, had also come to him from his predecessors in the faith as a term to encapsulate their message of what Jesus was doing, bringing salvation and help, particularly through healing. In Paul's hands the extension of the range of meaning of "gospel," which we have just noted, raised it to a central organizing concept for his theological construct, for his life, and for his work of ministry, a position the word has continued to hold until the present time for his Christian readers.

§5.3 "GOSPELLING": THE GOSPEL AS PAUL'S WORK

So far our conclusions about Paul's gospel have revolved around his use of the noun. His use of the verb "gospel" (εὐαγγελίζω) is also striking.

The importance of the gospel for Paul is set out in his statement: "I do all for the sake of the gospel" (1 Cor 9:23). Whereas once he was, as a Pharisee, set apart for the law he is now consecrated or set apart for the gospel (Rom 1:1; Phil 3:5). However, it is not simply the promotion of the gospel that is his life's work, the whole breadth of his work is "gospelling" (Rom 1:15). So "gospelling" becomes what Christ accomplishes through Paul (15:19–20). It is in Galatians that Paul expresses most clearly that what he does is to "gospel," which he probably takes to be fulfilling a command of Jesus to his followers (Gal 1:15–16; cf. 1 Cor 9:14). It is this identification of himself and his work with "gospel," rather than a change over time (which is not tidy or consistent), that is probably the explanation of its clustered use in his letters. Although there is, very roughly, a decrease in the use of the verb and noun over time, a closer examination of the distribution of the words suggests that it is when Paul is talking about who he is and his work that the "gospel" language is used most. This is particularly evident in Romans, probably his latest writing, where the overall use of "gospel" is low. However, where he is introducing himself and his work in the first two chapters there is a clustering of the vocabulary. The same clustering can be seen in 1 Thessalonians 2, Galatians 1 and 2, and 1 Corinthians 9, where he is reflecting particularly on himself and his work. In 2 Corinthians it is noticeable that the verb "to gospel" (εὐαγγελίζειν) is only used twice (2 Cor 10:16; 11:7). In this letter Paul is defending his ministry so we might expect to see a greater use of the verb. However, in his defense Paul has centered his attention around the gospel and his leadership rather than his "gospelling."

We noted the striking point that only on two occasions does he say that he was called to "preach" (κηρύσσω, Gal 2:2; 1 Thess 2:9). On a half dozen further occasions he uses "proclaim" (καταγγέλλω),[63] a synonym for "preach,"[64] which makes clear that he sees himself as involved in speaking or preaching. Notwithstanding, as if there is something about his work that is not captured in simply saying that he preached or proclaimed, his preferred way of describing his work is to say that he "gospelled."[65] In asking the Galatians, "does God supply you with the Spirit and work miracles among you by your doing the works of the law, or by your believing what you heard?" (Gal 3:5), the gospel in which Paul is involved is clearly more than his speaking; it includes, as we have just noted, the obvious supplying of the Spirit and the working of miracles. It is not that Paul performs the miracles; he never claims to have that gift.[66]

This point that Paul does not claim to perform miracles, yet they take place, is brought into sharp focus and explained in him saying, "the signs of the apostle were performed among you . . . signs and wonders and mighty works" (2 Cor 12:12a).[67] The aorist "were performed" (κατειργάσθη) links this activity to Paul's initial ministry in Corinth.[68] What is notable for our project is that "were performed" (κατειργάσθη) is also in the passive. In light of criticism he is countering, Paul could have been expected to say that, "Despite being nothing before God, I performed (κατειργασάμην) signs and wonders and mighty works."[69] But he does not. Paul, therefore, probably intends the passive to have theological significance, implying that God performed the miracles.[70] Indeed, saying the signs were performed

63. Rom 1:8; 1 Cor 2:1; 9:14; 11:26; Phil. 1:17, 18.

64. See p. 109n208 above.

65. Rom 2:21; 10:8, 14, 15; 1 Cor 1:23; 9:27; 15:11, 12; 2 Cor 1:19; 4:5; 11:4 (x2); Gal 2:2; 5:11; Phil 1:15; 1 Thess 2:9.

66. On Paul's use of the passive when referring to miracles in which he could be seen to be involved (e.g., κατειρλάσθη, "were performed," 2 Cor 12:12), see Twelftree, *Paul and the Miraculous*, 212–16.

67. This paragraph is dependent on Twelftree, *Paul and the Miraculous*, 212–16.

68. Barnett, *Second Epistle to the Corinthians*, 577, 581.

69. Cf. Plummer, *Critical and Exegetical Commentary*, 358.

70. Plummer, *Critical and Exegetical Commentary*, 358; Bertram, "κτεργάζομαι," 635; Schreiber, *Paulus als Wundertäter*, 275; Harris, *Second Epistle to the Corinthians*, 874.

"with utmost patience" (ἐν πάσῃ ὑπομονῇ, 12:12) would have brought to mind a characteristic of God (Rom 15:4-5; cf. Col 1:11).[71] On the other hand, Paul is happy to use the active form "accomplished" or "performed" (κατειργάσατο) when Christ is the subject of the verb (Rom 15:18).[72] He is also quite happy to use active terms in referring to Christ sending him to proclaim the gospel (1 Cor 1:17), and to write of his eagerness to preach the gospel (Rom 1:15), and to say that he proclaims it.[73] In fact, only once does Paul use the passive of his preaching the gospel, though he goes on to say it was he who was proclaiming it (Gal 1:11).

Thus, although Paul never claims to perform miracles or to have that gift, using the passive, to say signs and wonders "were performed," Paul has in mind God performing the miracles and the preaching being carried out by himself. In turn, rather, we can suppose, so intimately related did Paul see his speaking and the coming of the Spirit and the miraculous in the establishment and experience of the gospel, that he saw he was involved in that coming in a way that is not well expressed in describing himself as simply preaching. Hence he uses the verb "gospel" to describe his work.

§5.4 A CHANGING GOSPEL?

At the beginning of chapter 3 the question of change or development (or both) in Paul's ideas about the gospel was opened up. It was at least in view of exploring this question that the letters of Paul were examined in the order in which they are likely to have been written. However, there are significant challenges to detecting change or development in Paul. Aside from settling questions of, for example, the unity of Philippians and the Corinthian letters, not only is there a relatively short space of time over which they came from his pen or that of his amanuenses, the order in which his letters were written is also uncertain. If his letter to the Thessalonians was written in 50 or 51 CE[74] and if Romans was written in the winter of 57-58 CE,[75] only six to eight

---

71. Although in the New Testament "patience" is generally attributed to human beings (Luke 8:15; 21:19; Rom 2:7; 5:3, 4; 8:25; 15:4, 5; 2 Cor 1:6; 6:4; 12:12; Col 1:11; 1 Thess 1:3; 2 Thess 1:4; 1 Tim 6:11; 2 Tim 3:10; Titus 2:2; Heb 10:36; 12:1; Jas 1:3, 4; 5:11; 2 Pet 1:6; Rev 1:9; 2:2, 3, 19; 3:10; 13:10; 14:12; contrast 2 Thess 3:5 where Jesus is the subject), it was a gift of God given in the face of difficult circumstances (cf. Rom 15:5; Col 1:11). Cf. Radl, "ὑπομονή," 405-6.

72. Cf. Fee, *God's Empowering Presence*, 628n469.

73. Rom 10:8; 15:20; 1 Cor 1:23; 9:16; 15:11; 2 Cor 2:12; 4:5; 10:16; Gal 1:8, 16; 2:2; cf. Phil 1:15-16.

74. See §3.2 above.

75. See §4.4 above.

years separate his first and last extant letters. While this is not a great deal of time for intellectual development to take place, so intellectually creative is Paul, and so rich his ongoing experience and interaction with a variety of other people, that it would be surprising if there had not been change in Paul's thinking, even over this short time. Recognizing the difficulty in detecting changes over time in Paul's thinking about the gospel, a number of suggestions can be offered tentatively in this regard.

First, it is notable that in his earliest letters, those to the Thessalonians and Galatians, the two-part dimension of the coming of the gospel—in word and deed or in the message and the miraculous (1 Thess 1:5 and Gal 3:1–5)—is clearest and dominant. Though it is not absent elsewhere (e.g., Rom 15:18–19). The early prominence of the word-deed notion of the gospel and its coming can be readily understood. He is not far removed from the mid- to late-forties, the beginning of his ministry, which he describes as dramatic in its expression and impact. Though the coming of the gospel in word and deed remained essential to his ministry and his understanding of it (cf. 15:18–19), this now-routine experience perhaps no longer merited the mention it once did.

Second, in his earliest letter the gospel is characterized as something Paul is involved in conveying.[76] The gospel is also something that sums up his work (1 Thess 3:2; cf. Phil 2:22). In the later letters, however, there is a subtle though significant change: the gospel appears more all-encompassing; it dominates and determines his entire life. For example, he tells the Romans that he is set apart to the gospel.[77] Short though the number of years may have been, it appears that Paul has increased the complexity of the interconnections he makes between the ways he understood the gospel and his deepening relation to it.

Third, although the gospel and its propagation may have become increasingly important to his self-understanding, it is noticeable that, even with our limited evidence, his use of the noun broadly decreases over time.[78] We can suppose that, having inherited the term from other followers of Jesus, as he developed his theology and mission—including its theological complexity—he found new ways to add to the way he expressed his thinking.

Fourth, it seems that by the end of his short letter-writing career Paul is able not only to define the gospel succinctly (Rom 1:16), but then to explicate it in fulsome and complex ways, assuming that the letter to the

---

76. 1 Thess 1:5; 2:2, 4, 8, 9; 3:2.
77. Rom 1:1–3; cf. 1 Cor 9:16; Phlm 13.
78. See p. 80n6 above and the Appendix below.

Romans can be read at least in part as attempting that.[79] The increasing richness of his understanding of the gospel is apparent in, for example, "the righteousness of God" not appearing in 1 Thessalonians, Galatians, or Philippians, his earlier letters, but in Romans the term takes a decisive role (cf. 3:21-26) and is revealed in (ἐν) the gospel (1:16-17). In this the gospel is more closely equated with the powerful, salvific presence of God.[80] In turn, though it was not central to his purpose in his earliest letter to explicate the gospel message, from what can be read between the lines of his Letter to the Thessalonians (esp. 1 Thess 1:9-10), his description of the gospel appears rudimentary by comparison. Similarly, we have already noted in this section ([a] above) that the complexity of use of traditional material increases over time, perhaps as we become more adept at mining and representing it.

Fifth, reconstructing the message through which Paul introduced the Thessalonians to his gospel enabled us to see that he probably spoke about Jesus, God's Son in heaven, in light of his being raised to life by God. The Thessalonians were encouraged to live worthy of God, waiting for the Son who rescues them from the coming wrath.[81] In Romans, Paul's last extant letter, it is noticeable that he has considerably developed the implications of the gospel. On the other hand, little can be seen of waiting for the Son, and the *parousia* is no longer expected in the lifetime of the readers.[82] Though in some cases tentative, these observations suggest both a deepening and an increasing richness of his understanding of the gospel and gospelling, and his finding new ways to describe it and his relation to it. Though we made no attempt to reconstruct what Paul may have been saying later in his career, his later message probably no longer contained reference to an imminent expectation of the *parousia*.

§5.5 THE GOSPEL ACCORDING TO PAUL

This study has shown that contemporary views on Paul's gospel, understood essentially as his message, cannot be sustained in light of an examination of what Paul himself says about his gospel. We have seen that it is incorrect to say, with Gerhard Friedrich in his classic article on the gospel, that when Paul uses the absolute "the gospel" (τὸ εὐαγγέλιον) he refers to the act of proclamation.[83] Even to describe Paul's gospel as his God-empowered

---

79. See §4.4 above.
80. Cf. Hübner, "ἀλήθεια," 59.
81. See §§3.2 (a) 1 and 5.2 (e) above.
82. See §5.2 (e) above.
83. Friedrich, "εὐαγγελίζομαι, κτλ," 729, followed by, e.g., Jewett, *Romans*, 137.

message is a gross oversimplification and misunderstanding of his views. Also, even though there is a broad cosmic narrative substructure to Paul's message, and major points of the story of Jesus were at least part of his message, not only was he not a storyteller, his gospel was (primarily) neither a narrative nor his message.

We have already noted that it is not that the gospel is one thing described in many ways, but different things described in one way—the gospel. Paul's understanding of the gospel is so multifaceted, or of so many different realizations, that even his own definition of it for the Romans (Rom 1:16–17) or description of it for the Galatians (Gal 1:12, 15) do not suffice for capturing the richness of his varying expressions of it.

The gospel according to Paul is what he is dedicated to—he belongs to the gospel—and it is what can sum up his whole purpose and work. As we have seen, the gospel for Paul is the peripatetic preaching and healing ministry that Jesus carried out and called his followers to replicate. Paul considered his ministry to be in obedience to that call. So, the gospel becomes Christ himself and him expressed and experienced. In turn, the gospel becomes the minimal story or an elementary sketch of Jesus, particularly his status, death, and resurrection, and his salvific significance, handed on from earlier Christians. This material had been the raw material of their preaching and became the reservoir from which Paul chose his preaching topics. In turn, yet again, the gospel is not simply the life of Jesus but the saving act or drama of God reflected in it in which the gentiles become acceptable. God's saving drama in Christ is not only gospel but it is experienced as gospel in a saving event. The gospel takes place among the readers as they hear Paul's message express it and as they experience the gospel in God's activity in the miraculous. *If the declaration of the gospel put the gospel into effect*[84] *it is not because the words are empowered but because the words identify and (coincidently) describe the action of God.* Reasonably, then, Paul does not see his work as preaching but as "gospelling," being involved in experiencing and expressing (including in himself) God's salvific work in Christ. For Paul, this gospel of saving power with its own life and agency can (and should) be embodied and lived.

Even without the word εὐαγγέλιον ("gospel"), but more so with it, for Paul and his readers the gospel is subversive. Inherent in the popular use of the word is the assumption of complete allegiance to a savior figure filled with divine power for the benefit of the people. However, the allegiance was not to a political figure but to the Son of God. Notwithstanding, this

---

84. So Friedrich, "εὐαγγελίζομαι, κτλ," 723, followed by Spallek, "Origin and Meaning of Εὐαγγέλιον," 179.

point should not be overplayed or misunderstood. It is not that Paul is propagating a political gospel, declaring war on Caesar.[85] Paul never names a Roman emperor or governor. He can write of rulers, powers (Rom 8:38; 1 Cor 2:6, 8), and authorities (15:24), but they are never identified as Roman rulers. It is not, though, as John Barclay pointed out in a brief but brilliant essay, that there is a conspiracy of silence about an unmentionable opponent of the gospel. For Paul can refer to Rome (Rom 1:7, 15) and mention Caesar at least indirectly in referring to believers in his household (Phil 4:22).[86]

Rather, Paul maps his world and identifies his opponents differently.[87] Paul uses "reign" or "dominion" (βασιλεύω) not in relation to the Roman emperor or governors but the overthrow of sin and death by the "reign" of grace (Rom 5:12–21). Categories such as "rulers" and "powers" (Rom 8:38) might encompass the anthropological or political as well as the cosmic, but, as Barclay rightly puts it, they "defy our normal taxonomies."[88] Barclay notes: "Paul's language of 'powers' thus denotes comprehensive features of reality which penetrate (what we call) the 'political' sphere, but only as it is enmeshed in large and more comprehensive force-fields."[89] Paul's is not a political gospel; connotations are not to be confused with deeper denotations. His gospel has implications and ramifications across all realities for which he sometimes used political imagery.

In short, and to be clear, Paul's gospel can be: God's salvific drama; Jesus (Christ, the Son) himself, his life and character; the ministry of Jesus and, in turn, Paul's own work or ministry to which he is dedicated; Paul's message; and even the life of the believer. However, its coming or establishment makes clear that, at heart, *the gospel is God's salvation—the presence of God himself—in Christ, experienced in the symbiotic relationship between Paul's message about God's Son, Jesus Christ, and the activity of God in the miraculous.* It must be noted and clarified, however, that the miraculous was more than a proof or demonstration of the gospel; it was integral to it. In this way, consistent with the inherent meaning of εὐαγγέλιον ("gospel"), the

---

85. So Taubes, *Political Theology of Paul*, 16, followed by Bird, *Anomalous Jew*, 228–29. For a brief historical summary of the debate about the place of the Roman empire in Paul's polemics, and a counter to N. T. Wright's view in particular that Paul's theology is directly opposed to "Caesar's empire," see the important essay by Barclay, "Why the Roman Empire was Insignificant to Paul."

86. Barclay, "Why the Roman Empire was Insignificant to Paul," 375.

87. Barclay, "Why the Roman Empire was Insignificant to Paul," 384.

88. Barclay, "Why the Roman Empire was Insignificant to Paul," 384, noting (384n71) the longstanding hermeneutical challenge of Paul's categories, pointing to Caird, *Principalities and Powers*; Wink, *Naming the Powers*; and Wink, *Engaging the Powers*.

89. Barclay, "Why the Roman Empire was Insignificant to Paul," 384.

message and what it reported are equated.[90] Without the involvement and acts of God (in the miraculous), for Paul there would have been no gospel.

The richness—the polyvalence—of the term "gospel" for Paul challenges current views of the gospel as his message, even an empowered message. Our contemporary view of Paul's gospel only takes into account one aspect of what he had in mind and is, therefore, not only an inadequate description of it, but a crippling truncation and misrepresentation of it, denying the richness of what Paul had in mind. The fundamental challenge of this book is that we see Paul's gospel as more than his message. In their discussion of his gospel, Dunn, Wright, Schnelle, Gorman, Wolter, and Campbell, for example have each enhanced our understanding of Paul's message.[91] But they have not helped us see the breadth and depth of the use to which Paul put the term "gospel." Notably, current discussions are bereft of seeing the import of Paul saying the gospel comes in message and miracle (cf. 1 Thess 1:5).

Though Paul never brought them into direction relationship,[92] the term "gospel" functions in a similar way to how the phrase kingdom of God functioned in the ministry of Jesus. The kingdom of God was not the message of Jesus, but an eschatological act of God inaugurated in the ministry of Jesus, expressed, notably, in his healings, exorcisms, and radical acts of inclusion that had to be explained through the parables and in engagement with his opponents. Similarly, for Paul the gospel—which we have seen is a central and centralizing concept for him[93]—is the action of God in Christ his readers have experienced and which he explained to them, and which in his letters he needed to reiterate for them.

§5.6 CONTEMPORARY CODA

Paul was of such profound historical importance that he remains of profound contemporary importance. His impact on his time was so great that his influence continues to reverberate into our own time and can be expected to resonate beyond our time.

This has been an historical enquiry driven by questions of the historical Paul. However, so significant is Paul taken to be that, if the results of this

---

90. Cf. Friedrich, "εὐαγγελίζομαι, κτλ," 721. Cf. §2.1 above.

91. See §1.4 above.

92. Harnack, *Constitution and Law*, 294. However, we have seen at §2.2 (d) that Q appears to connect the gospel and the kingdom of God.

93. Cf. Becker, "Gospel, Evangelize, Evangelist," 111: "In Paul *euangelion* has become a central concept in his theology," also cited at p. 3n18 above.

reappraisal of his gospel are sound, the implications for historians, as well as for contemporary theology and praxis, are profound. Although it is beyond the scope of this study to draw out and develop all its implications, some suggestions can be offered.

If the argument of this book has been sound, we have seen that Paul's gospel is misunderstood. Limiting the understanding of Paul's gospel to his message—even an empowered message—is a disservice to the historical data. Historians wishing to do justice to "gospel" in Paul's vocabulary will need to broaden their enquiry and perspective, and look beyond the theological concerns of the Reformation to Paul's own writings. Doing so, they will discover a first-century Paul who was much more than a theologian and who was preoccupied with a different gospel. His gospel can be described but it is not captured in the text of his letters any more than love or a summer vacation can be captured in a postcard.

Paul's gospel was not only expressed in terms such as "grace," "in Christ," and "the righteousness of God." His gospel was also what was experienced in life-changing encounters with God that, in turn, caused lives to express the gospel in their character, activities, and eschatological orientation (1 Thess 1:9). In other words, attempts by historians to describe Paul's gospel[94] must take into account its polyvalence—including its experiential nature—and that the miraculous is as essential to its expression and experience as are the words. Simply put, Paul's gospel is not his message. In what can be seen from the evidence, in the simplest terms just noted above, for Paul "gospel" referred to God's salvation in Christ experienced in the symbiotic relationship between Paul's message about Jesus Christ and the activity of God in the miraculous.

A related point is that, while Paul's initial missionary message may not have been his gospel, it was an essential part of it in terms of its coming or taking place in the lives of people. It is surprising, then, that so little attention has been given to recovering that message. Instead, attention is given to what Paul subsequently writes to his churches. In this Paul's theology and practical concerns are too easily assumed to be his initial missionary message. Beyond the few studies in existence and what has been briefly attempted here,[95] there is important historical work still to be done in reconstructing in more depth and detail the "word" half of the "word and deed" pair that Paul describes as constituting the coming of the gospel (1 Thess 1:5).

---

94. Cf. §1.4 above.
95. See §3.2 (a) and especially note 50 above.

Unless historians make changes to their characterization of Paul's gospel along these lines a disservice to the historical data continues and, in turn, to the church as it takes a lead in its theology, preaching, and practice from that scholarship. For what historians discover and discuss about Paul is eventually heard and heeded by theologians, pastors, and preachers.

First, because of the significance of Paul's thought for the contemporary church, if his gospel is not understood the church will continue to presume what he would see as a truncated and diminished gospel centered around words that are, in turn, unable to have the divine impact Paul assumed, experienced, witnessed, and spoke and wrote about. For example, Paul would, to put it mildly, be surprised and probably infuriated—O! Foolish Westerners. Who has bewitched us?—at a notion of evangelism that is based on sermons or talks, and altar calls or centered around assent to propositions (cf. Gal 3:1–5). For Paul, this is another gospel (1:6–9). Paul would expect a person not simply to "turn to God from idols to serve a living and true God" (1 Thess 1:9). He would expect the person also to report a transformative encounter with God that was an experience "in power and in the Holy Spirit and with much fullness" (1:5). If Paul's gospel was to come to, or as he would say, be established and embodied in, lives and communities (1:5), more would be needed than the skill of an engaging preacher. Based on his own experience, Paul made that point most clear (1 Cor 2:1–5). The mission of the church depends not only on well-informed and highly educated leaders at all levels but on leaders who can report and provide evidence in their own experience and embodiment of the gospel that it is and comes in more than words.

Further, for those who would still "gospel," for Paul's perspective to be a model, it would be laughably tragic if their training was limited (as it generally is!) to an understanding of words and ideas that are to be conveyed to listeners. For, to repeat, *while the gospel can be explained in words it cannot be conveyed by words alone, for it is more than a message.* Also to repeat, for Paul, without the miraculous there is no gospel, only preaching. It is not, however, that miracle workers are required. Paul himself never claimed or even suggested he had that gift. Rather, Paul would require gospelling to be seen as explaining the trust (confidence or faith) a person needs in order to anticipate and encounter the miraculous, transforming presence of God, and then live a life embodying and expressing that gospel. In other words, conveying the gospel as Paul understood it would require individuals who grasped that the gospel comes, and is demonstrated, in a divine encounter, and is explained through a person whose life and words already anticipate, embody, and express that encounter. Søren Kierkegaard was right, then, to say, "When Christianity (precisely because it is not a doctrine) is not reduplicated in the life of the person presenting it, it is not Christianity he presents."[96]

This leads, second, to note that, although not explored in any detail in this study, we have seen that the gospel is not only what is encountered in "word and deed" (1 Thess 1:5), but is also the responsive expression in the life of the person encountered by the gospel.[97] That is, the extent to which Paul's perspective remains exemplary, what defines a Christian or believer needs to change in most contemporary Christian traditions. In most traditions a Christian is a person holding certain ideas, beliefs, or presuppositions. Reflecting a Pauline perspective, a Christian is also to be seen as a person who has had and continues to have an encounter with God (Gal 3:1–5) and responds to him in ways that transform bodies, beliefs, and behaviors, and causes others to conclude the person's life embodies, expresses, or reflects that of Jesus—who is also the gospel (Phil 2:1–13).

Thirdly, the gospel is culturally subversive. However, Paul's gospel is not subversive because he confronts imperial claims directly. Rather, to rely on John Barclay again, Paul confronts sociopolitical claims "by reducing Rome's agency and historical significance to just one more entity in a much larger drama." For, Barclay continues, "To oppose the Roman empire *as such* would be to take its claims all too seriously."[98] While the gospel's subversive nature reverberates in the word "gospel" itself, that subversion cannot be traced on a political map. Paul's gospel confronts and undermines political quests and claims for power "not by confronting them on their own terms, but by reducing them to bit-players in a drama scripted by the cross and resurrection of Jesus."[99] Readers are called to live their lives "in a manner worthy of the gospel of Christ" (Phil 1:27), an allegiance encompassing all of life and that subverts all other calls, and comes at great cost (including social and political), as it did in Paul's own life.[100] That is a challenge that continues to remain contemporary.

This leads, fourth, to the point that the embodiment, expression, or reflection of the gospel is extreme for Paul. He explains that a life living or expressing the gospel is modelling the humble, self-emptying, self-sacrificial attitude of Christ before God (Phil 2:1–11). According to Paul (3:7–11), the gospel calls for an allegiance to Christ that causes one to regard absolutely

---

96. Kierkegaard, *Papers and Journals*, 323 (48 IX A 208).

97. See Gal 2:14; 4:13; Phil 1:5, 13; 2:22; and the discussion above in §5.2 (f).

98. Barclay, "Why the Roman Empire was Insignificant to Paul," 386. Emphasis original.

99. Barclay, "Why the Roman Empire was Insignificant to Paul," 387.

100. E.g., see Rom 16:7; 1 Cor 15:32; Phil 1:12–26; 1 Thess 2:2; 3:4; Phlm 1, 23.

everything else as rubbish "because of the surpassing value of knowing Christ my Lord" (3:8). The implications of this self-emptying, sacrificial expression of the gospel for contemporary believers remain profound for any culture.

Appendix
The Vocabulary of "Gospel"

	Before Paul[1]	LXX[2]	NT	Paul	1 Thess	Gal	Phil	1 Cor	2 Cor	Phlm	Rom
ἀπαγγέλλω (verb, "announce")	459[3]	253[4]	9[5]	2[6]	1[7]			1[8]			
εὐαγγελίζω (verb, "bring or announce good news")	19[9]	23[10]	54[11]	19[12]	1[13]	7[14]		6[15]	2[16]		3[17]
εὐαγγέλιον (neuter, singular noun, "good news")	2[18]	1[19]	76[20]	48[21]	6[22]	7[23]	9[24]	8[25]	8[26]	1[27]	9[28]
εὐαγγελία (feminine, singular noun, "good news")	1[29]	5[30]									
καταγγέλλω (verb, "proclaim")	32[31]	2[32]	18[33]	6[34]				2[35]	3[36]		1[37]
προευαγγελίζομαι (verb, "proclaim good news in advance")	3[38]		1[39]	1[40]		1[41]					

NOTES

1. These figures (from TLG) do not include those from the LXX.
2. Figures from Lust et al., *Greek-English Lexicon of the Septuagint*.
3. Those using ἀπαγγέλλω ("announce") more than five times: Homer (ten); Aeschylus (nine); Thucydides (nineteen); Eurpides (eleven); Herodotus (twenty-one); Isocrates (six); Xenephon (eighty-two); Plato (thirty); Lysias (eleven); Hippocrates (eleven); Ctesias (nine); Demosthenes (eighty); Aeshines (twenty-nine); Aristotle (eleven); Polybius (eighteen); Diodorus Siculus (eighty-nine); Dionysius Halicarnassus (seventy); Nicolaus (ten); Philodemus (eight); Philo (thirteen); Strabo (ten).
4. LXX: Gen 12:18; 14:13; 21:26; 24:28, 49 (2x); 26:32; 27:42; 29:12, 15; 37:5; 38:13, 24; 41:8, 24; 42:29; 43:7; 44:24; 45:13; 46:31; 47:1; 48:1, 2, 3; Lev 5:1; Num 11:27; Josh 2:2; 10:17; Judg 9:25, 42, 47; 13:6, 10; 14:2, 6, 9, 12, 13, 14, 15, 16 (3x), 17 (2x), 19; 16:2, 15, 17; 9:25; 13:6; 14:2, 6, 9, 12 (2x), 13, 14, 15, 16 (3x), 17 (2x), 19; 16:6, 13, 15, 18 (2x); Ruth 2:11, 19; 3:4; 1 Kgdms 3:15, 18; 4:13, 14; 8:9; 9:6, 8, 18, 19; 10:15, 16 (3x); 11:9; 12:7; 14:1, 9, 33, 43 (2x); 15:12, 16; 18:20, 24, 26; 19:2, 3, 7, 11, 18, 19, 21; 20:9, 10; 22:21, 22 (2x); 23:1, 7, 11, 13, 25; 24:2, 19; 25:8, 14, 19, 36, 37; 2 Kgdms 1:4, 5, 6, 13; 2:4; 3:23; 4:10; 6:12; 7:11; 11:5, 18, 22 (2x); 13:4, 34; 14:33; 15:13, 28; 17:18; 18:11, 25; 21:11; 3 Kgdms 1:20; 2:29, 39, 41; 10:3 (2x), 7; 18:12, 13, 16; 21:17; 4 Kgdms 4:7, 31; 5:4; 9:12, 15, 18, 20; 10:8; 1 Chr 19:5, 17; 9:2, 6; 34:18; Ezra 3:16; 4:61; 5:37; Neh 2:12, 16, 18; 6:7; 7:61; Esth 1:15; 2:10; 4:12; 6:2; Jdt 2:7; 3:5; 6:17; 10:13; 11:19; 14:8; 15:4; Tob 8:14; 11:15; 1 Macc 4:26; 5:14, 38; 6:5; 9:37; 11:21, 40; 12:23, 26; 14:21; 15:32, 36; 16:1, 21; Pss 39:6; 54:18; 70:17, 18; 77:4, 6; 88:2; 104:1; 141:3; 144:4; 147:8; Prov 12:17; Eccl 6:12; 10:20; Song 1:7; 5:8; Job 1:15, 16, 17, 19; 12:7; 21:31; 23:5; 38:4; Wis 6:22; Sir 16:25; 37:14; 42:19; 44:3; Hos 4:12; Amos 3:9; 4:5, 13; Mic 3:8; Jonah 1:8, 10; Nah 2:1; Isa 30:7; 36:22; 44:8; 48:20; 57:12; Jer 40:3; Ezek 23:36; Sus 1:41; Dan 2:5, 9; 5:7, 8, 9; 8:19; Dan (Th) 2:6.
5. Matt 12:18; Luke 13:1; John 16:25; Acts 15:27; 1 Cor 14:25; 1 Thess 1:9; Heb 2:12; 1 John 1:2, 3.
6. 1 Cor 14:25; 1 Thess 1:9.
7. 1 Thess 1:9.
8. 1 Cor 14:25.
9. Aristophanes, *Eq.* 643; Demosthenes, *Cor.* 323.3; Lycurgus, *Leocr.* 18.2; Theophrastus, *Char.* 17.7.1; Menander, *Georg.* 83; Diogenes, *Epist.* 23.1.1; Nicolaus, *Fragmenta* 9.33; Philo, *Creation* 115.5; *Dreams* 2.281.1; *Joseph* 245.4; 250.4; *Moses* 2.186.3; *Virtues* 41.1; *Rewards* 161.4; *Embassy* 18.4; 99.6; 232.1; QG *(fragmenta)* Book 4 fragment 144.4; Περὶ ἀριθμῶν sive Ἀριθμητικά *(fragmenta)* Fragment 54.4.
10. 1 Kgdms 31:9; 2 Kgdms 1:20; 4:10; 18:19, 20 (2x), 26, 31; 3 Kgdms 1:42; 1 Chr 10:9; Pss 39:10; 67:12; 95:2; Pss Sol 11:1; Joel 3:5; Nah 2:1; Isa 40:9 (x2); 52:7 (x2); 60:6; 61:1; Jer 20:15.
11. Matt 11:5; Luke 1:19; 2:10; 3:18; 4:18, 43; 7:22; 8:1; 9:6; 16:16; 20:1; Acts 5:42; 8:4, 12, 25, 35, 40; 10:36; 11:20; 13:32; 14:7, 15, 21; 15:35; 16:10; 17:18; Rom 1:15; 10:15; 15:20; 1 Cor 1:17; 9:16 (x2), 18; 15:1, 2; 2 Cor 10:16; 11:7; Gal 1:8 (x2), 9, 11, 16, 23; 4:13; Eph 2:17; 3:8; 1 Thess 3:6; Heb 4:2, 6; 1 Pet 1:12, 25; 4:6; Rev 10:7; 14:6.
12. Rom 1:15; 10:15; 15:20; 1 Cor 1:17; 9:16 (x2), 18; 15:1, 2; 2 Cor 10:16; 11:7; Gal 1:8 (x2), 9, 11, 16, 23; 4:13; 1 Thess 3:6.

THE VOCABULARY OF "GOSPEL"   209

13. 1 Thess 3:6.

14. Gal 1:8 (x2), 9, 11, 16, 23; 4:13.

15. 1 Cor 1:17; 9:16 (x2), 18; 15:1, 2.

16. 2 Cor 10:16; 11:7.

17. Rom 1:15; 10:15; 15:20.

18. Homer, Od. 14.152 (εὐαγγέλιον); 14.166 (εὐαγγέλιον). The plural is used by Isocrates, Areop. (orat. 7) 10.4 (εὐαγγέλια); Aristophanes, Eq. 647 (εὐαγγέλια), 656 (εὐαγγέλια); Plut. 765 (εὐαγγέλια); Xenophon, Hell. 1.6.37.2 (εὐαγγέλια), 4.3.14.1 (εὐαγγέλια); Ctesias, Fragmenta, Jacoby#-F 3c,688,F fragment 26 line 16 (εὐαγγελίων), Jacoby#-F 3c,688,F fragment 26 line 20 (εὐαγγελίων); Aeschines, Ctes. 160.4 (εὐαγγελίων); Speusippus, Epistula ad Philippum regem [Sp.] Page 9 line 6 (εὐαγγέλια); Menander, Perik. 993 (εὐαγγέλια); 2 Kgdms 4:10 (εὐαγγέλια).

19. 2 Kgdms 4:10 (εὐαγγέλια, accusative, plural).

20. Matt 4:23; 9:35; 24:14; 26:13; Mark 1:1, 14, 15; 8:35; 10:29; 13:10; 14:9; 16:15; Acts 15:7; 20:24; Rom 1:1, 9, 16; 2:16; 10:16; 11:28; 15:16, 19; 16:25; 1 Cor 4:15; 9:12, 14 (x2), 18 (x2), 23; 15:1; 2 Cor 2:12; 4:3, 4; 8:18; 9:13; 10:14; 11:4, 7; Gal 1:6, 7, 11; 2:2, 5, 7, 14; Eph 1:13; 3:6; 6:15, 19; Phil 1:5, 7, 12, 16, 27 (x2); 2:22; 4:3, 15; Col 1:5, 23; 1 Thess 1:5; 2:2, 4, 8, 9; 3:2; 2 Thess 1:8; 2:14; 1 Tim 1:11; 2 Tim 1:8, 10; 2:8; Phlm 1:13; 1 Pet 4:17; Rev 14:6.

21. Rom 1:1, 9, 16; 2:16; 10:16; 11:28; 15:16, 19; 16:25; 1 Cor 4:15; 9:12, 14 (x2), 18 (x2), 23; 15:1; 2 Cor 2:12; 4:3, 4; 8:18; 9:13; 10:14; 11:4, 7; Gal 1:6, 7, 11; 2:2, 5, 7, 14; Phil 1:5, 7, 12, 16, 27 (x2); 2:22; 4:3, 15; 1 Thess 1:5; 2:2, 4, 8, 9; 3:2; Phlm 1:13.

22. 1 Thess 1:5; 2:2, 4, 8, 9; 3:2.

23. Gal 1:6, 7, 11; 2:2, 5, 7, 14.

24. Phil 1:5, 7, 12, 16, 27 (x2); 2:22; 4:3, 15.

25. 1 Cor 4:15; 9:12, 14 (x2), 18 (x2), 23; 15:1.

26. 2 Cor 2:12; 4:3, 4; 8:18; 9:13; 10:14; 11:4, 7.

27. Phlm 1:13.

28. Rom 1:1, 9, 16; 2:16; 10:16; 11:28; 15:16, 19; 16:25.

29. Diodorus Siculus, Bibliotheca historica 15.74.2.2 (εὐαγγελία).

30. 2 Kgdms 18:20 (εὐαγγελίας), 22 (εὐαγγελία), 25 (εὐαγγελία), 27 (εὐαγγελίαν); 3 Kgdms 7:9 (εὐαγγελίας).

31. Xenophon, Anab. 2.5.38.4; Lysias Δήμου καταλύσεως ἀπολογία 30.8; Hippocrates, De arte 10.21; Aristotle, Fragmenta varia Category 8 treatise title 44 fragment 538.12; Nymphodorus, Fragmenta 15.3; Polybius, Hist. 3.7.3.3; 4.53.2.6; 30.25.1.5; Bolus, Περὶ συμπαθειῶν καὶ ἀντιπαθειῶν (sub nomine Democriti) 5.2; [Aristides] Fragmenta 20.2; Diodorus Siculus, Bibliotheca historica 8.25.1.6; 8.25.4.3; 8.25.4.6; 12.78.1.6; 14.46.5.4; 14.68.4.4; 20.80.4.6; Antiquitates Romanae 9.60.6.4; 15.6.3.8; Ad Ammaeum 10.53; Philo, Creation 106.8; Migration 190.1; Abraham 261.9; Joseph 92.2; Good Person 65.1; 71.3; Eternity 69.1; Περὶ ἀριθμῶν sive Ἀριθμητικά (fragmenta) 41b.8; 49b.2; Strabo, Geogr. 14.1.31.11; Bruti, Epist. 30.3; 52.5 [Hercher, Epistolographi Graeci, 178–91].

32. 2 Macc 8:36; 9:17.

33. Acts 3:24; 4:2; 13:5, 38; 15:36; 16:17, 21; 17:3, 13, 23; 26:23; Rom 1:8; 1 Cor 2:1; 9:14; 11:26; Phil 1:17, 18; Col 1:28.

34. Rom 1:8; 1 Cor 2:1; 9:14; 11:26; Phil 1:17, 18.

35. Phil 1:17, 18.

36. 1 Cor 2:1; 9:14; 11:26.

37. Rom 1:8.

38. Philo, *Creation* 34.1; *Names* 158.4; *Abraham* 153.2.

39. Gal 3:8.

40. Gal 3:8.

41. Gal 3:8.

Bibliography

Abbott-Smith, Georges. *A Manual Greek Lexicon of the New Testament*. Edinburgh: T. & T. Clark, 1973.
Achtemeier, Elizabeth. *Nahum—Malachi*. Interpretation. Louisville: John Knox, 1986.
Achtemeier, Paul J. *Romans*. Interpretation. Atlanta: John Knox, 1985.
Alexander, Loveday. "Hellenistic Letter-Forms and the Structure of Philippians." *JSNT* 37 (1989) 87–101.
Allen, Leslie C. "Old Testament Background of προ ὁρίζειν in the New Testament." *NTS* 17 (1970) 104–8.
Allison, Dale C. *The Jesus Tradition in Q*. Harrisburg, PA: TPI, 1997.
———. "Paul and the Missionary Discourse." *ETL* 61 (1985) 369–75.
———. "The Pauline Epistles and the Synoptic Gospels: The Pattern of Parallels." *NTS* 28 (1982) 1–32.
Anderson, R. Dean. *Glossary of Greek Rhetorical Terms Connected to Methods of Argumentation, Figures and Tropes from Anaximenes to Quintilian*. CBET 24. Leuven: Peeters, 2000.
Ascough, Richard S. "Redescribing the Thessalonians' Mission in Light of Graeco-Roman Associations." *NTS* 60 (2014) 61–82.
Ashton, John. *The Religion of Paul the Apostle*. New Haven, CT: Yale University Press, 2000.
Asting, Ragnar Kristian. *Die Verkündigung des Wortes im Urchristentum dargestellt an den Begriffen 'Wort Gottes,' 'Evangelium' und 'Zeugnis.'* Stuttgart: Kohlhammer, 1939.
Atkinson, Kenneth. "Herod the Great, Sosius, and the Siege of Jerusalem (37 BCE) in Psalm of Solomon 17." *NovT* 38 (1996) 313–22.
Aune, David E. *Prophecy in Early Christianity and the Ancient Mediterranean World*. Grand Rapids: Eerdmans, 1983.
Balz, Horst. "προγράφω." *EDNT* 3:154.
Barclay, John M. G. "Why the Roman Empire was Insignificant to Paul." In *Pauline Churches and Diaspora Jews*, by John M. G. Barclay, 363–87. WUNT 275. Tübingen: Mohr/Siebeck, 2011.
Barnett, Paul. *Paul, Missionary of Jesus*. Grand Rapids: Eerdmans, 2008.
———. *The Second Epistle to the Corinthians*. NICNT. Grand Rapids: Eerdmans, 1997.
Barrett, C. K. *The Acts of the Apostles*. 2 vols. ICC. Edinburgh: T. & T. Clark, 1994, 2002.

———. *A Commentary on the Epistle to the Romans.* BNTC. 2nd ed. London: A & C Black, 1991.

———. *The First Epistle to the Corinthians.* BNTC. London: Black, 1971.

———. *Freedom and Obligation: A Study of the Epistle to the Galatians.* London: SPCK, 1985.

———. "I Am Not Ashamed of the Gospel." In *Foi et salut selon Saint Paul: Colloque Œcuménique à L'abbaye de S. Paul Hors Les Murs, 16–21 Avril 1968* (Épître aux Romains 1,16), 1, edited by Markas Barth, 9–41. AnBib 42. Rome: Institut Biblique Pontifical, 1970.

———. "New Testament Eschatology." *SJT* 6 (1953) 136–55.

———. *The Second Epistle to the Corinthians.* BNTC. London: Black, 1973.

Bates, Matthew W. *The Hermeneutics of the Apostolic Proclamation: The Center of Paul's Method of Scriptural Interpretation.* Waco, TX: Baylor University Press, 2012.

Bauckham, Richard. "Kingdom and Church According to Jesus and Paul." *HBT* 18 (1996) 1–26.

Baum, Armin D. "Synoptic Problem." *DJG*² 911–19.

Baur, Ferdinand Christian. *Paul the Apostle of Jesus Christ.* 2 volumes in 1. 1845; Peabody, MA: Hendrickson, 2003.

Beale, G. K., and Don A. Carson, eds. *Commentary on the New Testament Use of the Old Testament.* Grand Rapids: Baker Academic, 2007.

Beare, F. W. *The Epistle to the Philippians*, BNTC. London: Black, 1969².

———. "The Mission of the Disciples and the Mission Charge. Matthew 10 and Parallels." *JBL* 89 (1970) 1–13.

Beaudean, John William. *Paul's Theology of Preaching.* Dissertation Series 6. Macon, GA: Mercer University Press, 1988.

Beavis, Mary Ann. *Mark.* Paideia. Grand Rapids: Baker Academic, 2011.

Becker, Ulrich. "Gospel, Evangelize, Evangelist." *NIDNTTE* 2 (1976) 107–15.

Beetham, Frank. "The Aorist Indicative." *GR* 49 (2002) 227–36.

Behm, Johannes. "ἐκχέω, ἐκχύν(ν)ω." *TDNT* 2:467–69.

Beker, J. Christiaan. *Paul the Apostle: The Triumph of God in Life and Thought.* Edinburgh: T. & T. Clark, 1980.

———. "Paul the Theologian: Major Motifs in Pauline Theology." *Int* 43 (1989) 352–65.

Bell, Richard H. *The Irrevocable Call of God: An Inquiry into Paul's Theology of Israel.* WUNT 184. Tübingen: Mohr/Siebeck, 2005.

Belleville, Linda L. "Gospel and Kerygma in 2 Corinthians." In *Gospel in Paul*, edited by L. Ann Jervis and Peter Richardson, 134–64. Sheffield: Sheffield Academic, 1994.

Benoit, Pierre. "La deuxième visite de Saint Paul à Jérusalem." *Bib* 40 (1959) 778–92.

———. *Les épîtres de saint Paul aux Philippiens, a Philémon, aux Colossiens, aux Éphésiens.* Paris: Cerf, 1959.

Berger, Klaus. "χάρισμα." *EDNT* 3:460–61.

Bertram, Georg. "ἐπιστρέφω." *TDNT* 7:722–29.

———. "θαῦμα, κτλ." *TDNT* 3:27–42.

———. "κατεργάζομαι." *TDNT* 3:634–35.

———. "συνεργός, κτλ." *TDNT* 7:871–76.

Best, Ernest. *The First and Second Epistles to the Thessalonians*. BNTC. Peabody, MA: Continuum, 1986.

———. *The Letter of Paul to the Romans*. CBC. Cambridge: Cambridge University Press, 1967.

Betz, Hans Dieter. *2 Corinthians 8 and 9*. Hermeneia. Philadelphia: Fortress, 1985.

———. *Galatians*. Hermeneia. Philadelphia: Fortress, 1979.

Bird, Michael F. *An Anomalous Jew: Paul among Jews, Greeks, and Romans*. Grand Rapids: Eerdmans, 2016.

Bishop, Jonathan. "The Gospel(s) According to Paul." *ATR* 76 (1994) 296–312.

Bittlinger, Arnold. *Gifts and Graces*. Grand Rapids: Eerdmans, 1968.

Blakely, Hunter B. "The Gospel of Paul: A Study in the Prison Epistles." *ThTo* 3 (1946) 345–57.

Bloomquist, Gregory. *The Function of Suffering in Philippians*. JSNTSupp 78. Sheffield: JSOT, 1993.

Blumenthal, Christian. "Was sagt 1 Thess 1.9b-10 über die Adressaten des 1 Thess? Literarische und historische Erwägungen." *NTS* 51 (2005) 96–105.

Bock, Darrell L. *Luke 1:1–9:50*. BECNT. Grand Rapids: Baker Academic, 1994.

———. *Luke 9:51–24:53*. BECNT. Grand Rapids: Baker Academic, 1996.

Bockmuehl, Markus N. A. *Philippians*. BNTC. Peabody, MA: Hendrickson, 1998.

Bockmuehl, Markus N. A., and Donald A. Hagner, eds., *The Written Gospel*. Cambridge: Cambridge University Press, 2005.

Boers, Hendrikus W. "Form Critical Study of Paul's Letters: 1 Thessalonians as a Case Study." *NTS* 22 (1976) 140–58.

———. "The Foundations of Paul's Thought: A Methodological Investigation—The Problem of the Coherent Center of Paul's Thought." *ST* 42 (1988) 55–68.

Boesch, Paul. *Theōros: Untersuchung zur Epangelie griechischer Feste*. Berlin: Mayer & Müller, 1908.

Borgen, Peder. *Philo of Alexandria: An Exegete for His Time*. NovTSup 86. Leiden: Brill, 1997.

Bormann, Paul. *Die Heilswirksamkeit der Verkündigung nach dem Apostel Paulus: Ein Beitrag zur Theologie der Verkündigung*. KKS 14. Paderborn, Germany: Bonfacious Druckerer, 1965.

Bornkamm, Günther. *Early Christian Experience*. NTL. London: SCM, 1969.

———. *Paul*. London: Hodder and Stoughton, 1975.

Bortone, Pietro. *Greek Prepositions from Antiquity to the Present*. Oxford: Oxford University Press, 2010.

Bourke, Trevor J. "The Holy Spirit as the Controlling Dynamic in Paul's Role as Missionary to the Thessalonians." In *Paul as Missionary: Identity, Activity, Theology, and Practice*, edited by Trevor J. Bourke and Brian S. Rosner, 142–57. London: T. & T. Clark, 2011.

Bovon, François. *Luke I*. Hermeneia. Minneapolis: Augsburg Fortress, 2002.

Bowman, John W. "The Term *Gospel* and its Cognates in the Palestinian Syriac." In *New Testament Essays: Studies in Memory of T. W. Manson 1893–1958*, edited by Angus J. B. Higgins, 54–67. Manchester: Manchester University Press, 1959.

Bray, Gerald L., and Thomas C. Oden. *Romans*. ACCS, NT 6. Downers Grove, IL: InterVarsity, 2012.

Brewer, Raymond R. "The Meaning of *Politeuesthe* in Phil 1:27." *JB*; 73 (1954) 76–83.

Broer, Ingo. "καταγγέλλω." *EDNT* 2:256.

Brooke, Alan E. *The Johannine Epistles*. ICC. Edinburgh: T. & T. Clark, 1912.
Brown, Colin. *Miracles and the Critical Mind*. Grand Rapids: Eerdmans, 1984.
Brown, Michael Joseph. "Paul's Use of Δουλος Χριστου Ιησου in Romans 1:1." *JBL* 120 (2001) 723–37.
Brown, Raymond E. *The Birth of the Messiah*. Garden City, NY: Doubleday, 1977.
———. *An Introduction to the New Testament*. AB. Garden City, NY: Doubleday, 1997.
Bruce, F. F. *1 and 2 Corinthians*. NCB. London: Marshall, Morgan & Scott, 1971.
———. *The Acts of the Apostles*. Grand Rapids: Eerdmans, 1990³.
———. *The Epistle of Paul to the Romans: An Introduction and Commentary*. TNTC. London: Tyndale, 1963.
———. *The Epistles to the Colossians, to Philemon and to the Ephesians*. NICNT. Grand Rapids: Eerdmans, 1984.
———. *Galatians*. NIGTC. Grand Rapids: Eerdmans, 1982.
———. *Paul: Apostle of the Free Spirit*. Exeter, UK: Paternoster, 1977.
———. *Romans*. TNTC. London: InterVarsity, 1963.
———. *1 and 2 Thessalonians*. WBC 45. Waco, TX: Word, 1982.
Bryskog, Samuel. "Epistolography, Rhetoric and Letter Prescript: Romans 1:1–7 as a Test Case." *JSNT* 65 (1997) 27–46.
Büchsel, Friedrich. "παραδίδωμι." *TDNT* 2:169–73.
Bullmore, Michael A. *St. Paul's Theology of Rhetorical Style*. San Francisco: International Scholars, 1995.
Bultmann, Rudolf. *History of the Synoptic Tradition*. New York: Harper & Row, 1963.
———. *The Johannine Epistles*. Hermeneia. Philadelphia: Fortress, 1973.
———. *Theology of the New Testament*. 2 vols. Waco, TX: Baylor University Press, 2007.
Burk, Denny. "Is Paul's Gospel Counterimperial?: Evaluating the Prospects of the 'Fresh Perspective' for Evangelical Theology." *JETS* 51 (2008) 309–37.
———. "The Righteousness of God (*Dikaiosunē Theou*) and Verbal Genitives: A Grammatical Clarification." *JSNT* 34 (2012) 346–60.
Burrows, Millar. "The Origin of the Term 'Gospel.'" *JBL* 44 (1925) 21–33.
Burton, Ernest de Witt. *The Epistle to the Galatians*. ICC. Edinburgh: T. & T. Clark, 1921.
Buttmann, Alexander. *A Grammar of the New Testament Greek*. Andover, MA: Draper, 1873.
Byrne, Brendan. *Romans*. SP 6. Collegeville, MN: Liturgical, 1996.
Cabaniss, Allen. "Gospel According to Paul." *EvQ* 48 (1976) 164–67.
Caird, George B. *Paul's Letters from Prison*. NClB. Oxford: Oxford University Press, 1976.
———. *Principalities and Powers: A Study in Pauline Theology*. Oxford: Clarendon, 1956.
Calhoun, Robert Matthew. *Paul's Definitions of the Gospel in Romans 1*. WUNT 2.316. Tübingen: Mohr/Siebeck, 2011.
Cambier, Jules. "Paul and Tradition." *Conc* 10 (1966) 53–63.
Campbell, Douglas A. "Covenant or Contract in the Interpretation of Paul." *Participatio: Journal of the Thomas F. Torrance Theological Fellowship* Supp. Vol. 3 (2014) 182–200. https://www.tftorrance.org/journal/SuppVol3115.pdf.

———. *The Deliverance of God: An Apocalyptic Rereading of Justification in Paul*. Grand Rapids: Eerdmans, 2009.

———. "Determining the Gospel through Rhetorical Analysis in Paul's Letter to the Roman Christians." In *Gospel in Paul*, edited by L. Ann Jervis and Peter Richardson, 315–36. Sheffield: Sheffield Academic, 1994.

———. *Paul: An Apostle's Journey*. Grand Rapids: Eerdmans, 2018.

———. *The Quest for Paul's Gospel: A Suggested Strategy*. JSNTSupp 274. London: T. & T. Clark, 2005.

———. "The Story of Jesus in Romans and Galatians." In *Narrative Dynamics: A Critical Assessment*, edited by Bruce W. Longenecker, 97–124. Louisville: Westminster John Knox, 2002.

Carson, D. A. "Locating Udo Schnelle's *Theology of the New Testament* in the Contemporary Discussion." *JETS* 53 (2010) 133–41.

Casey, Maurice. *Jesus of Nazareth*. London: T. & T. Clark, 2010.

Cassidy, Richard J. *Paul in Chains: Roman Imprisonment and the Letters of St. Paul*. New York: Crossroad, 2001.

Catchpole, David R. *The Quest for Q*. Edinburgh: T. & T. Clark, 1993.

———. "The Question of Q." *STRev* 36 (1992) 3–44.

Chan-Hie, Kim. *Form and Structure of the Familiar Greek Letter of Recommendation*. SBLDS 4. Missoula, MT: Society of Biblical Literature, 1972.

Charlesworth, James H. "Can We Discern the Composition Date of the Parables of Enoch?" In *Enoch and the Messiah Son of Man. Revisiting the Book of Parables*, edited by Gabriele Boccaccini, 450–68. Grand Rapids: Eerdmans, 2007.

Ciampa, Roy E., and Brian S. Rosner. *The First Letter to the Corinthians*. PNTCS. Grand Rapids: Eerdmans, 2010.

Clark, Kenneth W. "The Meaning of ἐνεργέω and καταργέω in the New Testament." *JBL* 54 (1935) 93–101.

Coggins, Richard J., and S. Paul Re'emi. *Israel among the Nations: A Commentary on the Books of Nahum and Obadiah and Esther*. ITC. Grand Rapids: Eerdmans, 1985.

Cohen, Naomi G. *Philo's Scriptures: Citations from the Prophets and Writings: Evidence for a Haftarah Cycle in Second Temple Judaism*. JSJSup 123. Leiden: Brill, 2007.

Coleman, Rachel. *The Lukan Lens on Wealth and Possessions: A Perspective Shaped by the Themes of Reversal and Right Response*. Leiden: Brill, 2019.

Collange, Jean-François. *The Epistle of Saint Paul to the Philippians*. London: Epworth, 1979.

Collins, Adela Yarbro. "The Worship of Jesus and the Imperial Cult." In *The Jewish Roots of Christological Monotheism: Papers from the St. Andrews Conference on the Historical Origins of the Worship of Jesus*, edited by Carey C. Newman and James R. Davila, 234–57. JSJSup 63. Leiden: Brill, 1999.

Collins, John J. *The Scepter and the Star. Messianism in the Light of the Dead Sea Scrolls*. Cambridge: Eerdmans, 2010.

Collins, Raymond F. *First Corinthians*. SP 7. Collegeville, MN: Liturgical, 1999.

———. *Studies in the First Letter to the Thessalonians*. BETL 66. Leuven: Leuven University Press, 1984.

———, ed. *The Thessalonian Correspondence*. BETL 87. Leuven: Leuven University Press, 1990.

Conzelmann, Hans. "χάρισμα." *TDNT* 9:402–6.

———. *1 Corinthians*. Hermeneia. Philadelphia: Fortress, 1975.
Cosby, Michael R. "Paul's Persuasive Language in Romans 5." In *Persuasive Artistry: Studies in New Testament Rhetoric in Honor of George A. Kennedy*, edited by Duane F. Watson, 209–26. JSNTSupp 50. Sheffield: JSOT, 1991.
Cotter, Wendy. *Miracles in Greco-Roman Antiquity*. London: Routledge, 1999.
Cousar, Charles B. "Apostle Paul: His Life and Theology." *Int* 60 (2006) 478–79.
Cranfield, Charles E. B. "Changes of Person and Number in Paul's Epistles." In *Paul and Paulinism*, edited by Morna D. Hooker and Stephen G. Wilson, 280–89. London: SPCK, 1982.
———. *The Epistle to the Romans*. 2 vols. ICC. Edinburgh: T. & T. Clark, 1975, 1979.
Creed, John M. *The Gospel According to St. Luke*. London: Macmillan, 1930.
Cremer, Hermann. *Die paulinische Rechtfertigungslehre im Zusammenhange ihrer geschichtlichen Voraussetzungen*. Gütersloh, Germany: Bertelsmann, 1990².
Crossan, John Dominic. *The Birth of Christianity*. San Francisco: Harper, 1998.
Cullmann, Oscar. *The Early Church*. London: SCM, 1956.
———. "The Tradition." In *The Early Church*, edited by Oscar Cullmann, 59–99. London: SCM, 1956.
Dahl, Nils A. "Anamnesis: Mémoire et Commésmoration Dans Le Christianisme Primitif." *ST* 1.1–2 (1947) 69–95.
Dalman, Gustaf. *The Words of Jesus*. Edinburgh: T. & T. Clark, 1902.
Dalton, William J. "The Integrity of Philippians." *Bib* 60 (1979) 97–102.
Davies, William D. *Paul and Rabbinic Judaism*. London: SPCK, 1981⁴.
Davies, William D., and Dale C. Allison, *The Gospel According to Matthew*. 3 vols. ICC. Edinburgh: T. & T. Clark, 1988, 1991, 1997.
Davis, Basil S. "The Meaning of προεγράφη in the Context of Galatians 3.1." *NTS* 45 (1999) 213–29.
Dawson, Audrey. *Healing, Weakness and Power: Perspectives on Healing in the Writings of Mark, Luke and Paul*. PBM. Milton Keynes, UK: Paternoster, 2008.
De Boer, Martinus C. "The Composition of 1 Corinthians." *NTS* 40 (1994) 229–45.
De Jonge, Marinus, and Adam S. van der Woude. "11Q Melchizedek and the New Testament." *NTS* 12 (1966) 301–26.
De Silva, David A. *4 Maccabees: Introduction and Commentary on the Greek Text of Sinaiticus*. SComS. Leiden: Brill, 2006.
Debrunner, Albert. "λέγω, κτλ." *TDNT* 4:69–77.
Deissmann, Adolf. *Bible Studies*. Peabody, MA: Hendrickson, 1988.
———. *Light from the Ancient East: The New Testament Illustrated by Recently Discovered Texts of the Graeco-Roman World*. London: Hodder and Stoughton, 1910.
———. *Paul: A Study in Social and Religious History*. New York: Harper, 1957.
———. *The Religion of Jesus and the Faith of Paul*. London: Hodder and Stoughton, 1926.
Delling, Gerhard. "λαμβάνω, κτλ." *TDNT* 4:5–15.
———. "παραλαμβάνω." *TDNT* 4:11–14.
Denis, Albert-Marie. *Introduction aux pseudépigraphes grecs d'Ancien Testament*. SVTP 1. Leiden: Brill, 1970.
———. *The Letter to the Galatians*. NICNT. Grand Rapids: Eerdmans, 2018.
Dibelius, Martin. "The Apostolic Council." In *Studies in the Acts of the Apostles*, edited by Martin Dibelius, 93–101. London: SCM, 1956.

———. *Paul.* London: Longmans, 1953.
———. *An die Thessalonicher I, II, An die Philipper.* HNT 11. Tübingen: Mohr/Siebeck, 1937³.
Dickson, John P. "Gospel as News: εὐαγγελ- from Aristophanes to the Apostle Paul." *NTS* 51 (2005) 212–30.
Dines, Jennifer M. *The Septuagint.* London: T. & T. Clark, 2004.
Dobschütz, Ernst von. *Die Thessalonicher-Briefe.* KEK 10. Göttingen: Vandenhoeck & Ruprecht, 1909.
Dockery, David S. "The Use of Hab 2:4 in Rom 1:17: Some Hermeneutical and Theological Considerations." *WTJ* 22.2 (1987) 24–36.
Dodd, Charles H. *According to the Scriptures: The Sub-Structure of New Testament Theology.* London: Nisbet, 1952.
———. *The Epistle of Paul to the Romans.* MNTC. London: Hodder and Stoughton, 1932.
———. *The Meaning of Paul for Today.* New York: George H. Doran, 1920.
Donfried, Karl Paul, and I. Howard Marshall, *The Theology of the Shorter Pauline Letters.* Cambridge: Cambridge University Press, 1993.
Donge, Gloria van. "In What Way is Paul's Gospel (*euangelion*) of Freedom Theology of the Cross (*theologia crucis*)." *Colloq* 21 (1988) 19–33.
Donlon, Stephen E. "The Form-Critics, the Gospel, and St. Paul." *CBQ* 6 (1944) 159–79.
Doudna, Greg. "Dating the Scrolls on the Basis of Radiocarbon Analysis." In *The Dead Sea Scrolls after Fifty Years*, edited by Peter W. Flint and James C. VanderKam, 2:430–65. 2 vols. Leiden: Brill, 1999.
Downs, David J. "'The Offering of the Gentiles' in Romans 15.16." *JSNT* 29 (2006) 173–86.
Dunn, James D. G., ed. *The Cambridge Companion to St Paul.* Cambridge: Cambridge University Press, 2003.
———. *Christology in the Making: A New Testament Inquiry into the Origins of the Doctrine of the Incarnation.* London: SCM, 1980.
———. *The Epistles to the Colossians and to Philemon.* NIGTC. Grand Rapids: Eerdmans, 1996.
———. *The Epistle to the Galatians.* BNTC. Peabody, MA: Hendrickson, 1993.
———. "From Jesus' Proclamation to Paul's Gospel." *RCT* 34 (2009) 417–37.
———. "The Gospel According to St. Paul." In *The Blackwell Companion to Paul*, Wiley Blackwell Companions to Religion 53, edited by Stephen Westerholm, 139–53. Malden, MA: Wiley-Blackwell, 2011.
———. "The Gospel and the Gospels." *EvQ* 85 (2013) 291–308.
———. "How New Was Paul's Gospel? The Problem of Continuity and Discontinuity." In *Gospel in Paul*, edited by L. Ann Jervis and Peter Richardson, 367–88. Sheffield: Sheffield Academic, 1994.
———. *Jesus and the Spirit: A Study of the Religious and Charismatic Experience of Jesus and the First Christians as Reflected in the New Testament.* London: SCM, 1975.
———. "Jesus–Flesh and Spirit: An Exposition of Romans 1:3–4." *JTS* 24 (1973) 40–68.
———. *Jesus Remembered.* Grand Rapids: Eerdmans, 2003.

———. "Once More—Gal. 1.18 Ἱστορῆσαι Κηφᾶν' in Reply to Otfried Hofius." *ZNW* 76 (1985) 138–39.

———. "The Relationship between Paul and Jerusalem According to Galatians 1 and 2." In *Jesus, Paul and the Law: Studies in Mark and Galatians*, edited by James D. G. Dunn, 108–25. London: SPCK, 1990.

———. *Romans 1–8*. WBC 38A. Dallas: Word, 1988.

———. *Romans 9–16*. WBC 38B. Dallas: Word, 1988.

———. *The Theology of Paul the Apostle*. Grand Rapids: Eerdmans, 1998.

Dupont, Jacques. *The Sources of the Acts*. New York: Herder and Herder, 1964.

Eastman, Susan. Review of *Paul and the Hermeneutics of Faith*, by Francis Watson. *JBL* 125 (2006) 610–14.

Edwards, James R. *Romans*. NIBC. Peabody, MA: Hendrickson, 1995.

Edwards, Mark J. ed., *Galatians, Ephesians, Philippians*. ACCS NT 8. Downers Grove, IL: InterVarsity, 1999.

Eichrodt, Walther. *Theology of the Old Testament*. 2 vols. London: SCM, 1961 and 1967.

Elliott, James Keith. "A Tale of Two Missions." *NovT* 40 (1998) 295–98.

Elliott, Neil. *The Arrogance of Nations: Reading Romans in the Shadow of Empire*. Paul in Critical Contexts. Minneapolis: Fortress, 2008.

———. *The Rhetoric of Romans*. JSNTSupp 45. Sheffield: Sheffield Academic, 1990.

Ellis, Edward Earle. *Paul's Use of the Old Testament*. Eugene, OR: Wipf & Stock, 2003.

———. *Prophecy and Hermeneutic in Early Christianity*. Grand Rapids: Baker, 1993.

Esler, Philip F. *Conflict and Identity in Romans: The Social Setting of Paul's Letter*. Minneapolis: Fortress, 2003.

Evans, Craig A. "The Old Testament in the New." In *The Face of New Testament Studies: A Survey of Recent Research*, edited by Scot McKnight and Grant R. Osborne, 130–45. Grand Rapids: Baker Academic, 2004.

Eve, Eric. *The Jewish Context of Jesus' Miracles*. JSNTSupp 231. London: Sheffield Academic, 2002.

Fabry, Heinz-Josef. "The Reception of Nahum and Habakkuk in the Septuagint and Qumran." In *Emanuel: Studies in Hebrew Bible, Septuagint, and Dead Sea Scrolls in Honor of Emanuel Tov*, edited by Shalom M. Paul, 241–56. Leiden: Brill, 2003.

Fallon, Francis T. *2 Corinthians*. NTM 11. Dublin: Veritas, 1980.

Fee, Gordon D. *The First and Second Letters to the Thessalonians*. NICNT. Grand Rapids: Eerdmans, 2009.

———. *The First Epistle to the Corinthians*. NICNT. Grand Rapids: Eerdmans, 1987.

———. *God's Empowering Presence: The Holy Spirit in the Letters of Paul*. Grand Rapids: Baker Academic 2011.

———. *Paul's Letter to the Philippians*. NICNT. Grand Rapids: Eerdmans, 1995.

———. "Philippians 2:5–11: Hymn or Exalted Pauline Prose?" *BBR* 2 (1992) 29–46.

Fewster, Gregory P. "The Philippians 'Christ Hymn': Trends in Critical Scholarship." *CBR* 13 (2015) 191–206.

Findlay, George G. *St. Paul's First Epistle to the Corinthians*. EGT. Grand Rapids: Eerdmans, 1980.

Fishbane, Michael. *Biblical Interpretation in Ancient Israel*. Oxford: Oxford University Press, 1985.

Fisk, Bruce N. "Paul: Life and Letters." In *The Face of New Testament Studies*, edited by Scot McKnight and Grant R. Osborne, 283–325. Grand Rapids: Baker Academic, 2004.
Fitzer, Gottfried. "φθάνω, προφθάνω." *TDNT* 9:88–92.
Fitzmyer, Joseph A. *The Acts of the Apostles*. AB 31. Garden City, NY: Doubleday, 1998.
———. *Essays on the Semitic Background of the New Testament*. London: Chapman, 1971.
———. *First Corinthians*. AB 32. New Haven, CT: Yale University Press, 2008.
———. "Further Light on Melchizedek from Qumran Cave 11." In *Essays on the Semitic Background of the New Testament*, edited by Joseph A. Fitzmyer, 245–67. London: Chapman, 1971.
———. *The Gospel According to Luke (I–IX)*. AB 28. Garden City, NY: Doubleday, 1981.
———. *The Gospel According to Luke (X–XXIV)*. AB 28A. Garden City, NY: Doubleday, 1985.
———. "The Gospel in the Theology of Paul." *Int* 33 (1979) 339–50.
———. *Paul and His Theology: A Brief Sketch*. Englewood Cliffs, NJ: Prentice Hall, 1989.
———. *Romans*. AB 33. Garden City, NY: Doubleday, 1993.
Fjärstedt, Biörn. *Synoptic Tradition in 1 Corinthians: Themes and Clusters of Theme Words in 1 Corinthians 1–4 and 9*. Uppsala, Sweden: Teologiska Institutionen, 1974.
Fowl, Stephen E. "Know Your Context: Giving and Receiving Money in Philippians." *Int* 56 (2002) 45–58.
———. *Philippians*. THNTC. Grand Rapids: Eerdmans, 2005.
———. *The Story of Christ in the Ethics of Paul*. JSNTSupp 36. Sheffield: JSOT, 1990.
France, Richard T. *The Gospel of Mark*. NIGTC. Grand Rapids: Eerdmans, 2002.
Friedrich, Gerhard. "δύναμις." *EDNT* 1:355–58.
———. "εὐαγγελίζομαι, κτλ." *TDNT* 2:707–37.
———. "κῆρυξ, κτλ." *TDNT* 3:683–718.
Furnish, Victor P. *II Corinthians*. AB 32A. Garden City, NY: Doubleday, 1984.
———. "On Putting Paul in His Place." *JBL* 113 (1994) 3–17.
———. Review of *Paul*, by Günther Bornkamm. *JBL* 90 (1971) 501–2.
Garland, David E. *1 Corinthians*. BECNT. Grand Rapids: Baker Academic, 2003.
———. "The Composition and Unity of Philippians. Some Neglected Literary Factors." *NovT* 27 (1985) 141–73.
———. "Paul's Defense of the Truth of the Gospel Regarding Gentiles (Galatians 2:15—3:22)." *RevExp* 91 (1994) 165–81.
Gaston, Lloyd. *Paul and the Torah*. Vancouver: University of British Columbia Press, 1987.
Gathercole, Simon. *Defending Substitution: An Essay on Atonement in Paul*. Grand Rapids: Baker Academic, 2015.
Gaventa, Beverly Roberts. "'You Proclaim the Lord's Death': 1 Corinthians 11:26 and Paul's Understanding of Worship." *RevExp* 80 (1983) 377–87.
Gerhardsson, Birger. *Memory and Manuscript: Oral Tradition and Written Transmission in Rabbinic Judaism and Early Christianity* with *Tradition and Transmission in Early Christianity*. Grand Rapids: Eerdmans, 1998.

Gillespie, Thomas W. *The First Theologian*. Grand Rapids: Eerdmans, 1994.
Glombitza, Otto. "Der Dank des Apostels: Zum Verständnis von Philipper IV 10–20." *NovT* 7 (1964–65) 135–41.
Gnilka, Joachim. *Der Philipperbrief*. HThKNT 10.3. Freiburg: Herder, 1968.
Goldingay, John. *Isaiah*. UBCS. Grand Rapids: Baker, 2012.
Goodacre, Mark. *The Case against Q. Studies in Markan Priority and the Synoptic Problem*. Harrisburg, PA: Trinity, 2002.
Goppelt, Leonhard. *Theology of the New Testament*. 2 vols. Grand Rapids: Eerdmans, 1981, 1982.
Gorman, Michael J. *Abide and Go: Missional Theosis in the Gospel of John*. The Didsbury Lecture Series, 2016. Eugene, OR: Cascade, 2018.
———. *Apostle of the Crucified Lord: A Theological Introduction to Paul and his Letters*. Grand Rapids: Eerdmans, 2017.
———. *Becoming the Gospel: Paul, Participation and Mission*. Grand Rapids: Eerdmans, 2015.
———. *Cruciformity: Paul's Narrative Spirituality of the Cross*. Grand Rapids: Eerdmans, 2007.
———. *Inhabiting the Cruciform God: Kenosis, Justification, and Theosis in Paul's Narrative Soteriology*. Grand Rapids: Eerdmans, 2009.
———. *Reading Paul*. Eugene, OR: Cascade, 2008.
Goulder, Michael D. "Is Q a Juggernaut?" *JBL* 115 (1996) 667–81.
———. *Paul and the Competing Mission in Corinth*. Peabody, MA: Hendrickson, 2008.
———. *St Paul Vs St Peter: A Tale of Two Missions*. London: SCM, 1994.
Gräbe, Petrus J. *The Power of God in Paul's Letters*. WUNT 2.123. Tübingen: Mohr/Siebeck, 2008.
Grayston, Kenneth. *The Epistle to the Romans*. EC. Peterborough, UK: Epworth, 1997.
Green, Samuel G. *Handbook to the Grammar of the Greek New Testament*. London: Religious Tract Society, 1886.
Greenman, Jeffrey P., and Timothy Larsen, eds. *Reading Romans through the Centuries: From the Early Church to Karl Barth*. Grand Rapids: Brazos, 2005.
Grimm, Carl Ludwig Wilibald, and Joseph Henry Thayer. *A Greek-English Lexicon of the New Testament*. New York: American Book, 1889.
Grudem, Wayne A. *The Gift of Prophecy in 1 Corinthians*. Washington, DC: University Press of America, 1982.
Grundmann, Walter. "δύναμαι/δύναμις." *TDNT* 2:284–317.
Guillebaud, Harold E. "Paul's Gospel or Christ's?" *EvQ* 14 (1942) 281–90.
Guthrie, Donald. *Galatians*. NCB. Grand Rapids: Eerdmans, 1973.
Haenchen, Ernst. *The Acts of the Apostles*. Oxford: Blackwell, 1971.
Hagner, Donald A. *The New Testament: A Historical and Theological Introduction*. Grand Rapids: Baker Academic, 2012.
Hahn, Ferdinand. *The Titles of Jesus in Christology: Their History in Early Christianity*. Cleveland, OH: World, 1969.
Hall, David R. *The Unity of the Corinthian Correspondence*. JSNTSupp 251. London: T. & T. Clark, 2003.
Hannah, Darrell D. "Isaiah within Judaism of the Second Temple Period." In *Isaiah in the New Testament*, edited by Steve Moyise and Maarten J. J. Menken, 7–33. London: T. & T. Clark, 2005.

Hansen, G. Walter. *Abraham in Galatians. Epistolary and Rhetorical Contexts.* Sheffield: Sheffield Academic, 1989.
Hanson, Anthony T. *Living Utterances of God: The New Testament Exegesis of the Old.* London: DLT, 1983.
Hanson, Richard P. C. *The Acts.* NClB. Oxford: Oxford University Press, 1967.
Harnack, Adolf von. *The Acts of the Apostles.* London: Williams & Norgate, 1909.
———. *The Constitution and Law of the Church in the First Two Centuries.* London: Williams & Norgate, 1910.
———. "Das Alte Testament in den paulinischen Briefen und in den paulinischen Gemeinden." In *Sitzungsberichte der Preussischen Akademie der Wissenschaften*, 124–41. Berlin: Philisophiish-historische Klasse, 1928.
———. "Gospel in the Early Church." In *The Constitution and the Law of the Church in the First Two Centuries*, edited by Adolf von Harnack, 275–349. London: Williams & Norgate, 1910.
———. *The Mission and Expansion of Christianity in the First Three Centuries.* New York: Harper, 1962.
Harrington, Daniel J. "Paul's Use of the Old Testament in Romans." *Studies in Christian-Jewish Relations* 4.1 (2009). https://doi.org/10.6017/scjr.v4i1.1536.
Harris, Horton. *The Tubingen School: A Historical and Theological Investigation of the School.* Oxford: Clarendon, 1990.
Harris, Murray J. *Colossians and Philemon.* EGGNT. Nashville: B & H, 2013.
———. *Prepositions and Theology in Greek.* Grand Rapids: Zondervan, 2012.
———. *The Second Epistle to the Corinthians.* NIGTC. Grand Rapids: Eerdmans, 2005.
Harrison, J. R. "Paul and the Imperial Gospel at Thessaloniki." *JSNT* 25 (2002) 71–96.
Harrisville, Roy A. "The Life and Work of Ernst Käsemann (1906–1998)." *LQ* 21 (2007) 294–319.
Hart, Michael H. *The 100: A Ranking of the Most Influential Persons in History.* New York: Citadel, 1992.
Harvey, Anthony E. "'The Workman is Worthy of his Hire': Fortunes of a Proverb in the Early Church." *NovT* 24 (1982) 209–21.
Havener, Ivan. "The Pre-Pauline Christological Credal Formulae of 1 Thessalonians." SBLSP 20 (1981) 105–28.
Hawthorne, Gerald F., and Ralph P. Martin. *Philippians.* WBC 43 revised. New York: Thomas Nelson, 2004.
Hays, Richard B. *Echoes of Scripture in the Letters of Paul.* New Haven, CT: Yale University Press, 1989.
———. *First Corinthians.* Interpretation. Louisville: John Knox, 1997.
———. "Is Paul's Gospel Narratable?" *JSNT* 27 (2004) 217–39.
Hemer, Colin J. *The Book of Acts in the Setting of Hellenistic History.* WUNT 49. Tübingen: J. C. B. Mohr [Paul Siebeck], 1989.
Hengel, Martin. *The Charismatic Leader and His Followers.* Eugene, OR: Wipf & Stock, 2005.
———. *Crucifixion in the Ancient World and the Folly of the Message of the Cross.* London: SCM, 1977.
Hercher, Rudolphus. *Epistolographi Graeci.* Reprint. Amsterdam: Hakkert, 1965.
Héring, Jean. *The First Epistle of Saint Paul to the Corinthians.* London: Epworth, 1962.

Hiestermann, Heinz. *Paul and the Synoptic Tradition*. ABG 58. Leipzig: Evangelische Verlagsanstalt, 2017.

Higbie, Carolyn. "Cicero the Homerist." *Oral Tradition* 26 (2011) 379–88.

Hilgenfeld, Adolphus. *Messias Judaeorum: libris eorum paulo ante et paulo post Christum natum conscriptis illustratus, XI-XVIII*. Leipzig: R. Reisland, 1869.

Hofius, Otfried. "'All Israel Will be Saved': Divine Salvation and Israel's Deliverance in Romans 9–11." *PSB* 11 (1990) 19–39.

———. "Gal. 1.18: Ἱστορῆσαι Κηφᾶν.'" *ZNW* 75 (1984) 73–85.

Hollander, Harm W. "The Words of Jesus: From Oral Traditions to Written Record in Paul and Q." *NovT* 42 (2000) 340–57.

Holloway, Paul A. *Philippians*. Hermeneia. Minneapolis: Fortress, 2017.

Hooker, Morna D. "1 Thessalonians 1:9–10: A Nutshell—But What Kind of Nut?" In *Geschichte-Tradition-Reflexion: Festschriften für Martin Hengel zum 70 Geburtstag, Bd 3*, edited by Hubert Cancik et al., 435–48. Tubingen: J. C. B. Mohr, 1996.

———. *The Gospel According to St Mark*. BNTC. London: Black, 1991.

———. "A Partner in the Gospel: Paul's Understanding of Ministry." In *Theology and Ethics in Paul and His Interpreters: Essays in Honor of Victor Paul Furnish*, edited by Eugene H. Lovering and Jerry L. Sumney, 83–100. Nashville: Abingdon, 1996.

———. "Philippians 2.6–11." In *From Adam to Christ*, edited by Morna D. Hooker, 88–102. Cambridge: Cambridge University Press, 1990.

Horbury, William. "'Gospel' in Herodian Judaea." In *The Written Gospel*, edited by Markus N. A. Bockmuehl and Donald A. Hagner, 7–30. Cambridge: Cambridge University Press, 2005.

———. *Jewish Messianism and the Cult of Christ*. London: SCM, 1998.

Hornblower, Simon, et al., eds. *The Oxford Classical Dictionary*. Oxford: Oxford University Press, 2012.

Horsley, G. H. R. *New Documents Illustrating Early Christianity*. Vol. 3. North Ryde, NSW: Macquarie University Press, 1983.

Horsley, Richard A. *1 Corinthians*. ANTC. Nashville: Abingdon, 1998.

Hübner, Hans. "ἀλήθεια." *EDNT* 1:57–60.

Hughes, Philip E. *Paul's Second Epistle to the Corinthians*. NICNT. Grand Rapids: Eerdmans, 1962.

Hultgren, Arland J. *Paul's Letter to the Romans: A Commentary*. Grand Rapids: Eerdmans, 2011.

Hume, David. *Enquiries Concerning Human Understanding and Concerning the Principles of Morals*. 1748. Edited by Lewis Amherst Selby-Bigge. Oxford: Clarendon, 1902^2.

Humphrey, Edith M. "Glimpsing the Glory: Paul's Gospel, Righteousness and the Beautiful Feet of N. T. Wright." In *Jesus, Paul and the People of God: A Theological Dialogue with N. T. Wright*, edited by Nicholas Perrin and Richard B. Hays, 161–80. Downers Grove, IL: IVP Academic, 2011.

Hunter, Archibald Macbride. *Interpreting Paul's Gospel*. London: SCM, 1954.

———. *Paul and His Predecessors*. London: SCM, 1961.

Hurd, John C. "Good News and the Integrity of 1 Corinthians." In *Gospel in Paul*, edited by L. Ann Jervis and Peter Richardson, 38–62. Sheffield: Sheffield Academic, 1994.

Hurtado, Larry. "Jesus as Lordly Example in Philippians 2:5-11." In *From Jesus to Paul: Studies in Honour of Francis Wright Beare*, edited by Peter Richardson and John C. Hurd, 122-32. Waterloo, ON: Wilfrid Laurier University Press, 1984.
Jellicoe, Sidney. *The Septuagint and Modern Study*. Oxford: Clarendon, 1968.
Jeremias, Joachim. *The Eucharistic Words of Jesus*. London: SCM, 1966.
———. *New Testament Theology*. London: SCM, 1971.
Jervell, Jacob. "The Problem of Traditions in Acts." In *Luke and the People of God: A New Look at Luke-Acts*, edited by Jacob Jervell, 19-39. Minneapolis: Augsburg, 1979.
Jervis, L. Ann, and Peter Richardson, eds. *Gospel in Paul: Studies on Corinthians, Galatians and Romans for Richard N. Longenecker*. JSNTSupp 108. Sheffield: Sheffield Academic, 1994.
———. *The Purpose of Romans: A Comparative Letter Structure Investigation*, JSNTSupp 55. Sheffield: Sheffield Academic, 1991.
Jewett, Robert. "Conflicting Movements in the Early Church as Reflected in Philippians." *NovT* 12 (1970) 362-90.
———. *Dating Paul's Life*. London: SCM, 1979.
———. "The Epistolary Thanksgiving and the Integrity of Philippians." *NovT* 12 (1970) 40-53.
———. "The Redaction and Use of an Early Christian Confession in Romans 1:3-4." In *The Living Text: Essays in Honor of Ernest W. Sanders*, edited by Robert Jewett and Dennis E. Groh, 99-122. Lanham, MD: University Press of America, 1985.
———. *Romans*. Hermeneia. Minneapolis: Fortress, 2007.
Johnson, Allan C., et al., eds. *Ancient Roman Statutes*. Corpus of Roman Law II. Austin: University of Texas Press, 1961.
Johnson, Nathan C. "Romans 1:3-4: Beyond Antithetical Parallelism." *JBL* 136 (2017) 467-90.
Johnson, S. Lewis. "The Gospel that Paul Preached." *BSac* 128 (1971) 327-40.
Kaiser, Otto. *Isaiah 1-12*. OTL. Philadelphia: Westminster, 1972.
Käsemann, Ernst. *Commentary on Romans*. London: SCM, 1980.
———. "A Critical Analysis of Philippians 2:5-11." *JTC* 5 (1968) 45-88.
———. "Die Legitimität des Apostels Eine Untersuchung zu II Korinther 10-13." *ZNW* 41 (1942) 33-71.
———. "Ministry and Community in the New Testament." In *Essays on New Testament Themes*, edited by Ernst Käsemann, 63-94. SBT 41 London: SCM, 1964.
———. "The Pauline Doctrine of the Lord's Supper." In *Essays on New Testament Themes*, edited by Ernst Käsemann, 108-35. SBT 41. London: SCM, 1964.
———. "'The Righteousness of God' in Paul." In *New Testament Questions of Today*, edited by Ernst Käsemann, 168-82. London: SCM, 1979.
Kaye, Bruce N. "Lightfoot and Baur on Early Christianity." *NovT* 26 (1984) 193-224.
Kea, Perry. "Source Theories for the Acts of the Apostles." *Forum* 4 (2001) 7-26.
Keck, Leander E. *Romans*. ANTC. Nashville: Abingdon, 2005.
Keener, Craig S. *1-2 Corinthians*. NCBC. Cambridge: Cambridge University Press, 2005.
———. *Acts*. Vol. 1. Grand Rapids: Baker Academic, 2012.
Kelhoffer, James *Conceptions of Gospel and Legitimacy in Early Christianity*. WUNT 324. Tubingen: Mohr/Siebeck, 2014.

Kellermann, Ulrich. "ἀπολογέομαι." EDNT 1:137.
Kelly, J. N. D. *Early Christian Creeds*. London: Longman, 1972.
Kierkegaard, Søren. *Papers and Journals: A Selection*. London: Penguin, 1996.
Kim, Seyoon. "Jesus the Son of God as the Gospel (1 Thess 1:9-10 and Rom 1:3-4." In *Earliest Christian History: History, Literature, and Theology: Essays from the Tyndale Fellowship in Honor of Martin Hengel*, edited by Michael F. Bird and Jason Maston, 117-41. WUNT 2.320. Tübingen: Mohr/Siebeck, 2012.

———. *The Origin of Paul's Gospel*. WUNT 2.4. Tübingen: Mohr/Siebeck, 1981.

———. "Paul's Entry (εἴσοδος) and the Thessalonians' Faith (1 Thessalonians 1-3)." *NTS* 51 (2005) 519-42.

Kim, Yung Suk. "Reclaiming Christ's Body (*soma christou*) Embodiment of God's Gospel in Paul's Letters." *Int* 67 (2013) 20-29.
Kittel, Gerhard. "παράδοξος." TDNT 2:255.
Klaiber, Walter. "Ernst Käsemann as Theological Exegete and Ecclesial Rebel." *LQ* 26 (2012) 26-56.
Klein, Günther. "Paul's Purpose in Writing the Epistle to the Romans." In *The Romans Debate*, edited by Karl P. Donfried, 29-43. Rev. ed. Peabody, MA: Hendrickson, 1991.
Kloppenborg, John S. "An Analysis of the Pre-Pauline Formula in 1 Cor 15:3b-5 in Light of Some Recent Literature." *CBQ* 40 (1978) 351-67.

———. *Excavating Q. The History and Setting of the Sayings Gospel*. Edinburgh: T. & T. Clark, 2000.

Knibb, Michael A. "Isaianic Traditions in the Book of Enoch." In *After the Exile. Essays in Honor of Rex Mason,* edited by John Barton and D. J. Reimer, 217-29. Macon, GA: Mercer University Press, 1996.
Koch, Dietrich-Alex. *Die Schrift als Zeuge des Evangeliums: Untersuchungen zur Verwendung und zum Verständnis der Schrift bei Paulus*. BHT 69. Tübingen: Mohr, 1986.
Koehler, Ludwig., and Walter Baumgartner. *Hebräisches und aramäisches Lexikon zum Alten Testament*. Leiden: Brill, 1994.
Koperski, Veronica. "The Early History of the Dissection of Philippians." *JTS* 44 (1993) 599-603.
Kraft, Robert A. "The 'Textual Mechanics' of Early Jewish LXX/OG Papyri and Fragments." In *Bible as Book: The Transmission of the Greek Text*, edited by Scot McKendrick and Orlaith O'Sullivan, 51-72. London: British Library, 2003.
Kramer, Werner. *Christ, Lord, Son of God*. SBT 50. London: SCM, 1966.
Krentz, Edgar M. "Military Language and Metaphors in Philippians." In *Origins and Method: Towards a New Understanding of Judaism and Christianity: Essays in Honour of John C. Hurd*, edited by Bradley H. McLean, 105-27. JSNTSupp 86. Sheffield: JSOT, 1993.
Krodel, Gerhard. "The Gospel According to Paul." *Dialog* 6 (1967) 95-107.
Kruse, Colin G. "Paul and John: Two Witnesses, One Gospel." In *Paul and the Gospels: Christologies, Conflicts, and Convergences*, edited by Michael F. Bird and Joel Willitts, 197-219. London: T. & T. Clark, 2011.
Kümmel, Werner Georg. *Introduction to the New Testament*. London: SCM, 1973.

———. *The New Testament: The History of the Investigation of its Problems*. London: SCM, 1973.

---. *Promise and Fulfilment. The Eschatological Message of Jesus.* SBT 23. London: SCM, 1961.
---. *The Theology of the New Testament: According to its Major Witnesses: Jesus-Paul-John.* London: SCM, 1974.
Laffi, Umberto. "Le iscrizioni relative all'introduzione nel 9 A.C. del nuovo calendario della Provincia d'Asia." *Studi classici e orientali* 16 (1968) 5–98.
Lambrecht, Jan. "Thanksgivings in 1 Thessalonians 1–3." In *The Thessalonian Correspondence*, edited by Raymond F. Collins, 183–205. BETL 87. Leuven: Leuven University Press, 1990.
Lang, Friedrich Gustav. *2 Korinther 5,1–10 in der neueren Forschung.* BGBE 10. Tübingen: J. C. B. Mohr [P. Siebeck], 1973.
Lange, Armin, and Matthias Weigold. *Biblical Quotations and Allusions in Second Temple Jewish Literature.* JAJSup. Göttingen: Vandenhoeck & Ruprecht, 2011.
Langevin, Paul-Émile, "Le Seigneur Jésus selon un texte prépaulinien, 1 Th 1:9–10." *ScEccl* 17 (1965) 263–82, 473–512.
Lenski, Richard C. H. *The Interpretation of St. Paul's First and Second Epistles to the Corinthians.* Minneapolis: Augsburg, 1963.
Lewis, Naphtali, and Meyer Reinhold, eds. *Roman Civilization: Selected Readings.* 2 vols. New York: Columbia University Press, 1990.
Lietaert Peerbolte, L. J. *Paul the Missionary.* CBET 34. Leuven: Peeters, 2003.
Lietzmann, Hans. *An die Korinther I/II.* HNT 9. Tübingen: J. C. B. Mohr [P. Siebeck], 1949.
Lightfoot, J. B. *Biblical Essays.* London: Macmillan, 1904.
---. *Notes on Epistles of St Paul from Unpublished Commentaries.* Reprint. Eugene, OR: Wipf & Stock, 2001.
---. *Saint Paul's Epistles to the Colossians and to Philemon.* London: Macmillan, 1890.
---. *Saint Paul's Epistle to the Galatians.* London: Macmillan, 1881.
---. *Saint Paul's Epistle to the Philippians.* London: Macmillan, 1888.
Lincoln, Andrew T. "Ephesians 2:8–10: A Summary of Paul's Gospel?" *CBQ* 45 (1983) 617–30.
Lindars, Barnabas. *New Testament Apologetic: The Doctrinal Significance of the Old Testament Quotations.* London: SCM, 1961.
Lindemann, Andreas. *Der Erste Korintherbrief.* HNT 9.1. Tübingen: Mohr/Siebeck, 2000.
Linko, Jaakko. "Paul's Two Letters to the Philippians? Some Critical Observations on the Unity Question of Philippians." In *The Nordic Paul: Finnish Approaches to Pauline Theology*, edited by Lars Aejmelaeus and Antti Mustakallio, 156–71. LNTS 374. London: T. & T. Clark, 2008.
Linnemann, Eta. "Tradition und Interpretation in Röm 1:3f." *EvT* 31(1971) 264–76.
Litwak, Kenneth D. "Echoes of Scripture? A Critical Survey of Recent Works on Paul's Use of the Old Testament." *CurBR* 6 (1998) 260–88.
Locke, John. "A Discourse of Miracles." In *The Reasonableness of Christianity*, edited by Ian T. Ramsey, 79–87. Stanford: Stanford University Press, 1958.
Longenecker, Bruce W. "Narrative Interest in the Study of Paul: Retrospect and Prospect." In *Narrative Dynamics in Paul: A Critical Assessment*, edited by Bruce W. Longenecker, 3–16. Louisville: Westminster John Knox, 2002.
---. "Poverty and Paul's Gospel." *ExAud* 27 (2011) 26–44.

Longenecker, Richard N. *Biblical Exegesis in the Apostolic Period*. Grand Rapids: Eerdmans, 1999.

———. *The Epistle to the Romans: A Commentary on the Greek Text*. NIGTC. Grand Rapids: Eerdmans, 2016.

———. *Galatians*. WBC 41. Dallas: Word, 1990.

Louth, Andrew. *Discerning the Mystery: An Essay on the Nature of Theology*. Oxford: Clarendon, 1983.

Lüdemann, Gerd. *Early Christianity According to the Traditions in Acts: A Commentary*. London: SCM, 1989.

———. *Paul, Apostle to the Gentiles: Studies in Chronology*. London: SCM, 1984.

———. *Paul: The Founder of Christianity*. Amherst, NY: Prometheus, 2002.

Lundbom, Jack R. *Jeremiah 1–20*. AB 21A. Garden City, NY: Doubleday, 1999.

Lust, Johan, et al. *Greek-English Lexicon of the Septuagint*. Stuttgart: Deutsche Bibelgesellschaft, 2003.

Luz, Ulrich. *Matthew 1–7*. Edinburgh: T. & T. Clark, 1990.

———. *Matthew 8–20*. Hermeneia. Minneapolis: Augsburg Fortress, 2001.

———. *Matthew 21–28*. Hermeneia. Minneapolis: Augsburg Fortress, 2005.

Maccoby, Hyam. *The Mythmaker: Paul and the Invention of Christianity*. New York: Barnes & Noble, 1998.

MacGorman, Jack W. *The Gifts of the Spirit*. Nashville: Broadman, 1974.

Malinowski, Francis X. "The Brave Women of Philippi." *BTB* 15 (1985) 60–64.

Mansoor, Menahem. *The Thanksgiving Hymns*. Grand Rapids: Eerdmans, 1961.

Marcos, Natalio Fernández. *The Septuagint in Context: Introduction to the Greek Version of the Bible*. Leiden: Brill, 2000.

Marshall, I. Howard. *1 and 2 Thessalonians*. NCBC. Grand Rapids: Eerdmans, 1983.

———. "The Christ-Hymn in Philippians 2:5–11." *TynBul* 19 (1968) 104–27.

———. *The Gospel of Luke*. NIGTC. Exeter, UK: Paternoster, 1978.

———. *The Pastoral Epistles*. ICC. London: T. & T. Clark, 1999.

Martin, Dale B. *Slavery as Salvation: The Metaphor of Slavery in Pauline Christianity*. New Haven: Yale University Press, 1990.

Martin, Ralph P. *2 Corinthians*. WBC 40. Grand Rapids: Zondervan, 2014^2.

———. *A Hymn of Christ: Philippians 2:5–11 in Recent Interpretation and in the Setting of Early Christian Worship*. Downers Grove, IL: InterVarsity, 1997.

———. *Philippians*. NCB. London: Marshall, Morgan & Scott, 1980.

———. *Reconciliation: A Study of Paul's Theology*. Rev. ed. Grand Rapids: Zondervan, 1990.

———. *The Spirit and the Congregation: Studies in 1 Corinthians 12–15*. Grand Rapids: Eerdmans, 1984.

Martin, Ralph P., and Brian J. Dodd. *Where Christology Began: Essays on Philippians 2*. Louisville: Westminster John Knox, 1998.

Martyn, J. Louis. "Article Review." *SJT* 59 (2006) 427–38.

———. *Galatians*. AB 33A. Garden City, NY: Doubleday, 1997.

———. "Listening to John and Paul on the Subject of Gospel and Scripture." *WW* 12 (1992) 68–81.

Mason, Steve. "'For I Am Not Ashamed of the Gospel' (Rom 1:16) The Gospel and the First Readers of Romans." In *Gospel in Paul*, edited by L. Ann Jervis and Peter Richardson, 254–87. Sheffield: Sheffield Academic, 1994.

———. *Josephus and the New Testament*. Peabody, MA: Hendrickson, 1992.

Matera, Frank J. *II Corinthians: A Commentary*. NTL. Louisville: Westminster John Knox, 2003.
McFarland, Ian A. "Gospel." In *The Cambridge Dictionary of Christian Theology*, edited by Ian A. McFarland et al., 200–201. Cambridge: Cambridge University Press, 2011.
McKnight, Scot. "Atonement and Gospel." In *Church in the Present Tense*, edited by Scot McKnight et al., 123–39. Grand Rapids: Brazos, 2011.
———. *The King Jesus Gospel: The Original Good News Revisited*. Grand Rapids: Zondervan, 2011.
———. *Sermon on the Mount*. Grand Rapids: Zondervan, 2013.
McKnight, Scot, and Grant R. Osborne, eds. *The Face of New Testament Studies*. Grand Rapids: Baker Academic, 2004.
Meeks, Wayne A. "The Christian Proteus." In *The Writings of St. Paul*, edited by Wayne A. Meeks, 435–44. New York: Norton, 1972.
Metzger, Bruce M. *A Textual Commentary on the Greek New Testament*. New York: American Bible Society, 1994.
Meyer, Rudolf, and Hans Friedrich Weiss. "Φαρισαῖος." *TDNT* 9:11–48.
Michael, J. Hugh. *The Epistle of Paul to the Philippians*. MNTC. London: Hodder and Stoughton, 1928.
Michaelis, Wilhelm. "ὁράω, κτλ." *TDNT* 5:315–82.
Michel, Otto. *Der Brief an die Römer*. KEK. Göttingen: Vandenhoeck & Ruprecht, 1978[14].
Miller, Ernest C. "Πολιτεύεσθε in Philippians 1:27: Some Philological and Thematic Observations." *JSNT* 15 (1982) 86–96.
Milligan, George. *St Paul's Epistles to the Thessalonians*. London: Macmillan, 1908.
Minde, Hans-Jürgen van der. *Schrift und Tradition bei Paulus. Ihre Bedeutung und Funktion in Römerbrief, PthS 3*. Paderborn, Germany: Ferdinand Schöningh, 1976.
Molland, Einar. *Das paulinische Euangelion: Das Wort und die Sache*. Oslo: I kommisjon hos Jacob Dybwad, 1934.
Mommsen, Theodore, and Ulrich von Wiliamowitz-Moellendorff. "Die Einführungen des Asianischen Kalenders." In *Athenische Mittellungen* 24 (1899) 275–93. http://digi.ub.uni-heidelberg.de/diglit/am1899/0285.
Moo, Douglas J. *The Letter to the Romans*. NICNT. Grand Rapids: Eerdmans, 2018[2].
Moody Smith, D. "Ο ΔΕ ΔΙΚΑΟΣ ΕΚ ΠΙΣΤΕΩΣ ΖΗΣΕΤΑΙ." In *Studies in History and Text of the New Testament, in Honor of Kenneth Willis Clark*, edited by Boyd L. Daniels and M. Jack Suggs, 13–25. SD 29. Salt Lake City: University of Utah Press, 1967.
———. "The Pauline Literature." In *It is Written: Scripture Citing Scripture: Essays in Honour of Barnabas Lindars, SSF*, edited by Don A. Carson and Hugh G. M. Williamson, 265–91. Cambridge: Cambridge University Press, 1988.
———. "The Use of the Old Testament in the New." In *The Use of the Old Testament and Other Essays: Studies in Honor of William Franklin Stinespring*, edited by James M. Efird, 3–65. Durham, NC: Duke University Press, 1972.
Morris, Jenny. "The Jewish Philosopher Philo." In *The History of the Jewish People in the Age of Jesus Christ*, edited by Emil Schürer, 3.2:809–89. 3 vols. Edinburgh: T. & T. Clark, 1973–1987.
Morris, Leon. *1 Corinthians*. TNTC. Grand Rapids: Eerdmans, 1985[2].

Moule, C. F. D. *The Epistles of Paul the Apostle to the Colossians and to Philemon.* CGTC. Cambridge: Cambridge University Press, 1975.

———. *An Idiom-Book of New Testament Greek.* Cambridge: Cambridge University Press, 1959.

Moulton, James H., et al., *A Grammar of New Testament Greek.* 4 vols. Edinburgh: T. & T. Clark, 1908–1976.

Moyise, Steve. *The Old Testament in the New: An Introduction.* ABS. London: Continuum, 2015².

Moyise, Steve, and Maarten J. J. Menken, eds. *Isaiah in the New Testament: The New Testament and the Scriptures of Israel.* London: T. & T. Clark, 2005.

Müller, Jac. J. *The Epistles of Paul to the Philippians and to Philemon.* NICNT. Grand Rapids: Eerdmans, 1955.

Mullins, Terence Y. "Formulas in New Testament Epistles." *JBL* 91 (1972) 380–90.

Munck, Johannes. "1 Thess 1:9–10 and the Missionary Preaching of Paul: Textual Exegesis and Hermeneutic Reflexions." *NTS* 9 (1963) 95–110.

———. *Paul and the Salvation of Mankind.* London: SCM, 1959.

Murphy-O'Connor, Jerome. "Tradition and Redaction in 1 Cor 15:3–7." *CBQ* 43 (1981) 582–89.

Nanos, Mark D. *The Irony of Galatians: Paul's Letter in First-Century Context.* Minneapolis: Fortress, 2002.

———. *The Mystery of Romans: The Jewish Context of Paul's Letter.* Minneapolis: Fortress, 1996.

———. *Reading Paul within Judaism: Collected Essays of Mark D. Nanos.* Eugene, OR: Wipf & Stock, 2017.

Nanos, Mark D., and Magnus Zetterholm, eds. *Paul within Judaism: Restoring the First-Century Context to the Apostle.* Minneapolis: Fortress, 2015.

Neil, William. *The Epistle of Paul to the Thessalonians.* MNTC. London: Hodder and Stoughton, 1950.

Neuenzeit, Paul. *Das Herrenmahl: Studien zur paulinischen Eucharistieauffassung.* Munich: Kösel, 1960.

Neufeld, Vernon H. *The Earliest Christian Confessions.* NTTS 5. Leiden: Brill, 1963.

Neugebauer, Fritz. *In Christus Eine Untersuchung zum paulinischen Glaubensverständnis.* Göttingen: Vandenhoeck & Ruprecht, 1961.

Nguyen, Van Thanh. "Evangelizing Empire: The Gospel and Mission of St Paul." *SEDOS Bulletin* 41 (2009) 99–105.

Nolland, John. *The Gospel of Matthew.* NIGTC. Grand Rapids: Eerdmans, 2005.

———. *Luke 1–9:20.* WBC 35A. Dallas: Word, 1989.

———. *Luke 18:35–24:53.* WBC 35C. Dallas: Word, 1993.

Norden, Eduard. *Agnostos Theos; Untersuchungen zur Formengeschichte Religiöser Rede.* Stuttgart: Teubner, 1956.

Oakes, Peter. *Philippians: From People to Letter.* SNTSMS 110. Cambridge: Cambridge University Press, 2001.

O'Brien, Peter T. *The Epistle to the Philippians.* NIGTC. Grand Rapids: Eerdmans, 1991.

———. "The Importance of the Gospel in Philippians." In *God Who is Rich in Mercy: Essays Presented to Dr. D. B. Knox*, edited by Peter T. O'Brien and David G. Peterson, 213–33. Homebush, NSW: ANZEA, 1986.

———. *Introductory Thanksgivings in the Letters of Paul.* Eugene, OR: Wipf & Stock, 2009.
Okeke, George E. "1 Thessalonians 2:13–16: The Fate of the Unbelieving Jews." *NTS* 27 (1980) 127–36.
O'Mahony, Kieran J. *Pauline Persuasion: A Sounding in 2 Corinthians 8 and 9.* JSNTSupp 199. Sheffield: Sheffield Academic, 2000.
O'Neill, John C. *Paul's Letter to the Romans.* PNTC. Harmondsworth, UK: Penguin, 1975.
O'Rourke, J. J. "ΕΙΣ and ΕΝ in John." *BT* 25 (1974) 139–42.
Orr, William F., and James Arthur Walther. *1 Corinthians.* AB 32. Garden City, NY: Doubleday, 1976.
Panikulam, George. *Koinōnia in the New Testament: A Dynamic Expression of Christian Life.* AnBib 85. Rome: Biblical Institute, 1979.
Parry, R. St. John. *The First Epistle of Paul the Apostle to the Corinthians.* CGTSC. Cambridge: Cambridge University Press, 1926^2.
Pearson, Birger A. "1 Thessalonians 2:13–16: A Deutero-Pauline Interpolation." *HTR* 64 (1971) 79–94.
Perkins, Pheme. *First Corinthians.* PCNT. Grand Rapids: Baker Academic, 2012.
Pervo, Richard I. *Acts.* Hermeneia. Minneapolis: Fortress, 2009.
Peterman, Gerald W. *Paul's Gift from Philippi: Conventions of Gift-Exchange and Christian Giving.* SNTSMS 92. Cambridge: Cambridge University Press, 1997.
———. "'Thankless Thanks': The Epistolary Social Conventions in Philippians 4:10–20." *TynBul* 42 (1991) 261–70.
Pfitzner, Victor C. *Paul and the Agon Motif. Traditional Athletic Imagery in the Pauline Literature.* NovTSup 16. Leiden: Brill, 1967.
Pick, Bernhard. "Philo's Canon of the Old Testament and His Mode of Quoting the Alexandrian Version." *Journal of the Society of Biblical Literature and Exegesis* 4 (1884) 126–43.
Plevnik, Joseph. "The Center of Paul's Theology." *CBQ* 51 (1989) 460–78.
Plummer, Alfred. *A Critical and Exegetical Commentary on the Second Epistle of Paul to the Corinthians.* ICC. Edinburgh: T. & T. Clark, 1915.
Pogoloff, Stephen M. *Logos and Sophia: The Rhetorical Situation of 1 Corinthians.* SBLDS 134. Atlanta: Scholars, 1992.
Pokorný, Petr. *From the Gospel to the Gospels: History, Theology, and Impact of the Biblical Term Euangelion.* BZNW 195. Boston: de Gruyter, 2013.
Polhill, John B. "The Wisdom of God and Factionalism: 1 Corinthians 1–4." *RevExp* 80 (1983) 325–39.
Poole, Matthew. *Synopsis Criticorum Aliorumque Sacrae Scripturae Interpretum et Commentatorum: Summo Studio et Fide Adornata.* 5 vols. Utrecht: Ribb, van de Water & Halma, 1684–1686.
Porter, Stanley E. "Did Paul Speak Latin?" In *Paul*, edited by Stanley E. Porter, 289–308. Paul Studies 5. Leiden: Brill, 2008.
———. "Paul Confronts Caesar with the Good News." In *Empire in the New Testament*, edited by Cynthia Long Westfall and Stanley E. Porter, 164–96. Eugene, OR: Pickwick, 2011.
———. "Word Order and Clause Structure in New Testament Greek: An Unexplored Area of Greek Linguistics Using Philippians as a Test Case." *Filologia Neotestamentaria* 6 (1993) 177–205.

Poythress, Vern S. "Is Romans 1:3-4 a Pauline Confession After All?" *ExpTim* 87 (1976) 180-83.
Prat, Fernand. *The Theology of Saint Paul*. 2 vols. London: Burns, Oats and Washbourne, 1945.
Pretorius, Mark. "The Theological Centre of Pauline Theology as it Relates to the Holy Spirit." *HTS Teologiese Studies/Theological Studies* 62 (2006) 253-62.
Price, Simon R. F. *Rituals and Power: The Roman Imperial Cult in Asia Minor*. Cambridge: Cambridge University Press, 1998.
Pryke, Eric J. *Redactional Style in the Marcan Gospel*. SNTSMS 33. Cambridge: Cambridge University Press, 1978.
Rackham, Richard B. *The Acts of the Apostles*. WC. London: Methuen, 1901.
Radl, Walter. "ὑπομονή." *EDNT* 3:405-6.
―――. "Der Sinn von γνωρίζω in 1 Kor 15, 1." *BZ* 28 (1984) 243-45.
Räisänen, Heikki. *Paul and the Law*. WUNT 29. Tubingen: J. C. B. Mohr, 1987.
Rajak, Tessa. *Josephus*. London: Duckworth, 2002.
Ramsay, William M. *Pauline and Other Studies*. London: Hodder and Stoughton, 1906.
―――. "Tarsus." *The Expositor* 7.3 (1906) 258-77.
―――. "Tarsus XIV: Tarsus the Hellenistic City." *The Expositor* 7.3 (1906) 135-60.
Rappaport, Uriel. "The Letter of Aristeas Again." *JSP* 21 (2012) 285-303.
Reed, Jeffrey T. *A Discourse Analysis of Philippians: Method and Rhetoric in the Debate over Literary Integrity*. JSNTSupp 136. Sheffield: Sheffield Academic, 1997.
―――. "The Infinitive with Two Substantival Accusatives: An Ambiguous Construction?" *NovT* 33 (1991) 1-27.
Reichert, Angelica. *Der Römerbrief als Gratwanderung. Eine Untersuchung zur Abfassungsproblematick*. FRANT 194. Göttingen: Vandenhoeck & Ruprecht, 2001.
Remus, Harold. *Pagan-Christian Conflict Over Miracle in the Second Century*. PMS 10. Cambridge, MA: Philadelphia Patristic Foundation, 1983.
Rengstorf, Karl H. "ἀποστέλλω, κτλ." *TDNT* 1:389-447.
Reuf, John. *Paul's First Letter to Corinth*. PNTC. London: SCM, 1977.
Richard, Earl J. *First and Second Thessalonians*. SP 11. Collegeville, MN: Liturgical, 2007.
Ridderbos, Herman N. *The Epistle of Paul to the Churches of Galatia*. NICNT. Grand Rapids: Eerdmans, 1953.
Riesner, Rainer. *Paul's Early Period*. Grand Rapids: Eerdmans, 1998.
Robertson, Archibald T. *A Grammar of the Greek New Testament in the Light of Historical Research*. Nashville: Broadman, 1934.
Robertson, Archibald T., and Alfred Plummer. *A Critical and Exegetical Commentary on the First Epistle of St. Paul to the Corinthians*. ICC. Edinburgh: T. & T. Clark, 1914.
Robinson, William C. "Word and Power." In *Soli Deo Gloria: Essays for William Childs Robinson*, edited by J. McDowell Richards, 68-82. Richmond, VA: John Knox, 1968.
Roetzel, Calvin J. *The Letters of Paul: Conversations in Context*. Atlanta: Westminster John Knox, 1975.
Roller, Otto. *Das Formular der paulinischen Briefe. Ein Beitrag zur Lehre vom antiken Briefe*. Stuttgart: Kolhammer, 1933.

Ruemann, John. *Philippians*. AB 33B. New Haven, CT: Yale University Press, 2008.
Ryle, Herbert E. *Philo and Holy Scripture*. New York: Macmillan, 1895.
Saldarini, Anthony J. *Pharisees, Scribes, and Sadducees in Palestinian Society*. Edinburgh: T. & T. Clark, 1989.
Sanday, William, and Arthur C. Headlam, *A Critical and Exegetical Commentary on the Epistle to the Romans*. ICC. Edinburgh: T. & T. Clark, 1895.
Sanders, E. P. *Paul and Palestinian Judaism: A Comparison of Patterns of Religion* 40th Anniversary Edition. London: SCM, 2017.
———. *Paul: The Apostles Life, Letters, and Thought*. Minneapolis: Augsburg Fortress, 2015.
Saunders, Stanley P. "Letter to the Philippians." *NIDB* 4:503–7.
Scheck, Thomas P. *St. Jerome: Commentary on Ezekiel*. ACW 71. New York: Newman, 2017.
Schenk, Wolfgang. "Der 1 Korintherbrief als Briefsammlung." *ZNW* 60 (1969) 219–43.
Schilling, Othma. "בשׂר." *TDOT* 2:313–16.
Schippers, Reinier. "Pre-Synoptic Tradition in 1 Thessalonians 2:13–16." *NovT* 8 (1966) 223–34.
Schlatter, Adolf. *The History of the Christ: The Foundation for New Testament Theology*. Grand Rapids: Baker Academic, 1997.
———. *Romans: The Righteousness of God*. Peabody, MA: Hendrickson, 1995.
———. *The Theology of the Apostles: The Development of New Testament Theology*. Grand Rapids: Baker Academic, 1998.
Schlier, Heinrich. "βέβαιος, κτλ." *TDNT* 1:600–603.
———. *Der Brief an die Galater*. KEK. Göttingen: Vandenhoeck & Ruprecht, 1989.
———. *Grundzüge einer paulinischen Theologie*. Freiburg: Herder, 1978.
Schmithals, Walter. *Die Briefe des Paulus in ihrer ursprünglichen Form*. ZWB. Zürich: Theologischer, 1984.
———. "Die Korintherbriefe als Briefsammlung." *ZNW* 64 (1973) 263–88.
———. *Paul and the Gnostics*. Nashville: Abingdon, 1972.
Schnabel, Eckhard J. *Paul the Missionary: Realities, Strategies and Methods*. Downers Grove, IL: InterVarsity, 2008.
Schnackenburg, Rudolf. *The Johannine Epistles*. New York: Crossroad, 1992.
Schneemelcher, Wilhelm. "Gospel." In *New Testament Apocrypha*, edited by Edgar Hennecke, 71–84. 2 vols. London: SCM, 1973, 1975.
Schneider, Gerhard. *Die Apostelgeschichte*. 2 vols. HThKNT. Freiburg: Herder, 1980, 1982.
Schnelle, Udo. *Apostle Paul: His Life and Theology*. Grand Rapids: Baker Academic, 2005.
Schniewind, Johannes. "ἀγγελία, κτλ." *TDNT* 1:56–73.
Schniewind, Julius. *Die Begriffe Wort und Evangelium bei Paulus*. Bonn, Germany: Carl Georgi, 1910.
———. *Euangelion. Ursprung und erste Gestalt des Begriffs Evangelium*. Darmstadt, Germany: Wissenschaftliche Buchgesellschaft, 1970.
Schoeps, Hans J. *Paul: The Theology of the Apostle in the Light of Jewish Religious History*. London: Lutterworth, 1961.
Schrage, Wolfgang. *Der erste Brief an die Korinther*. 4 vols. EKKNT 7.1–3. Zürich Benziger, 1991, 1995, 1999.

Schreiber, Stefan. *Paulus als Wundertäter: Redaktionsgeschichte Untersuchungen zur Apostelgeschichte und den authentischen Paulusbriefen*. BZNW 79. Berlin: de Gruyter, 1996.
Schreiner, Thomas R. *Paul*. Downers Grove, IL: InterVarsity, 2001.
Schrenk, Gottlob. "γράφω, κτλ." *TDNT* 1:742–73.
―――. "προγράφω." *TDNT* 1:770–72.
Schubert, Paul. *Form and Function of the Pauline Thanksgivings*. ZNW Beiheft 20. Berlin: A. Töpelmann, 1939.
Schürer, Emil. *The History of the Jewish People in the Age of Jesus Christ*. 3 vols. Edinburgh: T. & T. Clark, 1973–87.
Schütz, John Howard. *Paul and the Anatomy of Apostolic Authority*. SNTSMS 26. Cambridge: Cambridge University Press, 1975.
Schweitzer, Albert. *The Mysticism of Paul the Apostle*. Baltimore: Johns Hopkins University Press, 1998.
―――. *Paul and His Interpreters: A Critical History*. London: Black, 1912.
Seager, Robin. *Pompey the Great. A Political Biography*. Oxford. Blackwell, 2002².
Seccombe, David Peter. *Possessions and the Poor in Luke-Acts*. SNTSU. Linz, Austria: Albert Fuchs, 1983.
Seesemann, Heinrich. *Der Begriff KOINONIA im Neuen Testament*. BZNW 14. Giessen: Töpelmann, 1933.
Seifrid, Mark A. "Romans." In *Commentary on the New Testament Use of the Old Testament*, edited by G. K. Beale and D. A. Carson, 607–94. Grand Rapids: Baker Academic, 2007.
Sherk, Robert K. *Rome and the Greek East to the Death of Augustus*. Translated Documents of Greece and Rome 4. Cambridge: Cambridge University Press, 1993.
Sherk, Robert K., and Paul Viereck. *Roman Documents from the Greek East: "Senatus Consulta" and "Epistulae" to the Age of Augustus*. Baltimore: Johns Hopkins University Press, 1969.
Shum, Shiu-Lun. *Paul's Use of Isaiah in Romans: A Comparative Study of Paul's Letter to the Romans and the Sibylline and Qumran Sectarian Texts*. WUNT 156. Tübingen: Mohr/Siebeck, 2002.
Silva, Moises. "ἀγγέλλω, κτλ." *NIDNTTE* 1:116–20.
―――. "ἐγκόπτω; ἐγκοπή." *NIDNTTE* 2:81–82.
―――. "εἰς." *NIDNTTE* 2:118–22.
―――. "εὐαγγέλιον." *NIDNTTE* 2:306–13.
―――. "παραλαμβάνω." *NIDNTTE* 3:79–85.
―――. "φρονέω." *NIDNTTE* 4:616–22.
―――. *Interpreting Galatians: Explorations in Exegetical Method*. Grand Rapids: Baker Academic, 2001.
―――. *Philippians*. BECNT. Grand Rapids: Baker Academic, 2005².
Sirinelli, Jean, et al. *La Préparation évangélique*. I. SC 206. Paris: Cerf, 1974.
Smalley, Stephen S. *1, 2, 3 John*. WBC 51. Rev. ed. Nashville: Thomas Nelson, 2007.
Snodgrass, Klyne R. "The Use of the Old Testament in the New." In *New Testament Criticism and Interpretation*, edited by David A. Black and David S. Dockery, 407–34. Grand Rapids: Zondervan, 1991.
Soards, Marion L. "Once Again 'Righteousness of God' in the Writings of the Apostle Paul." *BiBh* 17 (1991) 14–44.

———. "The Righteousness of God in the Writings of the Apostle Paul." *BTB* 15 (1985) 104–9.
Souter, Alexander. "Did St. Paul Speak Latin?" *The Expositor* 8 (1911) 337–42.
Spallek, Andrew J. "The Origin and Meaning of Εὐαγγέλιον in the Pauline Corpus." *CTQ* 57 (1993) 177–90.
Spicq, Ceslas. *Theological Lexicon of the New Testament*. Peabody, MA: Hendrickson, 1994.
Stählin, Gustav. "ἐγκοπή, ἐγκόπτω." *TDNT* 3:855–57.
———. "προκοπή, προκόπτω." *TDNT* 6:703–19.
Stanley, Christopher D. *Paul and the Language of Scripture: Citation Technique in the Pauline Epistles and Contemporary Literature*. SNTSMS 74. Cambridge: Cambridge University Press, 1992.
———. "'The Redeemer Will Come ἐκ Σιων': Romans 11.26–27 Revisited." In *Paul and the Scriptures of Israel*, edited by Craig A. Evans and James A. Sanders, 118–42. JSNTSupp 83 / SSEJC 1. Sheffield: JSOT, 1993.
Stanton, Graham N. *Jesus and Gospel*. Cambridge: Cambridge University Press, 2004.
———. "Paul's Gospel." In *The Cambridge Companion to St Paul*, edited by James D. G. Dunn, 173–84. Cambridge: Cambridge University Press, 2003.
Stendahl, Krister. "The Apostle Paul and the Introspective Conscience of the West." *HTR* 55 (1962) 119–215.
———. *Paul among Jews and Gentiles and Other Essays*. London, SCM, 1977.
Stettler, Hanna. "Die Bedeutung Der Täuferanfrage in Matthäus 11,2–6 Par Lk 7,18–23 für Die Christologie." *Bib* 89 (2008) 173–200.
Stevens, Gerald L. "The Righteousness of God: Frontiers of Pauline Research." *CTR* 12 (2015) 47–69.
Stewart-Sykes, Alistair. "Ancient Editors and Copyists and Modern Partition Theories: The Case of the Corinthian Correspondence." *JSNT* 61 (1996) 53–64.
Still, Todd D. *Conflict at Thessalonica*. JSNTSupp 183. Sheffield: Sheffield Academic, 1999.
———. "'Since We Believe that Jesus Died and Rose Again': The Gospel Paul Preached in Thessalonica as Evidenced by 1 Thessalonians." *ResQ* 54 (2012) 7–18.
Stolz, Fritz. "Zeichen und Wunder: Die prophetische Legitimation und ihre Geschichte." *ZTK* 69 (1972) 125–44.
Stone, Michael E. "Enoch's Date in Limbo; Or, Some Considerations on David Suter's Analysis of the Book of Parables." In *Enoch and the Messiah Son of Man: Revisiting the Book of Parables*, edited by Gabriele Boccaccini, 444–49. Grand Rapids: Eerdmans, 2007.
Stowers, Stanley K. *A Rereading of Romans: Justice, Jews, and Gentiles*. New Haven, CT: Yale University Press, 1994.
Strack, Hermann L., and Günther Stemberger. *Introduction to the Talmud and Midrash*. Minneapolis: Fortress, 1992.
Strandenaes, Thor. "Completing the Mission: Paul's Application of the Gospel to the Faith and Life of the Thessalonian Converts in 1 and 2 Thessalonians." *Svensk Missionstidskrift* 98 (2010) 69–98.
Strathmann, Hermann. "πόλις, κτλ." *TDNT* 6:516–35.
Strecker, Georg. "εὐαγγέλιον." *EDNT* 2:70–74.

———. "Das Evangelium Jesu Christi." In *Eschaton und Historie: Aufsätze*, edited by Georg Strecker, 183–228. Göttingen: Vandenhoeck & Ruprecht, 1979.

Strobel, August. *Untersuchungen Zum Eschatologischen Verzögerungsproblem: Auf Grund Der Spätjüdischurchristlichen Geschichte Von Habakkuk 2,2 FF*. NovTSup 2. Leiden: Brill, 1961.

Stuart, Douglas. *Hosea-Jonah*. WBC 31. Waco, TX: Word, 1987.

Stuhlmacher, Peter, ed. *The Gospel and Gospels*. Grand Rapids: Eerdmans, 1991.

———. "The Pauline Gospel." In *The Gospel and Gospels*, edited by Peter Stuhlmacher, 149–72. Grand Rapids: Eerdmans, 1991.

———. *Das paulinische Evangelium: Vorgeschichte*. FRANT 95. Göttingen: Vandenhoeck & Ruprecht, 1968.

———. *Paul's Letter to the Romans: A Commentary*. Louisville: Westminster/John Knox, 1994.

———. "The Theme: The Gospel and the Gospels." In *The Gospel and the Gospels*, edited by Peter Stuhlmacher, 1–25. Grand Rapids: Eerdmans, 1991.

Suggs, M. Jack "Concerning the Date of Paul's Macedonian Ministry." *NovT* 4 (1960) 60–68.

Sumney, Jerry L. *Steward of God's Mysteries: Paul and Early Church Tradition*. Grand Rapids: Eerdmans, 2017.

Suter, David W. "Enoch in Sheol. Updating the Dating of the Book of Parables." In *Enoch and the Messiah Son of Man: Revisiting the Book of Parables*, edited by Gabriele Boccaccini, 415–43. Grand Rapids: Eerdmans, 2007.

Swete, Henry B. *An Introduction to the Old Testament in Greek*. Cambridge: Cambridge University Press, 1914.

Tabor, James D. *Paul and Jesus: How the Apostle Transformed Christianity*. New York: Simon & Schuster, 2013.

Tasmuth, Randar. "Paul's *Gospel* to the Romans." In *Lux humana, lux aeterna: Essays on Biblical and Related Themes in Honour of Lars Aejmelaeus*, edited by Antti Mustakallio et al., 311–23. Helsinki: Finnish Exegetical Society, 2005.

Tatum, Gregory. "Galatians 2:1–14 / Acts 15 and Paul's Ministry in 1 Thessalonians and 1 Corinthians." *RB* 116 (2009) 70–81.

Taubes, Jacob. *The Political Theology of Paul*. Stanford: Stanford University Press, 2004.

Taylor, Lily Ross. *The Divinity of the Roman Emperor*. APAMS 1. Middletown, CT: American Philological Association, 1931.

Thayer, Joseph H. "Language of the New Testament." In *A Dictionary of the Bible*, edited by James Hastings, 3:36–43. 5 vols. Edinburgh: T. & T. Clark, 1900–1904.

Theissen, Gerd. *The Gospels in Context: Social and Political History in the Synoptic Tradition*. Minneapolis: Fortress, 1991.

Thiselton, Anthony C. *The First Epistle to the Corinthians*. NIGTC. Grand Rapids: Eerdmans, 2000.

Thrall, Margaret E. *II Corinthians, Volume 2*. 2 vols. ICC. Edinburgh: T. & T. Clark, 2000.

Tobin, Thomas H. *Paul's Rhetoric in its Contexts: The Argument of Romans*. Peabody, MA: Hendrickson, 2004.

Toher, Mark. "The '*Bios Kaisaros*' of Nicolaus of Damascus: An Historical Analysis." PhD diss., Brown University, 1985.

Torrey, Charles C. *The Composition and Date of Acts*. Cambridge, MA: Harvard University Press, 1916.

Tov, Emmanuel. "The Greek Biblical Texts from the Judean Desert." In *Bible as Book: The Transmission of the Greek Text*, edited by Scot McKendrick and Orlaith O'Sullivan, 101–22. London: British Library, 2003.

———. *Revised Lists of the Texts of the Judaean Desert*. Leiden: Brill, 2010.

———. "The Text of Isaiah at Qumran." In *Writing and Reading the Scroll of Isaiah: Studies of an Interpretive Tradition*, edited by Craig C. Broyles and Craig A. Evans, 2:491–511. VTSup 70.2. Leiden: Brill, 1997.

Tov, Emanuel, and Stephen J. Pfann. "Lists of the Texts from the Judaean Desert." In *The Texts from the Judaean Desert*, edited by Emanuel Tov and Martin G. Abegg, 27–89. DJD XXXIX. Oxford. Clarendon, 2002.

Trebilco, Paul R. *The Early Christians in Ephesus from Paul to Ignatius*. WUNT 166. Tübingen: Mohr/Siebeck, 2004.

Tuckett, Christopher M. "1 Corinthians and Q." *JBL* 102 (1983) 607–19.

———. "Isaiah in Q." In *Isaiah in the New Testament*, edited by Steve Moyise and Maarten J. J. Menken, 51–61. London: T. & T. Clark, 2005.

———. "Paul and the Synoptic Mission Discourse." *ETL* 60 (1984) 376–81.

———. *Q and the History of Early Christianity: Studies on Q*. Edinburgh: T. & T. Clark, 1997.

———. "Synoptic Tradition in 1 Thessalonians." In *The Thessalonian Correspondence*, edited by Raymond F. Collins, 160–82. BETL 87. Leuven: Leuven University Press, 1990.

Twelftree, Graham H. *Jesus the Exorcist. A Contribution to the Study of the Historical Jesus*. WUNT 2.54. Tübingen: Mohr/Siebeck, 1993.

———. "The Miracles of Jesus: Marginal or Mainstream?" *JSHJ* 1 (2003) 104–24.

———. *Paul and the Miraculous: A Historical Reconstruction*. Grand Rapids: Baker Academic, 2013.

———. *People of the Spirit: Exploring Luke's View of the Church*. London: SPCK, 2009.

Ulrich, Eugene. "An Index of the Passages in the Biblical Manuscripts from the Judean Desert (Part 2: Isaiah-Chronicles)." *DSD* 2 (1995) 86–107.

Usteri, Leonhard. *Entwicklung des Paulinischen Lehrbegriffs*. Zürich: Orell Füssli, 1834.

van Henton, Jan Willem. *The Maccabean Martyrs as Saviors of the Jewish People: A Study of 2 and 4 Maccabees*. JSJSup 57. Leiden: Brill, 1997.

Vincent, Marvin R. *Epistles to the Philippians and to Philemon*. ICC. New York: Charles Scribner's Sons, 1897.

Volf, Judith M. Gundry. *Paul and Perseverance: Staying in and Falling Away*. WUNT 2.37. Tübingen: Mohr/Siebeck, 1990.

Wagner, J. Ross. *Heralds of the Good News: Isaiah and Paul "in Concert" in the Letter to the Romans*. NovTSup 101. Leiden: Brill, 2002.

———. "Isaiah in Romans and Galatians." In *Isaiah in the New Testament*, edited by Steve Moyise and Maarten J. J. Menken, 117–32. London: T. & T. Clark, 2005.

Wanamaker, Charles A. *The Epistles to the Thessalonians*. NIGTC. Grand Rapids: Eerdmans, 1990.

Watson, Francis. "Is There a Story in These Texts?" In *Narrative Dynamics: A Critical Assessment*, edited by Bruce W. Longenecker, 231–39. Louisville: Westminster John Knox, 2002.

———. "The Law in Romans." In *Reading Paul's Letter to the Romans*, edited by Jerry L. Sumney, 93–107. RBS 73. Atlanta: Society of Bible Literature, 2012.

———. *Paul and the Hermeneutics of Faith*. London: T. & T. Clark, 2004.

———. *Paul, Judaism, and the Gentiles: Beyond the New Perspective*. Grand Rapids: Eerdmans, 2007.

Weatherly, Jon A. "The Authenticity of 1 Thessalonians 2:13-16: Additional Evidence." *JSNT* 42 (1991) 79-98.

Weaver, Paul R. C. *Familia Caesaris: A Social Study of the Emperors' Freedmen and Slaves*. Cambridge: Cambridge University Press, 1972.

———. "Social Mobility in the Early Roman Empire: The Evidence of the Imperial Freedmen and Slaves." In *Studies in Ancient Society*, edited by Moses I. Finley, 121-40. Past and Present Series. London: Routledge, 1974.

Wedderburn, Alexander J. M. *The Reasons for Romans*. SNTW. Edinburgh: T. & T. Clark, 1988.

Weiss, Johannes. *Der erste Korintherbrief*. KEK. Göttingen: Vandenhoeck & Ruprecht, 1910^9.

Wengst, Klaus. *Christologische Formeln und Lieder des Urchristentums*. SNT 7. Gütersloh: Gütersloher Verlagshaus Gerd Mohn, 1972.

Wenham, David. *Paul: Follower of Jesus or Founder of Christianity?* Grand Rapids: Eerdmans, 1995.

Westerholm, Stephen. "Law and Gospel in Jesus and Paul." In *Jesus and Paul Reconnected*, edited by Todd D. Still, 19-36. Grand Rapids: Eerdmans, 2007.

White, John L. "Introductory Formulae in the Body of the Pauline Letter." *JBL* 90 (1971) 91-97.

Whiteley, Denys E. H. *The Theology of St. Paul*. Oxford: Blackwell, 1974.

———. *Thessalonians*. NClB. Oxford: Oxford University Press, 1969.

Whitsett, Christopher G. "Son of God, Seed of David: Paul's Messianic Exegesis in Romans 2:3-4." *JBL* 119 (2000) 661-81.

Wilckens, Ulrich. *Der Brief an die Römer*. EKKNT 6. 3 vols. Zürich: Benziger, 1978, 1980, 1982.

Wilcox, Max. *The Semitism of Acts*. Oxford: Clarendon, 1965.

Wilk, Florian. *Die Bedeutung des Jesajabuches für Paulus*. FRLANT 179. Göttingen: Vandenhoeck & Ruprecht, 1998.

Wilson, Barrie. *How Jesus Became Christian*. New York: St. Martin's, 2013.

Wilson, Robert McL. *Colossians and Philemon*. ICC. London: T. & T. Clark, 2005.

Windisch, Hans. *Die zweite Korintherbrief*. KEK 6. Göttingen: Vandenhoeck & Ruprecht, 1924^9.

———. "καπηλεύω." *TDNT* 3:603-5.

Wink, Walter. *Engaging the Powers: Discernment and Resistance in an Age of Domination*. Minneapolis: Fortress, 1992.

———. *Naming the Powers: The Language of Power in the New Testament*. Philadelphia: Fortress, 1984.

Witherington, Ben. *Friendship and Finances in Philippi: The Letter of Paul to the Philippians*. NTCC. Valley Forge, PA: Trinity, 1994.

———. *Paul's Letter to the Romans: A Socio-Rhetorical Commentary*. Grand Rapids: Eerdmans, 2004.

Wojtkowiak, Heiko. "Unter der Herrschaft Christi: Ernst Käsemanns Paulusverständnis: Konstanten und Entwicklungen." *BN* 163 (2014) 103-20.

———. "Unter der Herrschaft Christi: Ernst Käsemanns Paulusverständnis: Konstanten und Entwicklungen, Teil 2." *BN* 165 (2015) 83-99.

Wolff, Christian. *Der erste Brief des Paulus an die Korinther.* THKNT 7. Berlin: Evangelische Verlagsandstalt, 1996.

———. *Der zweite Brief des Paulus an die Korinther.* THKNT 8. Berlin: Evangelische Verlagsandstalt, 1989.

Wolff, Hans Walter. *Joel and Amos.* Hermeneia. Philadelphia: Fortress, 1977.

Wolff, Peter. *Die frühe nachösterliche Verkündigung des Reiches Gottes.* FRLANT 171. Göttingen: Vandenhoeck & Ruprecht, 1999.

Wolter, Michael. *Paul: An Outline of His Theology.* Waco, TX: Baylor University Press, 2015.

Wrede, William. *Paul.* Reprint. Eugene, OR: Wipf & Stock, 2001.

Wright, N. T. "Gospel and Theology in Galatians." In *Gospel in Paul*, edited by L. Ann Jervis and Peter Richardson, 222–39. Sheffield: Sheffield Academic, 1994.

———. "In Full Accord: Paul's Social Gospel." *ChrCent* 128 (2011) 25–29.

———. "New Perspectives on Paul (2003)." In *Pauline Perspectives: Essays on Paul 1978-2013*, edited by N. T. Wright, 273–91. Minneapolis: Fortress, 2013.

———. *Paul and the Faithfulness of God.* Minneapolis: Fortress, 2013.

———. "Paul as Preacher: The Gospel Then and Now." *ITQ* 72 (2007) 131–46.

———. "Paul in Current Anglophone Scholarship." *ExpTim* 123 (2012) 367–81.

———. *Paul in Fresh Perspectives.* Minneapolis: Fortress, 2009.

———. "Paul's Gospel and Caesar's Empire." In *Paul and Politics: Ekklesia, Israel, Imperium, Interpretation: Essays in Honor of Krister Stendahl*, edited by Richard A. Horsley, 160–83. Harrisburg, PA: Trinity, 2000.

———. "Romans." In *The New Interpreter's Bible, Volume 10*, edited by Robert W. Wall et al., 393–770. 12 vols. Nashville: Abingdon, 2001.

———. *What Saint Paul Really Said: Was Paul of Tarsus the Real Founder of Christianity?* Grand Rapids: Eerdmans, 1979.

Wright, Robert B. "The Psalms of Solomon." *OTP* 2 (1985) 639–70.

———. *The Psalms of Solomon: A Critical Edition of the Greek Text.* JCTCRS 1. New York: T. & T. Clark, 2007.

Yeung, Maureen W. *Faith in Jesus and Paul.* WUNT 2.147. Tübingen: Mohr/Siebeck, 2002.

Zahl, Paul F. M. "A New Source for Understanding German Theology: Käsemann, Bultmann, and the 'New Perspective on Paul.'" *STRev* 39 (1996) 413–22.

Zeller, Dieter. *Der Brief an die Römer. Übersetzt und erklärt.* RNT. Regensburg, Germany: Pustet, 1985.

Zerwick, Maximilian. *Biblical Greek.* SPIB 114. Rome: Pontifical Biblical Institute, 1963.

Zetterholm, Magnus. "Paul within Judaism: The State of the Questions." In *Paul Within Judaism: Restoring the First-Century Context to the Apostle*, edited by Mark D. Nanos and Magnus Zetterholm, 31–51. Minneapolis: Fortress, 2015.

Ziegler, Joseph. *Isaias.* Septuaginta 14. Göttingen: Vandenhoeck & Ruprecht, 1983.

Ziesler, John. *Paul's Letter to the Romans.* TPINTC. London: SCM, 1989.

Zuntz, Günther. *The Text of the Epistles: A Disquisition Upon the "Corpus Paulinum."* Eugene, OR: Wipf & Stock, 2007.

Biblical and Ancient Literature Index

OLD TESTAMENT

Genesis

15:6	65n287
19:19	169n265
20:13	169n265
21:23	169n265
24:27	169n265
32:10	169n265

Exodus

2:3	173n291
14:31	158n192
24:1–11	143
34:10	96

Numbers

12:7	158n192
16:30	96

Deuteronomy

4:33	87n62
5:26	87n62
15:9	173n291
29:8	173n291
32:21	59n241
34:5	158n192

Joshua

1:1	158n192
1:15	158n192
3:10	87n62
8:21	158n192
8:23	158n192
18:7	158n192

1 Samuel

11:6	137n35

2 Samuel

7:5–8	158n192
7:14	65n283
7:16	161n212

1 Kings

11:36	158n192
8:66	158n192

2 Kings

5	40
10:10	158n192
19:34	158n192
21:10	158n192

1 Chronicles

6:49	158n192

2 Chronicles

1:3	158n192
23:18	66n295
24:6	158n192
25:4	66n295

Nehemiah

1:7	158n192
10:29	158n192

Esther

6:13	87n62

Job

2:9	88n70
7:2	88n70
21:24	173n291
29:14	168n259, 169n264
34:22	173n291

Psalms

2:7	161n211
9:18	41n131
33:6	100n150
33:9	100n150
36:10 (MT 36:11)	169n265
40:9	31, 30n45, 30n49, 31n61, 56n224
40:10	30n45, 30n48
51:11	162n223
68:10	41n131
68:11	30n45, 30n48, 30n49, 31n56
69:5	173n291
84:2	87n62
85:1	169n264
85:10 (MT 85:11)	169n265
85:13	168n259
89:3–4	161n212
89:14 (MT 89:15)	169n265
89:19–21	161n212
94:15	169n264
96:2	30n45, 30n48, 30n49, 31n61, 31n63, 56n224
97:2	66n292, 169n264
98:3	66n292
103:17	169n265
105:42	158n192

Proverbs

1:3	169n264
8:15	169n264
12:17	169n264
14:34	169n265
16:13	169n264
20:28	169n265
21:21	169n265

Isaiah

1–39	41
3:14–15	41n129
5:8	41n129
5:16	40n126
7:12	40n126
9:6	57n230
10:1–2	41n129
11:1	161n212
11:2	40n126
11:10	90n85, 161n212
14:13–15	40n126
20:3	158n192
25:1–5	41n130
25:4	40n126
26:9	169n264
26:19	40n126
26:29	40n125, 75n360
27:9	68, 68n309
27:12	40n126
28:17–19	40n126
29:14	40n126
29:18–19	40n126
29:18	40n125, 75n360
29:28	40n126
31:5	40n126
35:5–6	40nn125–26, 75n360
37:17	87n62
40–45	41
40:9	37
40:11	40n126
41:8–9	158n192
41:1	158n192
41:8–20	41n130
41:27	37
42:1	40n126
42:18	40nn125–26, 75n360
42:22	41n130
43:5–6	40n126
44:25	40n126
48:7	96
49:1–6	158n195

BIBLICAL AND ANCIENT LITERATURE INDEX 241

49:5	158n192	7:25	158n192
49:12	40n126	9:24	70, 70n327, 169n265
49:13	41n130	10:10	87n62
49:24–25	40n12652:7, 37	16:17	173n291
41:8–20	41n130	22:13	169n264
42:22	41n130	23:5–6	161n212
49:13	41n130	23:24	173n291
50:6	40n126	27:6	158n192
51:1	169n264	30:9	161n212
52:1–6	62	31:22	96
52:7a	76	31:31–34	143
52:13—53:12	158n192	31:31	143, 188
53:1	62	33:14–18	161n212
50:7–8	66n292	39:27	173n291
51:4–5	66n292	43:10	158n192
52:7	74		
52:7a	181	## Ezekiel	
52:10	66n292	8:12	173n291
53:12	40n126	34:23–24	161n212
52:15	70	37:24–25	161n212
52:15b	70n324		
54:10	97n129	## Daniel	
55:10–11	100n150		
56–66	41	5:4	86n59
58:2	169n264	5:23	86n59
58:4–7	41n131	6:21	87n62
58:8	40n126		
59:2–15	41n131	## Hosea	
59:19	40n126	1:10	87n62
59:20	68n310	2:1	107n195
61:1	26n8, 40, 40nn125–26, 41n131, 45, 75n360	2:19	169n265
		2:25	107n195
61:2	40	10:12	169n264
61:2–3	40n126		
62:4	41n131	## Joel	
62:8	41n131	2:12–22	59n239
63:10–11	162n233	2:28–32	59n239
63:16	40n126	2:28	59n240
64:7	40n126	2:31	59n239
65:2	69	2:32	30n45, 31n61, 31n63, 58n237, 59
65:7	40n126	3:5	74n353, 184n23
65:18–19	40n126		

Jeremiah

Amos

1:4	158n193	3:7	158n192
1:5	158n195		
1:10	158n195		

Nahum

1:15	30n45, 31, 61, 61n250

Habakkuk

1:3–13	67n303
1:5–11	67n303
1:14–17	67n303
1:15	67n303
2:1–8	67n303
2:2–3	67n303
2:4	66, 66n293, 66n299, 67, 67n300, 67nn303–4, 167, 181n12
2:5–11	67n303
2:13–20	67n303
2:18–20	67n303
3:1–19	67n303
3:9–15	67n303

Zechariah

11:7	41n131
11:11	41n131

LXX

Genesis

12:1–3	158n193
12:3	73n344, 73n346, 74n351
15:6	72n342, 73n343
18:18	73n344, 73n346, 74n351
22:18	74n351
26:4	73n344, 74n351
28:14	73n344, 74n351
32:11	169n265

Exodus

28	37n105
3:10	158n193

Leviticus

1–5	37n105
26	37n105
26:30	86n59

Numbers

3–4	37n105
21:29	71n329
33:52	86n59

Deuteronomy

11	37n105
29:17	86n59

Judges

8.17	88n70
13:6–7	34n85

1 Samuel

9:26—10:13	34n85

1 Kingdoms

1:42	31n58
4:7	71n329
4:8	71n329
4:21	71n329
13:26	87n62
18:31	30n48
31:9	30n45, 30nn48–49, 31n56, 31n59

2 Samuel

18:19	34n86
18:26	34n86
18:27	34n86
18:31	34n87

2 Kingdoms

1:15	192n53
1:20	30n45, 30nn48–49, 31n59
4:10	30n45, 30nn48–49, 31n53, 31nn59–60, 79n4, 192n53
18:19	30n45, 30nn48–49, 31n56, 31nn61–62, 56n224

18:20	30n45, 30nn48–49, 31n52, 31n56, 31nn61–62, 56n224	96:2	169n264
		97:3	66n292
		98:2	66n292
18:22	30n45, 31n53, 31n56	102:17	169n265
18:25	30n45, 31n52, 31n56	115:4	86n59
18:26	30n45, 30nn48–49, 31n56, 31nn61–62, 56n224	135:15	86n59

Proverbs

23:29	71n329

18:27	30n45, 31n52, 31n56
18:31	30n45, 30n49, 31n56, 31nn61–62, 56n224

Isaiah

3 Kingdoms

		1:4	71n329
1:41	158n193	1:24	71n329
1:42	30n45, 30n48, 30n49	3:11	71n329
1:49	158n193	3:9	71n329
7:9	30n45	5:11	71n329
12:24	71n329	5:18	71n329
13:30	71n329	5:20	71n329
		5:21	71n329
		5:22	71n329
		5:8	71n329

4 Kingdoms

7:9	31n52, 31n56	6:3	57n230
14:6	66n295	6:8	158n193
19:6	87n62	9:7	57n230
23:21	66n295	10:1	71n329
		10:5	71n329

1 Chronicles

		10:22	59
10:9	30n45, 30n48, 30n49, 31n56	11:1–9	57n230
		11:4–5	57n230
		13:3	57n230
		13:8	57n230
		14:3–23	57n230

Psalms

		17:12	71n329
14:7	68n309	18:1	71n329
18:5	59n241	21:3	57n230
35:11	169n265	24:16	71n329
39:10	30n45, 30n48, 30n49, 31, 31n61, 56n224	26:17	57n230
		28:1	71n329
67:12	30n45, 30n48, 30n49, 31n56	29:1	71n329
		29:10	64n278
68:6	173n291	29:15	71n329
71:17	73n344, 74n351	30:1	71n329
84:11	169n265	31:1	71n329
84:14	168n259, 168n264	33:1	71n329
88:15	169n265	34:5–6	57n230
93:15	169n264	37:19	86nn58–59
95:2	30n45, 30n48, 30n49, 31n61, 31n63, 56n224	39:12	57n230

Isaiah (continued)

40:9	30n45, 30n49, 57n225
41:28	86n59
42:1	57n230
49:1–7	57n230
49:1–6	71n330
49:1–6	71n330
52	61
52:7	30n45, 30n49, 31n61, 32n64, 56n224, 57n225, 59n241, 61nn248–50
52:13—53:12	57n230
52:7a	61
52:13	57n230
52:14	57n230
52:15	176
53:1–6	57n230
53:1	59n241
53:5	53n202
58:8	57n230
58:10	57n230
59:9	57n230
59:20–21a	68, 68n309
60:1	57n230
60:3	57n230
60:6	30n45, 30n49, 32n64, 57n225
61:1	30n45, 30n49, 31n61, 32n64, 56nn224–25
61:1–3	57n230
62:5	57n230
65:1	59n241
65:2	59n241
65:17	57n230
66:22	57n230

Jeremiah

1:10	71n330
1:5	71n330
4:13	71n329
6:4	71n329
9:23	70, 70n327, 169n265
10:19	71n329
13:27	71n329
20:9	71
20:15	30n45, 30n49, 31n57
22:18	71n329
26:19	71n329
27:27	71n329
28:2	71n329
31:1	71n329
31:33	68n309

Lamentations

5:16	71n329

Ezekiel

2:10	71n329
7:26	71n329
13:3	71n329
13:18	71n329

Ecclesiastes

4:10	71n329
10:16	71n329

Daniel

9:13 (Th)	66n295

Hosea

2:21	169n265
7:13	71n329
9:12	71n329
11:1	158n193

Joel

2:18—3:5	59
2:21–22	59n239
2:32	59
3:1–5	59n239
3:1	59n239
3:3–4	59n239
3:3	59n239
3:4	59n239
3:5	30n45, 30nn48–49, 31n61, 31n63, 56n224, 58n237, 59, 59nn239–40

Amos

5:16	71n329

5:18	71n329	16:17	95n112
6:1	71n329	19:5	95n112

Micah

7:4	71n329

Nahum

2:1	30n45, 30n49, 31n61, 56n224, 59, 59n241, 61, 61nn249–50
3:17	71n329

Habakkuk

2:4	67nn301–2
2:6	71n329
2:12	71n329
2:18	86n59
2:19	71n329

Zephaniah

2:5	71n329
3:18	71n329

Tobit

1:6	66n295
8:14	208n4
10:5	71n325, 71n329
11:15	208n4

Judith

2:7	208n4
3:5	208n4
6:17	208n4
10:13	208n4
11:19	208n4
13:13	95n112
14:8	208n4
15:4	208n4
16:17	71n329

Wisdom of Solomon

6:22	208n4
12:27	87n62
15.1	87n62
15:15	86n59

Sirach

1:30	173n291
2:7	88n70
2:12	71n329
2:13	71n329
2:14	71n329
6:19	88n70
16:25	208n4
17:15	173n291
17:20	173n291
30:19	86n59
37:14	208n4
39:19	173n291
41:8	71n329
42:19	208n4
42:20	173n291
44:3	208n4
44:19–21	72n335
44:21	73n344, 74n351

Baruch

6	37n105

Daniel

2:6 (Th)	208n4

Song of Three Young Men

9:13	66n295

Susanna

1:41	208n4
1:42 (Th)	173n291

Bel and the Dragon

1:4	86n59
1:5	86n59, 87n62
1:6	87n62
1:24	87n62
1:25	87n62

1 Maccabees

2:52	72n335

1 Maccabees (continued)

4:26	208n4
5:14	208n4
5:38	208n4
6:5	208n4
9:37	208n4
11:21	208n4
11:40	208n4
12:23	208n4
12:26	208n4
14:21	208n4
15:32	208n4
15:36	208n4
16:1	208n4
16:21	208n4

2 Maccabees

8:36	135n20, 142n78, 209n32
7:33	87n62
9:17	135n20, 209n32
9:24	95n112

1 Esdras

3:9	66n295
4:58	34n85

3 Maccabees

6:18	87n62
6:28	87n62

4 Maccabees

2:14	95n112

NEW TESTAMENT

Matthew

1:22	176n311
2:15	176n311
2:17	176n311
2:23	176n311
3:11–12	38n118, 59n239
4:14	176n311
4:23	38n114, 39n118
6:14	94n100
7:22	94n100, 98n132
7:28	39n118
8:17	176n311
9:2	59n239
9:10	39n118
9:32–24	94n101
9:35	38n114
10:7–8	140
10:13	49n178
10:23	96n118
11:1	39n118
11:2–6	94n100
11:5	26, 38, 39, 183
11:12–13	39n118
11:13	75
11:20	94n100, 98n132
11:21	94n100, 98n132
11:22	59n239
11:23	94n100
12:4	49n174
12:17	176n311
12:22–30	94n101
12:28	45n154
12:44	49n178
12:45	96n118
13:15	49n178
13:35	176n311
13:53	39n118
13:54	94n100, 98n132
13:58	94n100, 98n132
14:2	84, 94n100, 98n132
15:6	44n148
16:16	87n63
16:23	125n334
19:1	39n118
19:22	83
21:4	176n311
24:14	38n114
24:18	49n178
24:29	59n239, 94n100, 98n131
25:10	148n20
26:1	39n118
26:13	38
26:24	66n296
26:54	176n311
26:56	176n311

26:63	87n63	13:10	38n113, 176
26:62	43n141	13:16	49n178
27:9	176n311	13:24	59n239
27:27	29	13:25	98n131
27:43	50n189	13:34	59n239
27:52–53	162n221	14:9	38, 38n113
		14:21	66n296
		14:49	176n311
		15:16	29n39
		16:8	80n8
		16:15	38n113
		16:20	103n168

Mark

1:1	38n113, 50n183
1:2	60n245
1:9	38n118
1:14	38n113, 102n158
1:15	38n113, 38n117, 176n311
1:38	38n118
2:23	39n118
2:26	49n174
3:22–27	94n101
4:4	39n118
4:12	49n178
5:30	49n178, 93n100
5:33	11n216
6:2	94n100, 98n132
6:4	84n38
6:5	93n100
6:6	38n114
6:12–13	39n118
6:14	94n100, 98n132
6:34	38n114
6:50	59n239
7:4	52n200
7:13	44n148
7:29	83n33
8:31	53n202
8:33	125n334
8:35	38n113
8:38	166
9:1	54n212, 162n219
9:7	39n118
9:13	66n296
9:31	53n202
9:39	93n100
10:29	38n113
10:32–24	53n202
11:27	38n118
12:26	49n174
12:41	49n174
13:9–10	38n114

Luke

1:1	100n143
1:1–4	42
1:2	52n200
1:3	39n118
1:16	49n178
1:17	49n178, 94, 137n35
1:19	38n118, 43n146
1:29	83n33
1:35	94n101, 137n35
1:41	39n118
1:59	39n118
1:65	39n118
1:70	64n278
1:74	50n189
2:1–21	38n118
2:10	43n146
2:15	39n118, 145n104
2:17	145n104
2:23	60n245, 66n296
3:39	49n178
2:46	39n118
3:18	38n188, 43n146
3:22	40n126
4:12	40n126, 176n311
4:14	94nn103–4, 137n35
4:16–30	38n118
4:17–21	38n118
4:18	26n8, 38n118, 43n126
4:36	39n118
4:43	38n118, 43n146, 96n118
5:1	44n148
5:12	39n118

Luke (continued)

5:17	39n118, 93n100, 93n94
5:26	95n112
6:13	39n118
6:16	43n146
6:19 93n100	94
6:20	40n126
6:21	40, 40n126
6:29	40n126
6:38	40n126
6:49	40n126
7:2	45
7:11	39, 39n118
7:18	94n101
7:20	40n123
7:22	26n8, 38, 39, 40n126, 43n146, 48, 75n360, 76, 183
8:1	39n118, 43n146, 48n169
8:15	196n71
8:21	44n148
8:46	93n100
8:55	49n178
9:1	93n100
9:2	48n169
9:6	39n118, 43n146
9:18	39n118
9:29	39n118
9:33	39n118
9:35	40n126
9:60	48n169
10	39n122
10:1	96n118
10:2	38n114, 40n126
10:7	39nn121–22, 48, 140n58, 141, 189
10:8	39n122
10:9	48n169, 140
10:13	40n126, 94n101, 98n132
10:15	40n126
10:16	39n122
10:21	40n126
11:1	39n118
11:2	40n126
11:20	45n154
11:22	40n126
11:23	40n126
11:28	44n148
12:51	59n239
13:29	40n126
13:34	40n126
11:47–51	39n121
13:34	39n121
14:1	39n118
14:7	49n174
16:11	50n181
16:16	39n118
16:18	39n121
17:1–2	39n121
17:4	49n178
17:11	39n118
17:14	39n118
17:31	49n178
19:15	39n118
19:29	39n118
19:32	62n261
19:37	94n100
20:1	39n118
21:19	196n71
21:24	176n311
21:25	59n239
21:26	98n131
22:14	39n118
22:16	176n311
22:22	162:217
22:32	49n178, 96n118
22:61	44n148
22:66	39n118
24:4	39n118
24:15	39n118
24:30	39n118
24:44	176n311
24:51	39n118

John

1:9	50n181
2:22	83n33
2:8	50n181
3:33	87n63
4:23	50n181
4:37	50n181
4:42	90n80
4:51	80n8

5:20	50n181	5:11	39n118
6:32	50n181	5:42	38n116, 43n146
6:60	83n33	6:2	44n148
7:8	176n311	6:8	93n100
7:28	50n181	6:14	52n200
8:16	50n181	7:2	43n142
12:33	34n87	7:26	43n142
12:38	176n311	7:29	83n33
13:18	176n311	7:41	51n190
15:1	50n181	7:42	60n245
15:15	145n104	7:52	80n8
15:25	176n311	8:4	38n116, 43n146
17:3	50n181, 87n63	8:12	38n116, 43n146
17:12	176n311	8:13	39n118, 94n100, 98n132
17:26	145n104	8:14	44n148
18:9	176n311	8:19	94n103
18:28	29n39	8:25	38n116, 43n146, 44n148
18:32	34n87, 176n311	8:35	38n116, 43n146
18:33	29n39	8:40	38n116, 43n146
19:9	29n39	9:35	49n178, 86n52
19:35	50n181	9:40	49n178
19:36	176n311	10:1–48	6
21:19	34n87	10:1–11	18, 43
21:20	49n178	10:13	39n118
		10:36	26n8, 38n116, 43n146
		10:38	93n100, 94n103, 137n35

Acts

1:8	94nn103–4, 137n35	10:42	53n202, 55n218, 162n217
1:15	43n141	11:1	44n148
1:16	43n142, 176n311	11:4	39n118
2:2	39n118	11:13	49n174
2:17–21	59n239	11:20	38n116, 43n146
2:22	94n100, 137n37, 176n311	11:21	49n178, 86n52
2:23	162n217	11:27–30	149n125
2:25	73n347	11:29	162n217
2:28	145n104	13:5	44n148
2:29	43n142	13:7	44n148
2:31	73n347	13:15	43n142, 83n33
2:36	55n218	13:16	43n141
2:37	43n142	13:26	43n142
2:39	59n239	13:27	176n311
3:12	93n100	13:32	38n116, 43n146
3:18	80n8	13:33	55n218
3:19	49n178, 86n52	13:38	43n142, 143n83
3:24	39n118, 143n83	13:44	44n148
4:2	143n83, 162n221		
4:7	93n100, 94n103		
4:31	44n148		

Acts (continued)

13:48	44n148
14:7	38n116, 43n146
14:12	83n33
14:15	38n116, 43n146, 49n178, 86n52, 87, 87n63
14:15–17	88
14:21	38n116, 43n146
14:27	148n20
15	42n136
15:7	42n135, 43nn141–42, 44nn148–49, 76
15:11	90n80
15:12	42, 183
15:13	43n142
15:15	60n245, 66n296
15:19	86n52
15:20	51n190
15:23	63n269
15:26	54n211
15:35	38n116, 43n146, 44n148
15:36	44n148, 49n178, 143n83
16:4	52n200
16:10	38n116, 43n146
16:14	52n200
16:17	143n83
16:18	49n178
16:21	143n83
16:26	148n20
16:27	148n20
16:32	44n148
17:1	39n118
17:1–9	101n153
17:4	81n13
17:3	143n83
17:13	143n83
17:18	38n116, 43n146, 66n295, 80n8
17:23	143n83
17:26	162n217
17:31	55n218, 162nn216–17
18:1–3	132
18:1–5	80
18:4	132
18:6	132
18:7	132, 156n178
18:11	44n148, 132
18:18	132
18:23	39n118
19:10	44n148
19:11	94n100, 98n132
20:24	43n147
21:29	73n347
21:30	148n20
22:1	43n142, 121n292
22:16	62n258
23:1	43n142, 123n319
23:6	43n142
23:12–26	117n251
23:35	29n39
23:26	63n269
23:6	162n221
24:4	139n49
24:26–27	155
25:7	137n37
25:16	121n292
26:18	49n178, 86n52
26:20	86n52
26:23	143n83
26:25	111n216
26:27	86n52
28:17	43n142
28:22	125n334
28:27	49n178
31:33	55n218

Romans

1	4
1:1	3n4, 54n207, 62n262, 63n271, 64n275, 71n332, 74, 102n158, 158, 159, 160, 163, 171, 173, 175, 192, 194,
1:1–2	58n235, 63, 71n330, 182
1:1–3	108n197, 197n77
1:1–3a	19
1:1–5	157
1:1–6	24n151, 80, 164, 167, 177
1:1–16	85n50
1:1–7	163, 166

BIBLICAL AND ANCIENT LITERATURE INDEX 251

1:2	55, 63, 88n66, 116n245, 160, 173	1:16–17	15n117, 58n235, 65, 66, 66n291, 74n355, 134, 156, 165, 169, 173, 181n12, 190, 193, 198, 199
1:2–6	158		
1:3	50n183, 54, 55n217, 104, 160, 161, 163, 170n273, 186,192n56		
		1:16–18	166
1:3b–4	160	1:17	8, 60n245, 66n293, 66n296, 67n306, 165, 167, 177
1:3–4	156, 158n189, 160, 163, 172, 173, 188		
1:3–4a	53, 54n210, 76n365, 183n21, 186n29, 187	1:17a–b	169
		1:18	50n179, 111n215, 168, 170n275, 192n55
1:3–5	24n151		
1:3–7	173	1:18–32	166, 170
1:4	50n183, 54nn211–12, 55, 89n78, 94n106, 137n35,161, 162, 170, 192	1:25	111n215
		1:32	161n210
		1:59	160n214
		2:1—3:9	170
1:4b	163n228	2:2	111n215
1:5	63, 120n282, 186	2:21–22	50n190, 109n204, 170, 192, 195n65
1:5a	163		
1:5b–c	164	2:21–31	170
1:6	160, 164	2:24	60n245, 66n296
1:7	54n211, 200	2:25–29	157n184
1:8	104n174, 109n205, 135n19, 143n83, 195n63	2:5	170n27. 192n55
		2:7	196n71
		2:8	111n215, 170n275, 192n55
1:8–12	165		
1:8–15	106n181	2:9–11	157n184
1:9	3n4, 50n183, 54n207, 63, 161n210, 165, 170n273, 173, 175, 189n37, 192n56	2:16	3, 3n25, 20, 24n150, 45n155, 81n17, 173, 184, 192n55
		2:17—3:20	58n236
1:9–6	163n234	2:20	111n215
1:9–10	19, 165, 167	3:2	103n164
1:11–12	165	3:4	50n181, 60n245, 66n296, 87n61, 111n215
1:13	156, 157n184, 165		
1:13–14	165		
1:15	3n27, 4, 54n207, 19, 109n203, 159n203, 165, 177, 194, 196, 200	3:5	170n275, 192n55
		3:7	111n215
		3:10	60n245, 66n296
		3:10–20	170
1:16	3nn23–25, 12, 13, 15, 19, 54n207, 84n45, 156, 157n184, 165, 166,167, 168, 191n45, 197	3:21–26	198
		3:24	154n163
		3:25	88n67
		3:25	92n91
		3:26	90n82
1:16b	167n251	3:29	157n184
1:16b–c	169	4:1–25	170

Romans (continued)

4:3	60n245, 64n280, 65n287, 72n342, 73n343
4:6	55n217
4:9	65n287, 73n343
4:9–12	65, 74, 77
4:15	170n275
4:17	60n245, 66n296, 88n73, 107, 171n276, 192n58
4:21	100n143
4:24	50n187, 90n79, 90n84
4:25	90n84, 113n131
5:1	54n211, 170
5:3–5	60n243
5:3	196n71
5:4	196n71
5:5	59n240, 166n244
5:6	143n85
5:6–8	154n163
5:8	143n85
5:9	50n188, 170n275
5:10	50n183, 50n188, 161n210, 170n273, 192n56
5:11	54n211
5:12–21	200
5:15–17	154n163
5:21	54n211
6:1	171n276, 192n57
6:1–11	89n78
6:1–23	71n332
6:4–5	171n277, 192n58
6:4	50n187, 90n79, 90n84, 123n318, 162, 188
6:8	90n80
6:9	50n187
6:9	90n84
6:13	50n187
6:15–17	164
6:32	54n211
7:4	50n187, 90n84
7:24	50n189
7:24–25	68n318
7:25	54n211
8:3	50n183, 88n67, 88nn72–73, 107, 107n191, 161n210, 170n273, 192n56
8:4	123n318, 176n311
8:5	125nn334–35
8:11	50n187, 89n78, 90n79, 90n82, 90n84, 162, 171n277, 192n58
8:15	114n235
8:18–23	192
8:18–23	171
8:19	50n182, 88n68
8:23	50n182
8:25	50n182, 196n71
8:29	50n183, 170n273, 192n56
8:29–30	60n243
8:32	50n183, 13n131, 170n273, 192n56
8:34	90n84
8:36	60n245, 66n296
8:38	54n211, 98n131, 200
8:39	54n211
9:1	111nn215–16
9:4	143
9:6–29	59, 83n31
9:7	88n73, 107n195
9:9	83n31
9:11–12	107n191
9:12	88n73
9:13	60n245, 66n296
9:17	60n245, 64n280
9:22–25	107n191
9:22	145n103, 170n275
9:23	145n103
9:24–26	107n195
9:24	88nn72–73
9:25	60n246
9:26	87n60
9:27	59
9:30—10:21	58n236
9:30—11:25	68n307
9:31	70n325
9:33	60n245, 66n296, 166n244
10:1	168
10:2	58
10:4	58, 59
10:5–15	58

BIBLICAL AND ANCIENT LITERATURE INDEX   253

10:6	50n179	11:32	174
10:7	50n187	11:25b	68
10:8	109n204, 195n65, 196n73	11:25c	68
		11:25–28	58n235, 74n355, 182n14
10:9	50n187, 90nn79–80, 90n84, 150	11:25–32	68
10:10	150, 168	11:26	50nn188–89, 60n245, 66n296
10:11	60n245, 64n280, 68, 166n244	11:26a	68
10:12	59, 62n258, 157n184	11:26b–27a	68n309
10:13	58n237, 62n258, 74n353, 184n23	11:27b	68n309
		11:28	3n23, 20, 69, 177, 191n50
10:14–15a	60, 60n244		
10:14–21	59, 62n258, 109n204, 156, 195n65	11:29	95n113, 107n191
		12:1	171n276, 175, 192n57
10:15	20, 60n241, 60n245, 66n296, 109n203, 109n204, 177, 181n10, 195n65	12:3	120n282, 125n334
		12:4–8	99n137
		12:6	95n113, 99n139
		12:11	50nn184–85
10:15b	60, 61, 76	12:16	125n334
10:15–16	173	12:19	60n245, 170n275
10:16	3n23, 20, 24n150, 59n241, 62n256	13:4	170n275
		13:5	170n275
10:16a	62	13:9	83n31
10:16b	62	13:11	50n180, 90n84
10:17	114	13:11–12	171n278
10:18	59n241	13:11–14	176
10:19	59n241	13:13	123n318
10:20	59n241	14:5	100n143
10:21	58, 59n241	14:6	125n334
11:1	68n307	14:8	171, 192
11:1–6	71n330	14:11	60n245
11:2	60n245, 64n280	14:12	83n31
11:4	60n246	14:13	39n121
11:8	60n245, 66n296	14:15	123n318
11:9	55n217, 175	14:17	89
11:13	71n330, 157n184, 163n234	14:18	50n184
		15:1–7	124n325
11:13–36	156	15:3	60n245, 66n296
11:15	50n187	15:3–31	149
11:17	141	15:4	64n280, 196n71
11:20	125n334	15:4–5	196
11:21	69	15:5	125n334, 196n71
11:25	68, 174	15:6	54n211
11:25–28	68	15:7–13	157n184
11:28	174	15:8	111n215
11:28a	174	15:9–20	171
11:28b	174	15:9	60n245, 66n296

Romans (continued)

15:10–11	60n246
15:12	90n85
15:13	54n212, 94n106
15:14–29	3n25
15:14–33	156
15:15	163n234, 175
15:15–17	175
15:15–18	157n184
15:15–24	85n50
15:15b–16	20
15:16	3n24, 102n158, 108n197, 154n164, 159, 165n240, 174, 175, 177, 189n41
15:17–20	163n234
15:18	83nn32–33, 175, 192, 196
15:18–19	15, 20, 191n45, 197
15:18–20	175
15:19	54n212, 93n100, 137n35, 175, 177
15:19–20	165n240, 171n279, 175, 190, 194
15:20	3n27, 4, 20, 69, 109n203, 159n203, 167, 176, 177, 196n73
15:20–21	58n235, 69, 74n355, 182n14
15:21	60n245, 61, 66n296, 70n324, 176
15:22	139n49n 51
15:22–25	156
15:23	163n234, 176
15:24	156
15:25–32	149n125, 175n306
15:26	120n288
15:28	156
15:29	99n42
15:31	50n189
15:33	170
15:39	54n211
16:3	127n349
16:4	85n50
16:7	204n100
16:9	127n349
16:17–20	85n50
16:18	50n184
16:20	171n278
16:21	127n349
16:23	156n178
16:25	3, 20, 45n155, 81n17, 136n25
16:25–27	171
16:25–26	71n330, 172
16:25a–c	172
16:25d–26	172
16:26	63, 145n103
18b–19a	175

1 Corinthians

1:1	137n42
1:1	62n262
1:2	54n211, 59n240
1:3	54n211
1:4–9	106n181
1:5	83n31, 83n33
1:7	50n182, 54n211, 88n68
1:8	54n211
1:9	50n183, 54n211, 88nn72–73, 107n191, 108, 161n210
1:10–12	133
1:10–4:21	133, 137, 138
1:10–17	138n46
1:10	54n211
1:12	133
1:13	112n225, 113n226, 133
1:14	190n44, 156n178
1:17–18	133
1:17—2:16	96n121
1:17	3n27, 4, 13n130, 20, 83n33 109n203, 133n7, 134, 135, 138, 146, 159n203, 196
1:18	83nn32–33, 113n230, 134, 136, 167
1:19	60n245
1:21	97n128, 136n25
1:23	109n204, 112n225, 113n227, 113n230, 167, 188n35, 195n65, 196n73
1:26–27	107n191

1:27–28	167	5:7	88n67
1:31	60n245, 66n296, 70, 70n327	5:8	111n215
		5:9–11	133
2:1–5	93, 132, 135, 138, 203	5:19	83n32
2:1	83nn31–33, 109n205, 133n8, 135n19, 142n82, 143n83, 187n30, 195n63	6:1–11	138
		6:1–11	133n4
		6:9	89n75
		6:10	89n75
2:2	12, 92n91, 112n225, 113, 113n227, 113n230, 135, 167	6:11	54n211
		6:12–20	138
		6:14	90n79, 90n84
2:4	11n85, 83n32, 94, 94n33 136, 137, 146, 191n45, 192	6:16	60n246
		7:1–40	138
		7:1	133, 144n91
2:4b	83n31	7:10	39n121
2:5	14, 54n212, 97n128, 136, 193	7:15–24	107n191
		7:15	88nn72–73, 108
2:6	200	7:17	88nn72–73, 108n196, 123n318
2:8	112n225, 113n226, 200		
		7:18	88nn72–73, 107n194
2:9	60n245, 66n296	7:20–22	107n194
2:12	114n235	7:20	88nn72–73
2:13	83n32	7:21	88nn72–73
2:18–25	10	7:22	88nn72–73
3:3	123n318	7:23	71n332
3:4–5	133n4	7:24	88nn72–73, 107n194
3:5—4:21	138n46	7:25	144n91
3:5–9	103n167	8:1—11:1	138
3:5	50n180, 97n128	8:1–13	139
3:9	103, 127n349	8:1–3	96n121
3:10	120n282	8:1	133n4, 144n91
3:13–15	89	8:4	50n190, 53, 86n58
3:15	50n188	8:5	50n179
3:19	60n245	8:7	50n190, 96n121
4:1–21	3n25	8:9	139
4:3	137n42	8:12	138
4:9	62n262	8:13	39n121, 138, 139
4:14–21	137	9	39n122
4:15	3n23, 10n74, 20, 133n6, 138, 147	9:1–27	138
		9:1–3	137n42
4:17	126	9:1	138
4:19	83n33	9:1	62n262
4:19	84	9:2	62n262, 138
4:20	54n212, 83n33, 84, 89, 93n100, 94	9:3–4	138
		9:3	3n26
5:1–13	138	9:3–12	139
5:1	133n4, 144n92	9:4–18	153
5:5	50n188	9:5–11	138

1 Corinthians (continued)

9:5	53n202, 62n262, 188
9:9	60n245
9:10	60n245
9:12-23	138, 139, 141
9:12	10n74, 20, 71, 101n152, 103n169, 133n6, 138, 139, 140, 141
9:13-14	71
9:13	139, 140, 189
9:14	3n23, 10n74, 20, 24n150, 39nn121-22, 48n167, 101n152, 109n205, 133n6, 133n8, 135n19, 139, 140, 141, 183n21, 189, 194, 195
9:15	71
9:16	3n27, 20, 58n235, 71, 74n355, 109n203, 133n7, 139n48, 140n63, 159n203, 182n14, 196n73, 197
9:17-18	71, 140
9:17	46, 97n128 103n164
9:18	3n23, 3n27, 10n74, 20, 101n152, 109n203, 133nn6-7, 139n48, 140, 159n203
9:23	3n23, 10n74, 20, 104n173, 133n6, 141, 194
9:24-27	127
9:27	109n204, 195n65
10:7	60n245, 90n85
10:19	50n190, 86n58
10:25	29n39
10:27	39n122
10:31—11:1	124n325
11:2	52n200
11:17-34	142
11:18-19	133n4
11:18	97n128, 144n92
11:20	187
11:23-25	142
11:23-26	188
11:23	52n200, 109n207, 144n96
11:24	13n131, 143, 186n27, 188
11:25	143, 188
11:26	109n205, 133n8, 135n19, 142, 143, 187n31, 188, 195n63
11:27-29	142
11:33	50n182
12:1-15:40	138
12:1	144n91
12:2	50n190, 86
12:3	90n82, 145n103
12:4-7	95n115
12:4	99n139
12:6	84n38
12:7	97, 98
12:8-10	96, 99n137, 190n43
12:9-10	98
12:9	95n113, 96, 97, 98
12:10	94n100, 96, 98
12:18	95n115
12:24	95n115
12:28-29	97, 99
12:28-30	99n137
12:28	94n100, 95n113, 95n115, 98n132, 99n139
12:29	94n100, 98n132
12:30	95n113, 99n139
12:31	95n113, 99n137
13:1-3	9
13:2	97
13:3	97
13:4	188n35
13:6	111n215
13:7	97n128
13:11	125n334
13:13	97n128
14:6	98
14:9	83n33
14:16	98
14:21	60n245
14:22	97n128
14:27-29	98
15	47
15:1	3n27

BIBLICAL AND ANCIENT LITERATURE INDEX 257

15:1–2	21, 144	15:32	90n84, 144n93, 204n100
15:1–5	103n163		
15:1–7	64	15:35	90n84
15:1–8	24n151	15:39–41	96n120
15:1–58	51, 89n78, 138	15:42–47	91
15:1	10n74, 51, 52n200, 109nn203–4, 109n207, 133nn6–7, 145, 145n103, 159n203, 185	15:42	90n84
		15:43	54n212, 90n84, 162n219
		15:44	90n84
		15:45	60n245
15:2	50n180, 51, 52, 62n262, 83nn32–33, 97n128, 109n203, 133n7, 145, 159n203	15:47	50n179
		15:52	90n84
		15:54	60n245, 83n31, 83n33
		15:57	54n211
15:3	9, 52n200, 64n280, 109n207, 113n230, 143n85, 145	16:1–4	149n125
		16:1	144n91
		16:11	50n182
15:3–4	24n151, 52n201	16:12	133, 144n91
15:3–5	51, 52n198, 53n202, 55, 183n21, 186n27, 187	16:17	144n92
		16:9	148n20
15:3–7	146		
15:3–8	14n103	## 2 Corinthians	
15:3b-5	76n365, 144	1:1	62n262
15:4	53, 64n280, 90n84	1:2	54n211
15:5–8	24n151	1:3	54n211
15:5	9, 53n202	1:5	153
15:5b	52n199	1:6	196n71
15:6	52n199, 53n202	1:9	90n84, 153n159
15:7	53n202	1:10	50n189, 68n318
15:8	53n202, 76, 145	1:12—2:4	147
15:11	50n180, 97n128, 109n204, 144n93, 195n65, 196n73	1:18	83nn32–33
		1:19	50n183, 109n204, 161n210, 195n65
15:12	50n187, 90n84	1:21—12:10	153
15:13	90n84	1:24	127n350
15:14	90n84, 97n128	2:4	133
15:15	90n79, 90n84	2:12	10n74, 21, 103n169, 119n270, 119n279, 126n339, 147, 151n148, 154, 155n169, 196n71
15:16	90n84, 144n93		
15:17	90n84, 97n128		
15:20	50n187, 90n84, 162n221		
15:22	143	2:14—4:6	81
15:23	162n221	2:14–17	153n159
15:24	200	2:14	29n39
15:28	161n210	2:17	44n148, 83n32, 82n34, 148, 149
15:29	90n84, 144n93	3:3	87n60
15:31	54n211	3:16–17	89n78

2 Corinthians (continued)

3:16	49n178, 86n52
4:1–6	148
4:2	44n148, 83n34, 111n215, 123n318, 148
4:3–4	10n74, 21
4:3–5	148
4:3	3, 46n156, 81, 81n17, 148, 155n169, 171n280, 184
4:4–6	14n110
4:4	149, 155n169
4:5	109n204, 148, 195n65, 196n73
4:10	90n82, 153, 188
4:11	90n82, 153
4:12	84n38
4:13	60n245
4:14	90n79, 90n82, 90n84, 153n159
5:1	50n179
5:2	50n179
5:7	123n318
5:15	89n78, 90n84, 153n159
5:19	83nn32–33
5:20	14n110
5:21	88n67, 143n85, 153
6:1	103
6:2	60n246
6:4	196n71
6:7	54n212, 83nn32–33, 111nn215–16
6:8	111n215
6:16	50n190, 60n246, 87n60
7:1	54n212
7:5	120n282
7:8	133
7:14	111n215
8:1—9:15	149n125
8:1	145n103
8:2	120n285
8:6–9	124n325
8:7	83n33
8:9	54n211
8:15	60n245, 66n296
8:17	149
8:18–22	149
8:18	3n23, 10n74, 21, 149, 149n127, 154, 155n169
8:20–21	149
8:23	127n349
9:1–15	150
9:9	60n245, 66n296
9:13	10n74, 21, 03n169, 119n270, 119n273, 120n288, 150n140, 154, 155n169
10:1—13:10	153n158
10:1	153n158, 188
10:2	123n318
10:3	123n318
10:8	166n244
10:10	83nn32–33
10:11	83nn32–33
10:12–18	70
10:14–15	70n325
10:14	103n169
10:14	21, 70, 151, 154, 155n169
10:16	3n27, 58n235, 69, 70, 74n355, 109n203, 154, 159n203, 182n14, 95, 196n73, 21
10:17	70, 70n327
11:1–4	151
11:1–6	3n26
11:2	153
11:3	151
11:4	21, 90n82, 96n120, 109n204, 114n235, 151, 152, 153, 155n169, 195n65
11:5	53n202, 62n262, 153, 154
11:6	83nn32–33, 153
11:7	3n27, 21, 102n158, 109n203, 151, 153, 154, 155n169, 159n203, 195
11:8	153
11:10	111n215
11:13	152n152
11:19–21	152

BIBLICAL AND ANCIENT LITERATURE INDEX 259

12–18	151	1:10	63n271, 71n332
12:1	98	1:11–16	55
12:1–10	153	1:11—2:14	71, 129
12:2	29n37, 50n179	1:11–12	64n275, 103n160, 163
12:6	111nn215–16	1:11–16	160n204
12:9	98	1:11–17	107
12:11–13	153	1:11	3n27, 22, 46,76,
12:11	53n202, 62n262,		106n179, 109n203,
	153,154		110, 145n103,
12:12	10, 11n85, 62n262		159n203, 160, 196
	195n66, 196n73	1:12	46, 52n200, 98,
12:12a	195		109n207, 160, 184,
12:13	151		199
12:14	153n158	1:13—2:14	46
12:18	123n318	1:13—2:21	110
13:1	153n158	1:15–16	71n330, 76, 11,
13:4	90n79, 112n225,		126n337, 158n195,
	113n226, 162		194
13:8	111n215	1:15	54, 88nn72–73, 107,
13:11	125n334		199
		1:15b–16	22

Galatians

		1:16	3n27, 46,
1:1–5	106		50n183,106n179,
1:1—2:11	171		109n203, 159n203,
1:1	46, 50n187, 62n262,		161n210, 184, 196n73
	90n79, 90n84	1:17	62n262
1:3	54n211	1:18	46
1:4	113	1:19	53n202, 188
1:4:13	159n203	1:23	3n27, 22, 106n179,
1:6–7	21, 96, 107,		109n203, 159n203
	107n186111	1:3:8	163
1:6–9	3n25, 71, 105, 106,	2:1–5	191
	115, 192, 203	2:1–10	42, 72
1:6—2:21	106	2:2	22, 24n149, 98,
1:6	3n26, 106, 152,		101n155, 106n180,
	88nn72–73, 107		109n204, 110, 134,
1:7	103n169, 106, 108,		146, 195n65, 196n73
	113, 115, 53n202	2:3–14	110
1:8–9	21	2:5	106
1:8	3n27, 50n179106n179,	2:5	3n23, 22,110, 111,
	108, 109n203,		111n215
	159n203, 196n73	2:6–10	69
1:9	3n27,52n200	2:7	3n24, 22, 46, 103n164,
106n179	108, 109, 109n203,		106n180, 110, 183
	109n207, 159n203	2:9	46, 110, 120n282, 183
1:10–12	106, 109, 190	2:10	29n37, 149n125
1:10—2:21	107, 108	2:12	106n178, 110
1:10–12		2:14–16	111

Galatians (continued)

2:14	3n23, 22, 104n171, 106, 110, 111, 111n215, 193, 194, 204n97
2:16	50n180
2:20–21	13n133
2:20	50n183, 89n78, 113, 161n210
3:1–5	72, 108, 193, 197, 203, 204,
3:1—5:12	111
3:1–4	111
3:1–5	111, 115, 116n248, 190n44
3:1	112, 112n225, 92n91, 113, 113n227, 188n35
3:2–5	109
3:2	72, 114, 152
3:3–4	191n45
3:3	111, 114
3:3a	114
3:4–5	114
3:4	114n235
3:5	72, 84n38, 94n100, 94n106, 98n132, 112, 114, 115, 195
3:6–18	115
3:6—4:31	72
3:6–9	111
3:6–8	71, 74, 181n13, 182n14
3:6	72, 72n343
3:7	73
3:8	60n245, 64n280, 73n347, 74, 115, 160n205
3:10	60n245
3:11	67n306, 181n12
3:13–14	13n133
3:13	60n245, 143n85
3:14	82, 114n235
3:22	64n280
3:26	161n210
4:4	50n183, 161n210, 188
4:6	50n183, 161n210
4:9	49n178, 86n52
4:10	106n178
4:12–20	111
4:13	3n27, 22, 106, 106n179, 109, 109n203, 116, 13, 204n97
4:14–21	191
4:14	116
4:16	111n215
4:17	106n178
4:21–31	111
4:24	29n37
4:26	68n317
4:27	60n245
4:30	64n280
5:2–12	106n178
5:5	50n182, 88n68
5:7	111, 111n215, 139n49, 139n51
5:8	107n191, 108n196
5:10	125n334
5:11	109n204, 113n230, 195n65
5:12	105
5:13	107n191, 108
5:13	88nn72–73
5:16	123n318
5:21	89n75
5:24	112n225, 113n226
6:2	151
6:12–13	106n178
6:12	113n230
6:14	54n211, 92n91, 112n225, 113n227
6:17	90n82, 112n224
6:18	54n211
9:12–23	191
12:1–3	96
14:19	96

Ephesians

1:2	54n211
1:3	54n211
1:9	145n104
1:10	50n179
1:11	84n38
1:15–23	106n181
1:17	54n211
1:20	84n38, 90n79

2:3	170n275	1:14	83nn31–32, 122
3:2	120n282	1:15–16	196n73
3:3	112n220, 145n104	1:15–17	47
3:5	145n104	1:15–18	117n258
3:10	145n104	1:15	47, 109n204, 109n208, 122, 188, 195n65
3:11	54n211		
3:14	54n211	1:16	3n23, 3n26, 24n150, 47, 117n249, 188
3:15	50n179		
3:16	94n103, 94n106, 119n278	1:17	22, 47, 90n84, 109, 205, 117, 122, 135n19, 143n83, 188, 195n63
3:20	84n38		
4:10	50n179		
4:11	149n130	1:18	47, 109n205, 109n208, 111n215, 117, 122, 135n19, 143n83, 188, 195n63
4:13	50n183, 161n210		
4:25	111n215		
4:31	170n275		
5:6	170n275	1:19	117, 125, 126, 166
5:14	50n187	1:20	117n255, 166
5:20	54n211	1:21	166
6:9	50n179	1:22	145n103
6:19	145n104	1:25	122, 123, 165, 167
6:21	145n104	1:27—2:11	88n66, 123
6:24	54n211	1:27—2:18	118n262, 126
		1:27	3n23, 22, 104n169, 104n171, 117n249, 117n259, 117n261, 119, 119n276, 123, 124, 124n319, 124n320, 125, 127, 188, 204

Philippians

1:1	63n271, 71n332, 126		
1:2	54n211		
1:3–8	118, 127		
1:3–11	106n181, 117n260		
1:3	118n262, 118n269		
1:5	3n23, 22, 117, 119, 119n270, 120, 121, 126n339, 127, 128, 129, 149, 204n97	1:28–30	117
		1:28	124
		1:29	120, 122n304, 124
		1:30	120
1:6	119, 120	2:1–5	125n329
1:7	3n23, 3n26, 22, 117, 117n255, 119, 120, 121, 125n334, 166, 141	2:1–11	204
		2:1–13	204
		2:1	124n328, 125
		2:2–4	117n259
		2:2	123, 125, 127n346
1:8	188	2:3–4	125
1:12–14	117n255	2:5–11	110n211, 124, 125n332, 130, 155
1:12–26	104n171, 122, 188, 204n100		
		2:5	125n334, 126, 127n346, 188
1:12	3n23, 22, 117n249, 117n261, 121, 123		
		2:6–11	91, 122n304, 123n316, 125n332, 188
1:13	29n39, 117n252, 121n298, 122, 166, 193, 204n97		
		2:8	91, 134n14, 188

Philippians (continued)

2:9	89n78, 91, 155
2:10	90n82
2:12–16	188
2:12	117
2:13	84n38
2:15	130
2:16	121, 122, 127
2:17–18	117n255, 126
2:17	128n355
2:19	117n261, 126
2:20	117n261
2:21	125, 126
2:22	3n23, 22, 117n249, 118, 119n270, 125, 126, 127, 193, 197, 204n97
2:23	117n261
2:25–28	118
2:25–27	117n256
2:25	117n257, 127n349, 128n355, 141
2:30	117nn256–57, 128n355
3:1	117n261
3:1a	118n262
3:2–4	120
3:2–3	117n258
3:2	118n262
3:5	159, 159n197, 194
3:6	159
3:7–11	124, 130, 204
3:7	159
3:8	122n304, 205
3:10–11	155
3:10–14	127
3:10–11	89n78
3:10	122n304, 155
3:11	50n187, 155
3:12	71
3:14	107n191
3:15	125n334, 127n346
3:16	70n325
3:17–19	117n258
3:17	123n318
3:18–19	118n262
3:18	113n230, 123n318
3:19	125n334
3:20	50n179, 50n182, 88n68
4:1–9	127
4:1–3	127, 193
4:1	117nn260–61, 127, 144
4:2–3	117n259, 141
4:2	125n334, 127
4:3	3n23, 22, 117n249, 127, 127n349, 149n133
4:6	145n103
4:8	109, 111n215
4:9	109n207, 118n262
4:10–13	128
4:10–18	118
4:10–20	117n260, 118n262, 120
4:10	117n257, 118n262, 125n334
4:11–13	122n304
4:14	117n255
4:14	117nn256–57, 117n261
4:15	3n23, 22, 117n249, 117n261, 128, 129
4:17–18	128
4:18	117n256, 128
4:19	128
4:20	118
4:21–23	118n262
4:22	117n252, 200
5:15–16	117
9:13	126n339

Colossians

1:3–8	106n181
1:3	54n211
1:5	50n179
1:11	196n71
1:13	50n183, 50n189, 161n210
1:16	50n179
1:18	50n187
1:20	50n179
1:23	50n179
1:25	44n148
1:27	145n104

1:28	143n83		50n190, 76n365,
1:29	54n212, 84n38		81n13, 85, 86, 87,
2:2	99n142, 100n144		87n64, 88, 89, 91, 92,
2:6	52n200		93, 111n215, 151n144,
2:12	90n79		170, 183n21, 198, 202,
2:15	29n39		203
3:2	125n334	1:9b–10	49n175, 49n177,
3:6	170n275		185n26
3:8	170n275	1:10	48n172, 50n179,
4:1	50n179		50n183, 50n189, 51,
4:3	148n20, 155		68n318, 88, 89, 90, 91,
4:7	145n104		143, 161n210, 170,
4:9	145n104		171, 185, 187n30, 188,
4:11	127n349		192
4:12	100n143	1:12–14	104n172
		2:1–12	81, 85n49, 101, 102, 103,
1 Thessalonians		2:2–3	93
1:1	101n153, 158n190	2:2	22, 24n149, 24n151,
1:2–10	51		76n363, 80n11, 82,
1:2—3:13	48n172		87101, 101nn153–55,
1:2–10	48, 85, 192		101n160, 108n197,
1:2–5	106n181		154n164, 191, 197n76,
1:2	81		204n100
1:3	54n211, 196n71	2:3	82, 93n96, 102, 120
1:4–10	85n50, 103	2:4	3n23, 22, 24n149, 46,
1:4–5	81, 85, 99, 142n79,		76n363, 80n11 101,
	142n81, 152n154, 190		102n160, 102n162,
1:4	81		197n76
1:5	11n85, 12, 22, 24n151,	2:5–6	93
	46n156, 48, 54n212,	2:5	82, 82n25, 83nn32–
	76n363, 80n11,		33, 101n160
	81n17, 82, 83, 85,	2:7	62n262
	94n106, 99, 100n146,	2:8–9	108n197
	100n149, 100n151,	2:8	23, 76n363, 80n11, 87,
	101, 115n239,		101n152, 101n160,
	116n247, 137n35,		102, 154n164, 197n76
	162n219, 171n280,	2:9	23, 24n151, 76n363,
	185, 191n45, 192,		80n11, 82n28, 87,
	197n76, 201, 202, 203,		101, 102, 109n204,
	204,		110n212, 134, 146,
1:6–7	120n282, 120n284		154n164, 191, 192,
1:6	82, 100, 124n325		195, 197n76
1:7	82	2:12	85, 87, 88n69, 88n73,
1:8–9	104n174		93, 101n160, 107, 108,
1:8	83n32, 83n34, 142n81		123n318
1:9–10	48, 49n174, 49nn177–	2:13–16	103, 103n165
	78, 50nn180–82,		

1 Thessalonians (continued)

2:13	14n110, 12, 52n200, 83n32, 83n34, 87, 101, 109n207, 111n215, 192
2:14–15	103n165
2:14–16	39n121
2:14	81n13, 84, 120n284
2:16	70n325, 170nn274–75
2:17—3:13	103
2:18	139n51
3:2	23, 76n363, 80n11, 101n153, 103:2, 103n169, 108n197, 127n349, 191, 197, 197n76
3:4	85, 204n100
3:6	3n27, 7, 27, 76n363, 80, 101n153, 104, 104n176, 109n203
3:12	80
3:13	54n212
4:1–8	85
4:1	52n200, 80, 109n207, 123n318
4:7	88n73, 107n191, 108
4:8	39n122
4:10	80
4:12	123n318
4:13–18	88n69, 92
4:13—5:11	92
4:13	89
4:14	90, 91, 92
4:15–17	89
4:15	50n179, 70n325, 83nn31–32, 83n34, 90n85
5:1–11	88n69
5:2	89
5:3–4	89
5:9–10	91, 113
5:9–11	92
5:9	54n211, 89, 170nn274–75
5:10	91n86
5:20–21	98
5:23–24	107n191
5:23	54n211, 89
5:24	88n72, 108n196
5:28	54n211

2 Thessalonians

1:1	54n211
1:2	54n211
1:3–10	106n181
1:4	196n71
1:11	54n212
1:7	50n179
1:8	104n169
1:12	54n211
2:4	137n37
2:9	93n100
2:14	46n156, 54n211, 81n17, 100n51
2:16	54n211
3:1	83n34
3:2	50n189
3:5	196n71
3:6	52n200, 54n211
3:18	54n211

1 Timothy

1:11	103
1:2	54n211
2:7	111n216
2:8	170n275
3:15	87n60
3:16	55n216
4:10	87n60
4:15	122n307
5:18	60n245, 64n280
6:3	54n211
6:11	196n71
6:12–13	150n138
6:14	54n211

2 Timothy

1:2	54n211
1:3–7	106n181
1:7	94n106
1:8–9	107
2:8	45n155, 53n202, 157n189, 172
3:10	196n71
3:11	50n189

3:15	64n279	2:21	52n200
4:5	100n143		
4:16	121n292	**1 John**	
4:17	50n189, 100n143	1:5	80n8
4:18	50n189	2:8	50n181
Titus		3:11	80n8
1:3	103	4:1	98
2:2	196n71	5:20	50n181
3:6	59n23	5:21	51n190
Hebrews		**3 John**	
1:2	161n211	1:8	127n349
1:3–4	161n211	**Jude**	
1:5	55n218, 161n211	3	52n200
2:4	94n100	17	54n211
3:1	150n138	21	54n211
3:12	87n63	25	54n211
4:2	104		
4:6	104	**Revelation**	
4:7	162nn216–17	1:2	44n148
4:14	150n138	1:9	44n148, 196n71
6:5	98n131	1:12	49n178
6:11	99n142, 100n144, 103n168	2:2	196n71
8:2	50n181	2:3	196n71
9:14	87n63	2:19	196n71
9:24	50n181	3:7	50n181
10:22	50n181, 99n142, 100n144	3:8	148n20
10:23	150n138	3:10	196n71
10:31	87n63	3:12	68n317
10:36	196n71	3:14	50n181
10:38	66n299	3:20	148n20
12:1	196n71	3:21	68n317
12:22	68n317, 87n63	4:1	148n20
		6:9	44n148
1 Peter		6:10	50n181, 87n63
1:3	54n211	6:12	59n239
2:21–22	53n202	7:2	87n63
3:18–20	53n202	8:7	59n239
4:17	102n158	9:20	51n190, 86
		13:10	196n71
2 Peter		14:1	59n239
1:8	54n211	14:12	196n716
1:14	54n211	15:3	50n181
		16:7	50n181
		19:11	50n181

Revelation (continued)

19:2	50n181
19:9	50n181
20:4	44n148
21:5	50n181
22:6	50n181

OLD TESTAMENT PSEUDEPIGRAPHA

Apocalypse of Abraham

1–8	72n335

1 Enoch

38:2	57n230
39:3–14	57n230
45:3–4	57n230
45:4b–5a	57n230
46:1	3, 57n230
46:4–8	57n230
48:2–6	57n230
49:1–4	57n230
62–63	57n230
62:1	57n230
62:1–2a	57n230
62:2–3	57n230
62:3–5	57n230
62:4–5	57n230
62:6	57n230
62:9	57n230
62:11–12	57n230
108:7	41n133

Letter of Aristeas

	30n44

Jubilees

12	72n335
23:10	72n335

Odes of Solomon

10:8	71n329

Psalms of Solomon

2:25	57n227
2:26	57n227
4	57n227
7	57n227
8	57n227
10:5–6	41n133
11:1–2	61
12	57n227
15	57n227
17	57n227
17:23(21)	161n212
18:1–4	41n133

Testament of Naphtali

4.1	64n279
5.8	64n279

Testament of Solomon

23.1	97n129

DEAD SEA SCROLLS

1QHa

4.28–29	94n105
4.34–38	94n105
7.6–7	162n223
7.25–26	94n105
9.32	162n223
12.12	162n223
13.38	94n105
15.9–10	94n105
23.14–15	41n132

1QM

11.8–15	41n132
13.13–16	41n132
1QpHab	67n303

1QS

4.21	162n223
5.17	66n294
8.14	66n294
8.16	162n223

9.3	162n223	*Jewish Antiquities*	
4Q71	87n62	1.10–12	30n43
4Q82		1.152	87n62
		1.155–57	72n335
frag 102	67n303	2.15	142n78
4Q163		2.85	142n78
		2.91	95n112
4–7 II	18, 66n294	2.223	95n112
		2.245	73n348
4Q171		2.267	95n112
1.21	41n132	2.285	95n112
2.9–12	41n132	2.295	95n112
4Q174	161n212	2.333	97n129
1–2 I	12, 66n294	2.345	95n112
		2.347	95n112
4Q177		3.1	95n112
10–11.1	66n294	3.14	95n112
		3.30	95n112
4Q178		5.24	33n84, 34n88
3.2	66n294	5.28	95n112
4Q252	161n212	5.125	95n112
		5.277	33n84, 34n88
11Q13		5.282	33n84, 34n88
2.15–18	61	6.56	33n84, 34n88
		6.171	95n112
8Ḥev 1		7.245	33n84, 34n88
16–19	67n303	7.247	70n325
		7.250	33n84, 34n88
CD		7.251	34n87
3.2	72n335	8.102	145n105
7.19	66n294	8.130	95n112
19.9–10	41n132	8.326–27	87n62
		8.335	87n62
JOSEPHUS		8.337	87n62
		8.338	87n62
Against Apion		8.343	87n62
1.53	95n112	8.402	87n62
1.61	148n124	9.60	95n112
1.77	73n348	9.256	87n62
2.45	64n279	10.26–27	87n62
2.114	95n112	10.28	95n112
		10.117	93n97
		10.254	112n223
		10.263	87n62
		11.55	87n62
		11.65	33n84, 34n85
		12.51	63n269
		12.87	95n112

Jewish Antiquities (continued)

12.148	63n269
13.140	95n112
13.189	73n348
13.282	95n112
14.225	63n269
14.235	63n269
14.455	95n112
15.209	33n84, 34n88
16.29	28n33
16.343	95n112
18.228	33n8, 34n88
18.229	33n84, 34n88

Jewish War

1.42	73n348
1.518	95n112
1.607	33n84, 34
1.621	121n292
2.420	33n84, 34n88, 36n103
2.649	73n348
3.143	33n84, 34n88
3.503	33n84, 34n88
4.32	62n261
4.354	95n112
4.618	34n88
4.618–19	33n84
4.656	33n84, 34n88
5.271	73n348
5.273	73n348
6.102	95n112

Life

5	33n83
7	33n83
7.323	87n62
19	73n348

ODES OF SOLOMON

10:8	71n329

PHILO

Abraham

1.80	87n62
1.143	87n62
1.196	95n112
60–88	72n335
121	64n279
153.2	33n76, 180n6, 32n68, 73n345, 210n38
261.9	209n31

Agriculture

112	93n97

Cherubim

1.27	87n62

Confusion

1.31	95n112
1.59	95n112
1.132	95n112

Contemplative Life

28	64n279
75	64n279
78	64n279

Creation

1.124	95n112
5	70n325
8	70n325
34.1	210n38
34.2	33n77, 32n68, 73n345
54.4	32n68
115.5	32n68, 33n79, 208n9
106	142n78
106.8	209n31

Decalogue

1.8	64n279
1.59	87n279
1.81	87n279
37	64n279

BIBLICAL AND ANCIENT LITERATURE INDEX   269

Dreams

1.27	73n348
2.23	95n112
2.136	95n112
2.185	95n112
2.281	32n68, 33n71, 208n9

Drunkenness

1.66	95n112
1.178	95n112
1.160	73n348

Embassy

1.80	95n112
1.347	87n62
3.177	87n62
3.188	87n62
3.215	70n325
3.228	73n343
18.4	32n68, 33n74, 208n9
99.6	32n68, 33n70, 208n9
195	64n279
232.1	32n68, 33n71, 208n9
315.2	63n269

Eternity

1.48	95n112
1.109	95n112
68	142n78
69.1	209n31

Flight

| 1.180 | 95n112 |
| 4 | 64n279 |

Good Person

1.58	95n112
1.105	95n112
65.1	209n31
71.3	209n31

Heir

1.81	95n112
1.95	95n112
90	73n343

106	64n279
159	64n279
286	64n279

Joseph

92.2	209n31
245.4	32n68, 33n73, 208n9
250.4	32n68, 33n73, 208n9

Migration

44	73n343
139	64n279
190.1	209n31

Moses

1.2	70n325
1.23	64n279
1.143	95n112
1.202	95n112
1.203	95n112
2.125	95n112
2.186.3	32n68, 33n80
2.213	95n112
2.290	64n279
2.292	64n279
2.67	87n62
2.100	87n62

Names

| 158.4 | 32n68, 73n345, 210n38 |
| 186 | 73n343 |

Περὶ ἀριθμῶν sive Ἀριθμητικά (fragmenta)

41b.8	209n31
49b.2	209n31
54.4	208n9

Planting

| 1.62 | 95n112 |
| 1.69 | 95n112 |

Posterity

1.19	95n112
1.50	95n112

Preliminary Studies

1.3	95n112
1.103	87n62

Questions on Exodus

1.6	64n279
2.19	64n279

Questions on Genesis

3.18	95n112
4.144.4	32n68, 33n82, 208n9

Question on Genesis (fragmenta) Book 4 fragment

144.4	208n9

Rewards

72	73n348
79	64n279
161.4	32n68, 33n75, 208n9

Special Laws

1.65	87n62
1.176	87n62
1.214	64n279
1.309	87n62
1.313	87n62
1.332	87n62
1.345	87n62
1.99	73n348
2.104	64n279
2.159	64n279
2.238	64n279
2.255	87n62
3.125	87n62
3.127	87n62
4.192	87n62

Sacrifices

1.100	95n112

Unchangeable

1.127	95n112
4	73n343
6	64n279

Virtues

1.34	87n62
1.64	87n62
1.102	876n62
41.1	32n68, 33n72, 208n9
216	73n343

Worse

1.44	95n112
1.48	95n112
1.94	95n112
1.153	95n112

MISHNAH, TALMUD, AND RELATED LITERATURE

Babylonian Talmud

Baba Batra

3b	97n129

Berakhot

64a	97n129

Sanhedrin

24a	97n129
98a	68

Tosefta

Shabbat

13.1	64n279

Sanhedrin

7.11	67n305

BIBLICAL AND ANCIENT LITERATURE INDEX 271

OTHER RABBINIC WORKS

Rabbah Leviticus
9.9   61n251, n252

Rabbah Deuteronomy
5.15   61n251

Rabbah Song of Songs
2.33   61n252

Targum Isaiah
40:9   61n255

EARLY CHRISTIAN TEXTS

Athanasius
De incarnatione contra Apollinarium [Apoll.]
26.1161.40   64n279

Augustine
De Doctrina Christiana
4.32   60n243

Clement of Alexandria
Stromata
2.2.8.2.2   67n299
4.16.101.3.5   67n299

Eusebius
Commentary on Isaiah
1.96.25   64n278

Against Marcellus
1.2.17.4   64n279

Demonstration of the Gospel
6.14.1.6   67n302
6.14.3.9   67n302
6.14.8.5   67n299
6.15.2.4   67n302
7.2.53.3   64n279

Ecclesiastical History
5.20.6   94n100

Hippolytus
Refutation of All Heresies
7.23   94n100

Irenaeus
To Florinus   94n100

Jerome
Commentariorum in Michaeum libri II
    30n43

Homiliae XXVIII in Jeremiam et Ezechielem Graeco Origenis Latine redditae
5   30n43

Quaestionum hebraicarum liber in Genesim
31   30n43

John Chrysostom
Homiliae in epistulam i ad Thessalonicenses
1–11   104n175

Justin Martyr
First Apology
26.2   94n100

Dialogue with Trypho

11.4	94n100
35.8	94n100
115.4	94n100
119.6	73n343
132.1	94n100

Origen

Commentarium in evangelium Matthaei

11.11.15	64n278

Contra Celsum

1.46	94n100

Fragmenta ex commentariis in epistulam i ad Corinthios

15.57	44n149
76.5	44n149

Fragmenta in Psalmos

1–150	44n149
38-2-4.28	44n149

Homiliae in Jeremiam

10.8.27	44n149

Homiliae in Lucam

1.11.9	44n149
27.157.5	44n149

Procopius of Gaza

Commentary on Isaiah

PG 87.2253	line 34, 64n278

Pseudo-Clement

Homilies

17.19.7.4	128n352

Theodoret

Epistles

122.32	67n299

Interpretatio in xii prophetas minores

81.1820.18	67n299

ANCIENT WRITERS

Anthologia Palatina

9.229.1	148n124

Aeschines

Ctesiphon

160.4	209n18

Aeschylus

Agamemnon

21	27n15
262	27n16
264	27n17
475	27n15

Appian

Bellum Civila

3.13.93.12	36n103
4.4.20.9	36n103
4.15.113.17	36n103

Mithridatica

152.1	161n213

[Aristides]

Fragmenta

20.2	209n31

Aristophanes

Aves

450   112n223

Equites

643   208n9
647   28n23, 209n18
655–66   28n31
656   28n21, n22, 209n18

Aristotle

Ethica nichomachea

1.3   137n38

Fragmenta varia

Category 8 treatise title 44 fragment 538.12
  209n31

Bolus

Περὶ συμπαθειῶν καὶ ἀντιπαθειῶν *(sub nomine Democriti)*

5.2   209n31

Bruti

Epistulae

30.3   209n31
52.5   209n31

Cicero

Epistulae ad Atticum

2.3.1   28n27, 29n41 182n18,
2.12.1   29n41, 182n18
13.40.1   29n41, 182n18

De officiis

1.31.111   29n42

De oratore

2.36.153   29n42
3.207   60n243

Ctesias

Fragmenta

Jacoby#-F 3c   688,F fragment 26 line 16, 209n18
Jacoby#-F 3c   688,F fragment 26 line 20, 209n18

Demetrius

De elocutione

270   60n243

Diodorus Siculus

Ad Ammaeum

10.53   209n31

Antiquitates Romanae

9.60.6.4   209n31
15.6.3.8   209n31

Bibliotheca Historica

1.6.2   145n105
8.25.1.6   209n31
8.25.4.3   209n31
8.25.4.6   209n31
10.3.1   145n105
12.78.1.6   209n31
14.46.5.4   209n31
14.68.4.4   209n31
15.74.2.2   28n24, 209n29
20.80.4.6   209n31

Diogenes Laertius

Vitae philosophorum

7.45   137n38
9.49.3   64n279

Diogenes of Sinope

Epistulae

23.1.1	28n24, 208n9

Dionysius of Halicarnassus

Antiquitates romanae

1.51.3	64n279
19.10.1	63n269
44.22	161n213

Epictetus

Diatribai

3.1.28–29	112n223
3.13.12	93n97

Euripides

Electra

230	28n31

Orestes

1276	28n31

Phoenissae

975	70n325

Herodotus

Historiae

7.161	70n325

Hesiod

Opera et dies

554	70n325
570	70n325

Hippocrates

De arte

10.21	209n31

Homer

Ilias

24.173	28n29

Odyssea

5.393	73n348
5.480–85	97n129
14.152–53	27n13, 115n242, 179n4, 182n16, 193n61, 209n18
14.166	27n14, 115n242, 179n4, 182n16, 193n61, 209n18

Homeric Hymns

29.9	28n30

Isocrates

Areopagiticus

(orat. 7) 10.4	209n18

Lycurgus

Oratio in Leocratem

18.2	28n24, 208n9

Lysias

Δήμου καταλύσεως πολογία

30.8	209n31

Menander

Georgos

83	28n26, 208n9

Perikeiromenē

874	28n27
993	28n27, 209n18

Nicolaus

Fragmenta

9.33	28n24, 208n9
66.103	28n32
134–39	28n33

Nymphodorus

Fragmenta

15.3	209n31

Philostratus

Vita Apollonii

5.8.3	28n21

Plato

Phaedo

77c	137n38

Protagoras

313c d	148n124

Timaeus

40e	137n38

Plutarch

Agesilaus

33.5.1	36n103

Alcibiades

16.4	167n249

Camillus

11.2	112n223

Cato Major

1.2	145n105

Cato Minor

51.1.4	28n21

Demetrius

17	27n20
17.6.7	36n103
11.4.5	28n21

De facie

942.B.10	64n279

De Fato

570d9	161n213

De Gloria Atheniensium, 36n103

De Iside et Osiride

353.B.5	64n279
383.E.8	64n279

Fabius Maximus

21.3	145n106

Phocion

16.8.1	28n21

Praecepta gerendae rei publicae

799.F.6	28n21

Pyrrhus

6.7.4	63n269
21.3.3	63n269

Sertorious

11	28n23

Polybius

Histories

3.48.12	46n162
3.7.3.3	209n31
3.61.3	46n162
4.53.2.6	209n31
11.1–5	112n221
30.25.1.5	209n31

Publius Rutilius Lupus

De Figuris Sententiarum et Elocutionis

1.13	60n243

Quintilian

Institutio Oratoria

2.15.3	136n29
5.10.7	137n39
9.3.54–57	60n243

Rhetorica ad Herennium

4.25.34	60n243

Speusippus

Epistula ad Philippum regem [Sp.]

Page 9 line 6	209n18

Strabo

Geographica

14.1.31.11	209n31

Theognis

Elegiae

1.573–74	28n31
1.574	28n30

Theophrastus

Characteres

17.7.1	28n25, 208n25

Thucydides

History of the Peloponnesian War

1.23.5	112n220

Xenophon

Agesilaus

1.33	136n24

Anabasis

2.5.38.4	209n31
6.1.18	70n325

Hellenica

1.6.37.2	209n18
4.3.14.1	209n18
4.3.23	73n348

APOSTOLIC FATHERS

Barnabas

12.6	136n24
13.7	73n343

1 Clement

10.6	73n343
45.2	64n279
47.1	129n366
54.1	100n145
65.1	62n261

2 Clement

19.4	88n70

Didache

6.3	86

Ignatius

To the Magnesians

11.1	100n145

To the Philadelphians

1.1	100n145
5.2	88n70

To the Smyrnaeans

1.1 100n145

Polycarp

To the Philippians

5.2 124n319

PAPYRI

PCorn (Greek Papyri in the Library of Cornell University)

52 106n183

PMich (Michigan Papyri)

3.209.6	106n183
8.479.4–5	106n183

POxy (The Oxyrhynchus Papyri)

113.20	106n183
3063.11–16	106n183

Name Index

Abbott-Smith, Georges, 83n33, 139n50
Achtemeier, Elizabeth, 61n250
Achtemeier, Paul J., 65n288, 169n267
Alexander, Loveday, 118n268
Allen, Leslie C., 162n218
Allison, Dale C., 38n114, 39n121, 122, 97n129, 104n59
Anderson, R. Dean, 60n243
Ashton, John, 191n48
Asting, Ragnar Kristian, 7n44
Atkinson, Kenneth, 57n227
Aune, David E., 159n195

Balz, Horst, 112n223
Barclay, John M. G., 36n101, 99, 200, 204,
Barnett, Paul, 70n 326, 191n51, 195n68
Barrett, C. K., 42n138, 42n140, 43n144, 52n196, 70nn325–26, 71n331, 72n338, 127n350, 134n12, 138n47, 142n75, 142n77, 144n94, 147n115, 149n127, 151n147, 159n198, 161n209, 162n220, 162n225, 164n238, 165n239, 166nn242–44, 168n252, 174n298, 175n308, 176n312
Bates, Matthew W., 52n199, 54n213, 56n222, 69n323
Bauckham, Richard., 89n75
Baum, Armin D., 38n115
Baumgartner, Walter, 31n50
Baur, Ferdinand Christian, 6nn38–40, 103n165

Beale, G. K., 56n221
Beare, Francis Wright, 121n295, 124n321
Beaudean, John William, 54n209
Beavis, Mary Ann, 38n113
Becker, Ulrich, 2, 201n93
Beetham, Frank, 113n216
Behm, Johannes, 59n240
Beker, J. Christiaan, 11, 12n87, 79n3
Bell, Richard H., 103n165
Belleville, Linda L., 85n50, 188n36
Benoit, Pierre, 42n136, 119n281
Berger, Klaus, 95n114
Bertram, Georg, 86n51, 106n183, 127n350, 195n70
Best, Ernest, 48n171, 49nn174–77, 50n180, 50n182, 50n188, 50n190, 80n10, 83n30, 84nn39–40, 88n73, 90n83, 90n85, 91n90, 93, 100n50, 102n161, 104n175, 120n283, 170n269,
Betz, Hans Dieter, 72n335, 72n340, 73n344, 73n349, 114n237, 115n240, 150n137, 159n196
Bird, Michael F., 200n85
Bishop, Jonathan, 2n16
Bittlinger, Arnold, 96n117
Bloomquist, Gregory, 120n283,
Bock, Darrell L., 39n118
Bockmuehl, Markus N. A.,118n263, 118n265, 118n267, 118n269, 119n271, 121n294, 122n308, 123n313, 124n328, 126n340, 128n 357, 128nn359–60, 129n366
De Boer, Martinus C., 133n3

NAME INDEX

Boers, Hendrikus W., 2, 103n165
Borg, Marcus J.,
Borgen, Peder, 32n67, 32n69
Bormann, Paul, ix, 10, 19n142
Bornkamm, Günther, 10, 12, 17n136, 23n146, 142n77, 142n80
Bortone, Pietro, 84n43, 44
Bourke, Trevor J, 84n39, 95n108, 192n54, 59
Bovon, François, 38n118
Bowman, John W., 26n11
Bray, Gerald L., 6n33
Brewer, Raymond R., 124n320
Broer, Ingo, 135n20
Brooke, Alan E., 128n351
Brown, Colin, 95n110,
Brown, Michael Joseph, 63, 64n273,
Brown, Raymond E., 38n118, 78n, 117n252, 117n254, 133n3, 172n289,
Bruce, F. F., 1n2, 11n80, 43n144, 48n171, 50n181, 72n340, 83n35, 88n72, 92n92, 96n117, 101n153, 103n167, 108n200, 155n174, 176n313
Bryskog, Samuel, 63n268
Büchsel, Friedrich, 52n200
Bullmore, Michael A., 94n107
Bultmann, Rudolf, 9, 18, 26, 94n107, 99n138, 109n208, 128n352
Burk, Denny, 168n256
Burrows, Millar, 26n12
Burton, Ernest de Witt, 107n188, 107n192
Buttmann, Alexander, 29n37
Byrne, Brendan, 169n267

Caird, George B., 121n295, 123n317, 200n88
Calhoun, Robert Matthew, 160n207, 168n255
Cambier, Jules, 144n96
Campbell, Douglas A., 2,16, 17, 79n3, 85n50, 92n94,156, 157, 201
Carson, Don A., 55n221
Cassidy, Richard J., 35n99
Catchpole, David R., 38n115, 39n120
Chan-Hie, Kim, 149n128

Charlesworth, James H., 57n229
Ciampa, Roy E., 136n33
Clark, Kenneth W., 84n38,
Coggins, Richard J., 61n250
Cohen, Naomi G.,
Coleman, Rachel, 41n183–84
Collange, Jean-François, 127n344, 129n364, 130
Collins, John J., 57n227,
Collins, Raymond F., 49n177, 71n331, 97n124, 109n208, 138n43,
Conzelmann, Hans, 146, 52n199, 53n202, 95n114, 97n126, 136n26, 27, 141n68, 146n109
Cosby, Michael R., 59n240
Cotter, Wendy, 95n113
Cousar, Charles B., 14n108
Cranfield, Charles E. B., 46n156, 54n208, 59n240, 61n247, 63n265, 65n282, 65n290, 66n291, 68n308, 315, 317, 69n319, 161nn212–14, 162n215, 162n217, 162n220, 163n229, 164nn237–38, 168n256, 169n267, 171n281, 171n283, 172n285–86, 172n288, 174n302, 174n305, 175n309, 176n312
Creed, John M., 39n118, 43n145,
Cremer, Hermann, 169n260
Crossan, John Dominic, 95n111
Cullmann, Oscar, 17, 144n96

Dahl, Nils A., 142n80
Dalman, Gustaf., 37n106, 43n145
Dalton, William J., 118n262
Davies, William D.,17, 38n114, 97n129, 112n224
Davis, Basil S., 168n258
Dawson, Audrey, 116n246
Debrunner, Albert, 83n33
Deissmann, Adolf, 8, 9nn61–62, 26n12, 121n293, 179
De Jonge, Marinus, 61n252
Delling, Gerhard, 52n200, 99n142, 109n206
Denis, Albert-Marie, 41n133
De Silva, David A., 43n142

Dibelius, Martin, 9, 43n143, 50n195, 85n49, 122n302, 179
Dickson, John P., 26n12, 35n96
Dines, Jennifer M., 30n44, 30nn46-47
Dobschütz, Ernst von, 49n178, 87n64
Dockery, David S., 66n298
Dodd, Charles H., 8, 56n221, 67n300, 163n231, 163n233, 179
Donfried, Karl Paul, 80n9
Doudna, Greg, 57n226
Downs, David J., 149n125, 175n306
Dunn, James D. G., 1n5,6, 13, 14, 23, 26, 39n120, 42n134, 44n150, 46n160, 162, 163, 50n183, 54n212, 213, 54n, 59n238, 240, 242, 61n248, 62n260, 63n271, 64n277, 65n284, 66n297, 67n305, 72n335, 73n350, 91n87, 88, 96n121, 97n127, 107n192, 113n230, 113n234, 114n238, 116n244, 145n99, 155n170, 156n182, 159n199, 200, 202, 160n208, 161n210, 162n221, 222, 223, 224,162, 163n228, 230, 231, 232, 164n238, 165n239, 166n241, 167n250, 168n259, 169, 170n269, 171n282, 172n284, 173n290, 174n298, 299, 174n300, 304, 175n307, 188n36, 201
Dupont, Jacques, 42n136

Eastman, Susan, 74n357
Edwards, James R., 170n269
Edwards, Mark J., 126n341
Eichrodt, Walther, 96n116
Elliott, James Keith, 6n37,
Elliott, Neil, 17n144, 77n366
Ellis, Edward Earle, 58n234, 60n245, 66n297, 103n167
Esler, Philip F., 65n290, 141n72
Evans, Craig A., 55n221
Eve, Eric, 95n111

Fabry, Heinz-Josef, 67n303
Fallon, Francis T., 154n167
Fee, Gordon D., 49n173, 52n200, 59n240, 71n328, 96n123, 98n135, 103n167, 117n250, 117n261, 118n263, 119n270, 120n288, 290, 121n296, 123n310, 123n312, 123n325, 123nn330-331, 123n333, 127n346, 128n355, 129n361, 129n366, 130nn369-70, 130n377, 134n13, 135nn15-16, 136n33, 137n42, 139n52, 140nn61-62, 141n64, 141n66, 141n70, 142n77, 143n85, 143n89, 144n95, 145nn97-98, 196n72
Fewster, Gregory P., 123n316
Findlay, George G., 96n117, 96n120, 96n123
Fishbane, Michael, 181n8
Fisk, Bruce N., 159n195
Fitzer, Gottfried, 70n325
Fitzmyer, Joseph A., 12, 17n144, 19, 38n118, 42n136, 43n145, 147, 61n248, 252, 63n265, 66n294, 90n80, 137n41, 133n5, 138n45, 139n56, 142n76, 143n85, 165n239, 170, 174n305
Fjärstedt, Biörn, 39n122, 140n59
Fowl, Stephen E., 120n287, 122n305, 128n356, 129n368
France, Richard T., 38n113
Friedrich, Gerhard, 26n5, 26n12, 30n51, 30n54, 32, 37, 75, 93n100, 192, 198, 199n84, 201n90
Furnish, Victor P., 2n7, 4n28, 10, 18n141, 127n350, 147n116, 149n129, 149n132, 151n147, 152n155, 153n156

Garland, David E., 118nn264-65, 118n267, 135n16, 138n44, 139n54
Gaston, Lloyd, 17n136
Gathercole, Simon, 143n85
Gaventa, Beverly Roberts, 142nn78-79, 142n81
Gerhardsson, Birger, 52n200
Gillespie, Thomas W.,97n125
Glombitza, Otto, 129n363

NAME INDEX

Gnilka, Joachim, 121n295
Goldingay, John, 41n131
Goodacre, Mark, 38n115
Goppelt, Leonhard, 11
Gorman, Michael J., 2, 15, 16n121, 122, 193n62, 201
Goulder, Michael D., 6n37, 38n115, 175n308
Gräbe, Petrus J., 13n100
Grayston, Kenneth, 69n322
Green, Samuel G., 29n37,
Greenman, Jeffrey P., 6n33
Grimm, Carl Ludwig Wilibald, 145n106
Grudem, Wayne A., 98n133
Grundmann, Walter, 93n100, 94n100
Guthrie, Donald, 72n338, 107n192, 114n238

Haenchen, Ernst, 42n136
Hagner, Donald A., 78n1
Hahn, Ferdinand, 55n216
Hall, David R., 133n3
Hannah, Darrell D., 57n228, 229, 230
Hansen, G. Walter, 72n335
Hanson, Anthony T., 56n221
Hanson, Richard P. C., 42n139
Harnack, Adolf von, 7nn43–45, 17n136, 26n12, 48n136, 75n358, 86n54, 201n92
Harrington, Daniel J., 66n298
Harris, Horton, 6n36
Harris, Murray J., 82n26, 82n29, 84n41, 84n44, 147nn112–15, 148n119, 148nn121–22, 149, 126, 150nn141–42, 151n143, 151n146, 152n120, 154n165, 155n171, 195n70
Harrisville, Roy A., 156n175
Hart, Michael H., 1n1,
Havener, Ivan, 90n83, 91n86
Hawthorne, Gerald F., 118n269, 119n271, 119n280, 119n282, 123n310, 124n322, 125nn331–32, 126n342, 141n71
Hays, Richard B., 56n222, 58n233, 65nn282–83, 66n292, 72n334, 72n341, 74n352, 139n53, 143n84, 143n85, 167n246, 167nn247–48, 173n292
Headlam, Arthur C. 158n193
Hemer, Colin J., 42n136
Hengel, Martin, 48n169, 113n231, 167n245
van Henton, Jan Willem, 43n142
Hercher, Rudolphus, 209n31
Héring, Jean, 142n81
Hiestermann, Heinz, 39n121
Higbie, Carolyn, 29n42
Hilgenfeld, Adolphus, 41n133
Hofius, Otfried, 46n162, 188n34
Hollander, Harm W., 39n122
Holloway, Paul A., 117n252, 117n261, 118n262
Hooker, Morna D., 48n172, 49n177, 50n180, 50n105, 51nn193–94, 97n129, 124n326, 141n73
Horbury, William, 26n12, 37nn106–9
Hornblower, Simon, 35n99
Horsley, Richard A., 139n53
Hübner, Hans, 198n80
Hughes, Philip E., 70n326
Hultgren, Arland J., 13n100
Hume, David, 95n110
Hunter, Archibald Macbride, 144n96
Hurtado, Larry, 124n326

Jellicoe, Sidney, 30n47
Jeremias, Joachim, 53n202, 142n76, 143n88
Jervell, Jacob, 42n136, 104n174
Jervis, L. Ann, 156n179
Jewett, Robert, 42n137, 54n210, 54nn212–13, 55n214, 55n216, 60n247, 61n248, 62n257, 62n259, 62n264, 63n269, 64n273, 64n277, 65n281, 66n291, 66n297, 68n311, 68n314, 80n9, 120n283, 122nn300–301, 122nn303–4, 156nn177–78, 156n181, 159n196, 159n202, 161n213, 163n227, 163nn231–32, 163n234, 164n236, 167n249, 168n257, 169n266, 169n268, 171n282,

NAME INDEX

174nn301–2, 174n305, 175n310, 198n83,
Johnson, Allan C., 35n93
Johnson, Nathan C., 157n189

Kaiser, Otto, 41n129
Käsemann, Ernst, 2n8, 10, 61n248, 65n286, 66n291, 69nn321–22, 77n366, 99n139, 124n326, 142n77, 152n151, 152n156, 152n76, 168, 169n267, 172n284, 172n287, 174n303
Kaye, Bruce N., 6n41
Kea, Perry, 42n136
Keck, Leander E., 65n290
Keener, Craig S., 42n130
Kellermann, Ulrich, 121n292
Kelly, J. N. D., 52n198, 186n27
Kierkegaard, Søren, 203, 204n96
Kim, Seyoon, 49n177, 86n55
Kim, Yung Suk, 81n20, 125n332
Kittel, Gerhard, 95n112
Klaiber, Walter, 156n175
Klein, Günther, 156n179
Kloppenborg, John S., 38n115, 39, 119, 144n96
Knibb, Michael A., 57n230
Koch, Dietrich-Alex, 56, 58n234, 75n361
Koehler, Ludwig., 30n50
Koperski, Veronica, 118n262
Kraft, Robert A., 37n105
Kramer, Werner, 52n201, 55n216, 144n96
Krentz, Edgar M., 124n327, 127n348
Krodel, Gerhard, 26n6, 26n11
Kümmel, Werner Georg, 6n34, 9, 10, 11n79, 26n11, 156n183, 157n184

Laffi, Umberto, 34n91
Lambrecht, Jan, 51n193
Lang, Friedrich Gustav, 97n126, 149n131
Lange, Armin, 87n62
Langevin, Paul-Émile, 88n71
Larsen, Timothy, 6n33
Lenski, Richard C. H., 142n81, 143n87
Lewis, Naphtali, 34n91,

Lietaert Peerbolte, L. J., 191n51
Lietzmann, Hans, 142n81
Lightfoot, J. B., 6, 7n42, 13, 130, 72n335, 72n339, 100n151, 104n170, 104n176, 107n193, 112n219, 119n279, 120nn288–89, 122n299, 123n311, 129n364, 130n375, 150n174, 155n174
Lincoln, Andrew T., 2n15
Lindars, Barnabas, 56n221
Lindemann, Andreas, 71n332
Linko, Jaakko, 118n262
Linnemann, Eta, 54n212
Litwak, Kenneth D., xi, 56n222
Locke, John, 95n110
Longenecker, Bruce W., 14m107,
Longenecker, Richard N.,42n137, 56n221, 72n337, 106n177, 106n183, 107nn188–89, 107n193, 108n197, 113n230, 114nn236–37, 158n194, 161n211
Louth, Andrew, 190n44, 191n48
Lüdemann, Gerd, 1n4, 42n138, 48n171, 129n367
Lundbom, Jack R., 87n62
Lust, Johan, 208
Luz, Ulrich, 38n114,

Maccoby, Hyam, 1n3
MacGorman, Jack W., 96n117
Malinowski, Francis X., 127n348, 128n354
Mansoor, Menahem, 94n105
Marcos, Natalio Fernández, 30n44
Marshall, I. Howard, 38nn117–18, 80n9, 103n163, 103n167, 104n175, 124n326, 172n289
Martin, Dale B.,141n68
Martin, Ralph P., 2n9, 70n325, 96n117, 118n265, 118n269, 119n271, 119n280–81, 121n291, 121n295, 123n310, 123n316, 124n322, 124n326, 125nn330–32, 126n342, 127n343, 133n3, 141n71, 147n115, 148n121, 149n125, 149nn129–30, 151n147, 152n150, 152n152, 153n161, 154n167

Martyn, J. Louis, 75n358, 107n190, 107n192, 167n251
Mason, Steve, 33n83
Matera, Frank J., 153n157
McFarland, Ian A., 3n20
McKnight, Scot, 13n97, 19
Meeks, Wayne A., 47n166
Menken, Maarten J. J., 45n152
Metzger, Bruce M., 81n18, 103n166, 106n184, 199n108, 135n16
Meyer, Rudolf, 159n196,
Michael, J. Hugh, 123n309
Michaelis, Wilhelm, 46n159, 73n348
Michel, Otto, 62n260, 65n281, 159n201
Miller, Ernest C., 124n322
Milligan, George, 49nn177–78, 84n37, 86n55, 89n74
Molland, Einar, 172n288
Mommsen, Theodore, 34n90
Moo, Douglas J., 171n282
Moody Smith, D., 56n221, 57n232, 58n234, 60n245, 66n298
Morris, Jenny, 32n67,
Morris, Leon, 49n177, 86n55, 134n12
Moule, C. F. D., 84n42, 85n46, 114nn237–38, 121n298, 155n172
Moulton, James H., 29nn36–37, 29n39, 49n174, 84n41, 96nn118–19, 119nn277–78
Moyise, Steve, 45n152, 58n234
Müller, Jac. J., 123n309
Mullins, Terence Y., 106n183
Munck, Johannes, 9n68, 49n177, 51n192, 51n194, 81n192, 81n94, 86n53, 86n55, 86n57, 87nn64–65, 159n195, 176n312
Murphy-O'Connor, Jerome, 52n199, 53nn203–4

Nanos, Mark D., 18n136, 18n140, 107n188
Neil, William, 49n177, 51n195, 86n55, 171n282
Neuenzeit, Paul, 142n77
Neufeld, Vernon H., 55n215, 144n96, 163n231
Neugebauer, Fritz, 122n303

Nolland, John, 30n114, 38n115
Norden, Eduard, 55n210

Oakes, Peter, 120n283, 124n326, 126n336
O'Brien, Peter T., 48n172, 106n182, 118n269, 118n269, 119n271, 119n73, 119n76, 121n291, 121n294, 122n306, 123nn314–15, 125n332, 127n345, 128n353, 129nn365–66
Oden, Thomas C. 6n33
Okeke, George E., 103n165
O'Mahony, Kieran J., 150n137
O'Neill, John C., 171n282
O'Rourke, J. J., 82n29
Orr, William F., 71n328

Panikulam, George, 119n274
Parry, R. St. John, 141n69
Pearson, Birger A., 103n165
Perkins, Pheme, 136n22
Pervo, Richard I., 42n136, 43n143, 43n147
Peterman, Gerald W., 120n287, 128nn357–58, 129n368
Pfann, Stephen J., 57n226
Pfitzner, Victor C., 124n327
Pick, Bernhard, 32n69
Plevnik, Joseph, 2
Plummer, Alfred, 49n177, 96n117, 96n122, 96n123, 127n350, 134n12, 136n33, 137n40, 145n98, 154n162, 195nn69–70
Pogoloff, Stephen M., 136n30
Pokorný, Petr, 26, 76n364
Polhill, John B., 136n32
Poole, Matthew, 27n19
Porter, Stanley E., 29n40, 34n89, 121n290
Poythress, Vern S., 55n213
Prat, Fernand, 97n127
Pretorius, Mark, 2n10
Price, Simon R. F., 35n97
Pryke, Eric J., 38n113

Rackham, Richard B., 43n143

NAME INDEX 285

Radl, Walter, 145n101, 146n107, 196n71,
Rajak, Tessa, 33n83
Ramsay, William M., 29n36
Rappaport, Uriel, 30n44
Reed, Jeffrey T., 118n262, 118n267, 121n290,
Re'emi, S. Paul, 61n250
Reichert, Angelica, 156n179
Reinhold, Meyer, 34n91
Remus, Harold, 95n113
Rengstorf, Karl H., 62n261
Reuf, John, 134n12
Richard, Earl J., 48n171, 49n175, 49n177, 51nn191–92, 101n153, 101n157, 102n160, 103n166
Richardson, Peter, 156n179
Ridderbos, Herman N., 72n340
Riesner, Rainer, 79n2
Robertson, A. T., 29n37, 96n119, 147n113, 149n127
Robertson, Archibald, 96n117, 96n122–23, 134n12, 136n33, 137n40, 145n98,
Robinson, William C., 136n33
Roller, Otto, 164n236
Rosner, Brian S., 134n12, 136n33
Ruemann, John, 118n262, 119n275, 124n324, 129n366, 130n372
Ryle, Herbert E., 32n69

Saldarini, Anthony J., 159n196
Sanday, William, 158n193
Sanders, Ed P., 2, 11, 12, 19, 82n21, 85n47, 89n76
Sanders, Ernest W.,
Saunders, Stanley P., 118n266
Scheck, Thomas P., 30n43
Schenk, Wolfgang, 133n3,
Schilling, Othma, 31n50
Schlatter, Adolf, 7, 65n284
Schlier, Heinrich, 91n87, 108n201, 121n293,
Schmithals, Walter, 108n201, 133nn2–3,
Schnabel, Eckhard J., 191n51
Schnackenburg, Rudolf, 128n351

Schneemelcher, Wilhelm, 25n4
Schneider, Gerhard, 43n141
Schnelle, Udo, 1n5, 2, 14, 23, 201
Schniewind, Johannes, 135n18, 142n80, 143n83
Schniewind, Julius, 7, 31n50, 61n255
Schoeps, Hans J., 9, 10n69
Schrage, Wolfgang, 52n200, 134n9
Schreiber, Stefan, 195n70
Schreiner, Thomas R., 18n136
Schrenk, Gottlob, 64n279, 112n223
Schubert, Paul, 106n182
Schürer, Emil, 28n33
Schütz, John Howard, 139n55, 147n115
Schweitzer, Albert, 2, 8
Seager, Robin, 57n227
Seccombe, David Peter, 41n128
Seesemann, Heinrich, 119n272
Seifrid, Mark A., 61nn251–53, 61n256
Sherk, Robert K., 34n91, 35n92
Shum, Shiu-Lun, 68n314
Silva, Moises, 119n270
Sirinelli, Jean, 67n302
Smalley, Stephen S., 128n351
Snodgrass, Klyne R., 56n221
Soards, Marion L., 168n256
Souter, Alexander, 29n36
Spallek, Andrew J., 199n84
Spicq, Ceslas, 148n118
Stählin, Gustav, 112n308, 139n50
Stanley, Christopher D., 56n222, 68n310, 68n313, 72nn338–39, 72n342
Stanton, Graham N., 18, 26, 35
Stemberger, Günther, 67n305
Stendahl, Krister, 158n195
Stevens, Gerald L., 168n256
Stewart-Sykes, Alistair, 133n3
Still, Todd D., 81n20, 85n47
Stone, Michael E., 57n229
Stowers, Stanley K., 173n295,
Strack, Hermann. L., 67n305
Strathmann, Hermann, 67n305
Strecker, Georg, 26n12
Strobel, August, 167n247
Stuart, Douglas, 31n61

NAME INDEX

Stuhlmacher, Peter, 26, 46n163, 53n220, 61n251, 254, 255, 68n316
Suggs, M. Jack, 129n362
Sumney, Jerry L., 1n3, 47n165, 48n171, 52n199, 54n213, 154n168
Suter, David W., 57n229
Swete, Henry B., 30n46

Tabor, James D., 1n3
Tasmuth, Randar, 76n363
Tatum, Gregory, 42n137
Taubes, Jacob, 200n85
Taylor, Lily Ross, 130n374
Thayer, Joseph H., 145n106
Theissen, Gerd, 39n120
Thiselton, Anthony C., 52n196, 53n206, 97n126, 98n130, 98n134, 113n228, 134n9, 135n16, 136n22, 136n26, 138n43, 141n65, 141n74, 143nn85-86, 144n90, 145n98, 145n100
Thrall, Margaret E., 10n74, 46n156, 70n325, 120n285, 127n350, 133n3, 142n81, 147n112, 149nn127-28, 149n131, 150n137, 150n139
Tobin, Thomas H., 60n243
Toher, Mark, 28n33
Torrey, Charles C., 42n136, 43n144
Tov, Emmanuel, 37n105, 57n226
Trebilco, Paul R., 117n253
Tuckett, Christopher M., 38n115, 39nn121-22, 40n127
Twelftree, Graham H., xn2, 4n30, 39n121, 41n128, 46n157, 48n168, 71n330, 81n16, 93n99, 94nn101-3, 95n109, 99n136, 100n147, 107n186, 111n218, 116m246, 132n1, 135n16, 136n31, 140n59, 175n308, 184n24, 191nn46-48, 195nn66-67.

Ulrich, Eugene, 67n303
Usteri, Leonhard, 6,

Viereck, Paul, 34n91
Vincent, Marvin R., 120n286, 122n309, 123n311, 129n364, 129n366
Volf, Judith M. Gundry, 141n73

Wagner, J. Ross, 56n222, 61n256, 62n263, 63nn265-66, 68n312, 181n8
Walther, James Arthur, 71n328
Wanamaker, Charles A., 86n55, 91n86
Watson, Francis, 18n136, 73n343, 74, 93n95, 167n251, 173
Weatherly, Jon A., 103n165
Weaver, Paul R. C., 63n272, 64nn273-74
Wedderburn, Alexander J. M., 156n179
Weigold, Matthias, 87n62
Weiss, Hans Friedrich, 159n196
Weiss, Johannes, 142n81,
Wengst, Klaus, 55n216
Wenham, David, 18n136
White, John L., 106n183
Whiteley, Denys E. H., 9n68, 83, 89n74, 91n89
Whitsett, Christopher G., 55n213
Wilckens, Ulrich, 2n12
Wilcox, Max, 43n144
Wiliamowitz-Moellendorff, Ulrich von, 34n90
Wilk, Florian, 57n232, 61nn251-52
Wilson, Barrie, 1n3
Wilson, Robert McL., 155n170
Windisch, Hans, 147n115, 148n124
Wink, Walter, 57n232, 200n88
Witherington, Ben, 18n136, 118n269, 123n311
Wojtkowiak, Heiko, 156n175
Wolff, Christian, 135n16, 149n131, 152n153
Wolff, Hans Walter, 59n239
Wolter, Michael, 2, 16, 18, 19, 23, 179, 200n85, 201
Woude, Adam S. van der, 61n252
Watson, Francis, 17n136, 73n343, 74, 93n95, 167n251, 173,

Wrede, William, 1n4
Wright, N. T., 4, 9n65, 13, 14, 17, 23, 29n35, 146n109, 163n226, 200n85, 201
Wright, Robert B., 41n133, 57nn227–28,

Yeung, Maureen W., 97n129

Zahl, Paul F. M., 9n65
Zeller, Dieter, 62n260
Zerwick, Maximilian, 148n119, 152n150, 158n191
Zetterholm, Magnus, 18n140
Ziegler, Joseph, 68n312
Ziesler, John, 59n242
Zuntz, Günther, 60n247

Subject Index

Acts of the Apostles
   and Paul, 36, 42–45, 79, 87, 132
   "gospel" 38n116
"announce," (ἀπαγγέλλω), 207, 208n3
"association" (κοινωνία), 108, 119,
   120n289
atonement, 8
Augustus inscription. *See* Priene
   Calendar Inscription.
baptism, 138–45
Baur, Ferdinand Christian, 6, 103n165
Beelzebul Controversy, 94n101
Beker, J. Christiaan, 11–12
Bennett, Rachel, xi
Bornkamm, Günther, ix, 10, 12, 23
Bultmann, Rudolf, 9, 18, 26, 167

Campbell, Douglas A., xi, 2, 4, 16,
   17–18, 201
"charismata" (χαρίσματα), 95–99, 115,
   119, 138, 190
chronology of letters, 79
conversion, 6, 13, 43, 49–51, 86, 93,
   165
co-worker of God. *See* Fellow workers.
Corinthian church, 132–33
Corinthian letters, 132–55
   gospel in, 146–47, 154–55
creeds and creedal, 9, 47–56, 65, 69,
   74, 76–77, 78, 90, 91n86, 104,
   145, 160–61, 163–64, 185–86,
   200

Dead Sea Scrolls, 36, 41, 57, 67n303,
   94

Deissmann, Adolf, 8–9, 179
"demonstration" or "proof"
   (ἀπόδειξις), 94, 136–37, 146,
   192, 200
Dibelius, Martin, 9, 179
discernment, 96–98
Dodd, C. H., 8, 179
Dunn, James D. G., x, 4, 13–14, 23,
   26, 162, 167, 169, 201

Early Christians. *See* Gospel, Early
   Christian use.
embodied gospel, 15, 18–19, 22–24,
   85, 87–88, 92, 104–5, 111, 116,
   123–26, 128, 130, 154, 188,
   192–94, 198, 204
emperor (empire), emperor cult,
   25–26, 36–37, 55, 162, 200n85,
   204
   and gods, 35
   and gospel, 28, 34–35, 76, 162–63,
   180, 183
   savior, 75, 126, 130
Epaphroditus, 117, 128
eschatology, 2, 14, 35, 37, 40, 50, 61,
   74, 88, 105, 143, 167, 171, 176,
   201, 202
exorcism, 99, 190, 201
expiation, 170

faith, 8, 14, 16, 18–19, 22–23, 58,
   65–67, 72–73, 84n39, 99n141,
   104, 111, 114–16, 119, 123–24,
   136, 142n79, 155, 164–65, 170,
   173, 179, 181, 203

SUBJECT INDEX

faith *(continued)*
  charism, 96–98
  obedience of, 157, 164, 172
fellow workers, 22–23, 103n167, 119, 127
"fullness" (πληροφορία), 81, 99–100
Fitzmyer, Joseph A., 12, 19, 170

Galatian church, 105–106
Galatians, 105–16
  Gospel in, 116
Gentiles, obedience of, 15, 20, 175, 177
gifts (of the Spirit). *See* "charismata."
Goppelt, Leonhard, 11
Gorman, Michael J., xi, 4, 15–16, 18–19, 193, 201
Gospel
  בשורה (noun), 37
  בשר (verb), 30, 31n50, 37
  εὐαγγελία (feminine noun), 28–31, 33n84, 34n86, n88, 36, 79n4, 182, 207, 209n18, n19, n29, n30
  εὐαγγέλιον (neuter noun), 3n22, 7–8, 10n74, 11n86, 19, 27, 31n60, 32, 33n84, 34n88, 35, 37–38, 43–44, 48n167, 51, 54, 62, 64–65, 75, 79–82, 100n151, 101n154, 102, 104–105, 109–110, 115n242, 117, 119, 121, 126, 133, 139n48, 144, 146–52, 154–55, 158–60, 171–72, 174–76, 178–80, 182–83, 193–94, 198–201, 207, 209n18
  εὐαγγελίζω (verb), 3n27, 19, 28n24, 30–34, 36, 39, 54, 76, 80, 104–5, 109, 113n230, 140n63, 147, 151, 154, 165, 174–175, 177–78, 180, 182, 194, 207
    translating, 30–31, 54n209, 109n208, 134, 138
  antiquity, 115–16
  before Paul, 25–77
  beginning of, 22, 35, 128–29, 183
  brings salvation, 2, 6, 9, 11, 14–17, 19, 31–33, 41, 44–45, 47, 61–63, 65–66, 74–76, 84, 130, 134–35, 143, 145–47, 165–71, 173–74, 177, 180–84, 189–91, 193–94, 200, 202
  call of God, 59, 63, 88–89, 107–8, 116, 170, 173, 192
  change and development, 10, 46, 79, 169, 179, 189, 194, 196–98
  of Christ, 20–23, 103–4, 106–8, 123–26, 139, 147–48, 150–51, 175–76, 188, 191, 204
  coming, 11, 40, 51, 82–83, 100, 105, 107, 112, 147–48, 150n141, 151, 153, 164, 179, 185, 189–90, 199, 201
  complete (πληρόω), 175–76
  composite, 191–93, 195, 197, 200–201
  content, 5–8, 11, 15, 24n151, 37, 44, 48, 65, 124, 130n371, 134, 148, 180, 185–93
  defined, 13–19, 56, 58, 156, 165–66, 169, 173, 176–177, 184–94, 198–202
  different/another, 21, 106, 108, 112–13, 116, 151–54, 202–3
  early Christian use, 36–45
  embodied. *See* embodied gospel.
  embodying God's power, 4, 13, 17–18, 23–24, 78, 167, 178–79
  empowered message, ix, 4, 18, 24, 84, 178, 184–85, 190–92, 198–99, 201–202
  enemies of, 20, 68, 174
  ethical implications, 13, 89, 139, 147, 151, 193
  experienced, 72–74, 77, 85, 93, 100, 105, 111–16, 120–21, 146, 180–81, 184, 189–91, 193, 196, 199, 202–3
  of God, 16, 19–20, 22, 23, 63, 87, 101–2, 104, 108, 153–54, 157, 159, 174–75, 189
  loving kindness, 169, 177
  power, 14, 16, 19, 168, 190
  presence, 105, 148, 198, 200, 203
  salvation, 31n62, 41, 56, 76, 181, 200, 202
  salvific drama, 189–91, 193, 200

good news, 7, 12–15, 18n140, 27–29, 31–33, 35–37, 40, 58, 61–62, 80, 87, 115n242, 119n275, 146–47, 179–80, 183–84, 187, 207
heard, 40, 42, 44, 60, 62, 164, 199
Herodian Judean, 36–37, 44
of his Son, 19, 165
history of, 27–36
intellectual content, 6, 8, 10, 110
as Jesus Christ, 123–26, 130, 187–89, 204
Jewish source, 180–81
lived. *See* Embodied gospel.
of the Lord's death, 142–43, 187
as message, 191–93
military context, 28, 31, 33, 180, 182,
as ministry of Jesus, 189
and miracle, x, 6, 10, 72, 93–95, 98, 100–101, 109, 111–112, 114–115, 136–38, 146, 168, 184–85, 189–91, 195, 200–203
misunderstood, ix
narrative character, 12, 14–16, 53, 55–56, 92, 174, 177, 185–86, 199
nutshell, in a, 85–93
obedience to, 15, 20–21, 150–51, 164, 172, 175, 177
outline, 16, 18
origin of, 77, 179–84
  early Christians, 36–45, 47–55, 183–84
  Greek 27–29, 34–36, 182–83
  Jewish, 30–34, 180–81
  Latin. *See* Latin influence on Paul
  Revelation, 45–47, 184
  Scripture, 56–75, 181–82
of Paul, 184–94, 198–201
and Paul's message, 85–93, 113
and Paul's work, 113, 126–27, 129n366, 155, 178, 194–96
performative utterance, 15
political, x, 15–16, 28, 33–34, 124, 126, 161n213, 180, 199–200, 204
polyvalent, x, 5, 185, 201–202
power of God, 11, 13, 15–16, 19, 23, 65, 133–36, 137n40, 147, 165–71, 191
preached message, 4–6, 8–12, 16, 22–23, 47, 56, 83, 101–3, 109n202, 110–11, 116, 130, 134, 152, 176, 178–79, 183, 186, 191, 193, 195
presence of Christ, 148, 151, 189
presence of God, 2, 11, 32, 89n74, 100, 148, 182–83, 190, 198, 200, 203
purpose, 119–21, 163–64
realization of, 104, 138–42, 199
replication of Jesus' ministry, 189
revelation, 8, 46, 75n361, 76, 98, 110, 113, 116, 160, 172, 184
scriptural, 56–75, 77, 181–82
social dimension, 16, 204
spoken, 10, 42, 47, 49, 62, 83, 92, 111, 136, 174, 192–93
subversive, 184, 199, 204
in suffering, 123, 130
summary of theology, 14
traditions about Jesus, 47–55, 185–88
truth of, 9, 12, 22, 75, 106, 110–12, 116, 121, 193
Ugaritic background, 30–31
vocabulary, 3, 25–26, 35, 37–38, 42, 44–45, 66, 76, 79–80, 138–40, 163, 183–85, 194, 202, 207–10
as work, 115–16
"gospelled," 21–23, 41, 76, 104, 108–109, 116, 144–46, 154, 176, 195
"gospelling," 3, 20, 25, 48, 93, 109–110, 134–35, 147, 154, 165, 167, 173–74, 176, 179, 189, 194–95, 198–99, 203
grace, ix, xi, 16, 20–22, 43n147, 92, 99, 104, 106–108, 115–16, 119–21, 141, 150, 157, 163–64, 178, 186, 190, 192–93, 200, 202
Gradatio, 60

"hand on" (παραδίδωμι), 52n200, 144n96

Harnack, Adolf von, 7
healing(s), 41–42, 44–45, 77, 95–99, 115, 140, 182–83, 189–90, 194, 199, 201
Holy Spirit. *See*, Spirit, Holy.
Homer, 27, 36, 79, 182
Hymn to Christ (*Carmen Christi*), 91, 122, 124–25, 130, 188

initial message. *See* Missionary message.
idols, 49–50, 85–87, 92, 105, 133, 138–39, 170, 185, 192, 203
Isaiah, 26, 32, 40–42, 44–45, 57, 59–63, 68, 71n329, 74, 77n366, 176, 181–83
"it is written," 20, 60, 61n245, 173

Jesus
 ascension, 91
 crucifixion and death, 8, 12, 14n103, 15, 17, 53, 56, 88, 91–92, 111–13, 116, 135–37, 142–43, 145–46, 153, 166–67, 185–88, 199
 Davidic descent, 55, 157–58, 160–62, 172, 186, 188
 expected from heaven, 49, 86, 88, 91–92, 105, 171, 185, 187, 192, 198
 resurrection, 13, 17, 51, 53–56, 88–92, 138, 145–46, 153, 157, 160–62, 164, 170, 185–87, 192, 199, 204
 suffering, 153, 155
 tradition concerning, 37–42, 56, 140–42, 144–46, 166, 176, 188, 193
Josephus, 33–34, 36, 180–81
justification by faith, ix, 2, 13, 16, 69n322, 112, 170, 178

Kingdom of God, 8, 39n118, 45, 48, 84, 88–89, 94, 108, 140–42, 201
Kümmel, Werner, 9–11, 156

Latin influence on Paul, 29, 55, 76, 180, 182

law, ix, 56, 58, 72, 83n31, 106, 111–12, 114–16, 152, 157, 159, 164, 170, 177–78, 193–95
letters, greeting, 106, 164
 occasional, 79
Lord's Supper, 142–43, 187–88

message and miracles. *See* Miracle(s) and message.
miracle(s), 6, 10, 115, 137, 200
 defined, xn2, 95–99, 191n47
 by God, 191, 195–96, 201–202
 message and, 184–85, 191, 201
 "remarkable things" (παράδοξοι), 95
 workers, 153, 203
mission discourse, 39
missional hermeneutics, 15, 19, 23
missionary message, 5, 85–90, 92–93, 105, 146, 166, 170, 192, 202
mountains removed, 97
"my gospel," 3, 20, 22, 45, 81n17, 158n189, 171–73, 184

Nelson, John, xi
Nicolaus of Damascus, 28

obedience of faith, 157, 164, 172
olive tree metaphor, 141
oral tradition, 37, 42, 51
"our gospel," 3, 21, 22, 45–46, 81–82, 148–49, 171, 184, 190

parousia, 171, 176, 188n34, 192, 198
participationist theology, 2
partners in the gospel. *See* Fellow workers.
Paul
 apostle, 19, 46, 48, 62–63, 120n289, 138, 153, 157, 163–64, 186
 boasting, 20, 70, 153
 call, 11, 46, 48, 55, 74, 71, 77, 133–35, 140, 146, 158–59, 184, 189, 199
 center of his theology, ix, 2–3, 178, 184
 commission. *See* call.
 conversion. *See* call.

dedicated to gospel, 62, 159, 164, 194, 199, 200
defense, 3, 22, 106–7, 109–11, 121–22, 138, 148, 153, 156, 188, 195
development of thinking. *See* Gospel, change and development.
founder of Christianity, 1
illness, 116
impact, 1, 165, 184, 197, 201
imprisonment, 22, 117, 120–22, 155, 166
ministry strategy, 69, 135–37
miracle worker, 203
opponents, 47, 70, 105, 151, 153–54
Pharisee, 159, 194
slave, 63–64, 71, 126
suffering, 117, 101, 120, 122, 124
testimony, 36, 45–56, 76, 183–84, 189
Philemon, 155
Philippian church, 117–18
Philippians, 117–31
 gospel in, 129–31
 suffering, 120n283, 155
Philo, 32–33, 36, 180–81
Priene Calendar Inscription, 34–37, 180–83, 189
"power" (δύναμις), 84, 93–94, 167
"powers" (δυνάμεις), 94n100, 95, 98, 114–115, 137
"preach" (κηρύσσω), 47, 62, 93, 101n156, 109, 110, 116, 122, 134, 135, 152, 154, 173, 188, 195
preaching, 14, 60, 85, 129
 content, 5, 85n50, 199
 gospel, the, 7, 11, 19, 101–3, 177
 not the gospel, x, 11n86, 104, 116, 123, 127, 138, 147, 151, 159, 165, 168, 174, 178–79, 189, 191, 203
 Paul, 9, 11, 23, 85, 110, 113, 134–35, 139, 146, 152, 176, 179, 195–96, 199
"proclaim" (καταγγέλω), 20, 47, 54n207, 109, 113n230, 116–17, 122, 133, 135, 137, 139n48, 140, 142, 188, 195, 207

"proclaim good news in advance" (προευαγγελίζομαι), 32n68, 33, 73, 180, 207
priestly service, 174, 189
prophecy, 96–98

Q tradition, 38–42, 44–45, 48, 56–57, 76, 94n101, 140, 183, 189, 201n92
Qumran. *See* Dead Sea Scrolls.

"receive" (παραλαμβάνω), 52n200, 109, 144n96
reconciliation, 2
redemption, 8, 143, 170
Reformation, ix, 202
resurrection of the dead, 51, 54, 144, 162, 186
revelation (*charism*), 98
righteousness, 8, 16, 65, 72, 73, 168–69, 173, 181, 193
righteousness of God, 8, 56, 65–66, 165, 168–70, 177, 190, 198, 202
Roman church, 156–57
Romans, 156–77
 double character, 156–57
 doxology, 171–73
 gospel in, 177
 purpose, 156
 structure, 169–70
 theme, 169

salvation, 6, 7, 9, 11, 14–17, 19, 31–33, 41, 44–45, 47, 56, 61–63, 65–66, 74–76, 84, 91, 97, 126, 130, 134–35, 143, 145–47, 165–71, 173–74, 177, 180–84, 190–91, 193–94, 200, 202
salvation history, 16
Sanders, E. P., 2, 11–12, 19, 179
Schlatter, Adolf, 7
Schnelle, Udo, 2, 4, 14, 23, 201
Schweitzer, Albert, 7–8
Scripture, 4, 17, 19, 26, 30–33, 36, 45, 52, 56–78, 111–12, 115, 144, 157–58, 160–61, 163, 173, 178, 180–82, 184, 186
 interpreted by experience, 72, 181

Scripture (continued)
   shaped by Paul, 58, 61–64, 67–71, 74–75, 77, 160, 181–82
Semitisms, 53n202, 103n165
Septuagint, 30–33, 36, 41, 53n202, 56–75, 87n62, 169, 208n4
signs and wonders, 10, 15, 20, 175–76, 195–96
   signs of an apostle, 10, 195
spirit of holiness, 54, 157, 160, 162, 186
Spirit, Holy, 2, 10–15, 17–18, 20, 22, 32, 41, 45, 72, 81, 83–85, 93–94, 96–97, 99–100, 105, 109, 111–12, 114–16, 125, 135–37, 146, 152, 162, 164, 171, 175–77, 179, 189–90, 192, 195–96, 203
spirit, manifestations of, 11–12, 89n74, 179
Stanton, Graham, 18, 26, 35
super apostles, 152–54

Synoptic gospel traditions, 37–45

thanksgiving in letters, 48, 51, 82, 85, 92, 101, 106, 118, 120, 127–29
Thessalonian church, 80–81
Thessalonians, 80–105
   gospel in, 105
Timothy, 7, 23, 80, 101n153, 103–4, 126–27, 158, 172–73

Usteri, Leonhard, 6

Wolter, Michael, 4, 16, 18–19, 23, 201
"word" (λόγος), 44, 52, 83–85, 93, 101n156, 122, 133, 135–137
word and deed, 15, 20, 81–101, 175–76, 191–92, 197, 202, 204
wrath of God, 49, 86, 91–92, 105, 165, 168, 170, 185, 192, 198
Wright, N. T., 4, 13–14, 17, 23, 200n85, 201

www.ingramcontent.com/pod-product-compliance
Lightning Source LLC
Chambersburg PA
CBHW021650230426
43668CB00008B/577